The Dynamics of Divorce

A Life Cycle Perspective

FRONTIERS IN COUPLES AND FAMILY THERAPY
A Brunner/Mazel Book Series

Series Editor: Florence W. Kaslow, Ph.D.

The Dynamics of Divorce

A Life Cycle Perspective

By

Florence W. Kaslow, Ph.D.

and

Lita Linzer Schwartz, Ph.D.

BRUNNER/MAZEL *Publishers* • NEW YORK

Appreciation is given to the Faculty Scholarship Support Fund of The Pennsylvania State University which granted funds in support of the survey of separated and divorced adults and children of divorce.

This book is sold with the understanding that the authors and publisher are not engaged in rendering legal advice. Legal cases reported here may be modified or reversed on appeal. If legal advice or other expert assistance is required, the services of a competent attorney should be sought. Clinical cases have been disguised to protect the confidentiality accorded to clients and patients.

Library of Congress Cataloging-In-Publication Data

Kaslow, Florence Whiteman.
  The dynamics of divorce.

  (Frontiers in couples and family therapy)
  Bibliography: p. 307
  Includes index.
  1. Divorce. 2. Divorce—Psychological aspects.
3. Divorced people—Family relationships.
4. Life cycle, Human. I. Schwartz, Lita Linzer.
II. Title. III. Series.
HQ814.K37 1987   306.8′9   87-693
ISBN 0-87630-455-2

Copyright © 1987 by Florence W. Kaslow and Lita Linzer Schwartz

Published by
BRUNNER/MAZEL, INC.
19 Union Square
New York, New York 10003

MANUFACTURED IN THE UNITED STATES OF AMERICA

10 9 8 7 6 5 4 3 2 1

Foreword

The Dynamics of Divorce comes at an especially good time in the history of our study and understanding of divorce. By integrating a life cycle perspective with a family systems orientation, Florence Kaslow and Lita Linzer Schwartz have presented an important framework for reflecting upon the complex issues of divorce and the family. Rather than focusing narrowly upon one group of participants affected by the divorce, the authors have constructed a composite and balanced presentation of research and clinical observation that considers men, women, and children as individuals, as members of families, and as participants in the broader divorce process as it is currently shaped by the social, economic, and legal reality of our society.

In response to the need to create useful knowledge regarding a major and dramatic social phenomenon affecting millions of individuals and families in the past quarter century, social scientists have too often studied divorcing men and women in isolation from each other, and observed children and adolescents in isolation from their parents, extended families, peers, and other social supports. Although we have understood in other contexts that economic, health, and psychological realities shaped short-term as well as longer-range development and adjustment, only recently have these important variables been integrated with divorce-specific variables to assess the consequences and outcomes of divorce.

Other examples of the fragmentation in the divorce field abound. Until quite recently, for example, the effects of divorce on children were often measured without interviewing or assessing parents, without designing studies to enable analyses for age and sex differences, without controlling for socioeconomic and cultural differences and support. Strangely, data continue to be generated about fathers by talking only to mothers. Members of the clinical professions have made strong recommendations regarding custody dispositions or visiting arrangements without the additional insights achievable through an integrated process of evaluating all members of the family dispute. Researchers and clinicians alike have addressed psychological reactions to separation and divorce without simultaneously considering economic or social support variables. The earlier urgent search for reasonably simple answers to the question of the effects of divorce on family members has yielded to the understanding that we must be more disciplined in our quest and broader in our outlook.

The authors remind us that divorce occurs for individuals within families at different stages in the developmental life cycle, with varying predivorce marital and parental experiences, under quite diverse economic, social, and cultural circumstances. All the parties to the divorce experience bring not only their particular strengths and weaknesses to the process but also the fabric of interaction within the nuclear and extended family. There is no homogeneity among the individuals and families who are experiencing divorce. Unsatisfactory *marriages* that end in divorce have been found in many instances to be quite satisfactory *families* for children when the adult participants were able to set aside their marital difficulties sufficiently to provide a stable and nurturing environment in which children could thrive. Apparently as many as 25% to 30% of divorcing parents can successfully manage this separation of spousal and parenting function in their marriages. Given the fractionated approach and serious methodological problems in much child and adult divorce research, it is no wonder that the patchwork of divorce research and clinical observation is just now beginning to achieve some coherence. Through the use of standardized and objective measures, carefully drawn sample sizes, and increasingly sophisticated studies and analyses, we now see replication of results, encouraging leads, and a more solid data base from which we can more effectively assist families in the multiple transitions of divorce.

The Dynamics of Divorce is valuable because of its broad approach to advancing our understanding of divorce. Kaslow and Schwartz have reviewed the divorce research literature along the developmental or life cycle continuum, considering the effects of divorce not only on individual nuclear family members but also on parents and grandparents, other extended family, and friends of the participants. These psychological and social effects of the divorce transition, the economic issues and outcomes, the legal process in divorce, and the role of therapeutic and mediation interventions in assisting people in the divorce process are all considered. The effect of this more encompassing framework is to create links between these critical aspects of divorce more often dealt with in separate forums, publications, and professions. Mental health professionals are reminded that while psychic functioning is clearly deserving of attention during divorce, it is not operating in a vacuum. For lawyers there is the evidence that the legal process is played out in many extralegal arenas that directly affect the intensity and course of the divorce action. And divorcing families themselves can observe in this book that

they are not alone in their often overwhelming, confusing, and multifaceted response to divorce.

The presentation of information about the divorce mediation process
is particularly fitting within the family systems and life cycle perspective.
As Kaslow, Schwartz, and other practicing mediators have learned, divorce mediation is unique in addressing the multiple legal, financial,
psychological, and parenting issues from a perspective of the family
rather than the individual. At a time when attorneys, friends, extended
family, and indeed, our society as a whole are expecting and encouraging divorcing adults to press vigorously for their individual rights and
needs, mediation presents an increasingly attractive alternative of addressing individual and family needs and interests in an integrated manner. Knowledgeable mediators invite divorcing parents to consider
reaching agreements, for example, on grandparent visitations, simultaneously acknowledging the needs and interests of child, parent, and
grandparent. Such an approach anticipates and serves to minimize potential future conflicts within the family, and stabilizes relationships
known to be vulnerable to disruption after separation. Similarly, mediation discussions can explore the nature of future relationships of each
spouse with soon-to-be ex-in-laws and long-standing family friends. In
such sessions, divorcing men and women come to understand that they
have a choice as to whether they will destroy or preserve meaningful
links for themselves and their relatives. Discussions of who or how they
will continue in their church or Boy Scouts without undue tension or
more destructive open conflict lead to consideration of the needs of their
children and the nature of the postdivorce coparental relationship. How
will the division, or replication, of family photo albums be accomplished
so that each parent within the new binuclear family has memories of the
best that the family produced?

More so than the adversarial process, mediation assumes that despite
conflict and current high levels of marital dissatisfaction, there are some
positive aspects of the marital relationship which can be drawn on to
assist divorcing spouses in ending their relationship with dignity. Further, in mediating the future of parent-child relationships in discussions
of custody, shared parenting, and continued decision-making, couples
are given the opportunity to begin the process of restructuring their
marital relationship that has the possibility of continuing to serve child
and parental needs in each household in the postdivorce family.

There is a note of hope sounded in the book. While citing and acknowledging the deleterious effects of divorce on so many of its participants, Kaslow and Schwartz present the options that should be available
to assist divorcing family systems in their transition. They discuss the
need for and present a variety of therapeutic interventions as well as the

mediation alternative. The need of the child to continue a meaningful relationship with both parents is considered in contrast to the sober reality that children, too, are sometimes forced to divorce a parent. Kaslow describes a touching ceremony that would be healing for some families as they end their marital relationship. And they believe that despite the turmoil of the divorce process, with our increasing knowledge, with the availability of effective services, and with some thoughtfulness, couples can be helped to end their relationships with dignity and begin a life anew.

Joan B. Kelly, Ph.D.
Executive Director
Northern California Mediation Center

Contents

Tables

Figures

Preface

Since the 1950s, as the phenomenon of divorce continued its numerical upward spiral before beginning to level off in the 1980s, the number of books and journals in the field has become more plentiful. The contributions of such authors as Ahrons (1979, 1980a, 1980b, 1983a, 1983b), Bohannon (1970), Gardner (1976), Hetherington, Cox, and Cox (1977a, 1977b), Hunt (1966), Hyatt and Kaslow (1985), Kaslow (1979/80, 1981a, 1983, 1984a, 1984b), Kaslow and Hyatt (1982), Kaslow and Steinberg (1982), Kessler (1975), Krantzler (1974), Wallerstein (1985a, 1986), and Wallerstein and Kelly (1979, 1980) have helped shape the evolving knowledge base of the field as they have reported on research on and clinical observations about children of divorce, ex-spouses, and post-divorce families. Some have described stages and stations of divorce, tasks to be accomplished and appropriate therapeutic interventions; others have described the consequences of divorce in a more pragmatic manner.

The *Conciliation Courts Review*, the oldest journal which focuses on some of the emotional aspects of divorce and therapeutic considerations, primarily in the court setting, made its appearance in 1963. With the advent of the *Journal of Divorce* in 1978, it became clear that divorce had become a focal area of concern in the professional community of mental health professionals, sociologists, attorneys, and others dealing with divorce and was meriting special full attention rather than only occasional articles in other journals.

As the number of divorces increased, more people became aware of the devastating and far-reaching consequences of acrimonious litigated divorces. As a result of the efforts put forth at some Conciliation Courts in California and because of the pioneering work of Coogler (1978), the field of divorce mediation has mushroomed in the past decade. Books by Haynes (1981), Saposnek (1983), Folberg (1984), and others have helped the tide flow more swiftly. To the extent that appearance of a journal on a substantive area signifies its emergence as an important arena, the initial publication of the *Mediation Quarterly* in 1983 as the official journal of the Academy of Family Mediators is a benchmark event. Clearly, today couples have the option to choose whether to mediate or litigate their divorce.

In recent years, as we continually assessed developments in the many facets of the rapidly burgeoning divorce field, it seemed that few treatises had been written which conceptualized divorce within a life cycle framework: addressing where each member of the family is separately in his or her own developmental course and where the family as a unit is in its life cycle—before, during, and after the divorce. Questions that arose in our thinking were: What differential impact does divorce have on preschool children, on latency age children, on adolescents, on adult children? What variations occur that may be attributable to number of years of duration of marriage, age of each partner and age differential between them, socioeconomic status, marketable work skills of the female, whether the divorce was mediated or litigated, etc? Research was conducted to derive some fresh data on children of divorce in terms of age of occurrence and their retrospective reactions and current adjustment some years later. This study is reported in this volume (Chapter 4).

Our intent is to synthesize different mainstreams of the literature and to hopefully add some fresh insights and raise new questions based on our involvements in clinical and forensic aspects of the divorce process. Over the years we have probably worked with a combined total of close to 3,000 families of divorce. Thus clinical vignettes will be utilized illustratively in the text; hopefully they will amplify and enliven the discussions.

Consequently this volume has utilized a developmental life cycle framework—linking the life cycles of each of the divorcing adults, their children, and significant family of origin members with the developmental stage of the family as a unit to determine the multiple causative factors which eventuate in divorce and how this major life crisis is resolved. The tasks to be mastered at each stage of the divorce cycle and the kinds of therapeutic help which are likely to prove most efficacious have been highlighted.

It is our basic premise that, contrary to popular belief, the effects of divorce are not the same for everyone. There are, first of all, ripple effects of the separation/divorce that extend far beyond the nuclear family unit immediately involved. Second, the widespread stereotypes of the "gay divorcée," depressed and embittered divorcée, and the newly liberated bachelor are generalized images that do not necessarily reflect reality. Third, even within the ranks of one subgroup, such as rejected wives, there are differences stemming from self-perceptions (in the long term) as survivor or victim: attractive, independent woman or unwanted, helpless castoff.

Certain commonalities experienced by those dissolving their marriages will be explored, such as: some of the stages of uncoupling and mourning; the need to develop a new self-concept and life-style; role transitions; legal status changes affecting insurance coverage, taxation, and related responsibilities; economic issues; and the emotional roller coaster.

On the other hand, based on clinical experience and research, we find that the psychosocial effects of divorce are inequitably distributed, as measured by several variables. These include: gender, age, length of marriage, whether there are children or not and their ages if present, economic factors, self-image (mental set), emotional resources, relationships with extended family and friends, ethnicity, education, and availability of support networks and community resources.

This book is geared to a diverse audience—including psychological, psychiatric, and social service professionals who treat couples and families in conflict and in the process of restructuring their families, the professors and trainers who teach others "how to" do marital and divorce therapy, family sociologists, clergy, lawyers and judges, and lay people interested in a better understanding of their own and their friends' lives. Hopefully it will advance "the state of the art" and the knowledge of the divorce phenomenon.

I (Florence Kaslow) would like to express appreciation to Bernie Mazel, Chairman, Brunner/Mazel, Inc., for inviting and encouraging us to write this book, and to my secretaries, Priscilla Smyth and Lois Savage, for patiently typing and retyping the manuscript. To my husband of many years, Solis Kaslow, my profound thanks for his continuing to grow and change and keep our marriage dynamic and interesting and for understanding my desire to do the same.

My (Lita Linzer Schwartz) thanks to the administrators and librarians at the Ogontz Campus, Pennsylvania State University, who provided time, materials, and other support for this work, in addition to the Faculty Scholarship Support Fund; to Margaret Taylor, who typed the bibliographic references; and to the respondents to our survey, without whose input we would not have gained as broad a view of the varying effects of divorce on adults and children.

February 1987

Florence W. Kaslow, Ph.D.
Palm Beach, Florida
and
Lita Linzer Schwartz, Ph.D.
Elkins Park, Pennsylvania

The Dynamics of Divorce

A Life Cycle Perspective

CHAPTER 1

A Family Systems Framework and Life Cycle Perspective

A growing body of literature about divorce has appeared in the past three decades, but the approaches taken have fostered a patchwork quilt quality rather than an integrated, comprehensive, analytic perspective. We believe that enough is now known to present a synthesis of information about the divorce process—the precursors, the actual legal and economic aspects of formal dissolution, and the aftermath for all members of the postdivorce family. Our approach to such a synthesis utilizes a family systems perspective and a developmental lifecycle framework— linking the life cycles of the individuals involved, of the family as a unit, and of the divorce cycle itself.

It is our conviction that the effects of divorce are not the same for all adults, nor for all children. They vary according to the age, personality, family constellation, religious and ethnic heritage and attitudes, physical health, socioeconomic status and myriad other factors that make up the life of all those caught in the critical transitions divorce precipitates. There are ripple effects of the separation/divorce that extend far beyond the nuclear family unit immediately involved to the extended family, friends, work and school situations. It is often difficult for the parties involved not to "spill over" to others they are with and to bring their frustration, discontent or anger with them in everything they do for many months, even years. There may also be positive by-products for extended family members or friends who may derive courage from the divorced person's behavior to extricate themselves from various situations or relationships in which they have previously felt stuck (Kaslow & Hyatt, 1982).

The clichés of the "gay divorcée" and the "effervescent" new-bachelor are romantic images that more frequently conflict with reality than reflect it. Many recent divorcées are withdrawn, depressed, embittered, and not interested in the swinging singles scene. Many are preoccupied with concerns about children, jobs, and money. Even within the ranks of one subgroup, such as middle-aged "unwanted" wives, one sees variations stemming from self-perceptions (in the long term) as survivor or victim: desirable, autonomous woman or discarded, helpless castoff. Some newly single adults are exhausted, relieved, or baffled, sometimes all three simultaneously. Ambivalence is commonplace.

There *are* certain commonalities experienced by the central figures in divorce: the stages of the uncoupling and mourning processes; the need to survive and develop a new self-image and life-style; legal status changes affecting insurance coverage, taxation, and management of finances; and the emotional vicissitudes and accompanying identity crises that many experience. Yet, based on clinical experience and research, we find that the psychosocial effects of divorce are inequitably distributed in relation to several variables. These include: sex, age, duration of marriage, whether there are children and their ages (if present), financial status, self-image, emotional resourcefulness, relationships with extended family and friends, level of education, and access to community resources and support networks.

Although we have drawn on the extant research, we have also sought information from separated and divorced adults and their children across the country through a survey questionnaire which is described in Chapter 4. Their responses highlight many of the commonalities and differences cited above. It becomes apparent that to say "no two cases are alike" is virtually a truism.

DIVORCE RATES

According to the National Center for Health Statistics (1985), the number of divorces in the United States more than doubled annually between 1962 and 1982. In 1962, the rate was 2.2 per 1,000 population; in 1982, it was 5.0 per 1,000 population (see Figure 1). Similarly, there has been a marked increase in the number of children (per 1,000 children under 18 years of age) involved in divorce: in 1960—7.2; in 1982—17.6. The median ages at divorce for husbands were 32.6 and 33.6 years in 1972 and 1982 respectively; for wives, 29.8 and 31.1 years in the same time periods (National Center for Health Statistics, 1985). Generally the likelihood of divorce declines with the increasing number of children, but it also declines with the increasing age of husband and wife and the increasing length of marriage. Yet, as a result of changes in state laws which now permit "no-fault" divorces, making unfounded accusations or horrendous contested divorces legally unnecessary, persons who may have avoided divorce before might now seek it at a later point. Socially, attitudes toward divorce have become more permissive and accepting. These changes are reflected in very modest shifts in the divorce statistics in the direction of the median age of divorce becoming slightly older in the past 10 years, as reflected in the figures cited earlier.

The changes in divorce rates since the early 1960s, and even more since the 1930s, shown in the graph of Figure 1, reflect a number of factors. Economically, the nation was considerably more affluent in the post World War II period than during the Depression. This has even been true during the recession-recovery cycles of the past 20 years so that many of those who wished to separate could manage the increased expense of maintaining two households. Occupationally, the civil rights and women's liberation movements led to affirmative action in employment and thus more women in better paying jobs than formerly (despite continuing to receive lower wages than men in comparable jobs do), making them more independent. Socially, divorced women are no longer seen or shunned as pariahs in most communities, especially in urban centers. Furthermore, the "me-first" narcissistic attitude of the self-oriented 1970s led many husbands and wives to ask "Is this all there is?" as they found themselves bored after 15 to 25 years of marriage and realized they still had 30 to 40 years left in the future. They decided to "go for it" no matter what that elusive "it" was deemed to be—before it became too late. Many separated to "find" themselves. Indeed, divorce has become so common in many locales that people will ask someone who they see rarely, "How's the family?" rather than "How's ---?" referring to the person's spouse.

Staying together "for the sake of the children" is now less often deemed necessary or appropriate to emotional well-being than in earlier decades. In fact, some clinicians indicate that children raised in a tense and conflicted household where parents stay together for their sake fare much better when their parents separate and home is no longer a daily battlefield. Also, when the family split-up that they dreaded finally occurs, there may be a sense of relief and a chance to rebuild their lives— more peaceably. Still there appears to be an increase in the number of divorces occurring, as the youngest child graduates high school or leaves home for college, when parents no longer feel as obligated to keep the home intact for the benefit of their offspring.

Since there has been relatively little research done on these older divorced adults or the older children of divorce, we made a special effort to include such individuals in our study. These data will be described later along with a discussion on divorce among those in their middle and later years.

The mammoth number of people affected by divorce converge to form

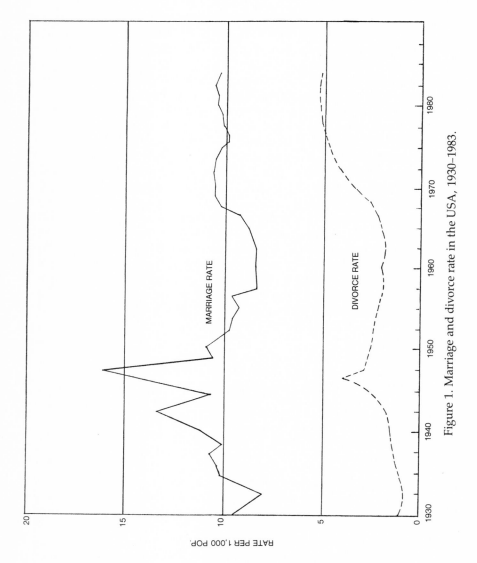

Figure 1. Marriage and divorce rate in the USA, 1930–1983.

a variegated, multihued, complex tapestry. For purposes of description and analysis we shall try to unravel the intertwined strands.

FAMILY SYSTEMS PERSPECTIVE

In brief, as in any system, in the family the various members have interlocking and interdependent functions. They are linked together with visible and invisible loyalties (Boszormenyi-Nagy & Spark, 1973) and mutual commitments and needs. Simply stated, what one member does impacts on all the other members. Whether their organization is primarily healthy, midrange, or dysfunctional (Lewis, Beavers, Gossett, & Phillips, 1976; Kaslow, 1981c, 1982a), their style of interrelating respectful and individuated, enmeshed or disengaged (Minuchin, 1974), their lives are intertwined so that decisions and actions of any member have implications for all the others. Within the family therapy field, a widely held premise is that causality is curvilinear and not linear so that what A does affects B, C, and D, and what they do in turn affects A. Feedback loops are recursive (Dell, 1982), relationships have multidirectional impact. As Satir (1964) indicated so aptly, if one member of the family is in pain, all members feel the pain in some way.

Clear evidence of this is visible to anyone observing the family of a chronic and terminally ill patient. The refrain "No man is an island" wells into consciousness. By way of example, consider:

The T Family
At the age of 48, Mrs. T discovered a lump in her breast and the surgeon felt a mastectomy was necessary. During the surgery it was determined that it was malignant and the cancer had already spread into her lymph nodes. Upon her release from the hospital, she began a series of radiation treatments and continued to work for seven months. By then her condition had deteriorated markedly and her energy was depleted. She resigned her position when she became unable to drive. Her husband and son often took off from work to take her for doctors' appointments and chemotherapy or radiation—whichever she was receiving. Evenings they spent with her, curtailing their activities. Friends took turns visiting and bringing her lunch. Eventually her daughter took a leave of absence from college to move home and help in whatever ways she could during the final months of her mother's life.

Everyone's lives were profoundly affected by Mrs. T's sad plight. They coped as well as a family can; indifference was not a hallmark of their family as it is not of other healthy families. (Kaslow, 1981c; Walsh, 1982)

Similarly, if there is child abuse, alcoholism or divorce, no one can emerge untouched.

Lewis et al. (1976) articulated eight variables that characterize all families. Where a particular family falls on the continuum of a specific variable determines whether a therapist or researcher will be likely to classify it as healthy, midrange or dysfunctional. As these variables will be alluded to throughout this text in the analysis of individuals, couples and families going through "the divorce process" (this phrase is used herein to connote pre-, during, and postdivorce), it appears useful to list the variables and elaborate upon one as an example of how those in the three broad categories differ.

1. Systems orientation
2. Boundary issues
3. Contextual issues (communication patterns)
4. Power issues
5. Autonomy and initiative
6. Affective issues
7. Negotiation and task performance (problem solving)
8. Transcendental values

A more in-depth view regarding boundary issues (#2) might reveal the following regarding three types of intra-family boundaries (Lewis et al., 1976).

Healthy	*Midrange*	*Dysfunctional*
1. Mr. & Mrs. Grendel have a 14-year-old son and a 16-year-old daughter. They often serve as chaperones for their son's band trips and enjoy watching their daughter's excitement over the flurry of activities for her Sweet 16 year. But they clearly remain in the parent generation and do not try to share as same age participants.	Mr. & Mrs. Grendel are very concerned about whether their son and daughter are associating with the right kind of children, want each person to be brought home so they can look them over, and Mrs. Grendel wants to go to the parties with her daughter—because she enjoys her friends too.	Every time their son or daughter takes off to participate in extra-curricular or social activities, Mr. or Mrs. Grendel yell that they are lazy, good-for-nothing kids who are only interested in a good time and don't care about their parents. Mr. Grendel is intensely jealous of his daughter's dating, says "nobody is good enough for my baby" and is insulting to her dates when they come to the house.
2. Julie keeps a personal diary. She knows that neither parent would invade her privacy and seek to read it. She can talk	Julie's mother searches for the key to her diary to ascertain "what's really going on" and if she's into pot or sex so she'll know	Julie is ridiculed for keeping a diary and everyone tries to get it and read it. Privacy is denigrated and violated—

(*continued*)

with friends after home-work is done without break-ins by other family members.	how to guide or discipline her. On occasion she eavesdrops on Julie's conversations with her friends.	someone is usually listening on another phone when she gets calls.

Duhl (1981) has evolved a Chronological Chart (see Figure 2) for use in general systems family therapy. It provides "a method for keeping track of family events and their impact on each of the family members" (Duhl, 1981, p. 361). It is a valuable tool for collecting and recording data so that the therapist can help family members become aware of and then inte-grate their differing perceptions of and reactions to the event and then enable them to formulate new options for mastery of any residual trauma or aftereffects.

We have found it to be extremely useful in working with divorcing and postdivorce families. It can be conducive to their becoming more attuned to the covert as well as overt meanings for *each* family member individu-ally of the dissolution of the nuclear family and its regrouping into two binuclear units (Ahrons, 1980b). It is a valuable device for keeping track of "multiple yet simultaneous events" and lends itself to the integration of "individual intrapsychic phenomena . . . with . . . interpersonal in-teractions and . . . systems transactions" (Duhl, 1981, p. 361).

Throughout this book the underlying framework is a family systems perspective. A recurrent theme will be the interplay of the needs, rights and responsibilities of the various individuals and subsystems involved. We accept the following premises as operational principles of systems that are applicable to families (Bertalanffy, 1968; Buckley, 1967), includ-ing transitional families during and after divorce. These will undergird much of the discussion which follows.

1. *Nonsummativity*. The family as a unit is more than the sum of its parts. It is inadequate to try to describe the family by summing up the characteristics of each member. It is important to observe the connecting patterns (Bateson, 1979) that comprise the family's structure and organization.
2. *Family rules*. These are the overt and covert norms and expectations which govern behavior and converge to shape the family's life-style. Families differ regarding the clarity of what is and is not permissible and the negative and positive sanctions used to bring about conformity.
3. *Homeostasis*. Some forces within the system seek to maintain the status quo and are therefore resistant to any push toward change that threatens the existing equilibrium. Extreme departure from the family's preferred modus operandi are stifled and repressive mea-sures may be enacted to preserve family tradition, status, stability and cohesiveness.

THE BOSTON FAMILY CHRONOLOGICAL CHART

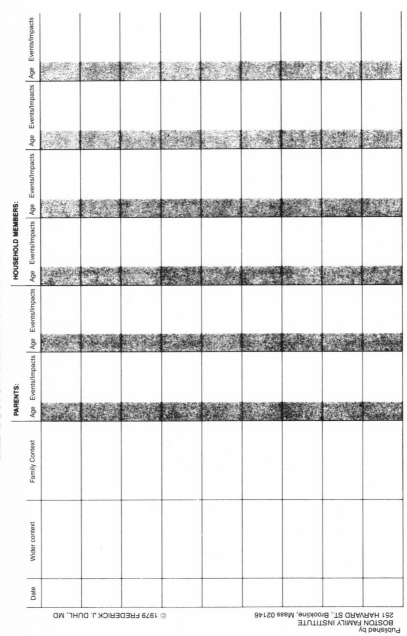

Date	Wider context	Family Context	PARENTS:		HOUSEHOLD MEMBERS:									
			Age	Events/Impacts	Age	Events/Impacts	Age	Events/Impacts	Age	Events/Impacts	Age	Events/Impacts	Age	Events/Impacts

Figure 2. The Boston Family Chronological Chart. (From Duhl, 1981. Reprinted with permission of the *Journal of Marital and Family Therapy*, 1981, 7[3], p. 366. Copyright 1981 American Association of Marriage and Family Therapy.)

4. *Morphogenesis*. However, the need and desire for growth and change in individual members of human systems, combined with external forces that impinge to promote or necessitate change, counterbalance the homeostatic pull and infuse the system with a more dynamic quality. Flexibility and adaptability are characteristics of healthy family systems both in regard to internal and external imperatives for change (Olson, Sprenkle, & Russell, 1979). "Second order change," or a modification of rules, is necessitated whenever members are in transition from one developmental phase to another because stage appropriate tasks and behaviors will be contingent upon evolving a new set of options and modified standards (Carter & McGoldrick, 1980).
5. *Circular causality*. Discussed earlier.
6. *Communication*. Behavioral messages are constantly being conveyed, verbally and nonverbally. Messages are interpersonal signals containing 1) content or substantive information about events, thoughts, or feelings; and 2) intent—the meta-messages which may or may not be congruent with the content and are concerned with defining the nature of the relational interaction (Reusch & Bateson, 1951). Messages may be clear or garbled, straight or deceptive, open to response, or direct commands requiring conformity, not amplification.
7. *Equifinality*. This premise rests on the proposition that the same occurrence or source may eventuate in different outcomes and the same outcome may eventuate from different origins or events. Thus, one set of parents may unknowingly adopt a learning disabled child and want to "give it back to the agency" once a diagnosis is made; another couple adopting a similar child will seek instead to find the best possible way to help the child master his/her environment.

In sum, utilizing a family systems framework enables one to derive a multidimensional view of a family at a given point in time. In order for the view to be dynamic and not static, a longitudinal perspective is needed and a life cycle approach provides this foundation.

THE LIFE CYCLE APPROACH: A REVIEW OF THE LITERATURE

It is erroneous to assume that the family life cycle conceptualization is a relatively contemporary one that had its genesis in modern psychoanalytic or psychodynamic thought. Rather, awareness of the evolutionary nature of the life cycle, repetitive across time and space, cultures and generations, is definitively depicted in an ancient source of wisdom, The Bible. In *Ecclesiastes* (Holy Bible, 1952) it is written (Chapter 3, Vs. 1–8, p. 740):

Unchanging Order of Events

There is an appointed time for everything; and a time for every affair under the heavens. A time to be born, and a time to die; a time to plant, and a time to uproot the plant. A time to kill, and a time to heal; a time to tear down, and a time to build. A time to weep, and a time to laugh; a time to mourn, and a time to dance. A time to scatter stones, and a time to gather them; a time to embrace, and a time to be far from embraces. A time to seek, and a time to lose; a time to keep; and a time to cast away. A time to rend, and a time to sew; a time to be silent, and a time to speak. A time to love, and a time to hate; a time of war, and a time of peace.

This solemnly written poetic verse recognizes the inevitable passage of time and individuals, by means of their own idiosyncratic yet typical time capsule, through life. Subliminally it seems to counsel acceptance of the changes wrought by time, perhaps more than acceptance, even guidelines for enjoying the richness of life as one season and stage replace another in harmony with changes in the cosmic universe.

Another significant and more sophisticated reference to the life cycle appears in Shakespeare's *As You Like It*, Act II, Scene VII, where the following crystal clear articulation appears:

All the world's a stage,
And all the men and women merely players:
They have their exits and entrances;
And one man in his time plays many parts
His acts being seven ages. At first the infant,
Mewling and puking in the nurse's arms.
And then the whining school-boy, with his satchel,
And shining morning face, creeping like snail
Unwillingly to school. And then the lover,
Sighing like furnace, with a woeful ballad
Made to his mistress' eyebrow. Then a soldier,
Jealous in honour, sudden and quick in quarrel,
Seeking the bubble reputation
Even in the cannon's mouth. And then the justice,
In fair round belly with good capon lin'd,
With eyes severe, and beard of formal cut,
Full of wise saws and modern instances;
And so he plays his part. The sixth age shifts
Into the lean and slipper'd pantaloon,
With spectacles on nose and pouch on side,
His youthful hose well sav'd, a world too wide
For his shrunk shank; and his big manly voice,
Turning again toward childish treble, pipes
And whistles in his sound. Last scene of all,

That ends this strange eventful history,
Is second childishness and mere oblivion,
Sans teeth, sans eyes, sans taste, sans everything.

Thus knowledge of the life cycle goes back to biblical times, has been incorporated into the thinking of great playwrights like Shakespeare, and resurfaces in modern psychology as a major organizing principle for interpreting the meaning of life events and experiences at a given point in time.

Of the modern theorists, Erik Erikson's (1963) formulation stands as one of the most complete creative works in stage theory of individual development. He identified stages of adulthood, as well as of childhood, expanding upon Freud's original model of children's psychosexual development. He delineated "Identity vs. Role Confusion" as a predominant theme in adolescence, "Intimacy vs. Isolation" in young adulthood, "Generativity vs. Stagnation" in middle adulthood, and "Ego Integrity vs. Despair" in older adulthood. Our own research and clinical observations corroborate that for people to be capable of achieving emotional and sexual intimacy, they must first achieve a good sense of their own identity, that is, who they are and what they believe. Only then is their ego sufficiently strong that they can risk becoming very close to another, at times merging in full union, without fear of loss of self. For a marriage to be a sound, healthy, and intimate one, both partners need to have arrived at a sense of their own unique identity and self-worth; only then can they respect and appreciate the wholeness of their mate.

Rice and Rice (1986) echo this theme and recast it in a contemporary version vis-à-vis divorce. They conceptualize both marriage and divorce as having specific implications for two ubiquitous developmental tasks: the formation of one's own clear identity (separation) and the achieving of intimacy (communion). They indicate that these tasks are never fully mastered; the need to achieve resolution of these parallel processes occurs periodically throughout one's life cycle, each time with somewhat different nuances. Divorce necessitates redefining one's identity and perhaps ultimately fulfilling one's desire for intimacy with a new partner.

While it is true that individual adults should be perceived in light of their progress along the developmental road, in considering families one must assess the interactions among adults (and their children) who may be at somewhat different points on the road. Erikson's work provided the basis and the inspiration for examining the family unit, where such multiple interactions occur, in terms of its stages.

Family life cycles are seen in slightly different perspectives by various authors. Much depends upon whether the family unit is begun in early adulthood or later, as part of a first or subsequent marriage for the partners, and whether there are children born within the marriage. Not all families follow the prototype thought of as normative: the couple alone, birth of children, children's school years, children's departure, couple alone. An examination of some models of family development will provide a basis for studying what happens when the unit's development is arrested or the cycle is interrupted by divorce.

Rhodes (1977), for example, sees the family adapting to the changes within it as family members grow and mature. Implicit in her view is continuing multigenerational and internal-external interaction as the family moves through the cyclic stages. Her first stage involves the marital coupling or dyadic relationship prior to birth of children. Either the couple develops an intimacy based on mutually realistic images, continues the romantic idealization of the mate or becomes disillusioned with the partner as unresponsive. Even if the last occurs, frequently the couple remain together because of religious or familial pressures, or their own inability to extricate out of fear of failure, loneliness or financial pressures. In this stage, however, two primary questions to be answered are: Can the spouses perceive each other's needs in the relationship as well as their attractions and what they have to give without being burdened by the "emotional baggage" brought from the family of origin? And, can they separate from dependence on the family of origin in a healthy way or is marriage perhaps their escape from the earlier family unit (Bowen, 1978)?

Rhodes' second stage is "replenishment vs. turning inward," which she describes as encompassing the period from the birth/arrival of the first child to the time when the last child enters school. Can the parents adapt to the care-taking parental roles and still replenish each other? Do mother and child(ren) become so allied with each other that they exclude the father? As the children move into the school years, the third stage— "individuation of family members vs. pseudomutual organization"—is reached. Can the mother develop as an individual? Is the father entering a "mid-life crisis" with questions about his identity and about his future expectations for himself? Are the children allowed to build relationships outside the family? Finally, can the family enlarge its world without its members feeling threatened? In terms of the healthy family model, is it an open system and does it encourage initiative and autonomy?

As adolescence is reached by the children, restructuring of the family recurs. The teenagers become more involved in peer networks and the parents must determine how far and in which directions to shift from the earlier more dominant parental authority role. Rhodes calls this stage "companionship vs. isolation," reflecting the modifications in the relationships between parents and children and between the spouses.

When the younger generation begins to move out of the family home and unit ("regrouping vs. binding or expulsion"), the strength of the marital relationship is again tested. The ability to permit, indeed to encourage, the separation and individuation of the grown children also tests the family unit in this fifth stage. How closely do the parents tie the children to the family gestalt? Do they need to cling to the adolescent to keep their marriage viable? Do they expel the adolescent/young adult who, in seeking a different path from what they want for him/her, acts in a manner that they find intolerable?

The postparental stages of "rediscovery vs. despair" and "mutual aid vs. uselessness" require further adaptation to the alterations in the family unit. The marital couple can discover new bonds and rediscover the attractions of their early years together, or they can drift apart, perhaps even divorcing. At the same time, they must again restructure and transform relationships with their children, who may be establishing their own family units. In healthy families, new relationships are created as children-in-law, *their* families of origin, and grandchildren are added to the family tree. In the final stage of the family's life cycle, from retirement to death, multigenerational bonds may be further strengthened or weakened but are unquestionably altered once more. In some cases, the deteriorating health of one or both marital partners may cause increased dependency, even role reversal, in relation to their children. In other instances, the grandparents may be viewed as rich resources—in other than a financial sense—to be enjoyed and cherished by the younger generations.

Hughes, Berger, and Wright (1978) have similarly adopted a seven-stage family life cycle model. These parallel the stages presented by Rhodes, although the focus is primarily on identifying those needs at each stage which may call for clinical intervention. Their labels for each stage are: 1) Beginning families, 2) Childbearing families, 3) Childrearing families, 4) Families with teenagers, 5) Families as launching centers, 6) Families in the middle years, and 7) Aging families. The areas in which needs or conflicts may arise at each stage may be physical, social, interpersonal, and/or intrapsychic. As families successfully meet needs at each stage, they become prepared to meet and resolve the tasks of the next stage more easily. Conflicts, unmet needs, and difficulty at one stage, however, are seen to negatively affect the family's ability to meet changing needs at the next stage; the family may have become *stuck*, unable to cope flexibly and may require professional help before they can make any progress. Hughes et al. point out that patterns and relationships evolve during the various stages and so must individual behaviors. What was appropriate behavior during courtship and early marriage, for example, may be quite inappropriate in the child-rearing stage, with consequent disharmony within the family unit if anyone perpetuates it or expects it to continue. (A word of caution—playfulness and fun together are important throughout the life cycle and should not be disparaged or necessarily interpreted as immature, juvenile, or the Peter Pan Syndrome). In transactional analysis terms, it's important to keep one's "spunky child" part alive and active.

In the significant life cycle work of Haley (1973), problems are viewed as symptomatic of a developmental impasse which occurs at a transition point, rather than as the result of family psychopathology. Therefore, for Haley and his followers, strategic intervention entails resolving the impasse rather than curing psychopathology. For successful movement to occur from one stage to another, Hoffman (1980) posits that the family must experience and ultimately integrate a discontinous process of change in the family organization. Such discontinous changes are irreversible, that is, the family cannot regress to the prior level of organization. Such change may be brought about therapeutically by first engaging the family and then unbalancing it to unfreeze the existing rigid organization. When a new, functional resolution of the impasse is reached, the crisis is overcome and growth can once again proceed within the milieu of a higher level of family organization.

Another significant contribution was made by Levinson, Darrow, Klein, Levinson, and McKee (1978), who specifically focused on *The Seasons of a Man's Life*. In their book they describe the "seasons" which became apparent in their longitudinal research study. One example will be used illustratively. The period during a man's mid 30s is characterized by the effort to establish his "niche in society" and to work toward career advancement. Intercorrelating this with what is likely to be going on in his children's life cycle at the same time, as one might do by using the Duhl Chronological Chart described earlier, it is in rhythm with the child's settling into a niche in school and concentrating on achievement there. If the woman is working, her tasks and goals may be similar to her husband's; if not, her concerns will likely revolve around affirming her identity and niche as wife, mother, and person in the community.

Levinson et al.'s (1978) work is multigenerational in nature so that they also evaluated what is likely to be going on concurrently in the grandparent generation. Given that most grandparents will by this point be in their 50s or 60s, they will have a fairly well-established niche in their world and may be redefining their relationship with each other, their children, and grandchildren as they consider the role they may want to play politically, socially, or philanthropically in their world. They may also have concerns and perhaps anticipation about possible retirement, relocation, health, and the ability to spend more time with grandchildren who have become more self-sufficient and accessible during their latency and teen years. In such a healthy family there is mutuality, reciprocity, closeness and individuality. In fragmented, chaotic, disengaged families a very different three-generational portrait would emerge, one of everyone struggling just to survive and feeling alienated or antagonistic rather than attached.

In *Adult Development: A New Dimension in Psychodynamic Theory and Practice*, Colarusso and Nemiroff (1981) proposed that adulthood is not a stable, static phase of life, devoid of developmental processes, but is instead a time of dynamic, ongoing change resulting from both childhood and adult developmental processes. The developmental tasks subsume and go beyond psychosexual and psychosocial tasks. Their work represents an excellent companion piece to that of Levinson et al. (1978).

Colarusso and Nemiroff have condensed their understanding of the nature of adult development into the following seven basic hypotheses:

1. The nature of the developmental process is basically the same in the adult as in the child.
2. Development in adulthood is an ongoing dynamic process.
3. Whereas child development is focused primarily on the formation of psychic structure, adult development is concerned with the continuing evolution of existing structure.
4. The fundamental developmental issues of childhood continue as central aspects of adult life but in altered form.
5. The developmental processes in adulthood are influenced by the adult past as well as the childhood past.
6. Development in adulthood, as in childhood, is deeply influenced by the body and physical change.
7. A central, phase-specific theme of adult development is the normative crisis precipitated by the recognition and acceptance of the finiteness of time and inevitability of personal death.

Conceptualizing the developmental process as lifelong and a crucial part of the psychology of adulthood, Colarusso and Nemiroff described the normal adult as in a state of constant dynamic change and flux, subject to the influences of the external and internal environment, reactive to previous life experiences from one's childhood and young-adult past, and engaged in such new phase-specific developmental tasks as responding to complex bodily changes and heightened awareness of time limitations and personal death.

They posit that the clinician is helped immeasurably by taking an adult developmental history as well as a childhood developmental history. Correlations between phase-specific adult developmental tasks and childhood events lend specificity and focus to psychotherapy.

To make their ideas more easily accessible, they have organized the developmental tasks of adulthood in table form (see Table 1).

Wynne (1984) approaches family development from a unique vantage

Table 1
Adult Developmental Tasks[a]

Early Adulthood (ages 20–40)	Middle Adulthood (ages 40–60)[b]	Late Adulthood (ages 60+)
1. Psychological separation from parents.	1. Dealing with body changes or illness and altered body image.	1. Maintaining physical health.
2. Accepting responsibility for one's own body.	2. Adjusting to middle life changes in sexuality (menopause, male climacteric).	2. Adapting to physical infirmities or permanent impairment.
3. Becoming aware of one's personal history and time limitation.	3. Accepting the passage of time.	3. Using time in gratifying ways.
4. Integrating sexual experience (homo- or hetero-sexual).	4. Adjusting to aging.	4. Adapting to losses of partner and friends.
5. Developing a capacity for intimacy with a partner.	5. Living through illness and death of parents and contemporaries.	5. Remaining oriented to present and future, not preoccupied with the past.
6. Deciding whether to have children.	6. Dealing with realities of death.	6. Forming new emotional ties.
7. Having and relating to children.	7. Redefining relationship to spouse or partner. (Our addition.)	7. Reversing roles of children and grandchildren (as caretakers).
8. Establishing adult relationships with parents.	8. Deepening relations with grown children or grandchildren.	8. Seeking and maintaining social contacts: companionship vs. isolation and loneliness.
9. Acquiring marketable skills.	9. Maintaining longstanding and creating new friendships.	9. Attending to sexual needs and (changing) expressions.
10. Choosing a career.	10. Consolidating work identity.	10. Continuing meaningful work and play (satisfying use of time).
11. Using money to further development.	11. Transmitting skills and values to the young. (Mentor relationship fosters generativity.)[c]	11. Using financial resources wisely, for self and others.
12. Assuming a social role.	12. Allocating financial resources effectively.	12. Integrating retirement into new life-style. (Our addition.)
13. Adapting ethical and spiritual values.	13. Accepting social responsibility.	
	14. Accepting social change.	

[a]Reprinted from Colarusso, C. A., & Nemiroff, R. A. (1981). *Adult development: A new dimension in psychodynamic theory and practice.* New York: Plenum. By permission of Plenum Publishing Corp.
[b]We would extend middle adulthood to 65 and begin late adulthood at 66+, based on our observations of adult life phases and activity.
[c]Items in parentheses inserted by current authors.

point. He focuses on the development of "relational systems" between the marital partners and the effect of their presence or absence on the family's development (see Figure 3). His exposition must be examined through the prism of history, highlighting the changing emphasis of different chronological eras. This view will enable us to look at contemporary marriage dissolutions with greater sensitivity.

The concept of attachment/caregiving, for example, in the era of arranged marriages assumed caregiving on the part of both spouses (though differentially demonstrated) with attachment developing after marriage, if one was fortunate, rather than before. More recently, as in the 1940s and 1950s, attachment usually preceded marriage and was the basis for the desire of both potential spouses to become mutual caregivers. Today, attachment continues to predate marriage in the United States, but the caregiving aspect, if present, may assume more assorted guises than formerly.

In the past when wives were perceived as chattel of their husbands, communication between the spouses tended often to have more disparate connotations for each partner than would be true today. There was little concern about deeper meanings of messages as long as the surface message was comprehended and socially correct. This could be extremely frustrating for the partner who indulged in subtlety and hoped that somehow his/her partner would intuitively grasp the underlying meaning of simple statements or actions. As Wynne points out, if communication skills are ineffective in the marriage, attachment and caregiving have difficulty growing, or, it might be added, being maintained at the highest level so far attained.

It is Wynne's perception that "without a background of attachment/ caregiving and communications skills, joint problem solving is doomed to be muddled and dysfunctional" (p. 19). In former years, when the husband's word was "law" and wives made independent decisions only in the absence of the husband, joint problem solving was rarely a consideration, let alone a stage of development in the family process or a potential issue (by virtue of its absence) in a divorce. Today, many expect to engage in joint problem solving in marriage, and to continue it even after divorce if there is to be co-parenting or joint custody of children. This generalization may be somewhat less true in very traditional marriages and somewhat more true among well-educated, "liberated" marital partners. Failures in joint problem solving tend to appear most frequently in regard to childrearing (and financial expenditures).

Joint problem solving leads to "mutuality." Early in a marriage, mutuality typically develops between partners despite divergent upbringings in their original families and periods of independent living prior to marriage. Recognizing that decisions must be reached in conjunction with

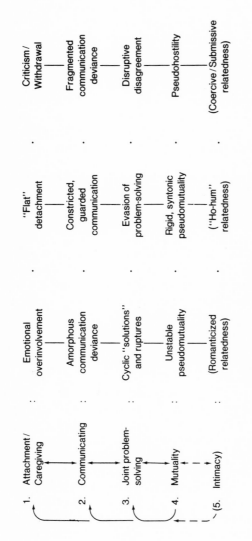

Figure 3. Major processes, and illustrative dysfunctions, in the epigenesis of enduring relational systems. The sequence may stop progressing at any stage. Intimacy is not essential for enduring relatedness, but if and when it becomes *reliably* available, intimacy is a subjective corollary of mutuality. (From Wynne, 1984. Reprinted with permission of *Family Process*, 1984, 23[3], p. 300.)

each other if the marriage is to endure, each partner must alter earlier patterns of solving problems and handling routine matters alone or with parental guidance and assistance. In most marriages that survive for any length of time, this does occur sooner or later in the relationship.

Wynne's final stage is "intimacy," perceived as mutual sharing and trust. Just as the infant in Erikson's schema (1963) learns trust or mistrust over time, so intimacy must be built over time in the marriage. Wynne quite explicitly states that his interpretation of intimacy takes it far beyond sexual passion. How important this expanded definition might have been in other eras is difficult to say. Wynne posits that it may have been "more a luxury than a developmental necessity in relational systems" (p. 309). But today, at least in the U.S., many crave intimacy. Wynne's expanded depiction of intimacy suggests that it is best characterized as "the inconstant, subjective side of relatedness, the sharing of personal feelings, fantasies, and effectively meaningful experience associated with each of the stages" (p. 310). Such interpersonal processes are relational but not necessarily symmetrical. His definition implies that "intimacy can be a deeply powerful, meaningful, humanizing experience, subtly and emotionally complicated, seductive and frightening." He further suggests that striving for and achieving intimacy may be incompatible with the values and life-styles of men in many cultures. Implicitly, this leaves women who desire and may be capable of an intimacy which encompasses and transcends sexuality baffled, frustrated and sometimes quite angry and disdainful. They perceive their partner to be insensitive to their emotional needs and incapable of giving; over a prolonged period of time, this may seem compelling grounds for divorce.

Looking at Wynne's stages from another vantage point, it is easy to see other conflicts which may arise, be unresolved, and lead to divorce. With respect to attachment, for example, if the spouses have a wide age difference, one partner's ideas may be rooted in the lifelong commitment to marriage inculcated in the 1940s and 1950s, while the other partner's feelings may be more reflective of the self-oriented 1970s and 1980s. The former may expect more caregiving than the latter can provide, leading inevitably to a clash in the relationship. The partner whose father was *the* voice of authority in the family of origin may be unwilling to listen to or communicate effectively with his/her spouse. The inability to communicate in a sharing manner and the concomitant inability to solve problems jointly is obviously a negative factor in the childrearing and subsequent years. If parents overtly or covertly differ in their responses to children's behaviors, not only are the children often confused, but they may become highly skilled at manipulating their parents by playing one against the other or become caught in schizophrenic type double bind messages.

This exacerbates the existing difficulties in the relationship. The couple's inability or unwillingness to negotiate solutions to problems, especially those involving children, often worsens after separation or divorce if and when each partner hardens his/her position.

In some instances, the unwillingness to solve child custody problems through negotiation may reflect an effort on the part of one partner to maintain the prior marital bond although the attachment has come to be perceived negatively. An example of this, drawn from our study, is seen in the ongoing disputes of a divorced couple even after several years, and although the husband had subsequently remarried.

The J's
    The former wife had instituted more than 100 court actions against the husband on child custody issues after the separation. Whether she could only perceive herself in terms of her bonds to him, or was carrying on a purposeful vendetta could be ascertained only with more complete knowledge of the marriage and divorce dynamics. The fact remains, however, that she has tried to maintain an attachment that is inappropriate, dysfunctional and detrimental to the welfare of the child involved.

In this case, there was certainly none of the kind of sound communication or mutuality Wynne defined as essential for functional relationships.

The models of development alluded to above are illustrative of the range of current thinking. Two recent fine volumes, which cover myriad aspects of the family life cycle in greater detail, are Carter and McGoldrick's *The Family Life Cycle* (1980) and Liddle's *Clinical Implications of the Family Life Cycle* (1983). These source books are recommended to the reader who is interested in pursuing this topic further.

It is vital that therapists and researchers take into account the stage in the family life cycle in which their patients-subjects fall as part of the salient identifying and diagnostic data. It is also vital, in attempting to understand the dynamics of divorce, that we address the interplay of the unfolding or deteriorating relational patterns within the context of the individual and family life cycle model, à la Wynne (1984). This is the synthesis being sought in this volume.

CHAPTER 2

Stages in the Divorce Process: Dynamics and Treatment —An Overview

All statistics in the decade and a half prior to 1984 have shown divorce to be increasing rapidly. Whether work is cited that sets the figures at 33% or 50% (both rates are bandied about), clearly the magnitude of the situation is great. Despite the fact that in many social circles the stigma of divorce has diminished as divorce laws have been liberalized and the frequency of marital dissolution has escalated, the traumatic impact of divorce does not seem to be lessened on the individuals who experience it. Also, a ripple effect occurs, profoundly affecting all members of the nuclear family and at least some of the family of origin of the separating spouses (Kaslow & Hyatt, 1982; Spanier & Hanson, 1981).

Although marital counseling began in a formalized way in the late 1930s and writings about family therapy began to appear in the professional literature in the early 1950s (Kaslow, 1980), the concept of divorce therapy as a substantive aspect of marital and family therapy did not begin to be discussed in the literature until the mid-1970s. Some of the attention has riveted on the impact of divorce upon children (Gardner, 1976; Hetherington, Cox, & Cox, 1977b; Kessler & Bostwick, 1977) and some on the adult's readjustment and re-entry into the singles' world (e.g., Froiland & Hozman, 1977; Hyatt, 1977; Kessler, 1975; Krantzler, 1974). Recognition of the special plight of couples who divorce, the impact on their children and their families of origin, and corresponding-

This chapter is a revision and expansion of F.W. Kaslow's "Stages and techniques of divorce therapy." In P. Keller & L. Ritt (Eds.). *Innovations in clinical practice: A source book,* Vol. 2, pp. 5–16. Sarasota, FL: The Professional Resource Exchange, Inc., 1983. Reprinted by permission of the publisher.

ly, recognition that many mental health professionals did not have a conceptual framework for understanding the dynamics and trauma of the divorce process nor training in effective intervention strategies, led Esther Fisher, a New York based therapist-educator also trained in law, to found the *Journal of Divorce* in 1977. The advent of this journal and the growing number of articles, chapters, and full books on divorce-related topics published since 1977 (e.g., Fisher, 1981; Kaslow, 1979/80; Nadelson & Polonsky, 1984; Stuart & Abt, 1981) are indicative of the fact that mental health and social service professionals have finally acknowledged the divorced individuals' needs for attention and assistance and have begun to concentrate their knowledge and skills on dealing with those affected by the divorce process.

Given the fact that a rising percentage of patients seen in public and private clinical practice are members of divorcing, divorced, or remarriage families, this contribution focuses on the stages of divorce and the practical aspects of divorce therapy. It is predicated upon the "diaclectic" conceptual framework which I (FK) have been evolving since 1977.

THE "DIACLECTIC" MODEL OF DIVORCE THERAPY

The term *diaclectic* was first coined to convey the fact that this paradigm draws eclectically from a variety of sources on behavior dynamics and stage theory, and seeks a dynamic, dialectic synthesis of what is known of the emotions experienced, actions exhibited, and tasks to be accomplished during the divorce process if reasonably successful resolution is to be achieved (Kaslow, 1979/80). Eclectic and dialectic were merged into diaclectic as a confabulated, yet simplified, labeling word (Kaslow, 1981a, 1981b).

What type of intervention is selected as the cornerstone of the treatment is contingent upon a clear understanding of where the patient(s) is in the divorce process sequence. Thus, a brief summation of two of the main stage theories of the divorce process, interwoven with some personal comments, will be given as a backdrop against which to view therapeutic strategies. Those interventions which have proven most effective in my clinical practice and which other clinician authors have also depicted as valuable will be discussed in relation to each stage—what is transpiring when, and what will help reduce the pain and chaos and maximize each involved person's capacity for fruitful living. My own current philosophical orientation is a blend of psychodynamic, object-relations and humanistic-existential theory; clinically the therapeutic approach utilizes analytic, gestalt, structural, strategic, family of origin, contextual, and behavioral techniques, depending on the presenting problem, personality dynamics, ego strength, and stage in the life cycle and divorce process (Kaslow, 1981a). In many ways, it is closely akin to

Lazarus' multimodal approach (Lazarus, 1981). All of this will be later integrated and incorporated in Table 2 (see pp. 30–31).

Bohannon (1973) clearly articulates a six "station" process. He emphasizes that, on both the individual and societal levels, the usual way of coping with devastating traumas such as divorce is to first try denial and hope the terrible problem will disappear. When this does not occur, the reality of the situation is slowly allowed into consciousness where it can gradually be accommodated. The stations do not occur as an invariant sequence, nor is the intensity the same at each phase or for all people. Inevitably, each stage must be experienced and its tasks mastered before a new equilibrium is established.

Emotional divorce is, in Bohannon's schema, the first station. During this period, the pair become increasingly aware of their disenchantment and dissatisfaction with one another, sense that their relationship is deteriorating, and may begin to distrust each other. One or both become disillusioned about the marriage being viable and worth keeping; they become critical and harp on the negative features of the spouse and the marriage.

The seeds of this dissatisfaction can be deeply sown. It can occur as an outgrowth of a long-standing and cherished childhood fantasy, nourished by fairy tales and motion pictures, that one will grow up, meet Prince Charming or the Beautiful Princess, fall in love, be awakened sexually by the lover's kiss, get married and ride off into the beautiful distance to "live happily ever after." Or, coming from an unhappy, abusive, or depriving household, one may enter marriage yearning for a second chance to be cared for and nurtured, craving parenting more than the reciprocal give and take of a healthy, adult, intimate peer relationship. If either of these scenarios predates the marriage and the unrealistic dreams remain present during the early years of marriage, disappointment and anger are the inevitable consequences when the needs continue to be unmet and the spouse feels cheated and unloved. When the deficiency needs (D needs) are tremendous (Maslow, 1968), clinging, pouting or more demanding spouses may be expecting their mate to be not only a parent but also their best friend, lover, confidante, helpmate, playmate, limit setter, mentor, and protector, all rolled into one, and capable of discerning which role to assume to harmonize with their mood of the hour. Such inordinate demands leave the caretaker spouse depleted and thwarted. In therapy they often say, and quite accurately, "Nothing I do is enough. It seems like a bottomless pit." The helplessness and dependency, perhaps originally great attractions, turn into infuriating deficits. The other partner's grandiose and authoritative manner, which was once perceived as exciting or which engendered feelings of security, deteriorates into a pompous and repetitious litany of promises never delivered.

Sometimes the early years go quite well, and conflict does not evolve until much later. At any moment in time, people choose exactly the kind of person they most need, consciously and unconsciously. Bowen (1978) posits that we each choose someone at the same level of individuation from their family of origin as we are from ours; to this I would add that we also tend to choose someone at the relatively same level of moral development (Kohlberg, 1969) and emotional health. A relationship capable of surviving is most likely one with a good balance between symmetrical and complementary elements (Pollack, N. Kaslow, & Harvey, 1982) and in which the partners agree that they should communicate openly, conveying clearly how they think and feel and what they want, and listening attentively and responsively to each other. In addition, some agreement to negotiate important differences and to accept each one's right to privacy and to being his or her own person, as well as part of a couple, is probably essential (Sager, 1976). Where these ingredients are not threads of the marital tapestry, the changes which inevitably occur as individuals grow in their life experiences are likely to disrupt the homeostatic balance, particularly if one grows while the other seems to stagnate, or if each grows but in incompatible directions. Problems related to the external environment, like job loss or job relocation, financial difficulties, death of a parent or child, sexual dysfunction or disinterest, severe injury, or other major life crises can place the couple under extreme stress for which they may blame each other, causing the relationship to become intolerable. Any one or a combination of the above factors can lead to disenchantment and unhappiness, and ultimately to the emotional divorce. Kessler (1975), who presents a seven stage model, labels Stages I and II *disillusionment* and *erosion*, respectively. These are both inherent in the emotional divorce.

It is during this period that the partner who does not want the divorce, or the one who is very discontent but ambivalent about the idea of divorce and all of its implications, may seek therapy. At this point, marital therapy should be seriously considered. Research indicates that couples who enter conjoint marital therapy are more likely to repair and improve their marriage (since the emphasis is on what is good for the couple as a unit as well as for each partner) than those in which one or both go into individual therapy (Whitaker & Miller, 1969).

PREDIVORCE STAGES IN THERAPY

In marital therapy, each of the member's complaints, criticisms, and disappointments should be heard first. Such ventilation provides some relief, at least temporarily, and gives them a chance to bring the sources of conflict out into the open in order to begin assessing and seeking solutions.

Meanwhile, the therapist can evaluate the couple and each individual (their strengths and weaknesses, quality of relationship, willingness to change, wellsprings of anger, whether the relationship is triangulated and, if so, with whom, sexual manifestations of the difficulty, personality integration). Asking partners to recount how they met, the basis of their attraction, and what positives still remain may enable them to break through the excessive negativism and realize that, despite the shattered dreams, they still care about one another and want to work at building or rebuilding a more solid relationship. Alternately, one or both may have feelings of being trapped and really be requesting help in extricating from the no longer wanted marriage. The therapist gets caught in a dilemma when one wants to save the marriage (and may even threaten suicide if the other leaves) and the other wants to dissolve the union. It is *ultimately the patients' decision*; however, the therapist can help them explore the consequences of both choices, can suggest temporary alternatives like a trial separation, and help them move toward feeling each has a part in the decision making. If one is determined to leave, then the therapist's role may shift to helping the partner who feels spurned and victimized take charge of planning his or her own future and enabling both of them to make divorcing as constructive an experience as possible.

Short-term couples group therapy is an efficacious approach at this point. Because of space limitations here, just a brief highlighting of this modality must suffice. (See Kaslow, 1981c, and Kaslow & Lieberman, 1981, for greater explication of this approach.) I prefer working with a group of five couples, all of whom are experiencing marital turmoil and none of whom have a member who diagnostically falls into either the severe psychotic or personality disorder categories (American Psychiatric Association, 1980). Each couple is first seen separately, and we jointly determine whether single couple or couples group therapy is likely to constitute the treatment of choice for them. If they find the idea of group therapy intriguing and I think they are good candidates, a contract is signed in which they both agree to attend 12 weekly sessions. Fulfilling the contract and terminating on time are crucial aspects, since many participants have not experienced others keeping their word or holding them accountable for fulfilling commitments. Because dependence-independence is customarily the main theme that emerges in this psychoanalytically oriented, closed end, short-term kind of group, the couples rapidly focus on the need for connectedness with and separateness from each other, their children, siblings, and parents. Through the group process, members become mirrors for one another, reflecting back what they see, and confronting each other's blind spots and rationalizations (Kaslow, 1982b). Healthy attachment, closeness, and individuation are supported; however, group members point out and challenge symbiotic clinging maneuvers and retreating into silence as a defense against self-disclosure and closeness.

The usual pattern is to have a heterosexual cotherapy pair as leaders. As a team they can: (a) structure their interventions to serve as role models for male-female interaction and constructive problem resolution; (b) function as parent substitutes from whom members can derive some nurturing, reducing the demands on the spouse and helping each member to realize that no one person can or should be expected to provide for all of their caretaking and gratification; (c) serve as parent surrogates against whom participants can ventilate some of their anger and distress, deflecting the stress from the marriage and enabling them to have breathing space in which to enjoy each other; (d) convey their belief that some of the problems predate the marriage and need to be worked through with each spouse's family of origin; and (e) communicate their belief that the couple is capable of deciding whether they prefer to stay together and improve their marriage, *with each taking responsibility for his or her own change process*, or whether they will ultimately fare better if they agree to separate, planning to do so in a way that will increase their self-esteem and respect rather than be demeaning. The preset time frame provides a useful structure for the group; since they have a limited time period in which to work on the problems which propelled them into therapy, they become more focused and learn techniques for problem resolution and decision making.

Couples group therapy is a lively, interesting modality that patients report they find exceedingly enlightening. It helps free up bound energy as they stop clinging to past hurts and battles and making excessive demands on each other and, instead, begin to create a larger resource network for fulfillment and enjoyment. It is also interesting and rewarding for the therapist!

Those couples who recognize and resolve the difficulties during Stage I, either with or without therapy, tend not to move on to the next phase. The prognosis is fairly good for their marriage at this point, and divorce therapy per se is not required.

Just as Kessler calls her Stage II *erosion*, I see a second phase of the predivorce period as a *time of despair* when the realization hits that the marriage is in severe jeopardy. It is a time of extreme ambivalence, wavering between denial, a pretense that everything is fine, attempting to win back the spouse's affection and perhaps to have one's own rekindled. Feelings of dread, chaos, confusion, inadequacy, and failure are prominent. Often one or the other may turn to family, friends, or clergy to entreat or pressure the spouse who wants to leave into staying. If they have been in marital therapy, one partner may no longer be willing to be seen in tandem. Individual therapy might well be in order here to help one deal with feelings of rejection and failure and the other with guilt over breaking up the marriage and hurting the spouse (or even for feeling relief that the ordeal may soon be ended).

THERAPY DURING DIVORCE

This period merges into Bohannon's second and third stations, *the legal and economic divorce*, when one or both parties seek legal counsel. Today, with the advent of divorce mediation (Coogler, 1978; Haynes, 1981), individuals who want to maximize their own input into the final agreement regarding custody and property distribution, and who dislike the prospect of litigation, are turning to this alternative form of dispute resolution. If they can decide to cooperate and seek a solution that attempts to embody what is likely to be in the "best interest" of everyone involved, then this period may be one in which they feel empowered to make their own choices and feel increasing self-respect as they exercise their own judgment and take responsibility for refashioning their own lives (Neville, 1984).

If adversarial proceedings are the route pursued, then the litigants are more likely to feel helpless, pessimistic, detached, and depressed since the negotiating is largely in the hands of the attorneys and the decisions regarding custody, parental responsibility, and division of assets rest with the judge. There is a great deal of anxiety emanating from uncertainty. From the admixture of confusion, loneliness, sadness, and grief over all losses entailed in the break up of the marriage and family, retribution may well become a dominant aim. The distribution of valued possessions, purchased or inherited as part of their dream of a fine life together, is a painful experience. Prolonged quarreling may represent unwillingness to let go of the last remnants of the union. Kessler (1975) designates Stage III as *detachment*, Stage IV as *physical separation*, and Stage V as *mourning*. On the master chart which appears in Table 2, these are interwoven with Bohannon's Station 2 and 3 and my discussion of feelings and tasks.

Invariably, I work from the theoretical stance of a family systems perspective, elucidated in Chapter 1, although often I will see subsystems or individual members of the system-in-flux. Like Isaacs (1981), I believe this is the most comprehensive and illuminating perspective for the divorce therapist. In this context, when the decision to separate has been made, it is often advisable to work with the couple around how

Table 2

Diaclectic Model of Stages in the Divorce Process

Divorce Stage	Station	Stage	Feelings	Actions and Tasks	Therapeutic Interventions
	1. Emotional Divorce	I	Disillusionment Dissatisfaction Alienation Anxiety Disbelief	Avoiding the issue Sulking and/or crying Confronting partner Quarreling	Marital therapy (one couple) Couples group therapy
Predivorce A time of deliberation and despair		II	Despair Dread Anguish Ambivalence Shock Emptiness Anger Chaos Inadequacy Low self-esteem Loss	Denial Withdrawal (physical and emotional) Pretending all is okay Attempting to win back affection Asking friends, family, clergy for advice	Marital therapy (one couple) Divorce therapy Couples group therapy
	2. Legal Divorce	III	Depression Detachment Anger Hopelessness Self-pity Helplessness	Bargaining Screaming Threatening Attempting suicide Consulting an attorney or mediator	Family therapy Individual adult therapy Child therapy
During Divorce A time of legal involvement	3. Economic Divorce	IV	Confusion Fury Sadness	Separating physically Filing for legal divorce Considering economic arrangements Considering custody arrangements	Children of divorce group therapy Child therapy Adult therapy

Stage		Emotions	Tasks	Therapies
4. Coparental Divorce and the Problems of Custody	V	Loneliness Relief Vindictiveness	Grieving and mourning Telling relatives and friends Re-entering work world (unemployed woman) Feeling empowered to make choices	Children of divorce group therapy Child therapy Adult therapy
5. Community Divorce and the Problems of Loneliness	VI	Indecisiveness Optimism Resignation Excitement Curiosity Regret Sadness	Finalizing divorce Begin reaching out to new friends Undertaking new activities Stabilizing new life-style and daily routine for children Exploring new interests and possibly taking new job	Adults individual therapy singles group therapy Children child play therapy children's group therapy
6. Psychic Divorce	VII	Acceptance Self-confidence Energy Self-worth Wholeness Exhilaration Independence Autonomy	Resynthesis of identity Completing psychic divorce Seeking new love object and making a commitment to some permanency Becoming comfortable with new life-style and friends Helping children accept finality of parents' divorce and their continuing relationship with both parents	Parent-child therapy Family therapy Group therapies Children's activity group therapy

Postdivorce
A time of exploration and re-equilibrium

they have been handling feelings and events with the children, and what needs to be done now. The therapist can help the adults understand the powerful impact of their actions on the children and indicate that the nature of their adjustment will correlate with the children's future adjustment (Wallerstein & Kelly, 1980). The children's needs to have access to both parents, to feel both parents continue to love them and will be actively interested in them, to remain loyal to both and not to be torn between them, and their right not to hear either parent denigrate the other (Bodin, 1982) should be highlighted. If the couple cannot be in conjoint sessions, and with dissolution of marriage their goal, it may be more valid to have separate sessions at this stage. The words "may be" are critical since, in some instances, this is a time for family sessions, including the children, so that feelings and wishes can be aired openly in the therapist's safe sanctuary, and all can have a say in shaping the evolving two single-parent families.

Sometimes, if the couples' parents are unduly pressuring them to make or alter a decision and they cannot contend with them alone, this is an appropriate occasion for two separate, multigenerational, family of origin sessions with each of their respective parents and siblings. In addition, since the children may well need total attention, empathy, and caring from a therapist, individual child therapy may well be in order, with play therapy an important modality so the child can act out his/her turmoil, hostility, and longings. Art therapy integrated into verbal psychotherapy also enables children and adolescents to draw out their internal conflicts, some of which they have great difficulty articulating. This can also provide the therapist with a better diagnostic understanding, an additional avenue through which to establish a therapeutic alliance, and a multipronged way of treating.

For Bohannon, the fourth station is entitled *"coparental divorce and the problems of custody."* In my paradigm, this is included in the "during divorce" stage and is closely intertwined with the legal and economic divorce, since often what is labeled a custody battle revolves around financial considerations. It is important for divorce therapists to be cognizant of the laws in their state regarding divorce (whether it is fault or no fault, the accrual of time for the required waiting period and when that begins to be calculated, how likely a temporary agreement is to become permanent) and child custody (whether there is a preference for joint custody, joint parental responsibility, or a sole/noncustodial arrangement), and what kind of guidance clients may be receiving from their mediator or attorney. It is essential for the therapist using any reality-oriented, here-and-now approach to make clear his or her own value stance (Abroms, 1978) regarding a "best interest of the child" position and the fact that emotional considerations are at least as salient and long lasting as financial ones.

Children often seem neglected in the "during divorce" stage when their parents are tense, hurt, and volatile, and their energies are being directed toward physically and financially separating, quarreling over provisos of the agreement, or perhaps taking on additional jobs to handle economic drain. There may be little time or energy left for the children and little sensitivity to their bewilderment and pain. Conversely, some parents become overly possessive, protective, and intrusive, trying to shield their children from additional anguish or feelings of abandonment, or trying to make them an ally against the other parent. For children at this time, group therapy with other children of divorce is a valuable approach. The therapist can create an environment in which they can ventilate their sorrow, explore their feelings, gain understanding of the crisis, derive support from each other through being with a sympathetic group of peers and a gentle, caring adult, and consider options for handling the difficult situations that are likely to arise. Kessler and Bostwick (1977) vividly describe the "how to" for children's groups. This modality may also be valuable in the postdivorce stage for children who still have many unresolved issues to deal with but who do not wish to do so when parents are present either because of fear of offending them or being inhibited by them.

POSTDIVORCE ISSUES

As the legal divorce nears completion, the kind of support system the individuals have is a critical factor. Do they have family to help them with their concerns and to fill the lonely void? What about friends? Are they accessible or does the divorce impinge on friends' religious convictions or threaten their own marriages? Bohannon labels his fifth station *"community divorce and the problem of loneliness."* Bach (1974) suggests that some kind of divorce ceremony helps facilitate closure. For the most part (except for Orthodox and Conservative Judaism which have traditionally performed a religious divorce ceremony using a tribunal of three Rabbis to convey sanction of the marital dissolution), there has until recently been a paucity of ceremonies or rituals to help mark and ease the divorce transition. For patients who need something specific and are religiously oriented, therapists can encourage them to talk to their clergyman about creating a special service (Kaslow, 1981b). (More on this in a later chapter.) Because of the dearth of community support, groups like Parents Without Partners arose. Later, social agencies and churches began running groups for divorced adults; the combined social-educational and support emphasis is appealing to many. It offers an alternative to the bar scene as a way of meeting people and serves as one of the passageways in the postdivorce period.

Once the divorce is finalized, two new family units begin to function. Ahrons (1983b) calls this the binuclear family. Visitation should slowly smooth out, new identities should begin to be forged, and the adults should be reentering the larger world. The rhythm which characterizes "letting go" of the past marriage and becoming involved anew or differently in work, recreation, and social activities is a very individual matter. The therapist must respect the person's unique tempo. It may be slow paced, as when the person is allowing the grieving process to be completed and getting the family and home reordered before entering into new relationships; or fast paced, as when he or she plunges into the social whirl to find excitement, prove sexual appeal and prowess, or as an antidote to loneliness. There is no one right way during the aftermath. If he or she is still extremely emotional and fragile, the therapist can help the person cognitively reframe and restructure perceptions about his or her new life. Conversely, if the individual is utilizing intellectualization as the main defensive mechanism of the ego against allowing his or her feelings into consciousness, the therapist probably should help the person get in touch with the various emotions buried within. As some balance is achieved between the affective and cognitive states, the individual can make sounder decisions about what actions to take.

For some, the immediate postdivorce period is one of exploration of the inner world as well as the outer environment (trying out new activities, pursuing interests that have been dormant or which have arisen as enticing, returning to school, reentering or changing jobs, and building new social relationships or changing existing ones). It is exciting, liberating, and stimulating. Individual or group therapy of "single-again" individuals can provide the "permission" needed to enjoy the pleasures of this heady new world and help them evolve the values and structure that will channel their pursuits. It can also assist them in learning to juggle the myriad aspects of their life (parent, friend, lover, worker, student, child's chauffeur, helper with homework, homemaker) and to mobilize their energy and optimism to utilize the opportunities inherent in their complex life.

For others it continues as a prolonged period of reactive depression, a time of unabated fury, desire for revenge, and a sense of hopelessness and helplessness. Those in this category are the ones most likely to malign their former mates, to try to influence their children against their former spouse, indulge in self-pity, and become "stuck" around the divorce as the most critical event in their lives. For them, individual therapy to work through the anger, to accept their own contribution to the marital discord and its eventual dissolution, to overcome the depression and to extricate the children from unhealthy bonding or becoming parentified, might well be in order. Only then can they, like the former group, complete what Bohannon calls the sixth station or *"psychic divorce."*

Kessler indicates that most divorcé(e)s pass through a *second adolescence*, which equates with what I have talked about as the *time of exploration*. Given their life experience, and often the fact of their parenthood and maturity, I do not find that everyone who reenters the single world "regresses" into an adolescent way of relating. Some are healthy adults whose ability to be creative and playful is reawakened (Maslow, 1968) as they attempt to "make up for lost time" (Hyatt, 1977). *Hard work* (Kessler, 1975) is essential as the person continues to resolve the psychic trauma and then reequilibrates into a wholesome integration that expresses his or her new identity and values in decisions and behaviors and takes full responsibility for the direction of his or her life (Kaslow, 1981b). Only after this occurs are most people ready and able to enter into a long-term committed relationship or capable of deciding that they prefer being single and alone for the foreseeable future. (Table 2 on pp. 30–31 summarizes the above in chart form to recapitulate and interrelate the foregoing concepts.)

Similar to the Bohannon, Kessler, and Kaslow models, yet more narrowly focused is Turner's (1980) analysis of stages in mid-life divorce. His first stage is *disenchantment*, based, as he put it, "on the psychological violation of largely known but unverbalized contracts" (p. 153). Disenchantment, similar to Bohannon's disillusionment, sets in as the result of one or more of the following: growth or change in oneself or the spouse, major life events (illness, changes in values, death of a parent), comparisons with others' marriages (or friends' divorces and their apparent freedom and happiness), a shift in the rewards/costs in the marriage, third party attraction/attachment, or gradual withdrawal from the spouse. Disenchantment is typically followed by *intrapsychic conflict*— "Should I stay?" "Should I go?" "Should I decide at all?" "Should I wait?" At some point, the individual makes a decision out of which a series of actions ensue. Assuming that the decision is to divorce, the individual seeks approval, first from those most likely to be supportive and later from significant others, such as family members. At some point, of course, the spouse also needs to be informed of the decision.

Turner deals very little with the legal and economic aspects of the divorce, so he skips from the *decision-making stage* to the *social transition stage* which encompasses those feelings and actions common to Kaslow's postdivorce period. His fifth and sixth stages—*restabilization and growth* and *postdivorce adjustments*—clearly belong to this period as well.

The unique aspect of Turner's model is that it is descriptive of divorcé(e)s who grew up and married at a time when values and practices differed from today's—pre-1960. In the "now world" of increased options for the young there remain more constrictions on the middle-aged because of their earlier socialization. In divorce, long-standing ties with the former spouse's family may be broken and this can be exceedingly painful if the relationships were positive and meaningful. The never-employed housewife may need to find employment in a highly competitive labor market for which she is unprepared; dating opportunities may be limited, especially for middle-aged women; and personal values and conservative behaviors may have to be modified. Although the middle-aged ex-partners may not have minor children about whom they engage in disputes over custody, if they are parents there are still involvements revolving around their children and each other when it comes to holidays, rites of passage, or other major life events, and finances. Thus Turner's focus is on a subgroup of the divorced and on a limited range of the effects of divorce on them rather than on the more generalized patterns seen by Bohannon and Kaslow.

For a divorced person, in the restabilization phase, reaching the level of intimacy described by Wynne (1984) with a new lover or spouse may depend upon the events of the separation or divorce. If one spouse abused the trust of the other, it will typically be more difficult for the "abused" party to become emotionally intimate with anyone else. (Of course, some adults are unable to reach full intimacy at any point in their life cycle for a variety of reasons.) There may be, however, some willingness on the part of the formerly abused partner to seek a more limited intimate relationship because of the desire to feel some attachment to another person. Obviously, the degree of closeness one is willing and able to obtain depends upon prior events and relationships and their consequences in terms of perceived levels of risk and vulnerability. Some spouses, as indicated, find it difficult to trust anyone as deeply as Wynne describes; others, perhaps with sharply diminished self-esteem as a result of the first partner's betrayal, place themselves again and again in a situation that repeats that pattern, as if to reinforce the negative self-image. The more fortunate find a new partner with whom, perhaps very cautiously, they can build a new and rather complete intimacy as they move through Wynne's stages anew.

If we now look back at the family life cycles described by Rhodes (1977), Hughes et al. (1978), and Wynne (1984), and superimpose the stages of divorce as delineated by Bohannon (1970, 1973), Kaslow (1979/80, 1981b, 1983), Kessler (1975) and Turner (1980), it appears obvious that the impact of divorce will vary somewhat depending on the point at which it intersects not only the adults' individual life cycles, but also the family's as a unit and each child individually. There has been some research over the past several years on the impact of divorce on children, with the majority of studies focusing on preschool and latency-age children who are at specific stages of their developmental cycles. Although all of the life cycles interact, we are unaware of any published effort to date to diagram the dynamic relationships accurately for the family as a whole at the moment of developmental trauma (divorce). As indicated earlier, we have utilized Duhl's Chronological Chart for this purpose and have found it to be a worthwhile tool.

Despite the fact that each family breakup has its unique aspects, the framework of family and divorce cycles fits virtually every case. Even among those who divorce after a year or less of marriage, and decide jointly to do so, there are some pangs of regret or guilt or failure. For those who have advanced to the children's departure stage, there are also feelings of regret, guilt, and failure with the addition, perhaps, of considerable mourning for the loss of a shared history and the end of a dream. It is our intent to demonstrate the similarities and differences of divorce experiences as they occur for males and females at different points in the individual and family life cycles. The principal paradigms used will be those of Hughes et al. for the family, Colarusso and Nemiroff for the adult individuals, and Bohannon and Kaslow for the divorce cycle.

This chapter has been written from a combined family systems and stage theory of development perspective. It suggests that the choice of what kind of therapy is likely to be most efficient and most efficacious in any given situation should be determined by assessing in which stage in the divorce process clients are when they seek treatment, their ego strength, cognitive functioning, and resources. It is predicated on an assumption of flexibility in the therapist's own style and philosophic orientation to either encompass modalities that are valid in the different stages (rather than rigid adherence to one purist truth) or refer patients to someone else who is likely to be more skilled. It recommends a dynamic, "diaclectic" paradigm of divorce theory and therapy, culled from various theoretical schools as clinicians of different disciplines and orientations pool their hypotheses, hunches, experiences, observations, and research findings to assist people in the community at large and in their patient populations to navigate through the divorce process.

CHAPTER 3

Literature Review: Clinical Findings and Research on Divorce

Generally this review of the literature will be sequenced in accordance with the stages of divorce elucidated in Chapter 2. Criticisms of contemporary research are discussed in the final portion of the chapter.

In the 1940s, college students studied marriage in terms of predicting "marital happiness." They considered what factors would be likely to strengthen marital bonds, and the answers given spoke of age, homogamy in educational and religious background, common interests, and similar items. In the 1950s, when those students married, the divorce rate was one in five or six marriages (Goode, 1956) as against the 1980s rate of one in every two or three marriages. It is hardly surprising, then, that the emphasis in courses dealing with marriage and the family has partially shifted to a study of factors contributing to divorce rather than to marital happiness.

CONTRIBUTING FACTORS

One of the earliest major studies of divorce was Goode's (1956) research with a sample of divorced mothers living in the Detroit metropolitan area in 1948. These women, aged 20–38 years, frequently experienced much social disapproval of their status even when they were divorced from abusive, alcoholic, rejecting, or unfaithful husbands. The moral atmosphere of the time was so stringent and condemnatory that there was no ethical imperative for relatives or friends to provide emotional or financial support for divorced parties. Goode's "Proneness to Divorce" Index, probably biased in the direction of this strict morality, found an inverse correlation between socioeconomic level and percentage of divorces, and thus reflected the popular view that divorce did not happen in "good" (i.e., middle-class and upper-middle-class) families. Divorce laws of that period also reflected the aura of moral judgement, granting divorces only on specific grounds such as adultery and making no allowances for a couple's common desire to separate because of incompatibility or extreme dissatisfaction with their union. Indeed, that would have been labelled collusion, a condition expressly forbidden by the statutes that negated any possibility of a divorce being granted unless "fault" could be shown and a guilty and an innocent (injured) party designated.

Although the husband has been the one most often seen as wanting the divorce, Goode suggested that "in our society *the husband more frequently than the wife will engage in behavior whose function, if not intent, whose result, if not aim, is to force the other spouse to ask for the divorce first*" (1956, p. 136). As a legal fiction and often a practical "courtesy," divorce suits were often instituted by the wife, preserving her "honor" as a wronged female.

According to Levinger's (1966) study, however, the "courtesy" may not have been such a legal fiction. In his study of 600 divorcé(e)s in the Cleveland area, all of whom had one or more children under age 14, wives—especially those identified as lower-class by the Hollingshead Index (1957)—filed divorce complaints citing physical abuse, financial problems, alcoholism, neglect of home and children, and mental cruelty, with each of these representing 26.5%–40.3% of the grounds cited. Although husbands who filed divorce complaints also cited mental cruelty (29.7%) and neglect of home and children (26.2%), they exceeded wives only in their citing of "sexual incompatibility" (20.0%) as grounds for divorce. Middle-class wives more often filed on grounds of "excessive demands" (2.5%), or infidelity (24.0%); lower-class husbands cited infidelity in 20.0% of complaints, or "lack of love" (22.8%); middle-class husbands—(13.5%). "In-law problems" were cited by husbands as a complaint almost three times as often as by wives (16.2% to 6.7%), and were the fifth most frequent husband-originated complaint.

Levinger concluded, "In general, the evidence indicates that spouses in middle-class marriages were more concerned with psychological and emotional interaction, while the lower-class partners saw as most salient in their lives financial problems and the unsubtle physical actions of their partner" (1966, p. 806). That is not to say that abuse did not occur in middle-class marriages, just that it was less often admitted by battered wives (or husbands) in the 1960s.

Kitson and Sussman (1982), who studied a multiethnic sample of divorced adults in the Cleveland area, found that women were more likely than men to cite "extra-marital sex, untrustworthiness or immaturity, being out with the boys, drinking, financial and employment problems . . . , and emotional and personality problems as major complaints" (p. 92). The ex-husbands, by contrast, were more apt to be

> unsure about what caused the breakup of their marriages and
> . . . to mention overcommitment to work, problems with relatives,
> and external events such as a death in the family, a job change, or a
> third party or thing . . . as reasons for the breakup. (p. 92)

It is instructive to examine not only the difference in complaints by gender, as Kitson and Sussman have done, but also differences by time period. Recalling that Goode's study was done in the immediate post-World War II period and that Kitson and Sussman's work reflects the social and psychological upheavals of the 1970s, Table 3 shows the priority ranking of marital complaints (ranked according to the ex-wives) by gender. (This ranking does not pertain to frequency.) The earlier study more frequently shows issues of nonsupport, conflicts in authority, and drinking as principal factors contributing to divorce, while the later study shows more affective complaints, such as personality, changes in values, and lack of communication. This is consistent with Kaslow's (1983) clinical observations.

A study by Spanier and Thompson (1984) supports this shift in factors. They report the chief sources of disagreement found in their sample to be:

1. Gender role performance (e.g., sharing in housekeeping tasks)
2. Quality of sexual relationship
3. Poor communication
4. Changes in involvement (e.g., values, time spent together)

Kelly (1982), on the other hand, reported a mixture of what might be considered the antithesis of the traditional "factors promoting marital happiness" and the more contemporary causes stemming from the social changes of the 1970s. She found the following factors associated with marital instability:

1. Socioeconomic and age factors
   a. Marriage before 18 for females and before 20 for males
   b. High school dropout
   c. Economic disadvantage
2. Premarital pregnancy
3. Work
   a. Instability of husband's work and income
   b. Marked year-to-year decreases in husband's income

Table 3
Marital Complaints by Rank Showing Changes Over Time

	Goode (1956)			Kitson & Sussman (1982)[a]	
	Wives	Husbands		Wives	Husbands
Personality	1	2	Lack of communication	1	1
Home life	2	3	Gender role conflicts (Intra couple)	2	8
Values	2	4	Not sure (Just fell apart)	3	29
Other	4	1	Incompatible	3	8
Authority	5	6	Interests/values changed	5	7
Drinking	6	9	Problems with relatives	6	19
Complex (multiple)[b]	7	10	Internal gender role conflict	6	2
Miscellaneous (including sex)	8	5	Too young to wed	8	12
Nonsupport	9	11	Overcommitment to work	8	25
Infidelity, husband	10	13	Not enough social life	8	12
(Money) consumption	10	8	No sense of family	8	10
Relatives	12	7			

[a]Kitson and Sussman (1982), Table 2 (p. 92) and Table 3 (p. 93) abridged.
[b]Parenthetical inserts by current authors—our interpretations.

    c. Wives with higher incomes (and therefore more independence)
4. Intergenerational transmission—negative effects of postdivorce arrangements on the children of divorce into their own adulthood

Turner (1980) cited as leading sources of "relationship disenchantment" in mid-life divorces such factors as growth or change in self or spouse, impact of life events (see Kitson and Sussman earlier), social comparisons, third party attraction or attachment, unhappiness that shifted the balance of rewards and costs of marriage, and an often unconscious gradual withdrawal.

A desire for "self-actualization" (Maslow, 1968), not specifically mentioned earlier as a major ground for divorce, became a contributory factor to many separations in the 1970s and 1980s. This was expressed by both men and women in therapy and in anecdotal comments on our questionnaires (to be described in Chapter 4). One woman, for example, who initiated her marital separation at age 27 (divorced at 32 and now age 44), wrote that "Had I not found the courage to go through separation/divorce, I'm positive that I would not be the happy, productive, confident woman that I am today" (Subject #49). Weiss (1975) noted this factor in his seminal book on marital separation, writing that "in several instances in which the pursuit of self-realization did not itself produce the separation, it seemed nevertheless to have contributed to marital strife" (p. 10).

Although affective complaints may be more often cited today as reasons for divorce, there are many other marriages that flounder due to financial issues (at all socioeconomic levels), spouse abuse (physical and/or verbal, and at all levels), substance abuse, and infidelity. In addition, gambling is more accessible to millions of people now than in prior decades, with some gamblers becoming as addicted to the gaming tables and other forms of gambling as alcoholics are to liquor.

The women's liberation movement has made more wives aware of what constitutes "abuse" and has even succeeded in having rape within marriage declared a crime by several state legislatures. Advocacy of "open marriage" (O'Neill & O'Neill, 1972) has permitted many unfaithful spouses to feel less guilty, although the implicit rejection of the betrayed spouse continues to damage the latter's sense of self-worth severely.

In general, however, it is more difficult to examine divorce petitions for specific complaints today, as the majority of state legislatures have enacted "no-fault" divorce statutes. In our own survey (Schwartz & Kaslow, 1985), we placed more emphasis on who initiated the separation and the responses of the other spouse than on specific contributing factors to the divorce. This was in part because of the difficulty of ascertaining the veracity of the responses and in part because of the possible variation by socioeconomic class (although our sample was broad, it was predominantly middle and upper-middle class), race (our sample was all Caucasian), and length of marriage (our sample's range was less than a year to more than 35 years).

ATTEMPTS AT REVITALIZATION

Couples who have become disenchanted and disillusioned (Stage 1 in the divorce process) with each other and/or with the state of being married respond in different ways. They also differ considerably in how long they tolerate their negative feelings prior to deciding to separate. One individual of the pair may tolerate marital malaise for five years, for example, at the same time hoping for a change for the better and being unwilling to break up the marriage. Another individual, with a lower threshold of tolerance, may be so discomfited as to propose separation and divorce within a few months.

In our study, one husband, who had initiated the separation, reported a 3-month period of disillusionment in a marriage that lasted less than two years. Another husband, also the initiator, reported no disillusionment in a 21-year marriage. A wife-initiator reported 5 years of disenchantment in an 11-year marriage, while another woman who was also married for 11 years indicated feelings of disappointment for the entire period. In that instance, there was a joint decision to separate. In all, 90.4% (N = 66) of our sample reported that there had been some disillusionment prior to the separation.

Pettit and Bloom (1984) concluded that there were gender differences in tolerance for marital difficulties, with men more inclined to propose separation when the problems were mild than when they were severe. "Women, on the other hand, tolerate relatively mild mental discomfort, but as their level of dissatisfaction increases, they become willing to risk marital disruption in order to achieve a more satisfying life" (p. 593). Thus, they may avoid the issues altogether, as one of the partners may withdraw into sulking, or one may confront the other—depending on individual temperaments and other factors, such as fear of confrontation, anger and eventual aloneness.

Whoever initiated the separation and however long the disenchantment may have lasted, in most marriages there is some attempt to revitalize the marriage—to save it. Many people, even today, "believe that divorce is evil. For them it is a stigma, a symptom of personal failure, a telling sign of poor judgement and an unwillingness or inability to make mature adjustments" (Lazarus, 1981, p. 15). The couple may sit down and try to work out compromises that will reduce the tensions and rekindle romance, affection, and their relationship in general. If there are minor children, they may resolve to make a "go of it" for the children's sake.

As the emotional estrangement proceeds, there may also be consultations with family members, clergy, or close friends, either to seek advice on how to repair the ongoing damage or on how to initiate a separation. This is, as Kaslow (1983) has indicated, a period of deliberation and despair for one or both partners. One partner *may* seek individual psychotherapy, hoping to correct his or her faults that are contributing to the difficulties. Or one or both partners may seek solace in an extramarital affair (perhaps believing the old "line" offered in this situation of "my wife—or husband—doesn't understand me" as they say it to the new romantic interest). Many couples decide at this point to enter marital therapy in an attempt to save the marriage. They may go to a weekend marital retreat sponsored by a religious or counseling group. In many cases, the more positive efforts *can* lead to reconciliation. On the other hand, Lazarus (1981) cited a case in which the couple came for marital therapy and discovered over several sessions that they really had few common interests. They then decided to mediate their divorce agreement. In Bloom and Hodges' (1981) sample, 44% had sought couples therapy and 52% went for individual therapy prior to the separation.

It is unfortunate that so many people contemplating divorce seek individual treatment, given findings like those of Whitaker and Miller (1969). They have indicated that psychotherapeutic intervention on one side or another, only when divorce is being considered, may serve to destroy the possibility of reconciliation. Despite the therapist's efforts to remain neutral, he inevitably finds himself thrust into the role of catalyst, judge or alternate mate (p. 57). Whitaker and Miller recommended that:

> Both partners, and often children and other family members, be included in the therapy as a way of averting an outcome that might ultimately prove deleterious to all. Although they have found involving other family members to be a "powerful helpful device" (p. 61), they are uncertain why. They hypothesize that it may be because: 1) it represents a symbolic proof that the therapist believes the marriage may dissolve and this is serious business (in which they all have a stake), and/or 2) it symbolizes their respect for the fact of the marriage. (In Kaslow, 1981b, p. 682)

Further these therapist-authors caution against seeing one spouse alone initially and aligning with that partner, as the other spouse quickly feels outnumbered and threatened by the coalition. When he/she enters treatment later, therapist and original patient already have a therapeutic alliance going and the spouse is an outsider. Some patients skillfully triangulate the therapist into the relationship just as they have done with a child or a lover (Rubenstein & Timmins, 1978), again making the spouse feel insignificant, excluded and/or furious. Rubenstein and Timmins indicate further that where one partner is in prolonged individual psychotherapy, this "therapeutic marriage" is what makes it tolerable to sustain a terribly empty marriage. The danger is, of course, that terminating the therapy means a double catastrophe, as both "marriages" will come to a sharp halt. Also, the therapist is not truly available to the patient as a replacement spouse-lover.

In treating both partners together, the diagnosis shifts from identifying one as a sick mate to establishing the existence of a relationship problem (Whitaker & Miller, 1969). This is a very different entry point and the therapy unfolds accordingly; that is, both consider their role in causing and perpetuating the problems and what each can do to hasten improvement. By way of illustration, Whitaker and Miller cite one case of a married couple who had not consummated their union. The husband was still deeply entangled with his mother and had acknowledged past homosexual episodes. Although he could have been diagnosed as presenting deep-seated pathology, the therapist chose to serve as a catalyst and build upon their feelings of love and desire by being reassuring and encouraging. He threw the weight of his therapeutic power on the side of the part of the spouses that was healthy and wanted to express their love sexually so that the marriage could flourish. In six weeks, they overcame their inhibitions and were thrilled with each other—and with the therapist!

Whitaker and Miller caution against permitting the spouse who is eager to break up the marriage to turn the unwanted mate over to the therapist with a message to the effect that "now that she's in good hands and I know you will take care of her, I can leave." If the therapist gets caught in the trap, he/she may well have to continue filling in as a substitute for the departing spouse for a prolonged period of time.

To summarize the issue of whether individual therapy for one or both spouses or conjoint marital therapy constitutes the treatment of choice when a couple is contemplating divorce, we again turn to Whitaker and Miller (1969), since they capture the core issue.

Where the marital tie is weak and divorce threatens, intervention with one of the pair seems routinely to be disruptive. We are impressed that moving unilaterally into a marriage relationship, taking one of the two as the patient and referring or ignoring the mate, is very often a tactical blunder. (p. 61)

Those asked for advice, especially if they are close relatives, often respond with shock to the possibility of a divorce by the couple. Some will offer constructive suggestions for rebuilding the relationship, while others may instead add fuel to the fire by suggesting that the individual's spouse really deserves to be left "because. . . . " Depending to some extent on one's generation reference group and social values, friends or family may counsel a speedy termination to the marriage, reasoning that no one need stay in a relationship that is deteriorating. Clergy, on the other hand, are more likely to try to persuade the couple to work at the difficulties and revitalize the marriage. Some members of the clergy are trained to do marriage counseling while others merely preach platitudes.

Another pattern emerges if one partner unilaterally decides to leave the marriage and neither discusses the reasons why nor makes any attempt to reduce the marital problems. Then there is little hope for salvaging or rebuilding the marriage. The departing spouse is usually not amenable to any pleas for reconciliation, no matter what the rejected spouse says or does. The despair of the latter, even if also somewhat disenchanted with the marriage, feels as one of our survey participants put it, "as if an atomic bomb had been dropped on me." Often, the rejected spouse will then enter individual therapy in an effort to cope with this traumatic event and to revitalize his/her life, if not the marriage.

ATTEMPTS AT RECONCILIATION

Where there has been an actual separation of more than a couple of days, any resumption of living together represents reconciliation. This sometimes occurs after the suit for divorce has been filed. The couple may, in fact, separate and reconcile a few times before they finally become recommitted to the marriage or ultimately legally terminate it. Kitson and Langlie (1984) found that 23% of participants in an earlier divorce study had withdrawn their petitions to divorce and reconciled. Upon investigation, responses to the authors' queries suggested that this reunion often occurred on a fragile basis. Kitson and Langlie's review of the literature indicated that a wide variety of characteristics were associated with withdrawal or dismissal of divorce petitions. Alcoholism and wife abuse were frequently cited as common factors in the couples who exhibited these vacillating behaviors.

Some of those who reconcile live separate and apart from the spouse although in the same house. Others part and reconcile several times, acting out their ambivalence. Kitson and Langlie (1984) found that the "reconciled are significantly less likely than the divorced to have sought help with personal problems from a clergyman, physician, psychiatrist or psychologist, marriage counselor, or social worker" (p. 482). They also found that "compared to the divorced and the married, those who reconcile with their spouses for at least a week have high levels of subjective distress and psychophysiological complaints, and more physician visits" (p. 486). Despite higher levels of domestic violence, the reconcilers are also more likely to view their spouses in a favorable light or they would not return to the marriage.

Our clinical observation is that many of those who reunite quickly are likely to be highly dependent, unable to cope with their internal and external world alone, and often fall, diagnostically, in the borderline or personality disorder category (American Psychiatric Association, 1980). There is another group of couples who, after separating, enter therapy and work through the impediments to an improved relationship, often softening a prior uncompromising stance or ending an extramarital affair. They may gain some insight into their contribution to the marital discord and may decide to alter their attitudes and/or behaviors. They may also find they miss their mate, children, and being a daily part of their own family and that being alone is not as appealing as they had fantasized it would be. After a "sabbatical" from marriage of some months to a year, during which some real soul-searching and emotional growth has taken place in both partners, they may achieve a fairly solid basis for reuniting.

THE DECISION TO DIVORCE

Kelly (1982) found that separation and divorce are rarely matters of mutual decision. Indeed, our own survey corroborates this, as only 15.1% (11/73) of the separated/divorced adults had made a joint decision to part. Even this is a substantially higher percentage than Wallerstein and Kelly (1980) had identified. Recent studies suggest that more women than men initiate divorce, a finding also corroborated in our sample where 57.5% of the initiators were the wives. Whoever makes the move generally does so as a result of a "last straw" phenomenon (e.g., infidelity, drinking, major life event), after psychotherapy, or as "the culmination of accumulated grievances, instabilities, and unhappiness accompanied by the growing recognition that the personal toll that the relationship extracts from the individual is no longer balanced by the security or gratification of being married" (Kelly, 1982, p. 376). It should be remembered, however, that the initiator is not necessarily the spouse who precipitated the turmoil or who files the divorce petition. In terms of the marital system and our family systems perspective, in some ways both precipitate the marital crises which culminate in the separation.

Spanier and Thompson (1984) divide the predivorce period into three phases: 1) foreboding of a possible breakup, 2) certainty about the end of the marriage, and 3) actual filing for divorce. They indicate more recognition of the impact of a sudden separation than many other researchers do, noting that "Not only are the timing and sequence of dissolution events related to the circumstances of marriage and its demise but also to the emotional impact of the breakup" (p. 51). Their perception is echoed by Oakland (1984), who pointed out that "The husband or wife who suddenly packs his or her bags, moves out, and employs a lawyer to handle all legal responsibilities, sets in motion a process likely to cause severe damage to him- or herself and the family" (p. 27). Their not having the courage or consideration to discuss their intentions or to be present when the unsuspecting spouse becomes aware of the impending breakup makes the impact of the mate's "disappearance" even more devastating. It has a destructive effect on any good memories that the deserted spouse may have savored to reassure him- or herself that at least for some time the marriage was valued and worth the personal investment of time, energy, caring, and trust.

The spouse who initiates the separation and divorce experiences greater stress prior to the separation, according to Kelly (1982), while the rejected spouse suffers more after the separation. This is because the initiator, after the anxiety of making the decision, is mentally prepared for the separation and, having made the decision to part, has a sense of control in the situation. Weiss (1975) agrees that the initiators and the "left" both suffer distress of different kinds, but distinguishes the nature of their suffering rather than the timing. He found that:

> those who initiated the separation tend to feel guilty, even anguished, at the damage their departure inflicted on those they were pledged to cherish. They may anticipate the condemnation of others and feel such condemnation to be partially deserved. . . . Those on whom separation was imposed, in contrast, have been the recipients of traumatic rejection, with what may seem to have been inadequate opportunity to retaliate. . . . They may feel that friends and neighbors who know they were left or forced to leave may have lost respect for them. . . . (pp. 64–65)

Most likely, both views have some truth in them, though some initiators may reject the burden of guilt and instead project full responsibility for the separation on the seemingly rejected spouse's abhorrent behavior in order to justify their decision to themselves as well as to others. Allowance should be made in considering these somewhat different perceptions for the rapidly changing society of the 1970s which altered value systems radically and left many people's attitudes in a continuing state of flux.

THE PHYSICAL SEPARATION—A PAINFUL PARTING

Sitcoms and films have shown a variety of actual separation scenarios. In one image, the wife leaves a note propped against the sugar bowl informing her husband that she has left him but that there's a casserole in the refrigerator for his dinner. In another, the couple discusses the timing and manner of the departure dispassionately as in the dialogue below.

> *She*: If you'll come by between 11 A.M. and 1 P.M., the children will be at school and I'll be at my aerobics class.
> *He*: But what will you tell the kids when they come home from school?
> *She*: Simply that we've agreed that this is best for all of us, and that you'll be in touch with them.
> *He*: I really don't like packing up and leaving without explaining it to them.
> *She*: Trust me. I'll explain it to them fairly. Then you can call them tonight to reassure them and to make plans to see them over the weekend.
> *He*: Well . . . All right. I guess under those conditions, I'll do as you suggest.
> *She*: Good! That's settled. Remember, between 11 and 1. And, oh yes, please leave the key on the hall table.

In a third scenario, the husband comes home while his wife is out, packs his things, and leaves without a word because he's unilaterally decided to "split." She comes home to an emptied closet. Yet a fourth plot shows the couple discussing the decision to separate with the children, explaining their reasons and answering the children's questions. All of these scripts have counterparts in reality, along with numerous variations on these themes.

Comedy shows that have the wife (usually) throwing the husband's clothes out the door or window, amid canned audience laughter, are rarely realistic in their portrayal. More valid is the perception that in whatever way the physical separation occurs, it tends to be one of the most painful aspects of the dissolution for one or both partners. At one time, after all, they cared enough for each other to commit themselves to a life together, "forsaking all others." For most, separation is an admission of failure to be able to make it work or of a grievous error in the original choice of mate.

It is natural that the thought of separation frightens people. Separation means starting over, alone. It means setting off without the partner on whom one has, perhaps for years, relied. It means new vulnerability, and perhaps isolation and loneliness. One cannot anticipate everything it will mean, and this too can be frightening. (Weiss, 1975, p. 25)

Oakland (1984), in describing men contemplating divorce, wrote that, prior to marriage, "A coming-together period extends over months, sometimes years. The disengagement period also should occur over time" (p. 28). Because the bonds of attachment underlying marriage can persist even in deteriorating marriages, time *is* needed to adjust to the separation with its concomitant changes in emotional and daily life patterns. Chiriboga and Cutler (1977) found that their interview respondents had become inured to facing marital problems over the years but felt they needed time to "shift gears" from "the state of couplehood to the state of singlehood" (p. 104), creating a need for time to learn and/or relearn behaviors appropriate to the new status.

During this predivorce period, many of the rejected or ousted spouses become enmeshed in an obsessive review of what went wrong in the marriage and what might have happened "if. . . . " Ruminating over the facts and accusations tends to interfere with concentration on other tasks at hand, contributing to disequilibrium and wildly fluctuating behavior at times. Other responses to this major life stress event include overwhelming anger, anxiety, and unipolar depression with its fatigue and sleeplessness, decreased self-esteem, and either lack of appetite with consequent rapid loss of weight or finding solace in overeating with subsequent obesity (Kelly, 1982). Bloom, White, and Asher (1979) found that the "maritally disrupted" are overrepresented in disease morbidity (with heightened alcoholism rates), suicide, homicide, and disease mortality. In their study, they particularly noted that automobile accidents occur at double the average rate for persons in the predivorce period (which they considered to be 6 months before to 6 months after the date of separation). One of our subjects commented that she used to sit at "STOP" signs waiting for them to turn green, although fortunately this did not cause her to become an accident statistic. Wertlieb, Budman, Demby, and Randall (1984) also found a marked increase in contacts with the health care system during the predivorce period. In fact, therapists alert to this predivorce phenomenon of increased health and accident risk usually warn their patients to take better than usual care of themselves because of the heightened risk factor.

Trafford (1984) has stressed the feelings of ambiguity and ambivalence of the separation period, a time when the individual is still married and yet isn't. Characterizing the separation as a "psychological earthquake," she also wrote that the "disorientation of the post-separation period is similar to the pain and confusion of adolescence. . . . Separating from a spouse is analogous to leaving home" (p. 40) (for the first time).

Although these generalizations have a great deal of truth to them, they do not reflect the primary emotions in all cases. If the physical separation follows a major argument, with one spouse hastily packing a bag and storming out the door, anger may supersede pain for both partners. If separation is an escape from recurrent spouse abuse, the dominant feelings may be relief or even exaltation at having successfully left a literally destructive situation. Or, if one spouse leaves to join a new partner with whom there is already an existing satisfying extramarital relationship, that spouse's principal feeling may be anticipatory joy. In each of these examples, ambivalence, regret, and/or pain may well surface somewhat later in the predivorce period.

CHILDREN'S RESPONSES TO SEPARATION

In addition to the emotional impact of the physical separation on the two partners, those with children are confronted with *their* unhappiness and potential adjustment problems. Parents are typically concerned about the effects of the separation on their children, about negotiating the custody arrangements, and, for a noncustodial parent, feelings of loneliness, guilt, and/or anger at being separated from the children.

The effects of divorce on children, both short- and long-term have been studied by many researchers (Coddington, 1972; Emery, 1982; Fine, Moreland, & Schwebel, 1983; Goode, 1956; Kalter & Rembar, 1981; Kelly & Berg, 1978; Lamb, 1977; Wallerstein & Kelly, 1980; Wynn & Brumberger, 1982). Contrary to the view of 20 years and more ago that parents should stay together for the sake of the children, no matter how turbulent and unhappy the marriage was, because the effects of divorce were so devastating, there is now some research support for the idea that the negative consequences of coming from a broken home may be minimal and/or potentially modifiable (Kulka & Weingarten, 1979). Further, it has been suggested that continuing childhood problems may derive more from long-term marital and preseparation interparental conflict than from the divorce itself (Emery, 1982). Nonetheless, in a review of the literature, Jacobs (1982) pointed out that "Although there is some disagreement among these authors as to which age group tends to show which symptoms, a consensus exists that poor self-esteem, depression, aggression, poor school performance, and antisocial actions are very frequently found" in children of divorce. Further, when these behaviors occur, noted the authors cited, their "families contained a distant, uninvolved, unsupportive, or angry noncustodial father and/or a chronically embittered, angry, vengeful custodial mother" (p. 1235). *Children's stress appears to be positively correlated with the parental stress and negative ex-*

spousal contacts, and inversely related to the length of time since the separation/ divorce occurred (Woody, Colley; Schlegelmilch, Maginn, & Balsanek, 1984).

That we are dealing with an increasing problem is easily discernible from data on the estimated number per 1,000 children under 18 years of age involved in divorces and annulments in the United States during the time period from 1950 to 1983 (National Center for Health Statistics, 1984). In 1951, the lowest figure of 6.1 per 1,000 was charted; the highest figure appeared in 1982—that of 18.7 per 1,000. The number declined to slightly under 18 in 1983.

Custody Decisions

Luepnitz (1982) asked in her research, "What are the advantages and disadvantages of maternal, paternal, and joint custody (a) from the adult's point of view and (b) from the children's point of view?" (p. 14).

Historically there have been biases, first toward paternal custody (child seen as property), then maternal custody ("tender years" doctrine), followed by a period of preference for determination of "the best interest of the child" (Goldstein, Freud, & Solnit, 1973). Current statutory and judicial biases have shifted somewhat in the direction of joint custody during the past five years. This had become legally possible in 22 states by 1984 (Howell & Toepke, 1984). Best interest of the child remains an overriding consideration; judicial preferences toward mothers and certain parental conduct factors may also be given weight. Howell and Toepke summarized the child custody laws in the 50 states in 1984 (pp. 58–59) (see Table 4).

Derdeyn and Scott (1984) responded to the shift toward joint custody by asserting, as have others, that "there is little basis for adopting as public policy the assumption that cooperation rather than conflict will ensue" from joint custody (p. 206). But sometimes it can and does work very well.

The issue of custody will be taken up in much greater depth later. It is touched on here only with respect to specific research findings. One question bears on whether the child was consulted about with whom he or she would prefer to live and about visitation arrangements with the noncustodial parent. Howell and Toepke found that children's wishes are supposedly considered in 33 states, with 2 states considering the preferences of children over 12 years of age only and 2 limiting this to adolescents 14 and older.

Clinically the issue of whether to ask for a child's preference, and if so how, is a particularly thorny question. What a dilemma for a youngster! To choose one parent is to fail to choose the other and subsequently to feel guilty of disloyalty, even betrayal. More on the emotional impact of this issue in the custody chapter. Springer and Wallerstein (1983) found that young adolescents resented not being included in planning the visitation schedule. This, too, will be elaborated upon later.

Gender Differences

In several studies it has been found that boys tend to react more poorly to divorce, both in intensity and in duration, than girls do (Emery, 1982; Hodges & Bloom, 1984; Kurdek & Berg, 1983). However, Reinhard (1977), Pett (1982), and Kinard and Reinherz (1984) found no gender differences in their subjects' postdivorce reactions, and Farber, Primavera, and Felner (1983) found that female adolescents suffered greater stress than male adolescents. Differences in sampling, locus of control, questions asked, respondents, and custody arrangements among the several studies are some of the factors that may account for conflicting results. Further, the ways in which girls and boys show their distress may differ.

> Girls are likely to be just as troubled by marital turmoil as boys are, but they may demonstrate their feelings in a manner that is more appropriate to their sex role, namely, by being anxious, withdrawn, or perhaps very well behaved. (Emery, 1982, p. 317)

Age Differences

Most of the research on effects of divorce on children has been focused on preschoolers and elementary school children. Relatively little investigation has been done on children of divorce who were adolescents and young adults at the time of parental separation. Yet the ways in which the same negative effects are expressed have been shown to differ by age. For example, the preschooler may demonstrate his anxiety and distress by regression, the latency-age child by aggression or withdrawal, the adolescent by sexual promiscuity, anger or running away, and the young adult by rebellion or depression. Younger children tend to blame themselves for the divorce; adolescents and young adults tend to disapprove of the behavior of one or both parents (Wallerstein, 1983). If the parent goes out on dates, younger children are likely to feel threatened by the parent's absence, while older ones look askance at the sexuality of their parents implied in such activity. Adolescents may feel quite competitive with their dating parent(s) and quite stirred up by the "sexier" overtones their parents are emitting with friends. Remarriage similarly affects children differently, depending on their age along with a host of other factors.

Table 4
Summary of the Child Custody Laws*

State	Psychological investigation may be ordered by court	Neither parent preferred because of that parent's sex	Joint[a] custody specifically allowed (if parents are suitable)	Access to child's records by noncustodial parent allowed	Similar relevant factors are used in determining custody	Wishes of the child considered by court	Parental conduct not affecting relationship with the child will not be considered	Grandparent visitation rights allowed
Alabama[b]								X
Alaska	X	X	X					X
Arizona		X			X	X		
Arkansas		X						
California[c]	X	X	X	X	X	X	X	X[e]
Colorado[d]	X	X	X		X	X		
Connecticut			X			X	X	
Delaware	X	X	X	X	X	X		X
Florida	X	X	X	X	X	X[f]		X
Georgia	X					X		X[e]
Hawaii	X		X			X		X
Idaho	X	X	X	X	X	X		X
Illinois[g]	X		X		X	X	X	
Indiana	X	X	X		X	X		X
Iowa			X			X		X
Kansas	X	X	X		X	X		
Kentucky[d]	X	X	X		X	X	X	X
Louisiana		X	X	X		X		
Maine[d]	X		X			X		
Maryland				X				
Massachusetts		X				X		X
Michigan			X		X	X	X	X
Minnesota	X	X	X		X	X[g]		
Mississippi					X	X		
Missouri	X	X			X	X		X

54

State						
Montana	X					
Nebraska	X			X		X
Nevada	X		X			X
New Hampshire	X		X			X
New Jersey	X		X			X
New Mexico	X		X			X
New York	X		X		X	X[f]
North Carolina	X					X
North Dakota	X					X
Ohio			X	X		X
Oklahoma						X[g]
Oregon	X				X	
Pennsylvania	X		X		X	X
Rhode Island			X			X
South Carolina						X
South Dakota	X					
Tennessee						X
Texas	X					X
Utah	X					
Vermont	X					X[c]
Virginia	X			X		X
Washington	X			X		X[c]
West Virginia	X				X	X
Wisconsin	X		X			X
Wyoming	X			X		X

[a] A number of other states may allow joint custody, but do not so specify in their law (e.g., Utah).

[b] If the wife abandons the husband, he may receive custody of the children over age 7. Also, the court may order an injunction to protect the safety of the wife or children if needed.

[c] Stepparents, relatives, or other interested parties may petition for visitation rights.

[d] If a parent leaves home because of spouse abuse or threat of spouse abuse, the leaving will not be considered abandonment and will not be held against the absent parent.

[e] Any person interested in a child's welfare may petition for visitation priviliges.

[f] Children over the age of 14 may choose which parent with whom to live.

[g] Children over the age of 12 may choose which parent with whom to live.

*Table from Howell and Toepke, 1984. Reprinted by permission of authors and *The American Journal of Family Therapy*, 1984, 12(2), p. 59.

Coddington (1972) did a cross-age study based on Holmes and Rahe's (1967) "Life Change Units" (LCUs), directed toward finding relationships between psychological changes and childhood disease, that demonstrates the differential impact of divorce-related events by age. Figure 4 and Table 5, adapted from Coddington's data, illustrate these findings. However, it should be noted that the impact of divorce (as measured in LCUs) rises to a peak in the elementary and junior high school years and tapers off at the senior high level, reflecting mid-teen progress toward individuation and concerns about their own futures. The latter preoccupations tend to reduce slightly the effects of the family's dissolution. Clearly marital separation and parental divorce rank a close second to death of a parent as extremely significant life change units. We perceive these to be events which have a tremendous impact on a child's present and future personality and interpersonal relationships.

In a study by Daniels-Mohring and Berger (1984), sex and age were shown "to relate to the emotional adjustment to divorce, with men generally experiencing more changes in overall mood as a result of divorce than women and older respondents tending to experience more stress from marital dissolution than younger ones" (p. 18). Among our own subjects, relevant to these findings, gender had little to do with depression at separation ($r = .093$) or with length of marriage ($r = .061$), and length of marriage (as a rough measure of age in the same correlation matrix) was inversely, but minimally, related to depression at separation ($r = -.073$). Albrecht (1980), in contrast to the Daniels-Mohring and Berger results, found that the divorce experience was significantly more stressful for the wife. These three conflicting reports, only a sample of those concluded in the past decade, reflect the fact that several additional variables must be considered, namely, 1) who initiated the separation? and 2) about which point and phase in the "predivorce" or "during divorce" periods are the questions about adjustment being asked?

RECOGNIZING THE INEVITABLE: COPING ALONE

Improved adjustment to the reality of the separation occurs over time with the support of friends, family members, and colleagues. As living arrangements become stabilized and if the individual gets involved in social interaction and can let go of anger and/or guilt, the individual can begin to cope with being without his/her ex-spouse (Raschke, 1977; Spanier & Casto, 1979). The time it takes for this to happen will inevitably depend on an interaction of the circumstances, the individual's personal characteristics and ability to be forward-looking and not be rooted in the past, and the opportunities for growth that are available or sought out. Probably for most people with a good measure of ego strength it takes 2

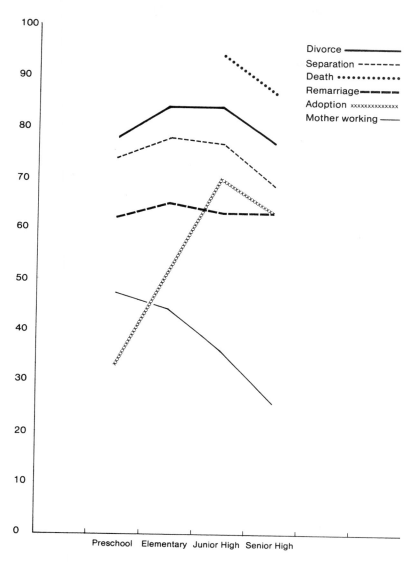

Figure 4. Life change units of events by age (after Coddington, 1972).

to 4 years from the time of separation; for dysfunctional individuals the critical event of divorce can remain a pivotal factor for the rest of their lives.

For someone who moved from the parental home directly to the marital one, the prospect of being alone and facing an unpredictable future can be overwhelming and terrifying. There are some, admittedly, to

Table 5

"Life Change Units" for Children of Divorce by Age[a]

Event	Preschool (N=806)			Elementary Age (N=887)			Jr. High Age (N=1,013)			Sr. High Age (N=911)		
	R	f	LCU	R	f	LCU	R	f	LCU	R	f	LCU
Decrease in number of arguments between parents	5	91	21	8	94	25	7	177	29	10	179	27
Mother begins to work	12	59	47	9	86	44	15	130	36	15	124	26
Increase in number of arguments between parents	16	31	44	16	51	51	13	141	48	13	149	46
Marital separation of parents	22	17	74	26	14	78	30	23	77	28	29	69
Discovery of being an adopted child	23	12	23	32	5	52	39	6	70	39	9	64
Divorce of parents	26	9	78	23	26	84	27	32	84	30	24	77
Marriage of parent to stepparent	29	5	62	28	10	65	31	22	63	33	19	63
Death of a parent[b]	25	12	89				32	22	94	37	10	87

Note. R = rank; f = frequency; LCU = Life Change Units (after Holmes & Rahe, 1967).

[a]Based on Coddington (1972); data are drawn from tables on pp. 206–209.

[b]"Death of a parent" inadvertently omitted from Coddington's elementary school questionnaire.

whom the prospect of independent living offers an exciting challenge, but such individuals are in the minority, at least in the early stages of separation. No matter how large one's support network, no matter how often the individual sees a therapist each week, there remain hours in the day when the individual has to "go it alone." Whether these are the late-night/early-morning hours spent tossing sleeplessly, or the formerly shared mealtimes, the individual wrestles either with the need to deal with the spouse's rejection and departure or with the need to accept the separation and begin to break away emotionally from the marriage.

What does being alone entail? It involves every aspect of one's life. The individual suddenly finds himself or herself solely and totally responsible for financial affairs, household management, social life, and rearing children (if physical custodian). For the woman, the total control of budgeting, expenditures, savings, tax matters, and handling investments is probably the least familiar arena on her list and may be perceived as overwhelming and beyond her competencies. Some women may have had little or no experience in decision-making beyond meal-planning and home-furnishing. For men, setting up and running a household and preparing meals is often the most foreign area.

Being completely responsible for the children if he has a shared parenting agreement or during visits if he is the noncustodial parent may be a new and even terrifying experience for the husband. Conversely, if the wife has handled all their financial affairs, he may be faced with overcoming reluctance to cope with the daily economic aspects of living. For one or both spouses, being alone in a couple's world is strange and possibly frightening. New friends, preferably divorced, widowed or never married, need to be found to supplement or replace those who were friends of the couple and who are now less attentive or less stimulating because they no longer have as much in common. New activities and interests must supplant those formerly engaged in with the spouse. New patterns of daily life have to be developed to minimize the time available to spend dwelling on the ex-spouse, the failed marriage, and the pervasive loneliness.

However, the decision to separate was made, the new world of "aloneness" in the first 4 to 6 months after separation poses difficulties for almost everyone involved. For those with a job, and who are able to focus on tasks, increased work-related activity often helps to dispel the anxieties of the predivorce period. For some, bitterness and anger may be the central themes of daily life, and these can be enervating and less than constructive in regeneration of the individual's equilibrium. For others, they may become overly invested in the children, clinging to them as a lifeline and engulfing them in an enmeshed relationship so that they won't also "abandon" the deserted parent. If all the available energy is expended in negative, vengeful activities, little is gained in the realm of confronting and coping with the situation of being alone.

Other individuals at this stage, however, use their anger as an energy-enhancing force. In effect, they say to themselves, "I'll show him (or her)! I'll manage better on my own than I ever did with that no-good rotten . . . !" The latter may be like the woman who, suddenly and without warning left alone, said aloud immediately, "I *will* survive." She does. Despite popular and professional opinion to the contrary, we have found some individuals *are* unaware of their spouse's discontent and intention to leave. Perhaps they have missed the signs or denied the covert messages, but it appears that sometimes there haven't been any; the disgruntled spouse has pretended all was fine. Thus the unsuspecting and "rejected" partner is shocked when the news is broken verbally or traumatized when he/she comes home to find that the mate has physically moved out in his/her absence.

The principal stumbling blocks that may arise for the newly-separated cover a broad range of life experiences. They may include feeling overwhelmed by having sole responsibility for the home and/or "problem" children and therefore becoming neglectful, dealing with work commitments, in-law problems, suspiciousness and jealousy, alcoholism, drug abuse, or physical abuse. Bloom and Hodges (1981) found that there were significant gender differences related to marital dissatisfaction, particularly in the areas of neglecting the home and alcohol and drug abuse, from wives about husbands. As their subjects gradually worked through their predivorce problems, however, Bloom and Hodges found some positives as "participants felt they had experienced substantial personal growth and increase in self-knowledge, some increased happiness and sense of independence (in each area significantly greater for females than males), and a moderate sense of relief from conflict" (p. 285).

Coping alone does not mean that the individual has to do everything alone. In legal matters, obviously he or she can consult an attorney. Similarly, if unfamiliar with financial affairs, the individual can consult a trusted accountant, stock broker, or knowledgeable friend. For the male unaccustomed to domestic routines, he can ask advice from female relatives or friends about how to do unfamiliar chores, whom to hire, where to buy household articles, etc. In the first several months postseparation, seeking guidance and assistance is almost expected and is not seen by anyone as a shameful admission of weakness. This *is* a period of instability, dependency, and vulnerability in most people's lives, and seeking help from others is quite normal under the circumstances. A good therapist, specifically, can assist the individual in confronting the trauma of separation, dealing with the questions that arise about "where did I go wrong?", the isolation of being alone, meeting practical matters capably, and treating a host of emotional ones—often including child custody and visitation—effectively.

Unless necessitated by financial need or other urgent factors, coping alone is facilitated by initially avoiding making major decisions. Being alone is a significant change in life pattern; selling or moving from the marital home (if the other partner has moved out) ranks as another significant stress factor (it was ranked anywhere from 24th to 35th among 42 critical life events by respondents in Rahe, Ryman, and Ward's [1980] study) and should be postponed until the divorcé(e) is feeling less shattered and more competent. This is especially true if the resident in the marital home is also primary custodian of the children. Children, already shaken by the marital split, need the stability and security derived from familiar surroundings, friends, and schools to help *them* weather the storm.

Coping alone, whether in the first few postseparation months or years later, means that the individual has full responsibility and decision-making power for a wide variety of situations. As a home owner, he/she has to decide when to buy appliances, when to have routine maintenance work done, whom to hire to do work, how many estimates to get, how to schedule the work. Often previously these were shared decisions, and perhaps the wife was at home to oversee the job. When there are errands and tasks to be done, there is now no one with whom to divide the labor. One person often feels overburdened by the myriad chores to be performed solo. Many middle-aged divorced people today also have aging parents who need attention, transportation, and assistance in decision-making. Where formerly there was a spouse with whom to discuss the problems engendered by aging, the individual now has no one with whom to talk about the problems—or the joys.

Perhaps coping alone can best be likened to becoming an informed generalist in life affairs rather than a specialist. Having to learn a great deal of information can provide a challenge and a constructive experience for the individual; for those who become anxious when confronted with the unfamiliar, especially under stressful circumstances, it can be overwhelming. In the process of learning, one also devises "shortcuts" in the interest of stretching time and energy to cover the increased number of obligations. Even if the divorced person never gets to the point of enjoying coping alone, a certain amount of self-esteem is (re)gained as a result of succeeding in these new and varied enterprises.

DIFFERENCES BETWEEN WIDOWED AND DIVORCED

The special plight of the divorcé(e) can be illuminated through contrast to that of the widow(er). Most of what follows is based on clinical experience; the literature on this topic is sparse.

Although there are certain similarities between widow(er)s' and divorcé(e)s' situations, there are also significant differences. Both groups find themselves alone and often lonely, solely responsible for the rearing and well-being of children, if present, and, perhaps for the first time, totally in charge of their own lives.

The widowed and divorced, however, do not share experiences from a common perspective. The widowed are not only permitted, but are expected to grieve openly. The divorced may have generalized social approval to grieve overtly for a brief time, but more often are expected to keep their feelings of sadness and/or anger private. Their emotionality and distress upset their friends and family, who may fear contagion or become overwhelmed by their sense of futility in easing the pain. And, they present a challenge to the security of others' marriages—might the same happen to them? If their spouse is unhappy, will this be a stimulus to take action and move toward marital dissolution?

The widowed are presumed to have had a relatively happy marriage and are therefore viewed as legitimately mourning its end. The divorced, on the other hand, usually see themselves as having failed at marriage, often have been rejected by the ex-spouse, and consequently suffer a loss of self-esteem that differs markedly from the widow(er)'s change in status (Schwartz & Kaslow, 1985). Consider the following from our case files:

> A woman in her 70s perceived herself as "nothing" after her husband's death. Her status had been tied to her husband's and her primary life role was as his wife. Without him, she suffered a substantial loss of self-esteem. This was, however, more related to her impression of others' perception of her than to any deficiency in herself.
>
> By contrast, a woman in her 50s was rejected by her husband in favor of another woman (of roughly the same age). *Her* drop in self-esteem was fundamentally related to interpreting this as a deliberate rejection of her as a satisfactory wife and sexual partner. It was perceived as an attack on her personally, and only secondarily related to how others would view her.

Clinically it appears that these disparate experiences often lead to differing views toward dating and later toward remarriage among divorced and widowed women who fall in the same age group, with the widow having a more optimistic outlook—if her memories of marriage are generally positive.

Although both the widowed and the divorced may suffer depression at the end of a marriage, the former can focus on happy memories while the latter tend to recall more of the negative marital experiences. The widow may be angry at her husband for dying and leaving her alone; the divorcée may be angry at her husband for failing to meet her needs, for not living up to her expectations, or for discarding her. If an extramarital relationship on the part of one partner preceded the divorce, the deception may cause the other partner to generalize the characteristic of deceit to all members of the opposite sex and therefore to be quite distrustful of them.

The widow may feel guilty for not having been as good a wife as she might have been, or for neglecting to do everything possible to extend the husband's life. She may vow to be much more devoted if she has a second chance. Conversely, if the marriage was unhappy or if she nursed an ailing husband for a long time, she may experience great relief from a burden and perceive the death as a freeing blessing. Some divorcées whose husbands became involved in extramarital affairs experience pangs of guilt over their possible contribution to this "unfaithfulness"—in the form of disinterest, coldness, sexual frigidity or unavailability, critical and/or demanding behavior, etc. From a family therapy framework, the behavior on the part of both parties must be considered within a context of circular and not linear causality (Dell, 1982).

A further difference between the widowed and the divorced lies in the matter of contact with the ex-spouse. Obviously the widow has no further contact with her late husband except in her own thoughts, in response to reminders of him, or in graveside visits. Also, she will usually have continuing communication with his family. Unless she murdered her husband or partially provoked his committing suicide, she is likely to have emotional and possibly financial support from her deceased husband's estate and family. As far as his family goes, they shared a love for the same man and also profoundly shared his loss. In the case of divorce, however, unless there is genuine affection between the woman and her former husband's relatives, it is far less likely that his family will be part of her support network. She may lose contact with them, except in regard to the children—even if she was genuinely fond of them (Schwartz & Kaslow, 1985). On the other hand, where an "in-law problem" was part of the marital friction, loss of contact can be a bonus of the divorce. This is true whether the divorce was based on a mutual decision or occurred because of the desire to sever the union by one of the partners. As Spanier and Thompson (1984) found, "it appears that [former] in-laws help out because they like the former family member and because of the children they share as relatives" (p. 177). The change in relationships with the late or ex-spouse's family can be equally complicated or friendly for the male in a comparable situation.

Both the widowed and the divorced may bemoan their loss of companionship and someone with whom to communicate closely and regularly. The widow, as noted above, can neither see nor speak to her husband ever again. This is indeed a source of sadness for her; yet since there is a finality in death the closure can permit healing to occur. Conversely, the divorcée, particularly one who has children, is likely to have lifetime contact with her ex-husband, whether she wants to or not. If they have joint custody and each wants to remain involved with their children, such contact is inevitable. They must both participate in vital decisions affecting their children's lives and later go on to attend and meet at their children's graduations, weddings, etc. In addition, if they live in the same community, they may inadvertently cross each other's path from time to time, with or without speaking. In the predivorce (separation) period and for the first few years after the divorce, these encounters can keep their negative feelings bubbling and can serve to reopen whatever wounds there may be.

This is not meant to imply that the widowed have life easier emotionally. Rather the desire for and experience of contact and communication are different for each of them. How deep the pain of the loss is (or the resurgence of pain through unwanted continuing communication and contact) depends on a number of factors such as length of marriage, quality of marriage, nature of the departure/loss, presence of "dates," and frequency of reminders and/or contacts.

Finally, widows typically are left with some income from life insurance policies, Social Security benefits, and maybe other tangible assets. Unless otherwise stated in the husband's will, the widow becomes undisputed owner of the marital home and property. Divorcées, on the other hand, frequently have to negotiate and/or battle for spousal support (alimony) or a flat up-front settlement and for child support payments. The marital home is merely one item of marital property (though it may be the principal asset) that they may or may not receive as part of the divorce agreement. In the majority of divorces, the former wife is economically in worse straits than she was during the marriage. (See Chapter 7 on economic aspects for a fuller account on this.) She is more likely than the widow to have to seek employment (if previously unemployed) or to find a more lucrative job if already working, for financial reasons as well as psychological ones. She is also more likely to be receiving public assistance than the widow (Bouton, 1984). And child support, though granted in a divorce decree, may not always be forthcoming or may prove woefully inadequate.

For men, there are many similarities to the foregoing situations. The grief, loneliness, anger, sense of life having been disrupted, and depression following death or divorce (if they were the one rejected) occur as they do for women, although men in our society are not expected to grieve as openly. In addition, in either situation, they have to adapt to running a home of some kind, which previously was probably more the wife's province. This may be their first experience in daily food preparation, changing bed linens, doing the laundry and cleaning bathrooms. If they cannot afford any domestic help, these new responsibilities can be awesome. They become more pressing after sympathetic friends and neighbors gradually stop pitching in and offering frequent invitations to "join us for dinner." Coming home to an empty pad or apartment, lacking a nurturing mother, an interested wife and/or energetic children can be a real jolt and a voyage into a silent abyss.

On the plus side, the widower rarely loses his sense of self-esteem. He still has his job and position in the community. He may be at least as well off financially as before his wife died, although men tend not to be the beneficiaries of their wife's life insurance (if she had any), if there are children. If divorced, he may or may not be in as good financial shape as during the marriage, depending on his postdivorce obligations to his ex-wife and to his children. Legally these vary from state to state as far as spousal support goes. In many states the practice of awarding (permanent) alimony to the wife until she remarries or dies has been discontinued. Short-term rehabilitative alimony has come into vogue, replacing permanent alimony. Child support usually continues until children gain their majority and/or complete their college education and is usually sent from husband to wife (although there are an increasing number of cases in which noncustodial wives send custodial husbands child support). If the husband was the rejected spouse, he may experience a double sense of loss of wife and children because he is no longer involved in their lives on a daily basis.

It is, even in today's more open society, easier for a lone male than for a newly single female to find companionship. His life changes as a woman's does, although the nature and quality of the changes may differ. Consider, for example, the divergent two views presented by Oakland (1984) and Bouton (1984), respectively.

Oakland (1984) states that communicating with the ex-wife may be difficult, even if the man sees the need to be civil and to compromise. He may feel that he has been pushed out of his home, deprived of his children, robbed of income, and whiplashed by an acrimonious divorce proceeding. At the time of separation:

men often realize how little power and authority they have. The courts and their wives seem to have constructed [sic] a strong, high narrow fence about them which severely restricts what they are allowed to do. Fairness is no longer considered. Try as they may, [men] may not be able to seek a proper solution to their concerns and grievances . . .

Examples are numerous. Children have freer access to their neighbors than to a non-custodial father. Children are even restricted from phoning him. Mothers may refuse to acknowledge legitimate visitation rights. Fathers who see child support payment frivolously spent on tobacco, liquor, and a mother's personal clothing, must continue to send money or face the possibility of being jailed. (p. 31)

In contrast, a study on sex bias in the courts made by a 23-person commission, and published in 1983 by the New Jersey Supreme Court, concluded that women are discriminated against in divorce court (despite a New Jersey equitable distribution law in effect for more than 10 years). Quoting the study, Bouton (1984) reports:

On a national scale, divorce portends long-term deepening poverty for a large proportion of women and their custodial children. Conversely, the study showed that the economic status of divorced men appears to follow a normal upward course with increasing age and experience. (p. 37)

Lenore Weitzman, a sociologist at Stanford, discovered that a woman's standard of living generally falls by 73% in the year following divorce, while a man's typically rises by 42% (Bouton, 1984).

In our survey, we found similar differences in point of view, with some men lamenting the unfair treatment they believed they had experienced in court and some women equally angry at the discrimination they felt they had suffered. These arguments, however, arise most often after the petition to divorce has been filed and reflect only one aspect of the entire divorce experience. At times, financial inequities develop during the separation period if one spouse uses the withholding of money, despite a legal obligation to continue supporting the other, as punishment. In the case of widowhood, financial hardship can be caused when there are delays in probating an estate or in insurance payments being issued.

Although both the widowed and the divorced may have post-event experiences that on the surface look very much alike, the causes and the emotional upheaval are different. Certainly the widowed do not have to suffer through the kinds of conflicts suggested by the excerpts above, nor do they have the custodial conflicts that the divorced parent has. The nature of support provided by family and friends differs for the divorced and widowed, and the nature of therapy needed—both supportive and rehabilitative—markedly differs also.

DIVORCE THERAPY

One or both parting spouses may seek therapy following the separation, or even as soon as it appears to be imminent. Even if the separation is or was a mutual decision, there are adjustments to be made in lifestyle, in future relationships with each other and with respective family and friends, in rebuilding a possibly weakened self-esteem, and, as noted above, in coping alone. When the decision was unilateral, the partner who was abandoned or rejected is likely to be acutely in need of professional assistance. Therapeutic intervention can effectively help the individual move through the stages of divorce to become once again a well-functioning person.

As in any therapeutic process, fact-finding early on is crucial. Not only the presenting problem, but pertinent biographical data must be collected in a low-key manner, giving the troubled client a chance first to get acquainted and establish a therapeutic alliance while responding unemotionally to less-threatening questions than those directly related to the separation. In the first few sessions a ventilation of the facts of the separation and the client's feelings about it should be elicited because that is the issue which propelled him/her into treatment. Tears may flow in abundance as the client mourns the death of a marriage, whether it was long or short, a love that existed and may yet persist, shared adventures, and the lost pattern of life that is considered normal in a world oriented to couples. There may also be frequent outbursts of anger, resentment, and/or guilt.

In this situation, the therapist must be, in turn as necessary, a willing listener, a "crying towel," or a sounding board. Perhaps the therapist's primary function, though, in this early stage is to provide support for the client's shaken sense of self-worth. Depending on the depth of the client's distress, the therapist may also deem it necessary to offer ideas as to possible options for coping with the crises of the moment, the tasks needing to be attended to and for channeling the emotionality into constructive activity.

Exploration of the dynamics of the marriage up to the point of separation can take place over many sessions, and need not occur in full during the first few hours of therapy. There is time later to consider the overt and covert reasons for the original choice of mate. More important is the client's need to be buoyed up in order to continue functioning, whether in the home and/or on the job. (That job, if there is one, is a key ingredient in the therapeutic process. The need to get up in the morning to face children, clients, colleagues, or customers keeps the individual emotionally "together" for much of the day.) As Kaslow (1979/80) has suggested,

"Working not only helps [the rejected spouse] to maintain some semblance of continuity in her [or his] life, but it also constitutes a neutral
arena in which adequate or superior functioning . . . can serve to repair
her [or his] damaged sense of self-esteem" (p. 724).

In the beginning stages of therapy there is also a need to confront the
traumatic aspects of the separation and, ultimately, the divorce to come.
Questions can be posed about immediate problems, their possible solutions, and implications of various choices. Even if these are asked toward
the end of a session, without resolution on the spot, they can direct the
client to a renewed awareness of alternatives and constructive thinking
between therapy sessions. Weiss (1975) has stated poignantly:

> The portrait of the client at this stage is not a happy one. Those on
> whom separation was imposed . . . have been the recipients of
> traumatic rejection, with what may seem to have been inadequate
> opportunity to retaliate. They may feel aggrieved, misused not only
> by the one man or woman who ended the marriage to them but by
> the entire human race. They may feel that friends and neighbors
> who know they were left or forced to leave may have lost respect for
> them. And they may have lost respect for themselves, they may
> question their capacity to hold the love of anyone. They may accept
> their spouse's accusations that they are unattractive or cold or dolt-
> ish or sexually inadequate, and decide that they are utterly without
> value. In addition, they may feel so hurt by the ending of their
> marriage that they are for a time reluctant to trust themselves in
> another relationship. (pp. 64–65)

Compounding the loss of self-esteem may be anxiety about being
vulnerable to sexual advances. Some are not in agreement with today's
rather permissive sexual atmosphere, yet they too have sexual desires
and they want to feel that someone "cares."

The loss of self-esteem may be so great in some clients that the therapist should be alert to the possibility of suicide. In our survey sample, for
example, almost 1/4 of the adults (16/73) contemplated suicide at some
point in the predivorce period or during the divorce process. Concern
with where one will be buried may arise, particularly for the wife, even
when there is no contemplation of suicide or prospect of imminent
death, particularly if the couple had formerly purchased two burial lots
together.

The rejected spouse may continue to regard the existing situation as
incredible, denying reality as too painful. All of these concerns intrude
on daily living, along with the very practical ones of finances, child
custody, relations with the existing spouse, place of residence, and simply facing each day. Eventually, the problems may be prioritized, with

the help of the therapist, with some of the concerns not recurring for several months while those of higher designation are worked through. One that grows, however, particularly for women (and some men but perhaps to a lesser degree) who reject the "singles" scene, indeed cannot yet conceive of themselves as "single," is loneliness—emotional isolation. This feeling is not reduced by outings with same-sexed friends, although such events do reduce social isolation. As one client expressed it, "You can't hug yourself!" Painful as this problem is, however, it has to be dealt with in its turn as more immediate matters, such as finances, take precedence.

Obviously life continues whether one loses a mate by death or by separation and divorce. For some of those left behind there is enough pride and/or professionalism for them to struggle along doing their jobs reasonably well, although functioning in other areas may deteriorate. These patients follow the refrain of "the show must go on." Reinforcement of such constructive behavior, by the therapist, is supportive and eventually leads to the resumption of other activities. Indeed, increased work activity is one of six factors seen as contributing to personal growth during the crisis of divorce (Kaffman & Talmon, 1982). In some cases, the reinforcement comes from colleagues as well, as seen in the following case:

> One woman, a chemist, said repeatedly over a period of months that she had no idea how she taught classes, worked in her laboratory, and fulfilled other obligations, social as well as professional, in the days and weeks after her unexpected separation. After several months in therapy, she concluded that she had functioned on "automatic pilot" rather than reduce her professional image and lose what little self-esteem she had left. She said that she had parked her pain and anger with the car each day and then went to work as if all was well. What she discovered was that her colleagues respected her for this and were able to offer sympathy and encouragement rather than pity for her situation. (Author LS's case file)

Playing one's accustomed role, even though it requires maintaining a facade, does help to overcome the devaluation felt or the rejection experienced. At the other extreme, though, are those who, feeling cast aside by the world as well as the spouse, hide out at home. Glasser (1983) cited the case of an abandoned male who ceased going to his office for a week or more following his wife's departure. When Glasser asked him in what ways this was helpful, the man had no answer. The following week he returned to work and, to his surprise, received much support from his colleagues.

Apart from the very intense personal pain (and often humiliation) the patient is undergoing, there is a need to help him or her realize (if this has not already occurred) that any children of the marriage are also experiencing confusion and a sense of having been rejected. If the client is the custodial parent (de facto or de jure), then he or she must supply, virtually single-handed, the nurturance and support required by the offspring, in addition to trying to work through his/her emotional crises. Whether or not the children are also seen in therapy, the therapist can assist the parent client to confront and deal with the children's problems in a constructive fashion. (More on this in Chapters 8 and 9.)

As suggested earlier, part of the work in therapy is to open up lines of thought and possible behavioral options that can be considered more fully between therapy sessions. Early on, for example, the therapist might take up the question of responsibility. Who is responsible for the client's feelings and behavior? Is my ex-spouse doing this to me or am I doing it to myself? Who is responsible for the former mate's behavior? Who can change the patient's feelings and attitudes? There is a need to move the patient from passive responsiveness to an action orientation, with assumption/resumption of responsibility for actions taken.

Another focal area has to do with reality-testing. The patient must come to recognize that past events cannot be undone and that *the former mate's present activities are also part of the real world over which she or he has no control*. One challenge here to the rejected spouse is confronting the insensitivity of the former mate to the feelings and consequences generated by his (or her) behavior. The ex-mate's concern may focus on injustices presumably done to him/her rather than on how current actions are affecting the rejected spouse. The thoughtlessness of the ex-mate tends to add to the patient's persistent depression. Both experience waves of anger and the left partner often feels helpless, pessimistic and stuck. Intellectualizing such events initially does little to resolve the depression, although over time it may be helpful. The client must be reminded of the questions posed with reference to responsibility and taught to ask them again and again until the noxious behavior can be ignored and the pain eased, if not totally relieved. Sometimes the ex-spouse is deliberately nasty and provocative and the patient needs to be helped to fend off criticism, vituperation, or other indignities—without decompensating or spilling over to the children.

Concurrently, the client needs to be stimulated to action. There may be resistance to suggested activities, which the therapist must explore and help overcome, with respect for the patient's capabilities and rhythm of recovery. Like a burned child, the client has to be taught how to handle fire, i.e., take risks, in ways that will minimize being burned again. Venturing out into the real world in unfamiliar settings is frightening for someone whose past has been blown into nothingness. Where there is a potential emotional involvement, for example, the client may feel not only vulnerable but inept, and may worry that loneliness and pain underlie responsiveness to the new person rather than genuine feelings of attachment and affection. It may be that the client will finally agree to risk participation in groups or to date, but only within certain limits where he or she feels some element of control. One example might be that a woman drives to the restaurant where she is to meet a blind date so that should she feel uncomfortable or distressed she can drive herself home rather than be dependent on the "date."

Discussion of goals in social-emotional areas and a review of past behaviors in interpersonal relations can be helpful in alleviating some of these anxieties and in avoiding repetition of past errors (Hyatt, 1977), including that the selection may well have been motivated by an unconscious desire to resolve underlying intrapsychic conflicts (Dicks, 1963) emanating from early unsatisfactory relationships in the family of origin. In addition, the mechanism of projective identification, which might subsume identification with the aggressor, projection, and self object transference, may well need to be addressed. Utilizing a psychodynamic concept of relationships, projective identification connotes that:

> the individual attempts to perceive his or her own repudiated qualities or impulses in the other, and may experience these qualities or impulses in the other vicariously. This implies a loss of good differentiation and a blurring of boundaries between self and object. (Berkowitz, 1984, p. 118)

When this has occurred the person may well need to control the object to ward off the breaking through of the projected aggressive impulses. The interpretation of such complex intrapsychic and interpersonal phenomena comes toward the end of divorce therapy when individuals have regained enough ego strength to comprehend and integrate the material on their own pattern of behavior and responsibility for same. This is particularly critical *before* they select another long-term partner if they are to avert the need for repetition of a similar choice and dyadic transactional pattern.

Each client, of course, has his/her own idiosyncratic way of handling anxiety and conflict, but forthright discussion can clarify perceptions that will underlie decision-making and new courses of action. For each client there are also collateral issues to resolve, such as who will be affected by the decisions and in what ways, and how much weight these considerations should carry in the decision-making process. The therapist should keep in mind that the whole idea of catering to one's own needs instead of those of the departed spouse may be in itself strange and unsettling, increasing, perhaps, the feelings of uneasiness.

With considerable effort, as the end of the first postseparation year approaches, the client should be able to confront reality with greater equanimity, although it may take several more months to a year more of therapy to be functioning at the individual's "normal" level. However, although it may take yet another year or more for the pain of the divorce and all of its implications to subside, once the bulk of anger is spent and the present situation is being handled reasonably well, it is time to work toward the termination of therapy. It may take several sessions to review changes in the client's outlook and behavior since the initial separation, focusing on strengths that have been developed and weaknesses that remain as challenges to overcome. The purpose of such a review is to bring these strengths and weaknesses to bear on future planning. In what directions is the client planning to move personally, vocationally, geographically? These plans are variable, of course, depending on whether there are children still at home, financial flexibility, local ties, or responsibilities for parents. Are the proposed moves realistic? Are they being made precipitously?

The review can also add to earlier efforts to rebuild the shattered ego. Presumably, during the course of therapy, the client has had to learn to function more independently in previously alien areas of responsibility. The therapist can then point to the increased competence and growing self-confidence that the client will now be able to bring to new situations and relationships. No longer constrained by the difficulties of a dying marriage, the client may be feeling more relaxed as well, and freer to participate in new activities. At the same time, there does have to be continuing recognition that one's social life has either no pattern or a new one and that this will require ongoing readjustments. Continuing contacts with the (former) spouse, if they occur, will also demand new skills to avoid resurgence of the earlier pain and anger.

As the therapist and the patient perceive growth behavior occurring, the suggestion to begin to phase out therapy can be made, perhaps initially reducing weekly sessions to alternate weeks for a month or two and then to no sessions at all. The client who may have been deeply involved in long-term therapy will doubtless feel more comfortable if told that the door will be open should a crisis arise—even if the privilege is never exercised. After supporting someone else's ego for years in marriage, then requiring support for one's own ego for months or years in therapy, such an open-ended termination of treatment is support in itself.

CRITICISMS OF RECENT DIVORCE RESEARCH

It is important to be alert to criticisms of much of the research on divorce. These can be subsumed under several headings: nonrepresentative samples, variations in time perspective, unsound or unstandardized psychometric techniques, debatable definitions, and nonindependent data.

Typically, samples are small and biased (Kurdek, 1983), often selected from "captive audiences" such as patient populations or groups similar to and including "Parents Without Partners" (Emery, 1982; White & Mika, 1983). Since participation in studies is voluntary, self-selection for various motives is a factor in the makeup of a research sample. In many studies, the number of divorces experienced by subjects is not controlled. In others, the sample is drawn from one socioeconomic level, such as upper-middle class, or from one geographic region, and is therefore not generalizable to the larger population (Kurdek, Blisk, & Siesky, 1981), particularly with reference to the economic impact of divorce on the parties. Also, some segments of the population affected by divorce are generally omitted altogether, such as the parents of divorcing couples (Hagestad, Smyer, & Stierman, 1984). Or, as Derdeyn and Scott (1984) have pointed out, joint custody research has generally been focused on the parents involved: the children living in such arrangements have been ignored. Or, gender and current age are not controlled, leading to erroneous conclusions in studies of children's psychological adjustment (Kalter & Rembar, 1981).

It is apparent from our own investigations and reports of divorcing partners that the most severe emotional problems are likely to arise prior to and at the time of separation (that is, in the predivorce period). At this stage, one is confronted by myriad changes in living arrangements, job, being a daily part of their children's lives and in one's relationships with the world outside the family unit. Still the first few years postdivorce are also ones of emotionality and reacclimitization (Kaslow, 1984a). Often it is unclear whether researchers are speaking of the predivorce stage or a later stage in their discussions. Some studies include no subjects in the first year of separation (Kurdek et al., 1981), while others focus only on the newly separated.

Although standardized scales such as personality inventories have been used in research on divorce, often the validity and reliability of measures can be questioned (Emery, 1982; Kurdek, 1983). Face-to-face interviews and mailed questionnaires are both dependent on how willing the respondents are to be "open" and objective, although integrity of responses can be assessed somewhat better in the former situation. A wide variety of investigative tools have been used in divorce research, making it more difficult to compare results.

Another criticism is that there is a lack of conceptual clarity in both the definition and measures of adjustment (White & Mika, 1983). In addition, difficulties in assessing individuals' functioning in many life roles and in interpersonal behaviors occur whether subjective or objective measures are used.

Finally, there is the problem of nonindependent data. One researcher asked, for example, "To what degree do parents in a volunteer, nonclinical sample have a bias toward reporting their children's adjustment as being more positive and healthy than it really is?" (Ellison, 1983, p. 79). Emery commented that often "the same judges rate both the marriage and the child, or, in the case of divorce, the judges of child behavior are aware of the marital status" (1982, p. 311). A third criticism is that control groups are often lacking or inappropriate (Kurdek, 1983).

Where the research is primarily focused on the question "What are the effects of divorce on children?" as much of today's research is, Levitin (1979) has indicated that there are many additional questions that must be asked (and many variables to be assessed). These include:

> Which children? What are their ages, gender, position in the family, personality characteristics and their needs? What are their coping strategies and typical responses to stress? From what families, with what sociodemographic characteristics? What was the nature of the parents' marriage and of their parenting? Was there open conflict and hostility? Was there a history of many separations and reconciliations before the divorce? What was the divorce like; what post-divorce and custodial arrangements have been made? Has the divorce been contested? Were children given the option to choose the parent with whom they wished to live; and, if so, how did this affect their relationship with the other parent? Is the custodial parent the mother or father? What patterns of visiting by the noncustodial parent have been established? Has either parent remarried? Are there stepsiblings? Are ties to the grandparents and other relatives of the noncustodial spouse maintained? What formal and informal support systems are available to parents and to children? What is the quality of supports such as day care centers? How well are the parents coping? Do they support each other as parents? What are the psychological consequences of various legal decisions such as joint custody? And so on. (p. 21)

A caution about drawing conclusions from studies of divorce was suggested some years ago by Weiss (1975) in his book on marital separation:

An account is not the same as an objective and impartial description, assuming that any such thing could be constructed. The accounts of a failed marriage offered by a husband and by a wife are likely to disagree, not only in that they report different versions of the same event, but even more in that they report different events. A listener who heard first the husband's account and then heard the wife's might not realize he had been told about the same marriage. (p. 15)

This premise must be kept in mind when assessing individual accounts of the why and what of divorce in both clinical and research interviews. Each person can only tell his or her own story, and at best, it is only part of their divorce composite.

CHAPTER 4
Schwartz–Kaslow Study

In our own study, alluded to throughout this volume, we were cognizant of the many criticisms mentioned earlier concerning research on divorce. Nonetheless, we found ourselves unable to control for all of the variables in an ideal way. The following material is presented with the realization that this constituted a pilot project only and that the results are descriptive. Various tests of statistical significance were performed on the data and these will be reported.

METHODOLOGY

To enhance our knowledge of divorce in the mid 1980s, we undertook a survey of divorced/separated adults and their children, seeking particularly to obtain a sample of older children of divorce, about whom there is relatively little in the professional literature. (See Chapter 9 for report on this aspect of the study.) We excluded from the study anyone who was already remarried.

The adult sample was drawn from several sources to try to get a more varied sample—particularly to go beyond individuals residing in one geographic area. Initially the prospective adult sample was drawn from 1) an outpatient clinical population of author FK's private practice in South Florida; 2) students, staff, faculty and alumni of the Pennsylvania

The study presented in this chapter was partially supported by the Faculty Scholarship Support Fund of The Pennsylvania State University. The authors express their appreciation for this support.

State University, Ogontz Campus (where LS teaches); 3) divorced acquaintances of both authors residing in various states; 4) participants in professional workshops on divorce mediation; and 5) then, via a "snowballing" effect, relatives and friends of the original subjects were recommended and sent the questionnaire. Each adult was mailed a covering letter, an explanation of the study, a questionnaire, an informed consent form, and a prestamped, preaddressed return envelope. Appropriate consent forms and questionnaires were included when the subjects had children (see Appendices A through H). One reminder was sent to prospective participants who did not respond by the deadline.

A parent responded to the open-ended questionnaire for children 10 years old or younger; older children of divorce answered their own questionnaires. All were asked to sign consent forms. Questions for all groups—adults, preadolescents, and older children of divorce—asked, apart from demographic information, about feelings and behaviors at the time of separation and the time of response (mid-1984 to April 1985), and also sought to gain information about support networks. Opportunity was given for free comments on problems or other aspects of separation and divorce, and many respondents took the time to express, sometimes vent, their feelings about attorneys, ex-spouses, the legal system, single parenting and personal growth. Some of their comments are used illustratively throughout this text.

STUDY POPULATION

Given how the subjects were gathered, the respondents were predominantly well educated. Our population ranged from the newly-separated to those 25 years postdivorce (and never remarried); subjects' ages ranged from their early 20s to senior citizens, and subjects' length of marriage from less than one year to those who had passed the 35-year mark. It included people in all of Hollingshead's socioeconomic classes (1957) at the time of separation and currently, those who were the ones who made the decision to divorce or others who did so jointly with the former spouse, as well as those whose spouse had sought the divorce. We utilized only Caucasian subjects to avoid confounding the data by introducing a racial variable, but members of all Western religions were represented in the sample. Both childless adults and those with children were included, with the children ranging in age from under 1 year to 40 years at the time of responding.

Responses were received from individuals residing in 17 states: Pennsylvania (45%); Florida (30%); Maryland, New York, Tennessee, and Wyoming (13%); and the remaining 12% from Arizona, Arkansas, California, Georgia, Iowa, New Jersey, New Mexico, North Carolina, and

Utah. These states are widely dispersed rather than concentrated in any one region. Of the 237 questionnaires sent, a total of 51.1% of usable responses were returned, with the breakdown shown in Table 6. Another 18 questionnaires that were returned could not be used because of such reasons as remarriage, advice from attorney not to respond, and incomplete answers. Various reasons were given for the low response rate of the older children, principally that they were living away from home or that the divorce had occurred when they were so young that they could not remember their feelings at the time. It is possible that parents did not mail them the forms, in order to avoid stirring up painful memories.

Of the 73 participating adults, 50 were females and 23 were males, with 50 (69.4%) having one or more children. These represent 72 marriages (6 were sent to formerly married pairs, but only one pair responded). Basic demographic data for this sample are included in Table 7.

It is important to keep in mind while perusing the data in Table 7 that: 1) 69.9% of the spouses were of the same religion; 2) that 34/73 respondents were Jewish and the number of Catholic (10) and Protestant (23) respondents combined was almost equal to the Jewish total 33 : 34; 3) that current mean assets were over $30,000; 4) that a large majority (49/73) of respondents were no longer living in the marital home; 5) that 90.4% suffered a period of disillusion preseparation; 6) and that 76.7% did not contemplate suicide postseparation. The last two findings are consistent with our clinical formulations in the material on stages of divorce, i.e., that the preseparation period is particularly disenchanting and depressing and that the majority of people experience relief as well as sadness and guilt after divorce—but they are not suicidal.

Some other interesting data obtained reveal that 33 individuals (45.2%) had not sought psychotherapy postseparation; 36 people (49.3%) had entered therapy. Four subjects (5.5%) did not respond to this query. In terms of how the issues were dealt with, 26.0% (19) had written their own agreements, an additional 23.3% (17) went for mediation, 32.9% (24) had undergone adversarial (litigated) divorces, 16.4%

Table 6
Questionnaire Responses

	Responses Received by Age Categories		
	Sent	Returned	Percent
Divorced adults (one marriage only)	122	73	59.8
Children aged 10 and under	32	16	50.0
Children aged 11 and older	83	32	38.6

Table 7
Demographic Data: Divorced Adults (N=73)

	Range	Mean	Median
Age at marriage	17–33	23.01	22.96
Age at separation	19–59	36.37	35.15
Age at time of response	26–70	42.01	41.37
Length of marriage (years)	<5–35+	13.37	11.63
Time since divorce (coded)	Not yet-6+	1.68 (=3 yrs.)	1.64 (=3 yrs.)
Respondent's education	HS Graduate–Professional degree	3.16 (=BA/BS)	3.55 (=College+)
Ex-spouse's education	HS Graduate–Professional degree	2.90 (Coll.incl.)	3.06 (=BA/BS)
Age of oldest child at separation	Unborn–32 years	9.34 years	6.00 years
Age of youngest child at separation	Unborn–24 years	6.00 years	1.42 years
Husband's occupation at separation (coded)	Professional to Unemployed (1–7)	2.89 (=Middle Management)	
Wife's occupation at separation (coded)	Professional to Unemployed (1–7)	3.93 (=Technical/High Clerical)	
Respondent's current assets (coded)	<$10,000–$100,000+ (1–9)	5.41 (more than $30,000)	

(12) were still "unsettled" at the time of our study, and 1.4% (1) did not provide information to this query. A preference for using nonadversarial pathways toward marital dissolution seems evident in these data.

Table 8 shows who initiated the separation by gender and age (using a dividing line of under 40 and 40+ years). What appears most striking is that in the under 40 category 62.5% of the divorces were initiated by the women. In the 40+ category, men and women each initiated divorce 48% of the time and only 4% were jointly initiated.

These data go against the commonly held view that women have the stronger nesting instinct in young adulthood and are more likely than men to cling to their marriages, even if they are not satisfying. The upward shift in male initiations of divorce in the 40+ age group goes along with ideas of male restlessness in the 40s and 50s, their desire to make any major changes necessary to make their lives more satisfying "before it's too late," with their greater willingness to extricate from a conflict-ridden marriage after the children have grown up, believing they have "served their time." It also ties in with the extra difficulties and resentments women face when they find themselves discarded and abandoned in mid and later life after having invested their high energy years, and the time when probably they were most attractive and desirable, in marriage, the family, and *his* career. They perceive their own chances of finding fulfillment, at least partially in a good heterosexual relationship, as being slim and may at least initially consider their ability to trust another man and risk future rejection as meagre.

The relationship between age at separation and anger at separation is much stronger in the 40+ group than in the younger group. The negative correlation is due to our scoring, with lower score being "more true" while age goes up. Therefore, the older one is at the time of separation,

Table 8
Who Initiated the Separation,
by Gender and by Age at Separation

Age	Total N	Husband N	Husband %	Joint Decision N	Joint Decision %	Wife N	Wife %
Under 40	48	8	16.7	10	20.8	30	62.5
40+	25	12	48.0	1	4.0	12	48.0
Total sample	73	20	27.4	11	15.1	42	57.5

$\chi^2 = 9.53$ (df = 2) p < .01 (Under 40 × 40+)

the angrier one is likely to be ($p < .01$). There is a statistically nonsignificant but stronger correlation between anger at separation and anger now, that is, the persistence of the feeling of anger, in the 40+ group than in the under 40 group. Wallerstein (1986) reports similar findings.

As we reviewed the professional literature about and some of the articles and books addressed to divorced persons, we found certain common threads. The bulk of the research and popular writing concerns fairly young families with preadolescent children. The usual assumption is that the divorce action is primarily adversarial, that the actual separation has been preceded by months or years of acrimony, and that there has been prior discussion of a possible divorce.

In reality, as can be seen in the foregoing tables, we found that what is assumed to be average or true is not always the case. There is a high frequency of divorce in the early years of marriage, often because the couple has discovered that they are more different and incompatible than either can tolerate. Even where there is a mutual agreement to part and this is fairly amicable, usually the parties still suffer emotional trauma in the predivorce and postdivorce periods. Open ended comments in questionnaire responses indicated that typically the couple had had a fairly large wedding, received the good wishes and gifts of family and friends, and at the time of separation had to face the humiliation of admitting their choice was a mistake. They may, in addition, have had to face the anger of parents who spent a good deal of money on the wedding and in setting up the household, and who also feared being confronted with embarrassing questions and comments when the divorce occurred within only a few months or years after the wedding.

In our sample of 73 separated/divorced adults, 20 (27.8%) had been married five years or less and an additional 14 (19.4%) had been married 6–10 years. The next largest group, 12 (16.7%) of the sample, had been married 21–25 years, typically being parents of adolescent or young adult children. Slightly more than 30% of the sample had no children. Although many of the respondents indicated that the marriage had been dissolved (or was in the process of being dissolved) by litigation, many others had made their own agreements or had used divorce mediation in preference to adversarial action. Not only did several respondents indicate that the separation and divorce took them by surprise, but periods of disillusion and discouragement rather than acrimony dominated the preseparation months and years.

Some of the comments by respondents illuminate their retrospective analysis quite poignantly and are therefore included herein.

Respondent #26—Male, 2 children, wife initiated separation. Father has primary physical custody.

Major problems:
   1. Suicide attempt by youngest child two months after separation.
   2. Money concerns—our before separation joint income
   ($80,000) seemed more adequate to run one household than
   two separate ones.

Comments:
   We have handled the separation and pending divorce (1-year)
with an intention of hurting our children as little as possible and
have handled property and custody by joint agreement and without animosity. It's hard to imagine what it would be like to go
through this experience with animosity, or in a family in which
only one spouse worked, or where both incomes were required just
to make ends meet. We have been able to make choices and have
been fortunate enough to have the resources to exercise choices and
take responsibility for them.
   I had heard that married couples don't know what to do with
you once you are divorced, but I wasn't prepared for how true that
would be. A number of couple friendships, some of 10–15 years'
duration, suddenly ceased to exist. Compensating for this were a
number of work colleagues (including our lawyer) who came forward and shared their experiences with their divorces or divorces
of their parents when they were children. All three (who did so), by
the way, were women.
   I am also very fortunate to have a close relationship with my
mother-in-law (who lives locally and sits for the girls when I'm on
business trips) and my brother-in-law. This past Christmas (1983)
he and I sat up all night one night and talked about our experiences
in Vietnam, something I had never been able to coax out of him
before. I assured him that I would not give up a 20-year friendship,
and one I valued, because of the divorce. We came out of that
experience closer than ever, and though we live 800 miles apart, I
expect to see him once or twice a year.
   To keep us in touch with one another and to assure joint parental
contact with the girls, we instituted a one night a week family
dinner at the girls' and my house. In addition, the girls have dinner
one night a week with their mother at her apartment.

Respondent #45—Female, no children, joint decision to divorce.

Major problems:
   1. Living alone in a city where you have no old friends of your
   own or relatives.
   2. Meeting new people for social relationships [age now 38].

3. Depression and lack of motivation [4 years postseparation; 3 postdivorce].
4. Money.

Comments:

I was very surprised to find out the difference in the way men of divorce are treated and women who are divorced. Men who are divorced are accepted by all without question and women are not.

I was not aware that all the friends I had as a married woman would also become divorced from me when I became single.

I would have benefitted from prior knowledge of the possible problems with divorce. I hope your study can enlighten society as to how divorced women are treated.

Respondent #63—Female, 4 children, wife initiated separation.

Major problems:
1. Finding and keeping work suitable to my educational background.
2. Financial problems.
3. Raising children myself—especially during teen years.
4. Finding suitable male companionship—I'm lonely [age now 49; separated at 37].

Comments:

Since I sought the separation for reasons of physical and emotional health, my ex-husband has been very vindictive. He has never been able to accept the fact that he contributed to the problems, and has, therefore, made an obstacle of every step, e.g., custody, visitation, child support payments, property settlement. Consequently, I've suffered serious energy drains, and have not seemed to have energy for doing all those things demanded of me. Also, he's seen to it that I should suffer financially, even to the extent of quitting his job so that he would not have to pay child support. This lack of financial support has kept me from getting more education, decent housing, more social life, and, until this year, a vacation. However, even though I'm much worse off financially, I'm much more emotionally contented.

For many years, I've shied away from male companionship, because I suffered a sort of "commitment phobia." However, I find at age 49 that I should like to spend my remaining years with an understanding, intelligent, sensitive male. Unfortunately, I cannot seem to find *any* single males within 5 years of my age, let alone any with the qualities I've described.

Table 9
Gender, Age at Separation, Age Now, Custodial Parent, and
Consultation on Custody for Two Groups of Children of Divorce

	10 years and under	11 years and older
	N = 16	N = 32
Gender		
Male	8	16
Female	8	16
Age at parental separation		
Mean	4.125	14.281
Median	4.000	16.100
Range	P[a]–9.000	1–32
Age now		
Mean	5.813	21.469
Median	7.000	20.500
Range	1–10	11–40
Custodial parent		
Father	2	0
Joint	12	3
Mother	2	22
Not applicable		7
Consulted on custody/residence		
Yes	5	9
No	11	18
Not applicable/no response	0	5

[a]Separation occurred during pregnancy (P).

Although the data on Children of Divorce will receive fuller attention in Chapters 8 and 9, the basic description and demographic material on the child respondents included in the Schwartz-Kaslow study are presented in Tables 9 and 10. We have divided the children throughout into two age groupings—10 years and younger and 11 years and older. For purposes of simplification of terminology and clarity, the former group have been labelled "babes" and the latter group "older kids."

Among the most illuminating findings are that the large majority of children in both groups were not consulted about custody/residence, there is decidedly more joint custody of the "babes" and more mother custody of the "older kids," and that in both groups the young people felt more confused, rejected and depressed, and less happy postdivorce. Obviously the impact of divorce on children is strong and long lasting. Kinds of interventions that may offset the negative impact have been alluded to earlier and will receive more attention later.

Table 10
Comparison of Strength of Feelings of
Older and Younger Children of Divorce

	"Babes"		"Older Kids"	
N	10		27	
Mean age at separation	3.900		16.296	
Mean age now	6.400		22.037	
	Mean	Range	Mean	Range
Angry				
At separation	3.700	2–5	2.593	1–5
Now	3.670	3–4	3.111	1–5
Feeling capable				
At separation	2.000	1–3	2.481	1–6[a]
Now	2.110	1–6[a]	1.889	1–6[a]
Depressed				
At separation	4.100	2–5	2.704	1–5
Now	4.110	3–5	3.704	1–5
Happy				
At separation	2.500	1–5	3.481	1–5
Now	1.780	1–2	2.481	1–6[a]
Feeling confused				
At separation	2.800	1–4	2.556	1–5
Now	3.780	3–6[a]	3.630	1–5
Feeling rejected				
At separation	3.800	3–5	3.296	1–5
Now	4.110	3–6[a]	3.593	1–5
Total change scores	8.560	−14–+30	15.460	−5–+30

[a]6 = Answer omitted.

Commentary

Our study population was drawn from many, rather than one or two locales. Both parents and children of separated and divorced families were respondents. We were concerned with both initial reactions to the family *qua* family's demise and with retrospective and current perspectives. Despite the limitations of the study due to the lack of a control group, a pre-post study design, and a fully representative sample, the data collected do indicate significant changes over time in perceived quality of life and emotional feelings in child and adult subjects. The survey findings suggest useful directions for future research.

CHAPTER 5

A Portrait of Key Issues: Their Impact on Resolution

Although, as we noted earlier, there are many commonalities in the divorce experience, there are also variations among and within subgroups of the divorced population. In this chapter, we will consider some important sources of these variations: specifically, self-image, gender, length of marriage, and chronological age. All of these are influenced by when the separation and divorce occur vis-à-vis one's personal and marital life cycle. Much of this discussion is based on findings from the aforementioned Schwartz-Kaslow study (Chapter 4).

SELF-IMAGE

Among divorcing parties, apart from those where the decision to separate is truly a mutual recognition of a marital mismatch and a joint decision to dissolve the union, at the overt level there may seem to be perpetrators (rejectors) and victims (rejectees). This view may partially flow from the way law is structured regarding civil disputes; i.e., there is a guilty party and an innocent one—a perpetrator and a victim—just as in criminal court in cases where there is an offense committed by one person against another. The person who decides to leave is often perceived as the guilty party, especially if he or she is involved in an extramarital affair.

This is a narrow and rigid perspective on the transactional dynamics that trigger divorce. Further, this view is antithetical to a systems perspective regarding marital interaction. Therapists and theoreticians holding this view usually find that the ostensibly rejected partner may indeed have been a provocateur—as in cases where they have been physically or emotionally abusive, alcoholic, drug addicted, frigid or impotent, continually rude or inaccessible, critical, frequently absent, overly demanding, too helpless and dependent, or exhibiting other noxious, repetitive behaviors that eventually help drive their spouse away.

There are, in addition, survivors and those who "fall apart," though not necessarily in the order just suggested. Let us consider these images and perspectives in different time frames and explore the implications of each.

First, a look at the perpetrators/rejectors. Even if their primary reason for initiating the divorce is, for example, a spouse who is so emotionally unstable as to make the marriage a "living hell," they may initially see themselves as failures for not having made a better choice of spouse originally or for not being able to intervene more effectively to "cure" their spouse's emotional problems. In the long term, these rejectors may well rebuild their lives and be survivors.

On the other hand, we see patients and research subjects like:

> a woman who divorced her husband after two years of marriage because he gambled away all of their assets. She dated and was on the verge of becoming engaged when her prospective in-laws rejected her because she was divorced. The engagement never took place. Today, some thirty years later, she is employed, still single, and definitely not a survivor in the sense of emotional stability, a "normal" social life, or a generalized feeling of contentment. The label and concept, an unwanted divorcée, became internalized and unshakable.

Among those who are classed as victims/rejectees, there are several possible outcomes. Many in the short term "fall apart" emotionally. They are unable to sleep, eat, or concentrate; they cry and lament; they are moderately to severely depressed. Yet even in this state of distress some may function adequately in their occupations, as we saw in the previous chapter. Those who do, and who seek therapy to help rebuild their shattered egos and lives, tend to become "survivors" in the long term. Others, sometimes bolstered by excessive sympathy of family members, continue the self-serving wail of victim. They may become the litigious ex-spouse who takes the second party to court repeatedly, with minimal justification. Their motto might well be "You did this to me and you'll pay for it forever!" They persist in seeing themselves as victims, eliciting "Poor ---!" comments along the way and keeping the children embroiled in the endless battle for as long as they can.

When we asked our subjects how their spouses had reacted to the initial separation, many responded that the "rejectee" had exhibited one or more of the following reactions: surprise, distress and/or frantic behavior (48/73). To judge by our sample, of whom 50% were rejectees, that initial reaction did not guarantee that the self-image of victim would persist in the long term.

What differentiates "survivors" and those who "fall apart"? One cannot easily say that the affluent, the employed, the male, or the better-educated are more likely to recuperate and go on to live fulfilling lives. Nor, looking at the question from a negative approach, do the data reveal that those who were most depressed at the separation were necessarily the most likely to continue suffering in the postdivorce period after several years. For example, we had 16 respondents who said that they had contemplated suicide after the separation. Of these, 8 had initiated the separation and 5 were rejectees. Today, 13 of them have "better" or "much better" emotional lives, 6 have improved financial lives, 9 reported better vocational/occupational lives, 9 were in better physical health, and 9 had improved social lives. So, despite considering self-destruction at the time of the crisis, 50% or more might be labeled "survivors" in the long term in four of five significant areas in their lives.

Further examination of this group indicates that 3 were males (of 23 in the sample) and 13 were females (out of 50); 7 were aged 17–20 at marriage and 9 married between the ages of 21 and 27; 8 were married 10 years or less, 4 were in the 11–20 year range, 3 in the 21–30 range, and 1 was married 31 years or longer. Ten of those who thought about committing suicide had children and the other 6 did not. Twelve had sought psychotherapy, although we do not know whether this was before or after they thought about suicide. Only 4 of those who had contemplated suicide reported that they had been both (very) bitter and depressed at the time of separation. Thus the factor of seriously contemplating death at the time of separation/divorce does not seem to be a good predictor of either long-term "falling apart," self destruction or the ultimate decision and ability to become a "survivor."

In the view of Kelly (1982), surviving is easier for older men than for younger men and for those who were better adjusted before the separation than for those who were emotionally disturbed prior to it. On the first point, older men (39 years of age and over) typically have more stability, more opportunities for gratification, and more sense of competence in their work lives than younger men do. These factors converge to provide substantial support for them which is lacking for the younger, less occupationally settled men. As for quality of pre- and postseparation emotional adjustment levels, those who were very dependent prior to (and during) marriage can be expected to maintain that characteristic in the separation and postdivorce periods. If they married in an effort to escape problems in and with their family of origin, more than likely they still have to deal with some or all of those same problems. Conversely, those who functioned comfortably and confidently in an independent fashion prior to separation can usually regain that capacity after the initial stress of the split-up.

It is pertinent to note from our own study data that when the population was subdivided by gender and having children or not, that "Emotional Life Now" score was strongly related to age at separation and age now in only one subgroup, albeit a small one. Men without children (N=7) who were younger at separation ($\overline{X}$ = 34.43) and are younger now ($\overline{X}$ = 41.57) than those with children ($\overline{X}$ = 40.81 and $\overline{X}$ = 43.38, respectively) had strongly inverse correlations with the emotional life score (with age at separation r = – .926; with age now r = – .818). Close inspection of the raw data, however, suggests that this may be a spurious correlation as only 1 male (age at separation = 59; age now = 70) said his emotional life was worse now, and only 5 males indicated that emotional life now was better, rather than much better, out of the 20 male subjects. For all four subgroups, on the other hand, there was a strong positive relationship (range of .625 to .885) between "Social Life Now" and "Total Quality of Life Now" scores. Even when divided by age at separation into an "Under 40" group and a "40 + " group, the correlation between "Social Life Now" and Total Quality of Life Now (TQUALN) score was very high (r = .797 and .792, respectively).

Spanier and Thompson (1984), examining immediate postseparation and current ratings of psychological well-being among their subjects (N = 205), drawn from a rural and small-city population in upstate Pennsylvania, similarly found that more than 75% evaluated their lives now as "pretty good" or "very good". This suggests that positive change does occur among both men and women over time in the more distant postdivorce period.

Some of the difficulty apparent in the throes of the separation and during the divorce periods for parents, however, arises from the continuing contact between the parties as they seek to resolve issues of finances, support, custody, visitation, child-rearing, and intimacy with others. Hetherington, Cox, and Cox (1979) found that the first year postdivorce was so stressful for parents that many began to regret the divorce. This changes markedly by the end of the second year postdivorce. Hetherington et al. noted that, although social life and self-improvement programs had "kept the parents busy and were associated with more positive emotional ratings, the most important factor in changing the self-concept two years after divorce was the establishment of a satisfying, intimate, heterosexual relationship" (p. 107).

Similarly, Raschke (1977), studying members of Parents Without Partners groups, found that the most strongly supported of her hypotheses was that "The more social interaction and/or involvement outside the home role relationships of the separated or divorced individual, with relatives, friends in organizations, and so on, the lower will be the stress associated with the separation and/or divorce" (p. 131). A similar hypothesis stated by Spanier and Casto (1979) was also strongly supported. Obviously the individual has to be willing to become involved with others and not dwell unendingly on the disturbing aspects of the divorce when with them. This is easier in some situations than others, and depends to some extent on having good support networks that encourage participation. For example, even in the more cocoon-like life of the kibbutz in Israel, Kaffman and Talmon (1982) found that, two or three years after separation, only half of the divorced adults they interviewed could be characterized as having "a healthy outcome in the sense of overall functioning, psychological equilibrium, acceptance of the reality of divorce and down-to-earth satisfaction with ordinary achievements" (p. 222). Another third gave evidence of not having completed the psychic divorce which hindered their functioning and psychological adjustment, while the remaining 15% were just beginning to move more positively toward personal growth and emotional restabilization. Kaffman and Talmon found that among the factors influencing postdivorce personal growth were reinvestment of mental energy into activities, mastery of anxiety as a precursor to establishing positive self-esteem, encouragement from individual friends and a larger support network, and a supportive love affair, much as Hetherington et al. (1979) had suggested.

In our study, we asked the divorced adult population to rate their feelings on 21 descriptors (e.g., angry, happy, jealous, relieved) at the time of separation, six months later, and now. Using the first and third ratings on a scale of "1 = very true" to "5 = very untrue," the maximum change in feelings in a more positive direction would be 4 points per descriptor, or a potential total change in feelings of +84. The actual range in total change scores was −8 to +67, with a mean of 27.90 and a median of 26.17, indicating that *for 50% or more of the sample there was noticeable improvement in feelings.* On the TQUALN score, based on rating emotional, financial, vocational/occupational, physical health, and social life now from "1 = much worse" to "5 = much better" (maximum TQUALN = 25), the mean was 19.12 and median = 19.37, suggesting that our subjects saw "life now" overall as "better" following separation. Obviously our subjects are, as a group, "survivors," yet their free comments as well as their lists of problems indicate continuing feelings of loneliness, concerns about children, and financial difficulties. Most had had support from family members, friends, colleagues, and therapists, enabling them to regain emotional and psychological perspective and equilibrium.

Table 11 offers means of descriptive statistics on divorced adults on the variables we were examining and compares these variables by gender and parental status.

Table 11

Comparison of Variables Among Divorced Adults,
by Gender and Parental Status (N=73)

Variables	Males With Children	Males Without Children	Females With Children	Females Without Children
N	16	7	35	15
Age at marriage	24.688	25.571	21.629	23.267
Age at separation	40.813	34.429	37.429	30.067
Age now	43.375	41.571	44.771	35.000
Emotional life now	4.688	4.286	4.429	4.133
Social life now	4.500	3.857	3.343	3.667
Total quality of life now	20.313	20.286	18.086	19.067
Anxiety at separation	1.875	1.857	1.486	2.200
Anxiety now	4.250	3.429	3.571	3.933
Length of marriage (coded)	3.500	2.286	2.800	1.733
Thoughts of suicide at separation	.125	.143	.229	.333
Psychotherapy since separation	.500	.286	.514	.467

Based on a review of relevant literature and our own study, therefore, we have concluded that there are numerous ways to reach the gestalt labeled "survivor." Internal ego-strength supported by others external to the marital dyad appears to be a constant in the gestalt. Clinically another element seems to be the level of one's emotional stability prior to separation, although we cannot substantiate that from our study. Other factors that can contribute to being a survivor might include psychological resiliency, i.e., the ability to bounce back from crises, experience in handling emotional issues even when they have not been as potentially shattering as a separation, unwillingness to allow someone else to maintain control of one's life in absentia, a sense of humor about the absurdity of life, the ability to go beyond the myopia of letting the divorce be and remain the critical event of one's life, and commitment to others besides oneself—like one's children and friends and the larger community where one may gain satisfaction and a sense of well being from making an unselfish or altruistic contribution to the larger world. All of this can aid in healing the sense of guilt/failure and/or narcissistic injury one has been experiencing.

GENDER

It should come as no surprise that divorce has differential impact by gender as well as by who initiated the parting. In the popular view, divorced males are seen as carefree and "eligible" while divorced females are perceived more negatively as "threatening" (potential castrators), too assertive, or failures in the wifely, womanly role in life. Of course, neither perception is universally accurate. Studies of divorced adults do, however, tend to show that divorce is more traumatic for females than for males (Albrecht, 1980; Kelly, 1982; Trafford, 1984). According to Trafford, the differences are due largely to cultural mores, with women having to learn to take financial responsibility, men having to establish a new and separate relationship with their children, and both having to deal with new social relationships. Men tend to be more sought after socially as there are fewer men than women; newly single women join the throngs of others seeking better paying jobs, more child support and alimony, and often, quality male companionship.

Divorcing Males

In a study of 40 well-educated men married from more than 6 months to 24 years and separated 1–6 months, White and Bloom (1981) found several problems endemic to the early predivorce stage. Learning to carry out household responsibilities such as cooking and laundry, and bearing the financial strain of supporting two households (reported by 22%) *are* among the initial shock waves of reality that confront many males in these early months. The moderate to severe difficulty of "integrating socially (53%) and sexually (58%) into a community in which they have been, by and large, stable, married members for a number of years" led to apparently unanticipated experiences of loneliness (p. 354). For those men who were fathers, they were distressed by the lack of involvement with their children and found that children were often the basis of friction with their wives. All of these problems led 70% of the men in the sample to seek psychotherapy before or after the separation. White and Bloom concluded, however, that age, fatherhood, length of marriage, residential stability, and even status as initiator of the separation did not differentiate among their subjects in terms of adjustment to separation. This may well be a function of the short, restricted time span of separation studied in this research.

On the other hand, acceptance of the separation (and presumably therefore better adjustment) was found by Thompson and Spanier (1983) to be significantly related to who was the source of the initial suggestion to separate. Level of personal commitment to the institution of marriage and whether parents approved or disapproved of the separation/divorce also were factors significantly related to one's ability to accept and cope with the end of the marriage.

Among divorcing fathers of preschool children, Hetherington et al. (1979) found what they called the "Hip, Honda, and Hirsute syndrome." Keeping in mind both the relatively younger ages of these men and the fact that they were studied in the mid-1970s, the syndrome is described this way:

> Men who had dressed conservatively began to appear in black leather jackets, boots, studded belts, or open shirts revealing beads or a medallion on a hairy chest. Facial hair, beards, bangs, mustaches, and sideburns sprouted. The divorced men also began buying motorcycles and sportscars. (p. 106)

According to Hetherington et al., this pattern, seen 10 years later in a slightly milder form and among older divorced males as well, was an effort to regain self-esteem. We would add that it is also an attempt to feel younger and recapture the years deemed to have been lost or wasted. Their principal concern, beyond feelings of rootlessness, guilt and anxiety, was the sense of loss of their children. This pervasive concern will be explored in greater depth a bit later.

As Oakland (1984, pp. 43–47, 54–57) explains it, divorcing males have several needs in common with those of children:

1. Close physical contact
2. Positive evaluations from important others
3. Feeling of competence
4. Assistance in overcoming and solving problems
5. Rules to reduce uncertainty
6. Control over their own lives
7. Balance between autonomy and affiliation
8. Stimulation
9. Congruence (reliability and integrity)

The same list could be applied equally well to divorcing females, a fact overlooked or ignored by Oakland. Indeed, the never-married and the still-married of both genders share these needs with divorcing males, although it may be in a more subtle form. The list is very close to Maslow's (1968) enunciation of affiliative and self-actualization needs of all humans.

Divorcing Females

High personal commitment to marriage, along with deep affectional expression and marital harmony, were hypothesized to be inversely related to acceptance. This was not proven in the data collected by Thompson and Spanier (1983) regarding females as well as male subjects. The more years of education, the greater the degree of acceptance of divorce among females, possibly because greater opportunities outside the home were available to the better-educated women. The length of marriage was found to have no bearing on ability to accept the termination of the union. For women "the crucial distinction is whether or not they were the recipients rather than the initiators of the suggestion" (to divorce) (p. 111).

According to Hetherington et al. (1979), newly divorced women, like their former husbands, also tended to change their appearance—via cosmetic surgery, changes in hair color and/or styling, and weight gains or losses of 15 pounds or more. The weight changes, particularly losses, may have been primarily related to postseparation depression, however, rather than to conscious efforts.

Divorced mothers in their sample "reported having significantly less contact with adults than did married parents and often commented on their sense of being locked into a child's world" (p. 107). Since they tended to have full responsibility for their preschool children, and often reduced financial resources, this no doubt accurately portrays their situation, especially if they had not worked since the children were born. The difficulties of divorced custodial mothers in the social arena were also noted by S.F.G. Schwartz (1984).

In another study, divorced women in Montreal (both French-Canadian and English-Canadian), with one to four minor children at home, tended to report higher stress scores as compared with their married peers who had adequate financial resources (Tcheng-Laroche & Prince, 1983). The Anglo-Canadians, in particular, reported more serious depressions, more stress symptoms, and significantly more use of professional therapists than either the French-Canadian or married subjects. Despite this, they are seen as being healthier in mind and body than women in lower income groups. Whether this was a factor of time since the separation or of socioeconomic status alone is difficult to determine.

Hansson et al. (1984) attempted to relate femininity/masculinity (as seen on the Bem Sex Role Inventory)* to women's potential and actual adjustment to divorce. In the section of their study with never-engaged, never-married female college students (N=66), they did find less concern for the potential trauma of divorce among those students who had higher masculinity scores. In their sample of divorced women, who were an average of 10 years older than the students and who had been married an average of 5.8 years, additional data were gained from the Beck Depression Inventory, a questionnaire on reasons for the divorce, and a biographical questionnaire. Here, masculinity was related positively to educational level and age at marriage, while femininity was related positively to both duration of the marriage and to age at divorce. This seems to suggest that "the more feminine subjects" were content to stay with their wifely role longer, perhaps due to less self-confidence. They also had higher depression scores in the early postdivorce period.

Another aspect of divorce adjustment is seen if one considers the effects of no-fault divorce laws (now extant in all states except South Dakota). Bahr (1983) found less bargaining power for wives, reduced awards of both spousal and child support to women, and an increase in the economic inequality of males and females to be consequences of no-fault legislation. (See Chapter 6 for fuller discussion of legal aspects of divorce.) Certainly, reduced income, with possible changes in residence and life-style, tend to make adjustment to divorce more difficult for women (and for men in some cases). For both sexes, the presence of children increases the complexities of the separation/divorce process and tends to increase the time needed to reacclimate successfully after it (Daniels-Mohring & Berger, 1984).

---

*The Bem Sex Role Inventory treats masculinity and femininity as independent dimensions (Hansson et al., 1984). By this Bem means the extent to which subjects identify with 20 positively valued masculine traits including dominance and aggressiveness. The same applies to women on femininity subscales and includes such traits as nurturance and empathy.

DIVORCED ADULTS

In our survey of 23 males and 50 females, all separated or divorced from a first marriage, we also tried to ascertain the effect of gender on adjustment to separation/divorce. Since we had already found significant differences between those with children and those without, we divided the males and females into childless and "with kids" subgroups. The three "Life Now" scores and the TQUALN (Total Quality of Life Now) score are based on self-ratings of 1–5 ("Much Worse" to "Much Better") for the individual aspects of life now as compared with prior to separation (see Table 12).

The data in Table 12 clearly show the disadvantage of the separated/ divorced mother in terms of financial position, social life, and her perception of the total quality of her life now. The mean length of marriage appears to be affected in this sample by the presence of children, and to a lesser extent by gender within the subset of parents. Whether it is affected by the femininity/masculinity dimension described by the Hansson et al. (1984) study cited is difficult to say. However, we do see that both mothers and fathers showed fewer tendencies toward suicidal thoughts than childless females and males respectively, and also that they sought psychotherapeutic help in higher numbers than did their childless counterparts of the same gender. The greater utilization of psychotherapy may be due to involvement of their children in therapy.

Childless females in the sample are appreciably younger than either females with children or males with or without children. In our society, where males tend to seek out younger women as dates or mates on remarriage, their Total Quality of Life Now scores are higher than those of separated/divorced women with children but lower than those of either male group. Childless female divorcées rate their Financial Life Now ($\overline{X} = 3.667$) higher than do women with children ($\overline{X} = 2.84$), which is not surprising in view of statistics that show lack of child support payments contributing to high rates of poverty in female-headed families, and the greater opportunity for full-time and possibly better-paying employment for childless women. On the other hand, childless females have the highest percentage of suicidal thoughts at the time of separation of any of the four subgroups (33.3%). This may be partially attributable to the fact that they do not feel responsible to or for anyone and that they may believe that no one of great importance cares whether they live or die.

The divorced women with children were the oldest of the four subgroups both at the time of separation and now. Although they are emotionally better off now than at the time of separation/divorce, they have the lowest mean score on Social Life Now and Total Quality of Life Now.

Table 12

Comparative Ages, Length of Marriage, Suicidal Thoughts After Separation,
Quality of Life Now Scores, and Psychotherapy by Gender and Parental Status

	Females		Males	
	Childless	With Kids	Childless	With Kids
N	15	35	7	16
$\overline{X}$ Age at separation	30.867	37.429	34.429	40.813
$\overline{X}$ Age now	35.40	44.771	41.57	43.375
Range	28–49	27–62	26–70	37–52
$\overline{X}$ Length of marriage (years)	6.80	15.80	8.86	14.88
$\overline{X}$ Emotional life now	4.333	4.429	4.286	4.688
$\overline{X}$ Financial life now	3.667	2.94	3.857	3.313
$\overline{X}$ Social life now	3.867	3.343	3.857	4.50
$\overline{X}$ TQUALN score	19.73	18.086	20.29	20.313
Range	14–25	8–25	17–25	16–25
$\overline{X}$ Suicidal thoughts	.333	.229	.143	.125
$\overline{X}$ Had psychotherapy	.600	.514	.286	.500
$\overline{X}$ Age of youngest child at separation	—	9.97	—	10.50

This is not surprising given that their male age-peers seek out younger women and when census data indicate that there are more unmarried middle-aged women than men all over the country (Westoff & Goldman, 1984). Only in the 20–24 age bracket are there more than 100 men per 100 women in the 38 largest metropolitan areas. The exception is the city of Houston, where women outnumber men. For the 35–39 age bracket, there is a range of 37 to 72 eligible men per 100 women; by 45–59 years, the range is 33 to 46 per 100 females; and by the 55–59 age bracket, the range has narrowed to 24–39 eligible men per 100 women. This imbalance is also reflected in a recently published study about why single women go out with married men (Richardson, 1985).

Male respondents fall between the two female subgroups of with and without children in Age Now, but rate their Total Quality of Life Now as better than either female subgroup. This appears to be due, in part, to higher scores on Financial Life Now than either female group has. In addition to changes in spousal support as a consequence of no-fault divorce laws, including general discontinuance of perpetual alimony, the difference in financial satisfaction is partly due to discrimination in salaries in favor of males, partly due to the higher level of positions held by males as compared with females (many of whom trail behind because of having entered or reentered the labor market after many years absence when they were functioning primarily as homemakers), and partly due to salary increments stemming from years of experience on the job that are therefore available to men but not to most women.

For all subgroups, Age Now is inversely related to Total Quality of Life Now scores, although the strength of the correlation varies. In some of the older subjects, this inverse relation reflects the census data above as well as perhaps increasing health problems, reluctance to become emotionally entangled again, and a now less satisfying social and financial life. The effect of age on adjustment to divorce is a separate area of investigation.

LENGTH OF MARRIAGE

In the 19th century, and even in the early decades of the 20th, marriages were more frequently terminated by death than by divorce, so that silver and golden wedding anniversaries were rare enough to stimulate community as well as familial celebrations. Numerous young women died in childbirth or as the result of too many pregnancies in too short a span of years. The widowers rapidly sought new wives to mother their half-orphaned children and to be companion-helpmates in life. Most women who outlived their husbands remarried if the opportunity presented itself, or lived with members of their family of origin or family of procreation rather than alone. "Living together" without the legal bonds of matrimony was either done very discreetly or the partners faced moral indignation and familial and communal opprobrium. Even common law unions were frowned upon.

Today the picture has changed markedly. Divorce rather than death is the dominant terminating factor in marriage. Living together although unmarried has become more acceptable in many communities as some individuals seek to avoid the possible emotional and financial complications and commitments of marriage and remarriage. Widowed fathers sometimes decide to raise their children alone rather than possibly subjecting their children to the trauma of living with a poorly chosen stepmother. Silver wedding anniversaries are rarities increasingly because of the high proportion of divorces that occur before marriages reach the 20-year mark. In 1981, for example, according to data compiled by the National Center for Health Statistics (1984), 37.7% of marriages were terminated by divorce before the 5th anniversary, 51.1% of divorces occurred in marriages that had lasted 5 to 19 years, and only 11.1% of the divorces occurred in marriages that had endured 20 years or more. Of the last group, many had continued longer than 45 years. In the group of divorces terminating marriages of less than 20 years' duration, 88.8% of the sample, there were usually minor children to consider as well as the wishes of the spouses. To what can divorces in these three periods be attributed?

Early divorces, defined as those occurring before five years have passed in marriage, occur sometimes because of the realization that the partners were a mismatched pair (as in the case cited by Lazarus earlier). Sexual compatibility, if present, perhaps has proven inadequate to compensate for incompatibility in other aspects of marriage. Or, belatedly, the pair discovered that one wanted a child and the other was adamantly opposed to becoming a parent. We have one such case in our sample, where the husband, furious about the pregnancy, left prior to the birth of the baby, and divorce followed soon thereafter. In another case, the husband gave his pregnant wife the choice of him (abortion) or the baby (divorce). As Sager (1976) indicated in his thorough analysis of the importance of open communication about expectations and goals for marriage prior to entering into matrimony, the process of contracting is a way of determining in advance if the couple are in agreement on major issues such as whether or not to have children. Such premarital explorations might well avert many marriages that seem, a priori, to be "destined for divorce."

Disillusionment with the mate, as suggested by Rhodes (1977), and/or with the responsibilities of the marital state, block the development of an intimate dyadic relationship between some couples. Likewise, once the romantic idealization of the mate diminishes in the light of daily reality, care-giving may be perceived as burdensome or as a violation of one of the partner's "rights" to independence. The lack of attachment and care-giving, combined with deterioration in the quality and/or quantity of communication, appears to inhibit the development of good relational systems in marriage (Wynne, 1984). Such a failure is among the principal contributing factors to early dissolution of marriage.

Even when a young couple has lived together prior to marriage, "emotional baggage" brought from the respective families of origin may become more apparent, and more disturbing, after the wedding. Intergenerational conflicts may erupt where they had been muted or ignored earlier. The two sets of families-in-law sometimes tug at the couple in such opposition that the younger pair argue endlessly over issues raised by their elders (Hyatt & Kaslow, 1985). Rather than turn against each other, another alternative would be to estrange themselves from one or both families in order to strengthen their marriage. Not all young marrieds are emotionally willing or able to do this and may not perceive the usefulness of therapeutic interventions. If they cannot cope with the parental pressure and are insufficiently emotionally differentiated from their parents or are financially dependent on them, they may choose the familiar, return "home," and get a divorce rather than remain with the spouse and in the marriage.

Whether in early divorce situations or later ones, behaviors that may have been hidden or controlled before marriage emerge and become disconcerting, even untenable. For example, the husband may have turned out to be a dedicated gambler, spouse-abuser or alcoholic. Many young women think that they can "reform" their boyfriends once they have married, only to discover that the behavior intensifies rather than disappears. In some cases, the wife stays in the marriage rather than admit her poor choice; in other instances, she leaves and seeks a divorce before her situation worsens (or before she has a child).

In the large middle group of marriages, there are also multiple causes of divorce. Developmentally, the expected pattern in this group of marriages lasting 5–19 years includes the child-rearing stage of family life. More couples in the past generation have opted for childlessness or for fewer children than was true in the past when large families were the norm, few women worked out of the home, birth control methods were less available and less certain, and children were viewed as a potential financial asset and not an economic burden, but their reasons for doing so may or may not be related to a subsequent divorce. In as much as the paradigms of Erikson (1963), Rhodes (1977), and Hughes et al. (1978) assume the normality of parenthood (whether as "generativity" or as "replenishment"), however, it seems appropriate to focus first on those broken marriages where there are children.

Were the spouses able to adapt to their new roles as parents yet still pay sufficient attention to each other? Were they in agreement on child-rearing philosophies and practices? Did mother and child(ren) form an alliance that excluded the husband-father? Did the husband and wife have unrealistic expectations of continuing preparental behavior patterns which, when these proved invalid, led to disharmony? Or did the husband-father continue *his* normal round of activities while his wife became increasingly restricted in hers? Did they grow in different and incompatible directions or did their life-style preferences and their values diverge irreconcilably?

As the children enter school and begin to expand their worlds, one or both parents may feel threatened by the new relationship the youngsters develop and the need to alter their own relationship to meet these changes. By the time the children near adolescence, fathers tend to be approaching age 40, the time when many men ask "Is this all there is?" or decide that they missed too much in life by marrying at too young an age. The adolescent's budding sexuality may arouse dad's fantasies about a new, younger, more titillating sex partner or mom's desire to also date and be sought after. This restlessness about the present and also the desire to enhance future expectations seem to account for a large number of separations and divorces among those married 10–19 years. As we shall discuss in the chapters on children of divorce, the breakup of the family at this point, while children are in latency or adolescence, comes at a particularly critical time for them.

Other factors contributing to breakups at this time include that the mother may have entered or reentered the labor force or college once the children were of school age, may have found stimulation and new interest there, and may have consciously or inadvertently become a threat to her husband, who has been accustomed to perceiving her in a more passive role. She may find him boring, tedious, dull or too domineering. The demands of her new role may also exacerbate smoldering conflicts elsewhere in the marital relationship; he may feel neglected and relegated to too low a position on her totem pole. Her new exposures and perspectives can alter her perceptions of her life and foster new interests that lead her on life paths that diverge markedly from what her husband wants.

Either or both of the spouses, given any of the above circumstances, or simply needing reassurance of their attractiveness to others as they anticipate the arrival of middle age, may have one or more extramarital affairs during this period. If the partner becomes aware of this infidelity, *this* may be the final blow to the marriage. There are marriages, however, where the partners agree to continue their relationship in public but to lead independent private lives. Or knowledge of the "playing around" may heat up the marital war, crystallize the discontent, and motivate them to resolve the problems that were conducive to the affair in the first place.

In childless marriages, whether both partners are working or not, there can be a wandering away from each other as their separate experiences outside the home place them in conflict. Where as parents they might have waited to separate "for the sake of the children," being childless they may simply decide to part—amicably or otherwise. Perhaps one partner has to travel a great deal as part of the job and the other no longer feels comfortable with this arrangement. Perhaps, as they matured, earlier similar philosophies or interests changed so that they have less in common, and maybe more in contention. One partner may no longer want to do the tasks that had not looked so onerous earlier in marriage. Or one may find the other unwilling to cooperate, not much fun, dishonest, too moody, unstable, cold, histrionic, narcissistic, etc. In any event, they lack the ability to meet each other's needs at this point and decide to separate rather than continue a relationship filled with friction.

Any and all of the problems discussed with respect to short-term and mid-range marriages may also affect long-term marriages. The tendency seems to be in this group, however, to stay together "for the sake of the children." Among our own subjects, for example, it was apparent that the separation and divorce often occurred when the youngest child finished high school and/or went off to college. In some respects, this made it easier for the children, since they were entering upon new and exciting aspects of their own lives. In other respects, it may have been more difficult growing up in a family where there was (although not uniformly the case) chronic conflict that was tolerated, sacrificially, for their sake. What kind of long range obligation and debt of gratitude are they then burdened with?

As the children begin to leave the parental home, the marital relationship again undergoes a period of testing. Can the partners regain their "twosomeness"? Can they adapt to the individuation of the children? They may, as already suggested, decide that this is the time for *them* to resume an independent life, to become a "different" individual. Why should their children have all the "fun"? One or both partners may feel "I've done my time" as provider, nurturer, dog-walker, cook, chauffeur, wife, or husband. The varied options available to women, especially, often look more attractive than another 20 or 30 years of the "same old routine."

Communication between the marital partners may have diminished over the years as each bore different responsibilities and conversation focused on the children and on the multiple minutia of daily life. Even in the area of social life, preferences may have stayed the same for one partner and changed for the other, again reducing communication. Tolerance for such changes may be weaker for one or the other resulting in reduced intimacy, trust, and affection. Long-neglected interests resurfacing after two or three decades may threaten the spouse who no longer "recognizes" his/her partner. The decline in the marital relationship of many years can be subtle or obvious, tolerable or unendurable. The difficulties of divorce tend to be greater for the older person because of economic, social, and often physical limitations imposed by society. Nevertheless, unilateral or joint decisions to divorce do occur in long-term marriages that appear to outsiders to be stable relationships, with 10% of the husbands aged 50 years or more and 7% of the wives being 50 or more at the time of the decree (National Center for Health Statistics, 1985). Does it make any difference how old they were when they married?

Age at Marriage

There is a general agreement in the literature that teenage marriages are at high risk for failure. Incomplete education (no high school diploma) contributes to low-level, poor paying jobs and/or a higher rate of unemployment, and these factors in turn tend to lead to less marital stability. Additionally, premarital pregnancy that results in a "shotgun" wedding increases the risk of marital discontent and eventual divorce (Bahr & Galligan, 1984).

Federal statistics support this pessimistic view of teenage marriages. In 1980, the rate of first marriages for females aged 15–17 years was 19.8/1000, and for those aged 18–19 years was 87.3/1000—collectively more than 1% of this age group. For males aged 15–17 years, the rate was 2.9/1000; at 18–19 years, 38.4/1000, or just over 0.4% of the teenaged male population. The figures changed only slightly in 1981 and 1982. The marriage and divorce rates for these three calendar years for persons under 20 years of age are shown in Table 13 and demonstrate the riskiness of teenage marriage.

Bahr and Galligan found further that "Of those young men who married in their teens and had not completed high school at the time of marriage, only 56% were still married after nine years. By comparison, 94% of those who were at least age 20 at marriage and had completed at least 12 years of schooling were still married" (1984, p. 396). Comparable figures for females are not available.

Youth and lack of education at marriage are not consistently factors

Table 13
Marriage and Divorce Rates for Teenagers,
1980, 1981, and 1982

	1980	1981	1982
Males			
Age at marriage[a]	0.043	0.039	Not available
Age at divorce[b]	0.8	0.7	0.6
Females			
Age at marriage[a]	1.07	0.99	Not available
Age at divorce[b]	3.4	2.9	2.7

Note: From "Advance report of final marriage statistics, 1981," *Monthly Vital Statistics Report*, 1984, *32*(11), p. 8; "Advance report of final divorce statistics," *Monthly Vital Statistics Report*. 1984, *32*(9), p. 11.
[a]Percent per 1,000 population.
[b]Percent of all divorces.

operative in divorce, however. The most popular ages of marriage for females in 1980 and 1981 were 20–24 years (11%) and 25–29 years (10 + %), and for males, 25–29 years (10 + %). The percent of all divorces for females in the 25–29 year age range (24.5%) and for males in this age group (22.6%) was the highest of all age groups in 1981 (National Center for Health Statistics, 1984). In our sample, we found this to be true as well, with the largest part of our sample (63%) having been married before age 29, and with 27% having separated by age 30. These were all at least high school graduates, with one exception, and more than half of our subjects and their former spouses had middle-level management or higher status occupations at the time of separation.

More important than the age at marriage for our purposes, however, is the age at separation and divorce. What are the major problems for divorced persons of different ages? Are there distinct patterns by age group? What are the chances for remarriage (or the contraindications to remarriage) at different ages?

Age at Separation/Divorce

In discussing the challenges of separation and divorce by age, we will divide our comments roughly among three groups: those aged 30 years and under, a middle group aged 31–50 years, and individuals aged 50 and over. These approximate the three subgroups arranged by length of marriage in our earlier discussion: under 5 years, 5–19 years, and 20 years and over (although many of those females who were married more than 20 years may actually be in their 40s now, given the earlier age of marriage in the 1950s and early 1960s). In one of the pioneering studies of divorce, Goode found that "with each increase in age the proportion falling into the high trauma class also *increases*, while the percentage falling into the low trauma class decreases" (1956, p. 192). Whether this is the effect of age alone, or of length of marriage, or the presence of one or more children of different ages, or some combination thereof remains to be seen.

It should be added that Kitson and Sussman (1982) found, echoing Goode's perceptions, that "those who have been married longer are more likely to complain of changes in interests and values and no sense of family, while those who have been married for shorter periods of time are more likely to mention problems with relatives and sexual problems due to health as complaints about their marriage" (p. 92). This conclusion supports the idea of a "mismatch" contributing to early divorce and the "drifting apart" phenomenon in much longer marriages discussed earlier.

In reviewing the literature on separation and divorce, we found relatively little information on young childless divorced couples. The bulk of the research appears to have been focused on single parents, and even in the middle and older groups, the emphasis is on those with children with perhaps passing reference to the childless. There are general statements to the effect that remarriage is easier for the young divorced adult who has no children (Bloom et al., 1979), and that the younger the individual is at the time of divorce, the easier it is to remarry (Albrecht, Bahr, & Goodman, 1983). Both statements seem to be supported by "common sense" or logic. If one looks at young divorced parents, however, as Hetherington et al. (1979) did, it becomes apparent that they are often "overwhelmed by the sheer number of tasks confronting them. [The young women] felt that they had neither the time nor the energy to deal with routine financial tasks, household maintenance, child care, and occupational and social demands" (p. 102). The childless divorcée not only has no child care tasks, but probably also has smaller living quarters and less complex financial matters to handle.

It is more likely today, moreover, that young childless divorcées are employed and can maintain a sense of self-esteem through competence on the job. For the single parent, especially one whose principal identity is associated with family and homemaking, this external source of self-image support may be missing. Hetherington et al. (1979) noted that:

> One of the most marked changes in divorced parents in the first year following divorce was a decline in feelings of competence. They felt they had failed as parents and spouses, and they expressed doubts about their ability to adjust well in any future marriages. They reported that they functioned less well in social situations and were less competent in heterosexual relations. (p. 106)

Life improved by the two-year mark following divorce for most of this sample, with the development of new relationships and a reduction in the stresses and conflicts over custody, finances, and intimacy. Childless young divorced adults, on the other hand, avoided many of these stresses altogether, but also experienced loneliness, fear of failure in future relationships, and the need to develop new social networks.

In mid-life, the decision to divorce "is often seen as a choice between two negatives: that is, the marriage is viewed negatively and divorce is viewed negatively. Yet, the pain in marriage is known whereas the pain anticipated in divorce is unknown" (Turner, 1980, pp. 172–173). For the divorced adult in the middle group, there is not only a need to redefine his/her identity, but also the trauma, or challenge for some, of reconstructing a social life beginning with dating. For many of the men, this is also a time of vocational change and/or reappraisal; for formerly nonemployed women, it is a time to enter the world of paid employment, using whatever skills they may have or may acquire following the separation. Today, alimony is being granted to women less often than formerly, with spousal support usually being provided only until the (ex)wife can become self-supporting. The concept of temporary rehabilitative alimony has replaced that of permanent alimony payable by the man to his ex-wife until her remarriage or death. The number of states in which lifelong alimony is handled as an entitlement has decreased markedly.

Even in the middle group, there are few studies that focus on the childless. Wise, (1980), for example, studied middle- and upper-middle-class divorced mothers who had been married 9–14 years, who were 30–35 years old at the time of divorce, who had custody of their children, and who had been employed before or during the early years of marriage. Like Hetherington et al.'s subjects (1979),

> all these women, one to four years post separation were experiencing considerable psychological distress: depression, anger, feelings of vulnerability, low self-esteem, preoccupation with loss, fears of loneliness and aging, awareness of loss of status, fears about financial security and lack of support systems, feelings of being incomplete without a husband, difficulties with parenting pressures, and reconciliation fantasies. (Wise, 1980, p. 151)

Similarly, Luepnitz (1982) reported that single parents in this middle group suffered from loneliness, the need to replace married friends, and changes in their support groups. She also found that more than twice as many of the fathers as mothers wished to remarry.

Baruch, Barnett, and Rivers (1983), who studied employed divorced mothers, ages 35–55, who had been divorced more than one year (with a mean of seven years), found many of the same signs of loneliness, problems in social and sexual relationships, and not having someone to share things with, as did other researchers, but also found these women to exhibit some positive traits. They tended to have a strong sense of personal growth and competence, a sense of mastery and being "in charge" of their own lives, and a feeling of satisfaction with having learned new skills and being able to manage their lives without having to answer to anyone. They did have problems related to being single parents, ranging from concerns because their children were upset, to difficult relationships with the ex-husband, to being women alone who could not comfortably go some places unescorted. The last point may be a by-product of the era in which they were brought up as compared with divorced women 20 years their junior, who are more comfortable being out without a male companion. For example, women in the middle group are usually more reluctant to attend a purely social dinner-dance alone or some similar "couples" event.

Finances for the majority of these women were either derived from fixed support allotments that were inadequate in light of continuing inflation or from low and/or part-time salaries. For a second group, those in high-prestige/well-paid positions, economic survival is not a serious concern—at least in the short term. With or without financial problems, however, Baruch et al. (1983) concluded from their study that:

> Divorced women all have something in common—surviving a difficult experience that tested their personal strength. They seem to draw their confidence from the fact of their survival rather than from how much they are enjoying or not enjoying the state of divorce . . . [we] believe that divorced women today are much less likely than before to blame themselves for the divorce, at least once it is over and behind them, or to feel stigmatized, worthless, or unfeminine because it happened. . . . they feel like whole people, competent, successful, and female. (p. 190)

They also found, as other researchers have, that these women were disinclined to remarry, both because it would necessitate once again accommodating to someone else's needs and because of the complications that a new marriage might have with and for their children. The idea of remarrying quickly so the children will "have a new daddy" and all will have a caretaker seems outdated in some segments of the population. Many women prefer to maintain their newfound separate identity and take charge of their own lives rather than risk becoming second in command.

Although many women in all age groups expressed the desire to have an intimate relationship, even one that did not lead to marriage, they expressed anxiety about their vulnerability and fear of being hurt by a man again. M.E., a young, attractive mother of two early adolescents, for example, was separated for 15 months when she became involved with a man who also had been previously married. When after several months the relationship was ruptured, she experienced renewed physical and emotional upset and determined that she would never put herself in such a vulnerable position again (author LS's case file).

When it comes to the oldest group, again the focus in the research tends to be on women, perhaps because their greater emotional and financial vulnerability makes them more interesting subjects. As one writer described the "gray divorcée":

> Women in their 60's belong to a generation committed to altruism and not narcissism, to stoicism not hedonism, to constancy not transiency. Ensconced in the daily exigencies of homemaking and caregiving, few of them had either the time or the inclination to monitor their own psychic temperatures, to gauge vicissitudes of their mental lives, to question whether or not they were self-fulfilled, self-realizing, or actualizing their potential. They held these truths to be self-evident: self-sacrifice, self-discipline and endless devotion would bring them their just rewards—the good health and well-being of their children, and the continuing loyalty of husbands, who would love, honor and cherish "till death do us part." (Cain, 1982, p. 90)

Although older divorcées share many of the problems of older widows—the aging process, loneliness, and a life that had been centered on marriage and family—they, like their younger counterparts, have to live with the knowledge that they were intentionally left.

Older women, as compared with younger divorced women, have fewer support groups, fewer employment opportunities (and often fewer skills), less opportunity to remarry, more difficulty in establishing credit in their own names because of lower incomes, and the loss of a share in the husband's medical insurance and pension plan. If the marriage lasted more than 10 years, they may be able to enter a claim for a share of his Social Security pension when they reach age 62, but the share will be inadequate usually to maintain the life-style they had had as married women. Spanier and Casto (1979) also found this economic concern a realistic one, considering the costs of illness today, among their older female subjects.

Each of Cain's subjects reported that the "husband's decision to leave home clearly coincided with his approaching retirement date" (Cain, 1982, p. 95). It is as if, threatened by impending old age, the husbands decided to make a complete break with the past and belatedly take up an entirely new life, one in which they try to act and look younger.

In another study of middle-aged and older divorced persons, Hagestad et al. (1984) interviewed men and women married 16–37 years who had at least one child aged 16 or older. Although 50% of the men had at least one college degree, only 8% of the women did, suggesting that the women had been primarily homemakers and hence would have greater difficulty in obtaining decently paying jobs. Half of their female subjects, as contrasted to one-quarter of the males, "said the time prior to the final separation and before any final decision has been made about the divorce was the most painful. For men, trauma was often reported *after* some movement towards divorce" (p. 11).

SUMMARY

In this chapter, we have tried to assess the impact of divorce on different people as they vary in age, gender, length of marriage, and self-image. Those who might be labeled "survivors" appear to have had strong support networks following separation and divorce (with an intimate relationship found to be especially helpful), to have been emotionally stable prior to separation, and to be psychologically resilient. Gender differences in response to marital dissolution were found, particularly with respect to having to learn to manage tasks formerly handled by the spouse, higher stress scores among the females, and, for our subjects, differences in quality of life now as compared to preseparation periods. Length of marriage and age at separation/divorce clearly have differential impact, partly as a result of generational differences in marital expectations and experiences and partly because of the ages of any children present. Typically, those who had been married longest experienced greatest trauma upon divorce.

Although some patterns were found, varying individual adjustments extended the range of these patterns considerably. Often the expected problems, for example, of men having great difficulty with housekeeping chores, were eased by special circumstances—frequently by the presence of a female with whom they had begun an affair prior to or shortly after the separation. Some older women, long married but employed during the marriage, had less difficulty in learning to make their own decisions and to manage their financial resources than younger women who had been totally involved with home and children. The most hard hit group, from the financial point of view especially, would seem to be women over 60 who had not been employed outside the home and who were cut off from medical insurance, retirement benefits, and a partner to share the remainder of their life with just when they were most likely to need him.

CHAPTER 6

The Legal Aspects
of Divorce

Now that the causes and effects of divorce have been examined, for a complete picture of this phenomenon it is also necessary to understand the "mechanics" of divorce—that is, how does a married couple become a divorced couple? What do the more than 1 million couples who divorce in the United States each year, with their more than 1 million children under 18 years of age, experience in terms of the actual legal procedures and final dissolution? In this chapter we will consider the legal requirements, machinations and options, including fault vs. no-fault grounds, contested vs. uncontested divorce suits, mediation vs. litigation as a means of reaching a settlement agreement, and the final decree and what it means. Custody and visitation arrangements, as part of the divorce agreement, will be discussed in more detail in the following chapter, but will be alluded to here when relevant.

FAULT VS. NO-FAULT

There is no uniform code of divorce law that is adhered to in all 50 states and the other jurisdictions of the United States. Just as each state has its own laws that articulate the necessary steps to obtain a marriage license and who may perform a marriage, so each state also has its own statutes for divorce proceedings. What has changed in the past two decades is the content of those statutes.

Reforms in family law appear to have emanated, at least in part, from changes in the larger fabric of society. Such social trends as the women's rights movement, greater participation of women in the higher education mainstream and the work force, greater sexual permissiveness, rising divorce rates, and the narcissism and self-actualization themes of the 1960s and 1970s, in combination, brought pressure on state legislators to alter the laws so that they would reflect contemporary realities. No doubt the fact that some legislators underwent tedious and painful divorces also contributed to their willingness to liberalize and modernize the laws.

As one attorney put it, "we cannot simply plug in legal devices which worked well in an earlier time and under different conditions" (Glendon, 1984, p. 1555). Consider the grounds on which divorce suits were based, for example. Historically, one party filed suit against the other on such grounds as: bigamy, adultery, mental cruelty, physical indignities, imprisonment of the other spouse, desertion, or other marital misconduct. The second party then had to respond defensively. A joint desire to divorce was simply not acceptable grounds and was, indeed, considered indicative of "collusion," which wiped out any possibility of obtaining the divorce.

We are all familiar, usually from old movies or from headlined stories in the newspapers, with cases where private detectives followed the suspected erring spouse to a motel and through the transom secretly took photographs of an adulterous relationship. Often the spouse's lover was then named as co-respondent in the divorce suit. Photos in hand, the injured wife as plaintiff could then win not only the suit, but also garner virtually lifetime alimony, more than half of the marital property, and custody of the children, all as punishment for the spouse's erring and "sinful" ways. The basis of "fault" divorces was that one party was all "right" and the other all "wrong," and that the one who committed misdeeds was to be punished. So it must be in an adversial system, predicated on linear causality, where one party to a dispute is judged guilty, and the other is innocent.

Divorce suits entered under "fault" premises frequently took many months or even years to resolve. To avoid such tension-filled delays, if one had the money and the time, a plaintiff could live in Nevada for six weeks and obtain the divorce more speedily. Mexico and some of the Caribbean republics were also divorce "havens," although decrees issued in those jurisdictions might not be recognized in the plaintiff's home state and could then be contested by the other spouse.

Since 1970, when California adopted "irreconcilable differences" as a policy, almost every state has adopted some form of "no-fault" divorce. This certainly does not mean that lawyers are no longer advocates for their clients, but it has reduced the need for both client and lawyer to engage in recrimination, connivance, or collusion (Perlman, 1982). All states still have bigamy as grounds for divorce, but it is now permissible in those states with "no-fault" divorce statutes to file on the basis of an "irretrievable breakdown" of the marriage.

To use Pennsylvania as an example of the reform in divorce laws, we need merely to consider that until mid-1980, "Pennsylvania had many grounds for divorce, all based on fault, blame, guilt, sin, the Judeo-Christian value system, fraud, vengeance, and high and low morality" (Hurowitz, 1981, p.1). This was fairly typical of provisions of pre-no-fault laws in other states as well. Although "irretrievable breakdown" of the marriage is now the prevailing policy where the parties both agree to the divorce and wish to expedite the process, if one spouse chooses to make the parting more difficult for the other, it is still possible to file on the grounds of "willful and malicious desertion," adultery, cruel and barbarous treatment, bigamy, imprisonment for two or more years for a crime, or "indignities to the person" (Hurowitz, 1981, p. 4).

One advantage to the no-fault divorce is that, if the parties mutually consent to a divorce, this is no longer labelled collusion. They are entitled to make the personal decision that their marriage is no longer viable. There is no "mud-slinging," no need to fabricate charges or evidence, and, since there is no need to present witnesses to substantiate the charges of adultery or one of the other still-existing grounds, it is also frequently less expensive than a divorce obtained on grounds of "fault." Yet another advantage, if the parties both agree to the mutual no-fault filing, is that the divorce decree can be obtained in 90 days. If they disagree, or if one refuses to consent, the proceedings take appreciably longer—up to three years in Pennsylvania.

There was concern, as states reformed the marital dissolution laws, that there would be an increase in the divorce rate. A number of studies cited by Bahr (1983) indicate that:

> the change to no-fault divorce has had no discernible effect on divorce rates. Three major changes have resulted from the reform of the divorce laws, however. First, the gender of the spouse who files for divorce has changed substantially, with many more husbands now filing than before. (p. 459)

A second change is that there has been a shift in weight economically from the stronger toward the weaker partner. And third, "monetary settlements are based increasingly on need and ability to pay rather than on misconduct" (p. 459). With reference to the second of these changes, wives, usually the economically weaker of the couple, used to be able to use their cooperation or lack of it as a bargaining tool in obtaining a better settlement in the divorce. This is no longer true, since either party can file for a no-fault divorce.

From a mental health point of view, there are pros and cons regarding no-fault divorce. A primary question, or criticism, is that the reasons for the divorce (e.g., adultery, spouse abuse) may never come to the fore publicly and therefore the negative feelings engendered may never be resolved (Perlman, 1982). It can be argued that the long drawn-out adversarial divorce that allowed the fault drama to be played out in full provided the necessary time frame and court arena for the feelings to be ventilated, each party's side to be heard, the former love object to be decathected, and ultimately enough distancing to take place that psychic closure could occur coterminous with the conclusion of the legal divorce. With the rapidity and lesser overt emotionality of no-fault divorce, the avenues for expressing, examining and ultimately resolving one's feelings of anger, wish for revenge, guilt, failure and myriad other emotions alluded to in earlier chapters, are one's family and friends—if they can tolerate the emotional vicissitudes, repetitive soul-searching, and criticism of self and/or former partner—or psychotherapy. The empathic and knowledgeable listening and skilled, strategic interventions of a therapist can be most helpful in working through the bewilderment, bitterness, sense of failure, and frustration with legal entanglements, and in assisting the divorcing person to put his/her life back together in a meaningful and satisfying way. Individual therapy with a systems-oriented therapist is probably the treatment of choice at this stage of the divorce process because of the utilization of a framework that recognizes the interaction of the individual's personality, needs and internal pressures, on the one hand, and the familial and larger environmental demands and expectations, on the other.

One other route emerges as a potential pathway for resolving animosity, albeit a less healthy one. Sometimes the "injured," rejected party may agree to obtain a no-fault divorce and then go on to express and try to work out the hostility and desire to retaliate hurtfully in the settlement negotiations or custody/visitation arrangements. When this is the course taken, the children are likely to become pawns in their parents' power struggle—rather than emerging as children of divorce whose best interest is truly at the heart of the custody/visitation plan.

On the positive side, no-fault divorce is concordant with the systems view of marriage delineated earlier. It also takes into account circular causality, recognizing that both parties, in some way, have contributed to the demise of their relationship. This becomes apparent in the case of Mrs. Simone.

Mrs. Simone became involved in an extramarital affair after many years of spending long evenings and weekends home alone with the children while her workaholic husband stayed at his law office or played golf to relax. Yet years back her desire for him to make "big money" so they could live in the best part of town contributed to the heavy work schedule he set up in order to push his earnings upward rapidly. (Author FK's case file)

How can one really determine who is to blame? Both shared responsibility for his workaholism, his absenteeism from the marriage, and her seeking affection from another. Neither was able to narrow the gap that had arisen. Under "no-fault" this joint contribution to the marital dissension becomes clearer. The same feelings may occur in a no-fault divorce as in a fault divorce and either or both parties may still be inclined to scapegoat the other. Yet in therapy we see those going through no-fault divorces have not been as stirred up by the legal system to think in terms of innocent and guilty and are therefore more likely to confront their own part in the marital war more directly and more quickly. When they come to grips with this and with ultimate acceptance that "they did the best they could," the prognosis for their postdivorce equilibration improves markedly.

CONTESTED VS. UNCONTESTED DIVORCE

The Divorce Itself

An uncontested case has been defined as "any suit for divorce, legal separation, or annulment in which the final judgment is entered *without the necessity of a trial*" (Friedman, 1984, p. 63). In practice, this means that one spouse files the suit and the other either files a mutual consent form (as in Pennsylvania) or waits out the statutory period (as in Pennsylvania's Three Year Unilateral No-Fault Divorce) (Hurowitz, 1981). An uncontested divorce does not mean that issues between the parties have all been resolved easily and to the satisfaction of both parties. It does mean that they have conferred about custody and the division of assets, working either through their attorneys or a mediator to draw up a mutually acceptable agreement. They do not seek a judge's determination about who should get and do what. Typically, however, a judicial proceeding still occurs in all states, required by administrative or statutory mechanisms, that results in the issuance of the legal divorce decree.

According to Mnookin and Kornhauser:

> The requirement of a judicial proceeding in undisputed divorce cases could easily be eliminated. Getting married does not require judicial proceedings, so why should getting a divorce? Some countries have eliminated the requirement that undisputed divorces go through court, and it therefore seems appropriate to examine the possible justifications for the requirement. (1979, p. 992)

They cite (pp. 992–994) the numerous functions the court proceeding (allegedly) serves: it represents a ceremonial function that demonstrates the seriousness with which the state treats divorce; it affords judicial approval of a divorce agreement that presumably ensures fairness between the spouses even if it is a private settlement negotiated originally out of court (between the lawyers or with a mediator) (Haynes, 1981); it ensures carrying out the state's interest in protection of any children of the marriage.

For each of these functions that the court proceedings serve, Mnookin and Kornhauser present a counterargument. Their purpose in so doing ostensibly was to stimulate consideration of alternative procedures that "might facilitate dispute resolution during a typically difficult and painful time in the lives of parents and children alike" (1979, p. 996). Indeed, in an uncontested divorce action, particularly those where the parties have "agreed to disagree" or at least to dissolve their marriage without rancor, and where there is no argument over child custody and visitation or monetary matters, they posit that the costs of the divorce would be reduced considerably in both time and money if there were no judicial proceeding required. This of course would appeal to the divorcing parties but could cut into the income derived by matrimonial lawyers quite substantially. (This may be one of the main reasons many trial lawyers still oppose mediation.)

A contested divorce suit is quite another story. In the first place, the contested divorce means that one of the parties is unwilling to agree to the divorce. A major reason for contesting the divorce action is that the second spouse wants a reconciliation and continuation of the marriage. He or she may believe he/she still loves the mate and that the marriage could again be viable, even pleasurable. Other reasons for delay include: 1) one spouse wants to impede the divorce as revenge against the rejecting, hurtful spouse obtaining his/her coveted freedom; 2) one spouse wants to block his/her partner from again getting his/her way and doesn't want to again be the one who "gives in"; 3) one spouse wants time to hide assets so that they will not be subject to equitable distribution at the time of the final divorce agreement; 4) the individual's religion does not permit divorce; and 5) philosophically the individual believes that marriage entails a lifetime commitment that is not cancelable. Technically, according to Friedman, a divorce case is "contested from the moment it is filed until a settlement has been reached. 'Contested' simply means that some issues relating to the divorce—custody, property, or support— have not been resolved" (1984, p. 63). Until the issues are all settled, the case proceeds as if it were going to court for a full trial.

Contested divorces can occur whether based on "fault" or "no-fault." If based on "fault," then the nonfiling party has to respond to the charge(s) within an allotted time period and defend him/herself regarding these. If based on "no-fault," there is no need for a "defense."

One of the difficulties in a divorce contested on the basis of disputed issues over child custody or distribution of assets is that the judge does not know the parties and rarely can allocate time to get to know them sufficiently well to make an informed ruling because of crowded court dockets. Sometimes the judge's lack of expertise in family dynamics and child psychology makes it difficult for him/her to weigh and evaluate the unique preferences and sentiments of the couple. Another difficulty is that the judge's allocation of assets, alimony/spousal support, and child support payments may not be the most efficacious in terms of tax burdens. Third, as joint custody gains in popularity as a preferential form for a resolution of that issue, the judge may order this arrangement, in the absence of any proof that one parent is "unfit" (Florida Dissolution of Marriage—Children Act, 1982), whether or not it is really in the "best interest of the child." This is not to imply that the judge is inept or incompetent, but rather that judges, like many other professionals, tend to follow "patterns" or "formulas" that have worked in the majority of cases in their experience, rather than to assess each child and set of parents individually in relation to specific needs and competencies. In actuality, the relationship between the two individuals, both in marriage and in divorce, tends to have unique qualities and characteristics in addition to those shared with other married and divorcing couples. Making decisions based on patterns and formulas rarely allows for the uniqueness. Thus, if issues are contested and brought to a judge for decision-making, it is likely that the decision will not be as good for the couple as one that is tailor-made for them through alternative means in which they actively participate. Fortunately, enlightened judges may turn to a psychologist or other mental health professional for a child custody evaluation and utilize the data obtained from such an objective assessment as a major piece of evidence upon which to base their decision.

The Child Custody Decision

Whether the couple seeks a contested or an uncontested divorce, if there are children, decisions will inevitably need to be made pertaining to their future lives. We hold as basic tenets that 1) children are not property; 2) they are not marital assets that can be traded or divided; 3) their living arrangements should not be conditional on the amount of child support paid or who possesses the greater wealth; and 4) children should not have their primary residence determined by which parent has been rejected and/or which one needs them more for company or as a caretaker.

In the best of all possible worlds, all parents would agree that their concern for their children's welfare is separate, apart from, and transcends any animosity, feelings of rejection or desire for revenge, or self-interest the parents may have with regard to each other. Since this is clearly not the case in reality, it becomes incumbent upon the professionals with whom the parents deal—attorneys as well as psychotherapists— to urge this position in their initial contacts with the separated couple. That is, the therapist who is working with a parent on the brink of divorce should raise the issue of "What do you think would constitute the most constructive arrangement for your child(ren) regarding such issues as: residence, school, medical care, and being with their other parent? What are your goals for your child(ren)?" Similarly, an attorney, at the first meeting with the client, could state that child custody matters are to be settled as promptly *and* as amicably as possible so that the child(ren) will feel as secure as possible and know implicitly that both parents love them and are concerned for them in spite of the conflict continuing between the parents.

In urging early settlement of the child custody issues, it is not proposed that one party suggest an arrangement and the other meekly assent. Rather, we encourage the parties, with their attorneys or a mediator, to consider together what is truly in the child's best interest rather than what is most convenient for each of them. If one parent chooses to contest the divorce action, on whatever grounds, this should not lead to a "push-pull" situation for the children. Children should never be permitted to be pawns on a divorce chess board!

Where the child is old enough to comprehend the marital conflict and its issues, the parent should explain why he/she is contesting the action or not contesting it. A parent, for example, who chooses not to contest the action, but opts for a 90-day mutual consent no-fault decree, may be doing so partly to minimize the friction for the child(ren). Other reasons might include a recognition that there will be no reconciliation and a desire under those circumstances to conclude what has become a nasty chapter in his/her life in order to start a new period. All of this can be explained to an intelligent 8-year-old or the average 10-year-old. Prolongation of the action without settling the custody issues, despite loud protestations of "I'm trying to do what's best for you," is less satisfactorily explained.

It is our contention that, no matter what the age of the child, he or she should not be asked, by therapist, lawyer or judge, "With which parent do you wish to be (i.e., have your primary residence)?" For a child to be placed in a position of making such a choice is to inherently make him/her guilty of disloyalty to the parent he/she does not choose; this constitutes an existential betrayal of a critical biological tie (Boszormenyi-Nagy & Spark, 1973). Rather, in our therapy and mediation practices, when working on custody issues, we seek to ascertain from the children their ideas and feelings about:

1. What are the reasons you might prefer to be with Mom or Dad as the primary residential parent?
2. What problems do you anticipate if you are with Mom? with Dad?
3. What activities and interests do you share with Mom? with Dad?
4. Who takes you to the pediatrician, dentist, and for other medical care?
5. Which parent assists in supervising what homework, when necessary?
6. Who takes you to scouts, little league, music and/or dancing lessons, other sports activities (or whatever this particular child is involved in)?
7. Who takes you clothes shopping, to the playground, to visit your friends? (Questions are always age appropriate.)

Obtaining such data and observing and hearing the emotions expressed as such information is given provide a kaleidoscopic picture of the child's perception of bonding. One must convey one's concern without forcing the child to reject one parent by having him/her express a preference for the other one. The information acquired from the child is incorporated into our suggestions to the parents as to what the optimal custody and visitation agreement might be and into any report we may be responsible for sending to the court.

PATHWAYS TO MARITAL DISSOLUTION

When an individual decides to move toward divorce today, there are several processes—litigation, mediation, arbitration, or an interdisciplinary panel—from which he or she can choose. This selection can be made before any action is filed in court or after the divorce complaint has been filed and served on the spouse. There are various documents to be handled and information to be secured. No matter what process is chosen, ultimately, the final decree is determined by the court and agreements must be acceptable under the laws of the state in which the divorce is granted. So, although the process may be nonadversarial, it is still carried out in accordance with legal stipulations governing custody arrangements, taxes, distributions of retirement and pension plan assets and other marital property, and the rights of all parties involved.

The parties should carefully select the process that best serves their interests and those of their children. Before making a final choice, they should gather information about what each process entails and determine which route will be most ego syntonic.

If the adversarial process is selected, each person should get a list of the family lawyers in the community and ascertain something about them *before* calling for an exploratory interview. Is the person reputed to be family oriented and humane? Or is he or she considered to be a "shark" or "barracuda" whose typical stance is "go for the jugular" and "demand all you can get" or "give away as little as possible"? Which type do the parties want?

If mediation is the method of choice, a list of mediators should be obtained. Here a similar selection process is needed. Do they want a therapist/mediator or a lawyer/mediator? Do they want someone very experienced or a novice?* Many private mediators are beginners, as this is a relatively new field. It is legitimate to ask, "How many cases have you mediated?" If sex of an attorney or mediator is important, this may also be a selection factor. How fees are charged, when they are payable and a guesstimate as to total cost are also valid concerns to be raised.

With this as a preview, let us look more deeply into what is involved in each approach to handling a divorce action.

Litigation

Each party takes his/her own case to separate counsel and indicates what he/she wants and is willing to give or not take. They make known their own needs, demands, assets and liabilities, and "their story" regarding the children.

Any issues in the divorce battle that cannot be settled between the parties, usually negotiating through their lawyers, such as property division, visitation, or support, are usually taken before a court for trial. It is possible that issues may be settled at a pretrial conference between the lawyers and judge, but if they are not, a date is set for the hearing and the matter proceeds. This can occur in both no-fault and fault cases, and in both uncontested and contested cases. Obviously, the "dirtiest" divorce cases are those citing "fault" as grounds for divorce, where one spouse accuses the other of adultery, abuse, addiction or desertion. If one spouse has chosen this route, it is likely that the other spouse will not only respond with anger, but also with great resistance to settling any issue in order to "get back" at the accuser (unless there are sudden surges of guilt feelings).

We need not go through all the steps leading up to the trial here. Nonetheless, it seems pertinent to note that litigation, or adversarial action, tends to be expensive in terms of legal costs, lengthy in time

---

*Whether the mediator is an attorney or a mental health specialist, he/she should have completed a specific basic training program in divorce and child custody mediation under a well-qualified training team or in a graduate school or law school with a definite course in family mediation.

spent in and out of court until the judge renders a decision, and highly stressful for both spouses. If one is advised not to move out of the marital home for either financial reasons or as leverage to force more concessions, the tension mounts even higher. If the wife's attorney advises her to withdraw from college, not get a job she was considering or to cut back on her working time so that she will appear less adequate and therefore be entitled to a more lucrative settlement, deception and gamesmanship characterize the dissolution, inflaming the ex-partner and contributing to a loss of self-respect. The children, too, often perceive the chicanery and find it distasteful, even reprehensible.

There is also no guarantee that what the plaintiff spouse is suing for in terms of distribution of assets, alimony, child custody or child support is what will be granted by the judge. As we indicated earlier, courts tend to be guided by formulas, and individual judges by their own conscious and unconscious biases, as well as informed prior experiences and readings on the topic. Unfortunately, not all judges have the wisdom, time and/or inclination to be responsive to the unique needs and characteristics of two specific individuals.

Furthermore, adults who decide to dissolve their marriage through adversarial action may prolong the agony of the conflict not only for themselves, but also for their children. Finding themselves unable to agree on one or more issues, and angered by each other's recalcitrance, they hurl accusations at each other, and denigrate each other at every opportunity—whether at a public court hearing or trial, in front of their children, or to relatives and friends. Meanwhile, the child, on the sidelines, is bewildered, angered, and frightened. He or she wonders anxiously if there will ever be an end to the conflict in which he/she is unwillingly embroiled, and often develops symptoms of physical and/or emotional illness. If the child physically resembles one of the warring parents, and perhaps has learned some of that parent's mannerisms as well, he/she may interpret attacks on that parent as being attacks on him/herself too.

In the view of Johnston, Campbell, and Tall (1985), adversarial conflicts serve the parents as defense against: 1) a narcissistic insult—protecting the injured self-esteem of the rejected party; 2) a sense of loss—as the relationship continues even in a negative way; 3) feelings of guilt; and 4) a sense of helplessness. All of these emotions may also be true of childless couples, of course. Where there are children, however, the children become the "trophies" of the battle. Gaining custody represents, "for some parents, retribution for the evil deeds of the spouse; for some, the children were a link, a last bridge, to the other parent" (Johnston et al., 1985, p. 126). It is clear that adversarial contests, whether over custody or over other issues, rarely, if ever, serve children's needs and interests well.

In keeping with the American Bar Association's (ABA) Model Code of Professional Responsibility (1981), an attorney is enjoined *only* to represent his or her client. The welfare and interests of the other partner (and the children) are not his/her concern since the assumption in law is that the former will be adequately represented by separate opposing legal counsel (and that the parents will both want and agree upon what is best for the children).

If for some reason, when the case comes to court, the judge determines that the best interests of the children are not receiving adequate and proper consideration and that the matter of custody needs greater illumination than can be obtained through standard adversarial channels, the judge may order a custody evaluation and/or appoint a child advocate or a guardian ad litem. In the latter instance, the three attorneys will each be representing a different perspective and "piece" of the dissolving and restructuring family. It remains for the judge to integrate all of the testimony and consider the future welfare of the unit as it moves toward becoming a postdivorce family, often linked economically and through the children emotionally for many years to come.

Further, inasmuch as the law governing divorce historically has cast the judge's role as one of ascertaining which party is "innocent" and which is "guilty," each attorney may still attempt to show his/her client in the best light—seeking to retain or obtain maximum benefits for the person he/she is representing. Sometimes the battle becomes hostile and demeaning, resulting in prolonged bitterness and anguish; children are traumatized by the continuing strife (Kessler & Bostwick, 1977; Wallerstein & Kelly, 1979, 1980), and everyone involved suffers a long-term loss of self-esteem and confidence.

ALTERNATIVES TO LITIGATION

Alternatives to adversarial proceedings include arbitration, mediation, and the use of an interdisciplinary committee or panel (in child custody disputes). The advantages of these methods for the parting pair lie in the potential reduction of pain, risks, financial costs, and the time delays involved in litigation. Advantages accrue to the children also and these will be discussed in greater detail later in regard to mediation.

Arbitration

Arbitration is less formal than a regular court proceeding, but still represents the imposition of a third party's solution to disagreements between the parting spouses. They usually try first to reach agreement and then those items that remain in contention are submitted to binding arbitration. The implication that one party is more "right" than the other, even where the arbitrated solution is a compromise, may leave both parties dissatisfied and the children little better off than they would have been, had the case been settled in court. An exception, for the children, may occur if there is an arbitration panel with a mental health specialist in child/adolescent development as a panel member. Said person may serve as a child advocate.

Proponents of arbitration emphasize that this is a speedier proceeding than a court hearing, permitting both spouses to get on with their lives. They also aver that the decision made will be more relevant to the specific couple than if the case were heard by a judge, since a panel is not concerned with setting judicial precedents for subsequent divorce cases. This alternative dispute resolution strategy has not yet obtained much popularity.

Parties contemplating the use of arbitration need to be reasonable to begin with and need to be willing to accept a decision over which they exercise limited control. Typically, both spouses are represented by separate counsel, are obligated to make full and frank disclosure of assets or other vital information, and may offer lay witnesses or expert witnesses as appropriate at the arbitration hearing. Although the arbitrators' decision is final, it is not the end of the matter. The decision is attached to the Divorce Complaint filed in court and is then incorporated into the final Divorce Decree.

Mediation

With the burgeoning of divorce mediation, following publication of Coogler's (1978) seminal work, and the expanding literature about the mediation process (see for example, Folberg, 1983; Haynes, 1981, 1982; Neville, 1984; Saposnek, 1983), couples who wish to optimize their choices in the critical matters of custody, visitation, and distribution of assets, and who abhor the idea of litigation, can consider mediation as a viable alternative to the adversarial process.

Some core principles of mediation, such as empowerment, consideration of the best interest of all family members, full and honest disclosure of all assets, cooperative problem solving, and equitable distribution of assets are congruent with the theory and practice of family systems therapy. The task orientation of jointly forging a mutually acceptable divorce agreement with the least possible distress is also conducive to coping constructively with the numerous problems and tasks at hand during the divorce process. Less energy is burned up in hostile, aggressive and retaliative behaviors. It also appears that the mediation process contributes to a more rapid and solid personality reintegration and life-style restabilization—that is, to some closure on and tranquility with the actual divorce—than does litigation. If the couple can cooperatively reach an agreement that takes into account the "best interest" of all involved parties, this period can be one during which they learn to express their desires and beliefs, and utilize their abilities more fully. As both come to trust "their own independent judgements, to negotiate assertively, to compromise effectively, and to take charge of redirecting and refashioning their own lives" (Kaslow, in press), their sense of self-sufficiency is augmented. (See Appendix I for sample contract for mediation services.)

Involvement in the mediation process can serve to diminish the feelings of despair, depression, hopelessness, helplessness, self-pity, fury and alienation that frequently characterize the legal, economic and custody phases of divorce. Innuendos and threats of contemplated self-destructive or vituperative behaviors lessen as the people are encouraged to decide for themselves how to distribute their assets and what residential and financial arrangements to make for their children. During the course of mediation it is not unusual for a client's perceptions and behaviors to shift from those of a victim and loser to those of a creator and winner.

The skills a mediator should possess exceed those typical of many fine mental health practitioners and many talented matrimonial lawyers. Mediation is a new specialty, which at best requires an amalgam of the sensitivity, empathy, and diagnostic and clinical acumen of the therapist; the knowledge of family law, property distribution, insurance, taxes and court procedures of the attorney; and the bargaining and negotiating skills of the labor arbitrator. Skill in such functions as power balancing, conflict management, negotiation management, agreement drafting and interprofessional communication are also vital (Haynes, 1982). Assisting mediation clients in this fashion is consonant with a philosophic orientation that values self-determination and self-actualization and believes these to be basic ingredients that enhance the recuperation from this often traumatic life event. Conversely, the adversarial process often erodes the right to self-determination, since it functions through lawyers doing the negotiating and making the tradeoffs, and judges making the final decisions regarding custody, visitation, child and spousal support, and property distribution.

Similar principles apply to the financial issues inherent in divorce. Those who are vague about their income and expenses, and their assets and liabilities, can be severely shaken when they recognize that in the near future they will have to live on a decreased income and will have to manage their own financial affairs. Such procedures as drawing up budgets, evaluating financial statements, and compiling a list of outstanding debts, which both partners are required to do, can be an illumi-

nating learning experience. From their successful completion, each partner can emerge with a greater sense of self-esteem and adequacy. To
realize one is capable of handling the finances contributes to a sense of
independence and autonomy—and decreases one's fear of financial chaos and aloneness. All of the above are core elements in an ability to
progress toward the psychic divorce (see Table 2, pp. 30–31). As the
separating former partners reach agreement on the equitable distribution of assets, principles of fairness and mutual consideration may become more a part of their modus operandi, thus enhancing their shattered self-respect, and ultimately making them less hostile and more
attractive in other interpersonal relationships.

The most valued asset in many marriages is the children. Both parents
may find the prospect of giving up full-time parenting untenable. Most
mediators are probably biased in the direction of children having easy
access to both parents and both parents staying integrally involved in
their children's lives. As the mediator explores the wishes, rights and
responsibilities of all family members, each adult is encouraged to see
and value the other's strengths as a parent and the children's need to
remain attached to both without worrying that loving one will be misper-
ceived as disloyalty to the other. When the children's responses to the
divorce, their developmental needs, hopes for the future, and changing
perspectives are carefully considered, and any parental selfish desire to
hurt the departing spouse by depriving him/her of access is worked
through, the agreement written will much more substantially incorporate attention to "the best interest of everyone." It will also be easier to
live with since everyone's needs and feelings will have been taken into
consideration (Hetherington et al., 1977b). When children and their parents remain closely involved with one another in co-parental arrangements, the sense of disruption, loss, and desertion is minimized. Grief
and mourning reactions, which are common for both children and the
noncustodial parent in many postadversarial divorce restructurings of
the family, are not as marked or long lasting in a mediated settlement.
This enhances everyone's potential for psychic well-being.

In relation to custody decisions it is suggested that mediators incorporate a family systems perspective. Often there is spade work to be done
with the couple to uncover how they have been dealing with the children's perceptions and reactions, to interpret the stages of what is happening to them, and to help them grieve and reintegrate. The mediator
can explain what a profound influence the parents' (and grandparents')
behavior will have on the children, that the nature of the two adults'
adjustment will correlate highly with the children's adjustment (Wallerstein & Kelly, 1980), and that the children need to know that both parents
will continue to cherish them and will be involved in their lives. Chil-

dren's "rights" include not having to listen to one parent criticize the other and not having to carry reports back and forth between the separate households.

In some instances what is revealed is that neither adult wants to be "saddled with" child care responsibilities. Children of course sense this, even when it is more covert than overt. When this is the case, the mediator helps them explore all the options and to evolve the most workable plan.

It becomes clear that in mediation, by contrast to litigation or arbitration, the parties work out the specifics of their own agreement. This approach is seen as a cooperative one that seeks to maintain each party's integrity and self-esteem and avoids fault-finding and attribution of blame. Not every couple can use mediation profitably, however. The individuals must be able to trust each other, to communicate reasonably and calmly, and to be willing to actually participate in formulating an agreement which becomes a map for the next years of their lives and their children's. If either is severely mentally disturbed or retarded, they are not good candidates for mediation and, in fact, need lawyers to represent their individual interests. The *mediator's function* is to find points of agreement and to suggest ways of reducing such conflicts as do occur, *but NOT to make decisions*. The mediator serves to empower them to negotiate with each other effectively; as a resource person, suggesting topics for discussion, sources of needed information, and possible alternatives for resolution; and as a facilitator, reinforcing positive moves toward agreement and shifting topics as needed to reduce growing conflict. Often the mediator teaches problem-solving skills and how to generate and consider options to the parties. The mediator may raise questions about the possible or probable consequences of proposals made—in effect forcing the couple to think about the outcomes of the decisions they are making. The mediator is not acting in a therapeutic role, nor a judgmental one, nor a legal one. Rather, he/she acts as a trained negotiator would, bringing the two parties to recognize realities and to compromise as necessary.

Divorce mediation is broader in scope than custody mediation, but may subsume it. It can be focused on any or all of the following issues: property division, spousal support and the form it takes (lump sum settlement or periodic short-term or long-term payment), tax liabilities and payments, child custody, visitation, and child support. The process is one of communication, negotiation, compromise, and tradeoffs.

As an example, let us suppose that both parties are employed, but that the husband has substantial holdings in stocks, bonds, and savings. In litigation, if he is furious with her, he may assert that her income is sufficient to take care of her needs and that he is willing to give her, in addition, 10% of the holdings for which he has paid over the years out of his earnings, but not a nickel more. She, on the other hand, points out what the marital life-style has been and that she cannot continue it or come anywhere near it with his offer. A judge, hearing that she makes $15,000 to $20,000 a year and thinking "that's a pretty good salary for a woman," may rule that her salary plus 20% of the husband's holdings is an appropriate and equitable distribution. A mediator, in contrast, will encourage more reasonable parties to discuss their life-style, the current and probable future cost of living, and whether 10% or 20% seems fair reimbursement for the additional unpaid contributions of the wife to the marriage of "x" years. This discussion, carried on in a spirit of compromise and commitment to principles of fair and equitable distribution of marital property rather than rancor, will likely lead to a distribution of these assets that is more of a win/win for each party, perhaps leaving each a touch dissatisfied. Through mediation the husband may pay a percentage more than he originally suggested, and the wife may accept a percentage less than she had originally requested (demanded?). In mediation there is rarely one clear "winner" and one clear "loser" as there is apt to be in litigation, and possibly in arbitration, since cooperation and consideration are emphasized as the pair strive to generate a mutually acceptable agreement.

Where children are involved, some mediators, especially those trained in the mental health professions, may invite the children to participate in a mediation session. The goal here is not to ask the child to make a choice between the parents as preferred custodian, but rather to ascertain the child's needs, interests, and quality of relationship with each parent. Children of school age often feel entitled to have a voice in determining their futures and, in some cases, this may be the first time that the parents, who have been preoccupied with their own conflicts, have really listened to their children's views. Knowing what is important to the child as a person may help them to reach a more rational agreement than would have been possible without this information. (More on this in Chapters 8 and 9 on children of divorce.)

Since the parents will have the responsibility of carrying out the provisions of a custody-visitation-support agreement, their voluntary and informed compromises are more likely to ensure the success of the agreement. Furthermore, the remediation mechanism can be included in the agreement as a means of reaching resolution regarding needed (future) modifications about arrangements for the children as they grow older or other conditions change (Hyde, 1984).

We believe, based on clinical observation, personal conversations with many divorcé(e)s, and the growing body of literature on mediation, that mediation often constitutes the dispute resolution strategy which best serves the current and future needs of children.

> When one is undertaking either divorce therapy or divorce media-tion with a couple, it is vital to ascertain such life cycle factors as: 1) where each is in his or her *individual* life cycle development in terms of chronological age, emotional maturity, cognitive functioning, ca-reer status and aims, and child rearing; 2) how long the *couple* had been together, what are the personalities and ages of the children, the nature of the couple's prior relationship to each other, the ex-tended family's response to the imminent divorce, the importance ascribed to independence/freedom vs. sharing one's life and being concerned about a partner's wishes, the level of intimacy sought and reached, the nature and frequency of arguments, the extent of ennui and disillusionment, the perceived friendship and career opportunities beyond the current marriage and job, and the eco-nomic circumstances; and 3) if they have already decided to divorce or where they are in this emotional and legal process—predivorce, during divorce, or postdivorce? (Kaslow, 1984b, p. 58)

It is important that the point of therapeutic entry and the selection of treatment strategies or the approach in divorce mediation be contingent upon etching a clear and accurate picture of the partners' individual and couple identity, rhythms, intrapsychic integration and interpersonal re-sources, and the life cycle stage in these intertwined aspects of living.

> The J's came for mediation self-referred. He was a successful engi-neer and she had recently finished her bachelor's work in political science. The children were 16 and 18 years of age. Custody and property distribution were easily agreed upon. The items under contention were spousal support and the children's education. Mrs. J wanted rehabilitation alimony for 10 years—during 2 years of part-time work until the second child entered college, 3 years for her to attend law school plus 5 years to establish her practice so she could be reasonably certain she could then afford to support herself in accordance with her accustomed life-style. She also wanted him to bear the complete cost of sending the children to expensive private colleges and whatever graduate schools they selected. When Mr. J balked, his wife threatened (and meant) she would report some of his shady dealings and drug trafficking to his boss.
> As the mediator, I (FK) helped Mrs. J examine the consequences of such an action, i.e., he might lose his job, and/or have to face drug trafficking charges and go to prison, and then, who would pay alimony, etc.? After discharging some of her wrath at his stingi-ness she backed down. After several sessions of proposals and

counterproposals, exploring and negotiating, they compromised on Mr. J paying a set rehabilitation alimony figure for 6 years, and then having it reduced by $3000 a year for the next 4 years. He also agreed to cover 4 years of undergraduate college—setting a realistic and generous maximum on what he could afford per year. If Mrs. J or the children believed something more expensive were warranted, they would have to contribute. She accepted this as a rational resolution and counteroffer. They agreed to reconsider graduate or professional school if and when the children expressed interest and if they could not work this out together—to then return for a brief additional period of mediation.

It was recommended that he seek therapy about his involvement with drugs—with emphasis on concern for his well-being and what he was modelling for his children.

Who in the family attends a mediation session should be determined not by hard and fast rules, but by discerning who is making an input into the decisions and who will be affected by the final agreement. Sometimes children should be included, but in most cases, as indicated earlier, it is imperative that they not be asked with which parent they prefer to live. Instead, helping them understand what is transpiring and the implications and consequences of the divorce may be in order, providing the discussion is consonant with the goal of enabling the parents to arrive at an agreement and that it does not become therapy. As parents decide on custody arrangements, queries about after-school chauffeuring, coaching teams, music lessons, doctors' visits, and care during illnesses should be asked to raise their level of consciousness to the demands of single parenthood. A clear and specific visitation plan should be written (Blau, 1984) and can be attached as an addendum to the memorandum of understanding drawn up jointly by the mediator and the couple and then taken by the parties to their respective attorneys for final drafting and filing.

If grandparents are to figure in the child care, financial support or housing, it may be advisable for them to participate in one or two mediation sessions. They can be instrumental in the implementation of the agreement; if spurned, they can sabotage it and serve as a negative influence by stirring up the children and inflaming their wrath against one parent.

As is true for therapists (Abroms, 1978), each mediator should clarify his/her own relevant values, indicating a preference for the "best interest of the child" precept. Mediators can indicate that parents' attention to their offsprings' emotional needs and future well-being are more compelling and far-reaching than financial concerns. Further, they can convey that the less argumentative and retaliative parents are, the better the prognosis for the children's emotional health. Such a position is likely to coincide with the one their therapist is taking (if they are in treatment) and will help diminish the level of bewilderment they are experiencing in other realms of their life where conflictual messages abound.

When the tentative memorandum of agreement is drawn up, each party should take it to his/her attorney to see that everything is legally correct and everything that needed consideration has been included, that their rights have been protected, and that the tax implications have been kept in view. At this stage any modifications needed are made; then the lawyers draw up and file the final agreement. It has usually been our experience that judges look favorably upon mediated documents and convert them into the divorce decree.

Occasionally participants in mediation will decide that some ceremony is warranted on the day they co-sign the agreement as they want it to read. Their judicious handling of a major stressful life event has culminated in a document of which they are proud. In the ambivalent mixture of feelings, there is an inkling of relief at this accomplishment. Marking this ceremonially facilitates their quest to bring closure to an important chapter of their lives and contributes to the movement toward growth and positive reintegration. The ceremony may take place co-terminous with the legal agreement or anytime in the months to come. Completion of the mediation agreement, underscored in a ceremonial marker event may represent a vital success experience at a time when so much else has felt like failure and may well provide needed momentum for entering the postdivorce stage with more of a spirit of optimism and a determination to meet challenges that lie ahead. (See chapter 11 for more on ceremonies.)

Some mediators routinely ask their clients to return at periodic intervals after the legal divorce is final. Three-month, 6-month and 1-year follow-up sessions can provide clients with a formal opportunity to assess how the agreement is working out and to renegotiate any nonfunctional clauses. I (FK) also recommend that clients meet with me conjointly again when one or both are about to be remarried and the postdivorce family is again being restructured—necessitating another series of alterations and accommodations in relationships. Sometimes, when a particular child's developmental or personality needs are such that a change of primary physical residence might be advisable or if there is a great change in a parent's circumstances warranting such a shift, and the couple have difficulty reaching agreement on their own, a return to mediation might break through the impasse (as in the J case cited earlier). What is being advocated here is rational continuity and the ability to plan ahead, without total guarantees of "forever," since some flexibility is usually "in the best interest of the child." Changes should be planned for and should not occur out of desperation, rejection, anger or impetuosity. When major changes are made, the court should be asked to formalize a change of custody order.

It appears crucial that solid research be undertaken to assess whether those who enter and complete mediation restabilize better and more rapidly than those who undergo an adversarial divorce and perhaps remain foes long after the legal divorce is final. It is the tentative hypothesis being advanced here that this is so.

An Interdisciplinary Committee

A third alternative to litigation, useful when the issue is custody, is an interdisciplinary committee, chosen in advance by the parents. The panel might include an educator, a clergyperson, an impartial attorney, and a child psychology specialist (Hyde, 1984). Ideally, these panel members should be or become familiar with the family and the needs of its various members.

The interdisciplinary committee would represent a compromise process between the purely voluntary nature of mediation and the third-party decision-making of arbitration or litigation. It constitutes an attempt to consider what is best for the child(ren) from several points of view rather than solely from a legal, moral, or psychological position. According to Kubie, such a committee system would "save both the parents and the court money and resources" (Hyde, 1984, p. 34). (To our knowledge this approach is not being used.) As with other alternatives to adversarial proceedings, however, a committee's decision would only have the status of a recommendation to the court as, to date, a nonjudicial panel has not been accorded the authority to make a final decision.

CONTRAINDICATIONS FOR EACH APPROACH

Despite the positive publicity mediation has been receiving, it is not a panacea, nor is it the marital dissolution route of choice for all. For example, when one party is mentally retarded, brain damaged, psychotic, or has a severe character disorder, he or she may well need a tough attorney to forcefully represent his or her interests. Sometimes there is a tremendous power disparity and the weaker partner cannot or will not be assertive. If the mediator has to throw too much weight on the side of the weaker member of the couple, he/she may lose the neutrality and objectivity so essential to fair mediation. In such instances recourse to a lawyer may be advisable so that the more aggressive, demanding partner cannot take advantage of the more placid, less articulate one. Sometimes the parties are so embittered that equity is not at all what they seek.

Rather, they may, in fact, need to fight viciously and prolong the divorce in order to 1) punish their ex-spouses, 2) ventilate and work through anger, 3) achieve concessions as the price of achieving closure, and 4) stall for time until they are better able to "let go" of the relationship and the vituperation and heal psychologically. Litigation, not mediation, can offer this.

Conversely, individuals embarking on divorce can be educated to the fact that when adversarial proceedings are undertaken, the antagonists are likely to feel

> much more helpless and pessimistic than in mediation as the nego-
> tiating devolves on the attorneys, with final authority for all deci-
> sions resting with the judge. Much anxiety and apprehension col-
> ors the ambiguity of the turbulent waiting period until the final
> decree. A combination of bewilderment, loneliness, anger and grief
> over all the losses wrought by the breakup of the marriage/family
> may be further stirred up until a state of depression prevails.
> (Kaslow, in press)

The decreed distribution of valued possessions, amassed as part of their life together, is often a disturbing and disorienting experience.

THE AFTERMATH

After the marriage has been legally dissolved by the divorce decree, if one of the parties is dissatisfied with the judge's ruling in a litigated suit, that party can appeal the decision. Mere dissatisfaction with the distribution of assets, however, tends to have limited success on appeal. "If, on the other hand, the trial judge has committed some legal procedural error which has substantially affected the outcome of the case, the chances of the appeal's succeeding are far greater" (Friedman, 1984, p. 126). An appeal is very costly in attorney's fees and may take a year or more to be heard and decided.

A second possible negative event in the aftermath of the divorce decree being granted is that one party does not abide by its provisions. (This seems less likely to occur after mediation since it is their own personalized agreement they are implementing.) Postlitigation, the other party's attorney may apply to the court for relief, and the offending party may be held in contempt of court until the provisions are met. Different states handle this type of problem differently, although some kind of punitive action may be taken, up to and including imprisonment for contempt of court. If the default involves child support payments, there is now a federal law that makes provision for enforcement of such payments. (See Chapter 7.) Resorting to such tactics may serve to antagonize and make shared parenting responsibilities more difficult.

Yet a third outcome of the divorce has to do with communication between the ex-spouses. Once the divorce agreement has been finalized, childless couples may be able to avoid contact with each other. However, if there are children, especially minor children, there is a continuing need for communication and occasionally to see each other. Depending upon the hostility generated during the separation and divorce periods, the maturity of the parties, and many other factors, this continuing— though limited—relationship can be amicable, "civilized" but cold, or a continuation of the earlier bitter war. Clearly, if there are children, it is not in their best interest to continue the battle. This does not mean that the parents have to like each other or even be friendly, but they should be able to be civil. Outbreaks of hostility can occur, even in a courteous relationship, but should be limited in scope if they are not to be damaging to the children—of whatever age.

There are other considerations in the aftermath of divorce. The parties must build new lives alone or with a new partner, conclude the psychic divorce if possible by working through the anguish, blame and guilt, continue working or find a job, and help the children to adjust to the new circumstances. These variable outcomes of divorce are considered in Chapter 10.

SUMMARY

This chapter on the legal aspects of divorce has been written utilizing the "diaclectic" model of stages in the divorce process, which serves as the framework (Kaslow, 1984a). This model is contingent upon incorporation of knowledge about the individual's growth and development through the epigenetic phases (Erikson, 1968), a comprehension of marital dynamics and conflicts, which may lead to disenchantment and, eventually, dissolution, and the utilization of a family systems perspective.

This philosophic orientation embodies a melding of psychodynamic, object relations, holistic/systems, and humanistic-existential theory. In divorce therapy, the treatment approach which evolves from it may incorporate analytic, gestalt, structural, strategic, family of origin, contextual, and behavioral techniques. The approach selected is contingent upon the couple's presenting issues, personality dynamics, ego strengths, amount of time to be allocated to mediation (or therapy), and developmental stages in the life cycle and in the divorce process (Kaslow,

1981a, 1983). (Table 2 on pp. 30–31 delineates the model in chart form. Please refer back to it for a base point in the ensuing discussion.)

The "stations" (Bohannon, 1970) or phases of the divorce process do not occur in an invariant sequence, nor are the turmoil and distress the same at each phase or for all people. Each stage must be experienced, its obstacles surmounted and its challenges faced before a new, more satisfying equilibrium can be established.

> Both individually and societally, the usual way of dealing with the overwhelming phenomenon of divorce is first to try to deny it and hope the crisis will be averted. When the situation continues to deteriorate, the magnitude of the catastrophe permeates one's total being. Once the likelihood of divorce is fully confronted, it can be framed and addressed as a problem to be solved. (Kaslow, in press)

The phase called "During Divorce" encompasses Bohannon's second (legal), third (economic), and fourth (coparental divorce and problems of custody) stations. It is advantageous for purposes of analysis, understanding, and skillful interventions in therapy and in mediation to consider these complex, intertwined aspects separately. This period officially commences when one or both parties initiate action legally to dissolve their marital union. Traditionally this has occurred when the services of an attorney have been retained and the adversarial process of a litigated divorce is launched with "papers being served" by one spouse to the other. Today, as shown in this chapter, it may begin with the entrance of the parties into arbitration or mediation also.

Divorce as a process has many variations. It can be contested or not contested (mutual consent); it can be fought out in court by attorneys on behalf of the two adversaries (litigation), mediated, arbitrated, or negotiated in some other fashion; it can be accepted as the judge rules or appealed; and it can have an ugly aftermath or a relatively peaceful outcome. As a legal process, it is carried out by the judicial system on behalf of the State. As a human life event, it is produced and shaped by all the individuals involved and affects the divorcing parties, their children and other significant others in a variety of ways to which they must adapt as best they can. Even those who believe themselves to have been victims shape part of their present and future destiny through the process they select for obtaining their divorce, the kind of litigator, arbitrator or mediator they choose, and their own behavior during the proceedings.

CHAPTER 7

Financial and Economic Aspects of Divorce

We can consider economic factors from a variety of perspectives. One aspect is socioeconomic class. What do marriage and divorce mean economically to poor and lower-class people? How do these impact to change their life circumstances, sense of security or of uncertainty, ability to plan or need to be concerned daily about survival at the most meager level of existence? How does this differ from the perspective of middle-class and upper-class individuals? Another approach is to view economic factors in terms of distribution of marital assets and liabilities at divorce. A third aspect is the transfer of money from one ex-spouse to the other, usually ex-husband to ex-wife, for child and spousal support in the postdivorce period. These are the principal issues to be discussed in this chapter.

SOCIOECONOMIC CLASS

In the opinion of Daniels-Mohring and Berger (1984), "Socioeconomic level is directly related to the ability to recover from divorce with individuals in higher income brackets having an easier general adjustment process" (p. 18). (Our discussion of socioeconomic class and status is done in terms of general categories and descriptive characteristics, with full realization that these are not universally applicable.) Apart from the basic factor of amount of money available, why should this be so?

Even before marriage, there are differences in dating patterns and in expectations regarding marriage between blue collar, middle-class, and upper-class individuals. Courtship tends to be shorter in the blue collar working-class, with the initial meeting of the couple occurring in high school or at some neighborhood gathering place, followed by a short engagement period after graduation, and then marriage. It is more probable that the couple will live in the same community or neighborhood as their parents than is true for middle-class or wealthy, upper-class couples and that they may share quite similar family, ethnic and religious backgrounds. Both working-class parties tend to anticipate a rigid division of labor in marriage, related to traditional sex-role stereotypes. In the matter of child-rearing, for example, the expectation is likely to be that the wife is the primary caregiver and the husband is the authority figure and earns the money to support the family. In the matter of sexuality, emphasis is on physical relief for the husband with little or no concern for the wife's desires and pleasure (L'Hommedieu, 1984).

When this division of "classes" is made, the general perception is that members of the blue collar working-class have a high school education or less, and that their occupations are in clerical, retail sales, skilled or semi-skilled labor positions. By contrast, members of the middle-class, who also live predominantly on income earned through their own efforts, have typically attended college for two years or more (especially among today's younger generation), and are employed in semi-professional or middle-management positions. In L'Hommedieu's (1984) study, lesser educated working-class women related their self-esteem to their status as married women and discussed it only in terms of their emotional reactions to the divorce. Middle-class women, on the other hand, questioned their feelings of self-esteem or lack of same as a vital part of their dissatisfaction within the marriage prior to the divorce. Some of their sense of identity may be derived from their contribution in the workaday world and not solely from their status as "Mrs." Somebody. They may well be working for emotional as well as economic reasons and may obtain gratification in both arenas—just as their husbands and upper-class female counterparts may.

With individuals from upper-middle- and upper-class families, or those aspiring to upward mobility, there is a high likelihood that both have completed undergraduate college and that one or both have graduate degrees. They may have met in college or graduate/professional schools away from home and may each come from a different home town. There may be more diversity in terms of family structure, values, heritage, and expectations of marriage. With the expectation of that small percentage of the population who don't work because of vast inherited wealth, the others enter and participate in the job market in middle- and upper-management positions, and/or at the professional and executive level. Some go into parents' firms, businesses or professional corporations. Many possess the requisite education and technical skills to consider positions in a vast array of geographic locales and so are less apt to marry someone from their local high school and settle down near their respective families of origin. Also the better-educated tend to marry later. Between their higher earning power, some working time before marriage during which they have accumulated some material possessions and savings, larger weddings and bigger wedding presents, plus possibly some inherited wealth in the form of securities, trusts, etc., they bring more into the marriage financially. They may or may not want to have a prenuptual agreement written regarding the distribution of these assets in the event of divorce. And they may or may not wish to put everything in joint name, keep it in separate name or do a combination of both depending on their views about protecting their claim to nonmarital property, how much in love they are, and how total a commitment they want to make to the marriage.

Differences among lower-class, middle-class and upper-class individuals are also seen in the complaints made about the marriage. Women with less education and lower socioeconomic status tend to focus their complaints on the physical and/or psychological abuse they are subjected to, and the frequency with which their husbands go out with male friends. Women with more education and higher socioeconomic status are more likely to cite as sources of marital dissatisfaction such items as changes in interests, internal gender-role conflict, lack of communication and understanding, "incompatibility," and the husband's overcommitment to work (Kitson & Sussman, 1982). Similarly, we have seen, clinically and in our own research, that husbands of well-educated career women also cite their wives' overcommitment to work as a complaint. Such "overcommitment" leaves the other spouse, of either sex, feeling undervalued and neglected—whether it is paid work, community or political involvements, golf or other athletic activities, or deep friendships that frequently detract from time for each other.

There are also differences in life-style and expectations during marriage among the several general groups. To those in lower socioeconomic brackets, going out to dinner at anything other than a fast-food restaurant is a rare treat. Watching television is much less expensive, and therefore a more frequent, pastime than going to a movie, play, or concert. Wives may work in order to help the family pay bills for essentials, but their lack of higher education and enormous home responsibilities tend to necessitate that their on-the-job hours remain structured and specific and that the job does not entail taking work home or other spillover. They rarely spend an evening "out" with female friends in the way that their husbands spend evenings or even weekends with male friends. Domestic help, part-time or full-time, is not part of their experience except for the occasional teenager who serves as babysitter. They may do volunteer work for the church or local school, or serve as a local political leader but such activity is squeezed into time left after family and domestic chores have been completed. Their husbands are the ones with the time to work in politics or as volunteer firemen as they tend to take on only those household tasks that their macho-oriented peers consider gender-appropriate (e.g., painting the house, mowing the lawn, electrical repairs).

The difficulties for the poorer woman, particularly after divorce, are legion. If she had relatively few financial assets during marriage, she is likely to have virtually none after divorce, and may end up on the welfare rolls because she is unable to hold a job, or is only prepared for a marginally remunerative one, while caring for her children and the household, too. At the bottom of the socioeconomic ladder, being on welfare may not be quite as disgraceful or harmful to one's self-respect as it is for the middle-class woman, particularly if many of her neighbors are and it is an acceptable status in her reference group.

Although a generation and more ago it was considered unseemly for a middle- or upper-class woman to work, as her working would be construed to mean that her husband was unable to support her adequately, implying failure on his part, this is no longer true. Desire to utilize their educational preparation, the emotional desire to "be somebody" and make a respected contribution to the world, and economic factors have pulled many women into the labor market. However, middle- and upper-class women more often have at least part-time domestic help to relieve them partially of both household chores and child care. Having put in a busy day in a career, they expect to go out to dinner at least once on the weekend and perhaps occasionally during the week as well. Through family background or education, they look forward to going to the theater, movies, sporting events, or concerts once a week or more as a normal part of life. Many nonworking middle- and upper-class women are active volunteers, not only in local circles like their poorer sisters, but in state and national organizations on behalf of the ill or aged also. They may serve on a local school board or as chairperson of a philanthropic group. Their husbands, too, frequently are community leaders in charitable and political affairs. Middle- and upper-class couples usually have amassed tangible assets to be divided at divorce. However, some middle-class couples can barely make ends meet in the postdivorce financial arrangements. As Weitzman (1985) has indicated, the woman's economic status may decline markedly. She may have to resort to "going on welfare" because of an unintended combination of circumstances. For her, becoming a welfare recipient is perceived as a total disgrace and is severely damaging to her self-esteem. This is, of course, not an issue in upper-class families where there are ample financial resources so that neither divorced spouse suffers a serious downward spiral in his or her life-style.

DISTRIBUTION OF ASSETS

When one begins to look at assets in the context of divorce, what is surprising is not only what is considered an asset, but also the amount of conflict that can be engendered by a single small item such as a souvenir from a long-ago vacation. At a minimum, the following items may be classified as marital assets:

1. Homes, if owned, with or without mortgage
2. Contents of marital home
3. Income—salary, dividends, interest
4. Personal property
5. Pension plans and retirement plans including Social Security retirement income and Individual Retirement Accounts (IRAs)

    The Retirement Equity Act (REA) was signed into law on August 23, 1984 as P.L. 98-397. The Act's avowed purpose is to improve the delivery of retirement benefits and provide greater equity under private pension plans for workers, their spouses and dependents, by taking into consideration alterations in work patterns, the status of marriages as an economic partnership, and as a substantial contribution made to that partnership by mates who work both in and outside the home and for other purposes (REA, 1984). There has been widespread agreement that REA provides new and much needed pension protection for (divorced) spouses; the legislation has at times been dubbed "the women's equity act." It imposed new participation and vesting rules, new methods for testing breaks in service and introduced qualified domestic relations orders (QDROs) which place a participant's retirement benefits into pay status long before his or her normal retirement age (Smith, 1985). Smith (1985, p. 8) believes that "REA . . . has guarantee(d) an inalienable right to pension benefits for both the participant and his/her spouse." REA permits a former spouse to anticipate the tax consequences of each of several distribution alternatives; knowledge of these can guide the parties' decisions regarding a more equitable distribution of retirement benefits. (See Fall 1985 issue of ABA's *Family Advocate* on "Pension Plans and Divorce" for a fuller discussion of this issue.)

6. Cars
7. Life Insurance
8. Profit Sharing Plans ⎫
9. Professional Degrees ⎬ Some states have held these to be divisible assets
10. Professional corporations or wholly ⎭ owned businesses
11. Trust funds
12. Stocks and bonds
13. Savings

From these assets, of course, the couple must subtract their liabilities and decide how to deal with those. Liabilities include:

1. Mortgages
2. Loans
3. Charge account bills
4. Other outstanding debts

In addition, the couple should assess, with the aid of an accountant or attorney, the tax implications if one spouse pays off the debts of the other. Tax consequences for each, now and in the future, are also a major consideration in negotiating the distribution of assets. Those working with mediators or attempting to draw up their own agreements should seek guidance from a person knowledgeable about IRS rulings and the most current Tax Reform Act so that they can follow the principle of equitable distribution while maximizing the portion of their assets that they retain.

A perusal of the foregoing lists provides some idea of how many potential sources of conflict there can be in the issues of division of assets and payments of debts. Dealing with the marital house is often one of the simpler matters to resolve. Most couples share ownership as "joint tenants in the entireties" or as "joint tenants in common." Either the parties concur on the current value of the house or will agree to abide by the valuation of a mutually acceptable independent real estate appraiser. If, for example, the husband does not want the house but the wife does, his half of the value can be given to her as part of the total settlement or credited in a ledger against items he wants as his share in the equitable distribution arrangements. If neither party wants the house, they may agree to sell it and divide the proceeds of the sale on some percentage basis (in relation to other parts of the total agreement of allocation of all items) after paying off any mortgage. If it takes a long time to sell, and/or is sold at a loss from the original purchase price, they may run into some immediate cash flow problems. If the wife continues to live in the house, the decree should stipulate who pays the rent or mortgage, utilities, other maintenance costs and taxes, when and to whom these are to be paid, and other such details so that each month the parties are not arguing because of ambiguity at the time of settlement.

For some, dividing up the furnishings of the house may be a difficult matter. In some cases, premarital ownership of certain pieces of furniture may remove those from the negotiating table. Where the furniture was purchased after the marriage by the couple, they may agree that one is to have the bedroom furniture and the other the living room furniture, one to have the breakfast room pieces and the other to have the television.

Unless they can come to a reasonably amicable agreement, however, it may be necessary to have a furniture appraiser engaged to assess the value of each piece if the division is to be along dollar lines rather than simple preference. Other household contents, such as dishes, flatware, serving pieces, paintings, art objects, musical instruments, and the like, may be divided by preference or according to an assessment. Where there are valuable collections, these may be divided by "favorite" pieces, by dollar value, or by selling the collections and dividing the proceeds. The fact that one party, frequently the husband, had been the principal purchaser tends to be irrelevant if the collections were intended to be a joint holding. Indeed, since presumably the collections were acquired after the marriage, they are by that fact marital assets. Usually items purchased for current use and as investments are divisible marital property.

Income that has been put into joint bank accounts is assumed to be a common marital asset. The same is true of investments held in joint name. Rulings on individual earnings kept in separate bank accounts and securities held in one name vary more and need to be checked carefully with legal counsel.

Personal property includes such items as jewelry, furs, and clothing. Even if the husband purchased all of the wife's jewelry and furs, one would assume that these were gifts to her and that he did not own them and merely allow her to wear them "rent-free" as it were. Usually items purchased as gifts belong to the recipient. It may be necessary to provide sales receipts or a note accompanying a gift to validate a claim that this was, indeed, the intention. Jewelry and furs would be saleable assets for the wife, however, and many women, finding themselves in dire financial straits following a divorce, have sold all or part of these possessions in order to pay bills.

Cars are also personal property, unless owned by a corporation or rented. Again, if the husband purchased a car for his wife's use, even though the title might be in his name, the weight of reason would be on the side of the wife retaining the car and having the title changed to her name. If they are a one-car family—this becomes a very ticklish issue, particularly if both "need" the car.

Rulings change from time to time on whether or not an ex-wife is entitled to any part of her former husband's pension plan or Social Security income, or vice versa. In late 1984, for example, it was announced that if the marriage had lasted for more than 10 years, an ex-wife at age 62 was entitled to draw on her ex-husband's Social Security account. At any given time, it would be wise for an ex-wife to verify this and all other items discussed here with an attorney knowledgeable and current in this aspect of law.

Life insurance policies may exist on either party's life and with either spouse as owner. That is, for example, a policy on the husband's life, naming the wife as beneficiary, may be owned by the husband or by the wife. The owner is free to change beneficiaries, so that a wife, for instance, who has taken out insurance on her own life, may substitute a child for the husband as beneficiary, or another relative, or at some point, a new spouse. Life insurance policies can also be part of the final agreement, taken as security for one partner's future obligations toward the other. If at the time of settlement either partner agrees to name children as beneficiaries, and the other partner and the children plan around this and it gets changed—a major dilemma ensues. Thus care must be taken to "guarantee" that such provisos are irrevocable.

In the matter of professional degrees, there have been a number of court cases with different outcomes regarding whether these constitute divisible marital property. If the wife worked to support the husband through law school, for example, possibly foregoing her own graduate education to do so, and the couple decided to divorce shortly thereafter, she might have a legitimate claim to funds from him not only to support her through her own further education so that she can qualify for a higher level, more appropriate job (rehabilitative alimony), but she may also have a legitimate claim to a share of a portion of (all) future earnings. The rulings vary from state to state, and appear in some cases to depend upon such factors as the length of the marriage and the wife's contribution to her husband obtaining a degree. In the first *O'Brien v. O'Brien* decision (1982), for example, it was held that the wife is precluded from sharing in the projected value of the license obtained during the marriage because, invariably, professional licenses have always been held not to be "property." Mrs. O'Brien was awarded $7,000 and appealed the decision. It was reversed by the 2nd Department on February 11, 1985 (Cohen & Hillman, 1985)—a decision heralding the advent of consideration of professional degrees to be marital property. Similarly, if the husband has established a professional corporation, the wife may be entitled to a share of its value, depending on the state in which the divorce is granted and her contribution to the practice. (This was a New York case and its holdings are not applicable in other states, although some believe it has precedent-setting ramifications.)

It is important to emphasize that with an increasing number of husbands helping to finance their wives' costly graduate and/or professional educations, they too may have a claim to a portion of the wife's corporation (like a law practice) or to future earnings—or to child support—if the father becomes the primary residential parent.

Similarly, if the husband owns a business, the wife may claim a share in its value. If he owned the business before the marriage, any gain in its value subsequent to the marriage is likely to be regarded as a marital asset. Thus, if the business was worth $1 million at the time of the marriage, and is worth $10 million at the time of the divorce, her claim is to a portion of the $9 million only. Whether she invested time working in or for the business may also be a consideration. (As indicated earlier, the services of a knowledgeable attorney in the particular state of residence may be needed to determine the validity of her claims to a share in the professional husband's future earnings, or his corporate or business assets.)

Trust funds and inheritances often have legal constraints that may remove them entirely or in part from the financial negotiations. If one partner inherited x dollars from a parent, even during the marriage, that is typically exempt from the bargaining except as its value may have increased. The increase is regarded as a marital asset.

In dealing with liabilities, standard operating procedure is to determine how each one was accrued and who is responsible for them. For example, did both parties agree upon and sign for a home improvement loan? If there is a mortgage on a house, typically both spouses have signed papers; this may be less true for a boat, business property, or charge accounts. It is often difficult to establish that responsibility only falls upon the one whose name appears on the bills.

The higher the economic status of the pair, the more assets to consider. Tax shelters may be in the picture; if so, which of the pair will ultimately be responsible for paying the delayed tax on these funds? The more assets there are, the more essential it would seem to be for a tax accountant to be consulted about the wisest and fairest distribution plan. This holds true as well in deciding another issue—long-term support (alimony) vs. lump-sum settlement.

Other assets that often need attention are health insurance policies, contents of safe deposit boxes, and "hidden" bank accounts. To consider the more mercenary assets, first, if one spouse suspects that the other has been "burying" assets in safe deposit boxes and semi-invisible bank accounts, an independent investigator is sometimes hired to prove or disprove the hypothesis, or this information may be sought by counsel in the discovery and deposition phases of the divorce process. "Hiding" assets is not necessarily a typical practice, but does occur when one spouse is contemplating a divorce, long before the mate suspects or is aware of this possibility, and plans for it carefully. Obviously, the more a spouse knows about his/her partner's business dealings and/or investments, the more leads he or she can provide to an investigator or his/her attorney.

In mediation, each would be morally bound by their agreement to fully disclose all assets. The fact that prior secrets existed between the couple regarding nonrevealed assets usually is indicative of a long-standing lack of trust, and lack of sharing and commitment to the relationship and therefore that tension, fear of withholding or seeking to "fleece" and recrimination will be high. When investigators have been utilized, suspicion and acrimony are likely to be intense and the divorce a bitter one. A therapist may need to help patients decide if they really want to hire a detective and/or how to respond if the spouse already has.

Where the wife has co-signed joint income tax returns, but has not examined said returns nor questioned items on them because she trusted her husband's integrity or was discouraged by him from being inquisitive and becoming well-informed, her lack of knowledge about their finances will place her at a decided disadvantage that will need to be addressed. If there is a real gap between what she vaguely recalls and what the husband claims they own at the time of divorce negotiations, copies of past income tax returns can be obtained by requesting them from her husband. If he refuses, they can be secured through an attorney's intervention from the Internal Revenue Service directly. The more that is shared voluntarily, the less antagonistic the process of divorce is likely to be, so this is preferable and to be recommended from our point of view.

In therapy and in mediation, the wife's lack of knowledge about finances and its myriad implications are a salient issue. Why did she collude to maintain her husband's supremacy in the power-laden area of marriage represented by financial knowledge and control? Why did he choose to exclude her from a partnership arrangement in this domain? Was she disinterested, incapable of learning or disenfranchised? How did both of them feel about this extremely unequal distribution of power and responsibility? How could she sign such an important document as an income tax return without understanding what the figures signify?

Sometimes, having learned that her husband failed to disclose all income to the IRS, an irate wife, eager to increase her bargaining leverage to get a better settlement, will threaten to report him to the IRS unless he accedes to her demands. By way of illustration in one of FK's mediation cases, the following occurred.

Mr. Green was a successful attorney who had not filed their income tax returns for several years. During the mediation process he was also engaged in trying to catch up, in conjunction with his accountant, on filing these. Part of the difficulty was undeclared income— he sometimes represented drug dealers and was paid part or all in cash. There were veiled hints that he may have done some dealing himself also.

His wife, a highly intelligent woman, had returned to graduate school two years earlier. She detested his procrastination, the pressure of being in arrears, and his often less than ethical behavior. She threatened to report him to the IRS unless she got 75% of all property assets and $35,000 a year for 10 years of rehabilitative alimony although she only had one more year of course work plus dissertation to go and was herself already earning $25,000 per year.

I suggested we consider the implications of her doing this in terms of several factors. First her own culpability. Did she know about the undeclared income? She vacillated and said not the full extent—but admitted closing her eyes because she enjoyed their luxurious life-style. She knew their standard of living far exceeded their combined declared income. Thus, in some ways she had colluded in his defrauding the government on earlier tax returns when she co-signed. Secondly, he said he would rather go to prison than pay the exorbitant amount she was asking, while trying to also pay off high back taxes, and it seemed likely he'd be willing to harm and spite himself by being incarcerated rather than give in to her pressure. In fact he attributed his desire to extricate himself from the marriage to wanting to avoid her continual nagging and excessive materialistic demands. I asked her to consider that if indeed he went to prison, she would receive nothing—certainly not the outcome she sought. (I encouraged both of them to act ethically regarding disclosures to each other, to me as specified in their original agreement to mediate, and with their accountant and indicated I could not continue to mediate with them if they did not do this.)

Hospitalization insurance constitutes a different sort of problem. Let's assume that one partner has carried Blue Cross/Blue Shield coverage with the mate also insured through the policy and that the other spouse either has no independent coverage or has private hospitalization insurance as part of his/her employee benefits. At the time of the divorce, the second spouse ceases to be covered by the Blue Cross/Blue Shield contract unless special provision is made for continuation of the coverage in the divorce agreement. If the second spouse has no other hospitalization coverage, it is essential that this be arranged promptly given the high costs of medical and hospital care. If there is private coverage or employer-related coverage, it should be reviewed to see whether it is adequate. Medical insurance also needs to be arranged for any children who are eligible for inclusion in a parent's insurance policy. When this is not done, as when the husband drops his coverage of ex-wife and children and she is not employed, worries about cost of care during illness mount and legitimately cause much fear.

From the foregoing, it should become obvious that it is more psychologically sound and much less expensive if the two parties can participate maximally in planning the distribution of assets in consultation with their mediator, accountants or attorneys, than if they go through formal adversarial procedures. Both routes produce tension; it's likely to be less if done between the two parties. The emotional pain of litigation, its risks and uncertainties as to outcome, and the time and money it takes can all be reduced. If there aren't a great many assets (or liabilities), the negotiations obviously will be less complicated, but still must consider equity and tax ramifications no matter whether the agreement is self-written, mediated or litigated. The Court's role is to be certain of the fairness of the agreement and then to include it in the final divorce order.

The equitable distribution laws passed in recent years by a number of states have not always worked to the advantage of women, although some thought that these new laws would rectify earlier unbalanced awards of assets to ex-wives. At a seminar on Pennsylvania divorce law in 1984, for example, the divorce masters (nonjudges) who hear divorce cases and make recommendations to judges) from several counties indicated that wives could expect to receive about 35% of the assets if distribution was determined by the courts. "Equitable distribution" is clearly not a 50-50 division of assets. The wife's income is figured into the financial negotiations, and the life-style to which she has become accustomed in marriage by virtue of her husband's income (with or without hers) may decline. Or she may receive more than half if she is primary parent for a handicapped child.

Increasingly, it is recognized in some quarters that (usually) the wife's contribution to the marriage and her ex-spouse's welfare ceases at the time of divorce. Why then should the ex-husband's responsibility, in the form of financial support, continue for many years or until her death? How does this lopsided postdivorce responsibility tie in to current principles of equity? How long does one have to be married to accrue entitlement to "forever" postdivorce support? If the ex-wife's income goes up considerably and the ex-husband becomes incapacitated and has no income—should he still have to pay spousal support or should she now send the monthly check to him? Such moral and ethical questions have not yet been addressed in the psychological or legal literature. We hope that the issues raised here will lead to dialogue and research on these complex matters.

For now, what is apparent is that as a consequence both of a United States Supreme Court ruling in 1979 and the new "no-fault" divorce and equitable distribution laws, awards to wives have tended to be lower in recent years. "Contrary to popular belief, the major effect of recent changes in divorce law has been to increase the economic inequality between males and females" (Bahr, 1983, p. 464). This conclusion is echoed by Albrecht (1980) and Bouton (1984), and in the reports we received from some of our study respondents.

In a study of divorcing couples in Los Angeles County in 1977–78

Weitzman (1985) found that the net worth of assets (including debts) of more than half her sample was below $20,000. The median net worth of these couples, $11,000 in 1978 was only $18,000 in 1984 dollars. This reflects, of course, the high proportion of young couples seeking divorce who have not yet acquired considerable marital property and who are frequently paying off debts incurred for higher or professional education.

In the eight community property states (Arizona, California, Idaho, Lousiana, Nevada, New Mexico, Texas and Washington), there is an assumption "that both spouses have contributed equally to the economic assets of their marriage, whether by homemaking or by earning a salary, and that each is entitled to an equal share of the total assets" (Weitzman, 1985, p. 54). The starting point for division of assets is at 50-50 in these states.

In the other 42 states, separate or common law property is the rule, modified in most states by the "equitable distribution" provision in statutes governing divorce. Here,

> the starting point for an "equitable distribution" is typically one-third of the property to the wife, two-thirds to the husband. The underlying assumption is that the property really belongs to the husband because he was the one who earned it. The court then has to decide what would be an equitable share of "his property" for the wife. (Weitzman, 1985, p. 54)

We doubt this was the intention of the legislators who enacted these laws.

POSTDIVORCE STATUS

Although the marriage may be legally dissolved, and the parties may have completed some of the resolution of the psychic divorce, they are still bound by the divorce agreement's provisions for the postdivorce economic entanglements. This subsumes any lump-sum settlement, alimony or spousal support, child support and future college costs. It may also take time to divide certain assets such as government bonds that cannot be cashed in prior to a certain date, or the marital home and/or other tangible property when the sale is delayed. Such continuing residuals mean that the economic divorce postdates the legal divorce—often by many years. Economics often remain a continuing battlefield as when child support payments stipulated in an agreement do not come through on time.

Some states, like Pennsylvania, require both parents to be responsible for child support, to the best of their ability, no matter which parent has custody. The amount of child support awarded varies with the age and needs of the specific children, ability to pay, number of children, and life-style. Children with specific medical problems, such as diabetes or asthma, must have the cost of this care provided. So, too, if a child is learning disabled or emotionally disturbed. Costs for postsecondary education might also be embodied in the agreement and should be honored.

Since reports from all over the country indicate that 40%–60% of fathers fail to pay child custody on a regular basis, the federal *Child Support Enforcement Amendments* were passed in 1984. One aspect of this law is that financial incentives are provided to states that adopt more efficient systems of enforcing child support orders. Another provision is that employers can be ordered to withhold wages if the parent is in arrears on custody support payments for more than a month. This law is responsive to the plight of parents and children who, not having received any or all custody support due, request a court order after a few months of not receiving support payments. It traditionally may then have taken a few more months until the order was implemented. Meanwhile, there was no income. The new law appears to be reducing this problem. All state withholding laws must be in compliance with Federal statutes for both in-state and out-of-state child support cases to be enforced through the Federal/State Child Support Enforcement Program. To date, experience nationally has shown that among its benefits are (U.S. Department of Health and Human Services, 1985, pp 5–6):

1. Wage withholding is the most effective tool for enforcing child support obligations.
2. It reduces the amount of time employees are absent from work for court appearances or administrative reviews.
3. It reduces the amount of psychological distress custodial parents experience with missed payments.
4. It enables the paying parent to regularize payments and encourages better allocation of financial resources.

The U.S. Department of Health and Human Services (1985) literature does not address the impact of violation of the employee's right to privacy, the concomitant embarrassment and resentment, nor whether there may be legitimate reasons for nonpayment. Of course a court decree is legally binding, and if untenable, one can go back to court to renegotiate the amount—particularly if financial circumstances have changed markedly.

There are, in many states, two kinds of alimony. During separation, there is what is called Alimony Pendente, or support awarded until the divorce is final. The amount varies, but is awarded to the spouse with no or lesser earnings, usually the wife, in order for her to be able to pay housing, food, and other essential bills *until she is in a position to support herself.* This may also, depending on whether it is granted during separation or for the postdivorce period, be termed "rehabilitative alimony."

A second kind of alimony, and the type commonly thought of when the word is used, is final or permanent alimony. Such payments continue until the paying spouse dies or the receiving spouse remarries or dies. A relatively new development is that some agreements specify alimony will continue for one or two years after remarriage, as an incentive for marriage. After all, if alimony is high and automatically terminates with remarriage, one might decide it is financially advantageous to stay single. Other agreements having a totally different thrust may contain a cohabitation clause; that is, alimony ceases if the recipient spouse cohabits. Often what constitutes cohabitation (how often, how long) is left vague and contributes to later arguments.

Today permanent alimony is less often granted than formerly to younger women, nor is it awarded automatically to any ex-wife. The trend is for continuing alimony to be given to older women who have not worked outside the home and who are unlikely to be able to obtain paying jobs because of their inexperience and advanced age. There is a risk attached to alimony payments. Suppose the ex-husband remarries, becomes incapacitated, or simply gets tired of paying his ex-wife hundreds or thousands of dollars each month, and decides to stop payment. Although it is possible for his ex-wife to take him to court to force him to continue the payments, this is a time-consuming and expensive procedure without any guarantee that he won't hold back again at a later date or disappear out of the country and begin life under a new name.

Generally, "alimony payments are taxable to the recipient and deductible by the payer . . . Further, since alimony payments are an adjustment to gross income, they can be deducted even if a taxpayer doesn't itemize." Under the Tax Reform Act of 1984 *"only cash payments qualify as alimony"*; transfer of services or property do not (*Financial Planning Update*, 1986, pp. 3–4). (See article entitled *Reconciling Differences in Divorce Taxation Rules* for further discussion of this complex topic.)

To minimize the risk of alimony payments being withheld, and also to reduce dependence on and contact with the ex-husband, some women waive alimony in exchange for a cash lump-sum settlement. The funds received can then be invested to provide a continuing income. Although the husband may grumble about having to turn over large sums of money at one time, and may try to keep the amount down as much as possible, in the long run he will probably be relieved at not having to write a monthly check to someone with whom he no longer lives and for whom he may no longer care. This route also facilitates culmination of at least one part of the economic divorce and so has much to recommend it.

EMPLOYMENT FOR THE DIVORCED WOMAN

One problem that may not be amenable to legal correction, despite civil rights and antidiscrimination legislation, is the ability of some divorced women to get a job. Since this is clearly more of a problem for females in that they have been either out of the labor market for years or may not have very marketable skills, the discussion to follow will focus on women to the exclusion of men.

> If one thinks of the common marital pattern in which a housewife and mother supports her husband's career . . . , it is evident that marriage can vastly alter the employment prospects of the two spouses in different directions. His career prospects may be enhanced, while hers are impaired; his earning capacity may grow, while hers diminishes. . . . Their opportunities are not, in fact, equal. (Weitzman, 1985, p. 36)

Let's begin with a consideration of the divorced woman in her 60s or older, for her plight is typically the most difficult. For her, the new ease of divorce and the changed distribution of marital assets constitute a violation of the "contract" she made at marriage with her husband and with the approval of society. Marriage was to be a partnership in which the parties shared equally. Instead the courts have changed the rules in the middle of the game—after she believes she has fulfilled her part of the bargain. (Actually, it is the last quarter of the game because she can never recapture the years that she invested in her family and usually she has passed the point where she can choose another pathway in life [Weitzman, 1985].)

If she is eligible for her own Social Security payments or to draw on her ex-husband's, she may be able to live a very modest life-style. If she has never worked outside of the home, the likelihood of anyone hiring her now is slim in any field other than child care or live-in companion. Outside of this domestic arena, what skills does she have that will tempt a strange employer to hire her, for what will likely be only a few years at most, instead of a younger person with better skills and possibly job-related experience? Few employers are willing to invest time (=money) in training a new employee who is probably going to be working only a short time. (This is reminiscent of the employer practices in the 1950s, when young women were not hired for responsible jobs because it was believed that they would get married, then become pregnant, and leave the job; so it was not deemed worth the expense to train them.) The silver-haired divorcée, unless an unusually talented/skilled/experienced person, becomes a candidate for welfare if she has no other source of income. If her husband had an income sufficient for them as a couple, but not sufficient to maintain two households at the former standard of living, her alimony is going to be minimal, and her golden years quite tarnished. If she is no longer eligible to be included on her ex-husband's medical/hospitalization insurance, she may be in dire straits at the very point in life when medical problems tend to increase. It is understandable why those older women who did not initiate or want a divorce become embittered, depressed and pessimistic. Their reality may be quite grim as they feel engulfed by loneliness, rejection and poverty. Friends can help by comforting, supporting emotionally and encouraging them to pick up the threads and build a new life—and possibly to seek the guidance of a skilled mental health professional. If they do enter therapy, the therapist's goal may be to help them accept the divorce and their own contribution to the demise of the marriage, and to seek pathways to emotional contentment and financial self-sufficiency.

> Mrs. S. was divorced by her husband when she was 61. He decided to "trade her in" because at 63 he still had "a lot of living to do" and preferred to do it with his attractive 40-year-old secretary. Furious at being discarded after 38 years of marriage, 4 children and 6 grandchildren, Mrs. S. withdrew and sulked. Her eldest daughter insisted she enter therapy and volunteered to pay for it. After her overwhelming sense of pain, futility and anger was ventilated and worked through, the therapist (FK) broached the possibility of her finding satisfaction in working in an area that would enable her to utilize her compassion and parenting skills and provide her with housing and a network of contacts. A bright woman, she recognized this would be a good pathway for her and she was able to find a position as a house mother in a campus-based sorority house in her home community so she was not isolated from old friends and 2 of her children who resided there.

Dropping down a decade or two to women in their late 40s and 50s, if they have no outside work experience, even anti-age discrimination laws will not guarantee them a job. Some may be able to transform extensive volunteer, child care and homemaking experience into marketable skills and obtain employment; some may be attractive enough and knowledgeable enough to be hired as saleswomen in specialty shops; others may brush up on secretarial or nursing skills that have been dormant.

Some may be put off in job interviews by a variety of excuses that avoid any show of discrimination, but that are in fact related to age. They, too, like their older sisters, must be concerned about health insurance, and about having 30 to 40 years of paying rent, buying food, and keeping themselves clothed to which to look forward. Unless they have or can quickly acquire technical, professional or business skills, salaries are likely to be low or mid range. Yet a job may almost be an emotional as well as a financial necessity. Many divorced and widowed people have learned that work is good therapy. Thus the inability to get a job, even if there is rehabilitative or continuing alimony, can contribute to impaired mental health and impede one's ability to recover from the trauma of the divorce.

Many of the women in both age groups just discussed were married in an era when middle- and upper-class wives did not work, at least not for pay, and they need to consult with specialists in career or vocational guidance to find out what options they have. The woman of lower socio-economic status may have always worked and contributed to her family's support—but her earning capacity might be quite limited.

Younger women, in their late 20s and 30s, are more likely to have been employed before and/or during marriage, and to have had more education than the older women. The chances of their already having a suitable position or being hired for a job, given a reasonably good labor market, are better than the older women's chances. Many may already be quite career-oriented so there is less need for a shift in thinking to accommodate to working than there is for many older women. They may have some difficulty if their previous work skills have become outdated, as in a scientific or computer-related field. The younger woman who has to support herself may have to reorder her priorities in terms of what is acceptable to her in a job, placing congenial surroundings and co-workers into a lower priority than salary, hours, and location.

For young women who have children at home, there is an even more critical problem. Due to inadequate alimony/child support payments, they may have to work in order to provide for the child(ren) and themselves. At the same time, many want to be on site, effective nurturing mothers. Most of them are well aware of the criticisms leveled at mothers who leave their school-age children alone after school hours, even when the necessity for doing so is real. They themselves want to be available for the children; they recognize that the divorce has caused problems for the children, who may already feel "abandoned" by the departed parent. They do not want to compound the sense of loss or neglect. Finding a job that permits her to be away only during school hours isn't easy. Finding one that allows for childhood emergencies and the need, perhaps, to stay at home with a sick child for a few days, is even more difficult. If the child or young adolescent gets into some kind of trouble, the mother feels guilty for not having been at home, yet she must work so that they all can have adequate housing, food, clothing and other essentials. Thus the divorced woman of this generation, although more able to get a job than someone 10 or 20 years older, is sometimes in an almost untenable position. She cannot be in two places at one time, nor can she be held solely responsible if, despite all her efforts, a child acts out his/her feelings about the divorce or any other problem in living in an aggressive or illegal manner while she is not at home but on the job. We know that an antisocial act can take place when mother is home all day and all evening; her absence, though, is held against her by some, despite the fact that this may not be her choice. Curiously, the father who chooses to move out seems to be held less accountable for what happens to the children. It is "mom" who is labelled negligent, self-centered, or worse. There are no easy answers to this situation with its built-in ambivalences, especially when social services and welfare funds for such exigencies are being cut rather than expanded.

Looking at divorced women with good prior work experience, they may remain in an existing job because they enjoy it and it meets their financial and other needs. Indeed, co-workers may constitute a strong support network during the postdivorce period and the ego-gratification derived from the job can help a battered sense of self-esteem to heal. However, unless women are unusually accomplished or well-known in a profession, for example, they may not have the option to change jobs or work part-time instead of full-time, should that be necessary for one reason or another.

In addition to being employed, of course, many women suddenly find themselves financially responsible for everything in their lives, and often that of their children. If they've never handled the family checkbook, this is a new skill to be mastered. Beyond that, however, they need to be concerned with other things that they may have been aware of but not responsible for in the marriage, such as car insurance, home owner's insurance, taxes of all kinds, home maintenance, and even basic budgeting. If they are fortunate enough to have a friend, accountant, therapist, parent or sibling who can furnish sound advice, this is clearly a big help. If not, there are women's resource agencies in large cities where they can learn the rudiments of handling these responsibilities—what questions to ask of insurance agents, how to budget, and similar items. If these are not available, an adult class at a local high school may provide essential information, or a sympathetic and patient bank officer can often be helpful. This will be particularly important if getting a bank loan or making other arrangements for credit poses a stumbling block for the woman.

If the woman's income is low enough to use standard deduction forms, she may be able to manage taxes with minimal assistance. If her income is higher, she may find it wise to consult an accountant. A divorce lawyer may be willing to help her get organized initially. If she has funds to invest, as from a lump-sum settlement, then she needs to seek out a trustworthy stock broker or bank officer. The key point here is that she must be willing, and must develop the courage, to ask for assistance in a realm with which she is unfamiliar.

THE MAN'S POSTDIVORCE ECONOMIC STATUS

Men, during and subsequent to divorce, may well be paying child support and/or alimony. If they have paid out a large amount for a lump-sum settlement, their reserves have dwindled. Many report the shock of realizing how much more expensive it is to support two households than one and to not be able to say "No, we can't afford camp or private school because my earnings haven't kept pace with inflation" because the court has ordered him to pay for these items. If and when he wants to remarry, he may find he has to place himself under great pressure to earn a sufficient amount to contribute to the upkeep of two distinct families. If in the past his ex-wife handled the budgeting and check writing, he will be the one who has to learn economic survival skills. Nonetheless, Weitzman (1985) reported that men in middle income brackets retain 75% of their postdivorce income and are much more upwardly mobile in the financial sphere than their ex-wives, who are likely to be downwardly mobile.

The category of men who may experience greatest postdivorce hardship are those who have histories of unemployment and who were financially dependent on their wives. If they are alcoholic, chronically ill, or unemployable for other reasons, welfare may also be their main option. If employable, they may find problems similar to those encountered by never employed women or those lacking marketable skills in locating a job.

Oakland (1984) indicated that:

> While divorce often brings economic hardships, some men have more spendable income or choose to live more heavily on credit, thus allowing themselves to spend their way to happiness. . . . Fun-filled weekends with the children, good restaurants, and expensive shopping trips are but a few ways fathers attempt to impress their children, and perhaps attempt to punish their former wives. A visible mark of success comes with his financial success. (p. 33)

SUMMARY

Whether or not money is the root of all evil, as it is alleged, it is a major issue in divorce and its aftermath. Socioeconomic level affects both marital expectations and postdivorce life-style. Income affects what assets the couple has to divide, and hostility between the parties influences the ways in which they distribute them.

A number of the legal complications involved with deciding what is a marital asset and how it should be divided equitably, in accord with most current state laws, were discussed in this chapter. It is important to emphasize that equitable does not mean equal!

Further financial considerations are spousal support (alimony) and child support. A number of the problems dealing with these two items were explored, with special emphasis on the maintenance of child support.

Finally, the job-hunting woes of newly-divorced women were discussed. This was done by age groups since the problem of finding employment hinges on past work experience and education or marketable skills which typically vary among women of different generations. Related to all of the above is coping with financial responsibility, possibly yet another new task for the woman. Items of responsibility and resources for getting assistance with them were discussed here in order to alert divorced women and their therapists to what they may face.

The economic divorce is rarely coterminous with the legal divorce. It does not end until all financial support is terminated and all jointly held property sold or transferred to single name, which may be several decades or for as long as the ex-spouses live. The cost of separating into two households is also high and long lasting. The emotional correlates of the legal severance and residual economic commitments are weighty and distressing for all. No wonder arguments over money are the battleground for continued returns to court and/or postdivorce family animosities.

Weitzman's (1985) well-researched and documented study on *The Divorce Revolution: The Unexpected Social and Economic Consequences for Women and Children in America* revealed the following facts:

1. The husband's per capita income is almost 200% above what it was when he married—while his children and former wife are left with half of their former income.
2. One year after the divorce (in marriages that last fewer than 10 years) husbands have postdivorce incomes equivalent to at least three-fourths of the family's total income before the divorce.
3. The contrast is most pronounced among middle- and higher-in-

come families. The wife's income is reduced to 39% of the family's former standard while her husband maintains 75% of their pre-divorce income, if it was between $30,000 and $40,000 a year.

4. Among low- and average-income families, the husband has about twice as much money as his former wife and each of his children.

5. The husband experiences rapid upward mobility after divorce. His wife and children experience rapid downward mobility.

6. The older and longer-married woman suffers the most, economically, after divorce—because her divorce award is likely to establish her standard of living for the rest of her life. Judges expect her to become self-sufficient even though job placement, retraining and low self-esteem are likely to pose severe problems.

7. Life after divorce is hardest for the long-married woman who has devoted her life to raising children who are now grown. She will experience the greatest downward mobility after divorce if she shared a family income of $40,000 or more before divorce. She is expected to live at less than half of her former per capita standard—42%—while her former husband advances to living at 142%.

8. Downward mobility means moving to less comfortable housing in a poorer neighborhood, losing neighborhood and friendship networks, establishing credit and finding services in new communities, cutting back on family recreation, helping out with the financial problems of children who are legally grown but not financially self-sufficient, and having far less to offer younger offspring.

9. A divorced woman's newly restricted income means she must withdraw from activities she can no longer afford. Within a year, the dissociation from marital friends is typically much greater for women than for men—particularly if a woman's social life revolved around her husband's career.

Weitzman's findings reinforce our clinical observations and are similar to those reported by Cohen and Hillman (1985) in the *Equitable Distribution Reporter*. Cohen and Hillman analyzed 70 reported decisions after trial, from the time New York's equitable distribution law went into effect, July 19, 1980, through October 15, 1984. The purpose of this study was to ascertain whether there was gender bias by the courts in application of the law.

With the exception of dispositions of marital homes, liquid properties and, to some extent, pensions, judicial dispositions of marital property at the time of dissolution of a marriage reflect that property is not being distributed equally to the spouses. Except in rare instances,

dependent wives, whether they worked in the home or in the paid marketplace, were relegated to one or a combination of the following in an aggregate of 49 out of the 54 cases susceptible of this analysis: Less than a 50% overall share of marital property; short-term maintenance after long-term marriage; *de minimis* shares of business and professional practices which, in addition, the courts undervalued; terminable and modifiable maintenance in lieu of indefensible equitable distribution . . . awards; and inadequate or no counsel fee awards. These findings demonstrate that the marriage partners' contributions to each other and to the marriage itself are not being viewed as of equal value. (Cohen & Hillman, 1985, p. 94)

In regard to maintenance, the dispositions analyzed in Cohen and Hillman's (1985) study reflect a prevalent and unfounded judical assumption that women who have devoted much of their adult lives to the marriage partnership can quickly and readily relocate from the marital home and find suitable paid employment. These court decisions reflect a judicial preconception that wives, whose own career opportunities were often sacrificed and lost as part of a tacit or express marital partnership plan, can easily be recycled into the paid marketplace. The preconception is not grounded in fact.

The above two sets of findings reveal that our current laws are not conducive to either truly equitable or equal distribution of assets and that further rethinking and rewriting of legislation appear warranted in the immediate future.

The advent of the computer may herald the wave of the future. Mediators, attorneys and accountants who help clients figure out their budgets and financial statements based on an analysis of past expenses, present commitments, and projections of future needs as these relate to future income potential from all sources, have a much more accurate and comprehensive data base upon which to generate recommendations for equitable settlements.

CHAPTER 8

Effects of Divorce on Young Children

Much of the data on children of divorce is generic to children of all ages and so will run through the next two thematic chapters on this topic. To make the material more cohesive, we have chosen to divide the discussion, as best we could, into younger and older children of divorce. The two chapters are a unit, weaving back and forth with comparisons and contrasts.

Children may be separated involuntarily from a parent by illness, war, death, and/or divorce. In the case of the first two painful situations, there may be anxiety about the parent's well-being, but there is a measure of hope and confidence that the parent will return safely home. In the case of death, there is a finality that minimizes fantasies about the family reuniting, and there is a time set aside for mourning rituals that ultimately help the child to accept the loss. Friends and relatives cluster about as a sympathetic and available support system, and grieving is acceptable behavior. Conversely, there is no traditional mourning period for children of divorce, which makes coping with parental departure and sometimes almost total loss much more disturbing and difficult (Laiken, 1981). When one parent leaves his/her spouse, the child is confronted with the fear that he or she will also be abandoned as unworthy and undesirable. There may be unconscious or conscious fears that the other parent will also leave, and a perception that adults are not honorable and reliable. Over the years, from the time of separation and well into the postdivorce period, relationships with the departed parent change, as do the children's images of both parents (parent imagos) and of themselves.

As indicated earlier, the number of children involved in divorces and living with a single divorced parent has increased since 1950 from

6.3/1,000 children under 18 years of age to 18.7/1,000 (or 1 in 53 children) in 1981, 17.6/1,000 in 1982, and 17.4/1,000 in 1983 (National Center for Health Statistics [NCHS], 1984, 1985). Apparently no similar data exist to indicate how many legally adult children were involved in divorcing families, although 11% of divorces in 1981–1983 terminated marriages of 20 years' duration or longer (NCHS, 1985).

PSYCHOLOGICAL TASKS

Just as the couple must go through stages of divorce (Bohannon, 1973; Kaslow, 1979/80, 1983), so must the children. Wallerstein (1983) itemized six psychological tasks children of divorce need to master. The first two tasks need prompt attention and resolution within the first year, while the others may need to be reworked several times. Task I is the acknowledgment of the reality of the marital separation, which may, as indicated above, involve fears of abandonment and/or ego regression. Task II is to disengage from the parental conflict so that customary pursuits, like school and sports, can be resumed. Adequate resolution of Task II means that children do not become or remain triangulated (Bowen, 1978). Wallerstein indicates that inability to disengage is reflected in lower learning achievement, higher dropout rates from school, and some acting-out behavior. Clinically we note that continued enmeshment is also reflected in depression, indecisiveness, and feeling torn asunder—since being loyal to one parent may spark untenable feelings of disloyalty to the other (Boszormenyi-Nagy & Spark, 1973).

The third task has to do with "resolution of loss"—the cessation of family traditions, the loss of one parent on a daily basis, and feelings of rejection and being unloved. Task IV, resolution of anger and self-blame, heightens some children's inability to believe in the legal concept of no-fault divorce. According to Wallerstein, "divorce characteristically gives rise to anger at the one parent who sought the divorce or both parents for their perceived self-centeredness or unresponsiveness to the wishes of the child to maintain the intact family" (1983, p. 239). She found the anger to be especially intense and long-lasting among the older children of divorce.

The fifth task is to accept the permanence of the divorce, which tends to be easier for older than younger children. The final task, according to Wallerstein, is to achieve realistic hope regarding one's own future relationships. She concludes that young adults may fear (and shy away from) love relationships because of the recurrence of the residues of sadness, anger, and anxiety about intimate and would-be "permanent" relationships at critical times during their adult years; the painful memories of the process of family dissolution and restructuring may inhibit their ability to risk entering into a committed relationship.

There is now some support for the idea that the negative consequences of coming from a "broken home" may be potentially modifiable and need not be permanent (Kulka & Weingarten, 1979). Indeed, it has been suggested that continuing childhood problems may derive more from preseparation interparental conflict than from the divorce itself (Emery, 1982), or from continuing to live in a two-parent household marred by continuing strife and/or abuse. This contention is supported by a survey of 400 psychiatrists who reported that they believe that children living with their parents who have an ongoing unhappy marriage may be victimized by their parents' conflicts (Pietropinto, 1985). Where such children cannot be spared the parents' angry confrontations, they may be much better off if the parents separate and the level of turmoil decreases. (Several respondents in the Kaslow-Schwartz study, already alluded to, verify this as a personal experience.)

Kinard and Reinherz (1984) found that "the type, severity, and persistence of problems manifested by children experiencing marital disruption may be mediated by a number of demographic and situational factors" (p. 91). The factors include: sex and age of the child; characteristics of the family—size, ethnicity, socioeconomic status; maternal employment; reason for the disruption; length of time since the separation; conflict in the family before and after separation; child's relationship with the noncustodial parent; and social support systems available for the single parent. (We would add to this list religion or spiritual framework for meaning and value in life.) In a review of the literature, Jacobs (1982) wrote that the negative effects of divorce on children tend to be found where their families "contained a distant, uninvolved, unsupportive, or angry noncustodial father and/or a chronically embittered, angry, vengeful custodial mother" (p. 1235). Children's stress appears to be positively correlated with parental stress and negative ex-spousal contacts, and inversely related to the length of time since the separation/divorce occurred (Woody et al., 1984). Little (1982) has pointed out that if the child *is* spared the parental conflicts, the child-parent relationship suffers less disruption, and the maintenance of a warm relationship with at least one of the parents reduces the negative consequences the child experiences during separation and divorce. Wallerstein and Kelly (1980) indicated that children's postdivorce adjustment parallels that of their parents; i.e., if parents cope well and can live in the present and future and not get stuck in the past, so, too, will the children.

Garber (1984) found that parents may rationalize not telling school personnel about an impending divorce when they believe that the teacher may become prejudiced toward the child and judgmental toward them; such parental fears are often justified. Many parents and teachers expect the child to continue to function well in school despite the turmoil at home. Teachers may actually become impatient when the child day-dreams or falls behind in his/her work. Parental divorce is, therefore, generally not accepted as a valid excuse for doing poorly in school. These inappropriate expectations of the child by parents and teachers probably stem from two sources. The latency-age child is idealized by the adult because he/she seems to embody the essence of childhood and is often (from our point of view erroneously) perceived as devoid of instinctual conflicts and as one whose total energy is focused on learning. Consequently, he or she is expected to function, academically, in spite of a collapsing environment. The second reason for the high expectations is the adults' need to deny the profound impact of divorce on the child. The child's good school performance is interpreted to mean that the child is not experiencing the trauma of the divorce which in turn diminishes the parental guilt. It would seem reasonable to assume that the more teachers know about what goes on in the life of the child, the more helpful and supportive they could and would be.

It is critical for the teacher (and sometimes school administrators) to know about the status of visitation. Frequently a child returns from a weekend with a noncustodial parent in a state of overstimulation. The child may be unable to function on Monday, but may settle down later on in the week. Teachers can be helpful to the child who manifests this behavior. Also, the teacher can be prepared for the sullen and disappointed child whose noncustodial parent failed to visit. The school might be asked to assume some responsibility for monitoring that a child is only permitted to leave school with the parent(s) or their clearly designated representatives so that the school does not inadvertently play into a "child-snatching" drama.

CHILD CUSTODY

Although we have discussed some aspects of child custody arrangements as part of the legal phase of divorce, other aspects bear discussing here. It is apparent from research studies that postdivorce custodial arrangements do have an impact on the children of divorce. There are many questions to be raised when deciding with whom the child(ren) will live, whether siblings are to be raised together, how much access or visitation and under what circumstances it takes place for the nonresidential parent, what "joint custody" or co-parenting means in practice, whether physical care of the children is to be equated in a dollar-value as child support is, and so on.

Luepnitz (1982) explored, "What are the advantages and disadvantages of maternal, paternal, and joint custody (a) from the adults' point of view and (b) from the children's point of view?" (p. 14). Historically, there have been biases toward paternal custody (the child seen as property) until the second decade of this century, and toward maternal custody (the "tender years" doctrine) well into the 1960s. The paternal preference was also linked to an agrarian society where men had the money and were around the farm, and if the wife/mother left there were other women such as a paternal grandmother or aunt to handle the mothering role. Maternal preference superseded this by virtue of a confluence of forces including: the industrialization of America and the shift from an extended to a nuclear family system leaving the mother the only person available in the household for child-rearing, the psychiatric deluge stressing the importance of a strong mother-child bond, and the continued evolution of the macho culture for men in and out of the workplace. Although the "best interest of the child concept" was probably enunciated as early as 1925 by Justice Brandeis, it did not become popular until the late 1960s (Goldstein, Freud, & Solnit, 1973). In the shift to preference for the custody arrangements to make the child's interest paramount, the desires and rights of the parents ceased to be of overriding import. In the 1970s and early 1980s, another doctrine was enunciated—that children need access to and involvement with both parents (California Assembly Bill, 1979; Florida Dissolution of Marriage—Children Act, 1982).

Current statutory and judicial biases favor some form of joint custody that emphasizes "the best interest of the child." Several researchers have asserted that there is, in actuality, little basis for adopting as a public policy the assumption that cooperation rather than conflict will eventuate from joint custody arrangements (Derdeyn & Scott, 1984). However, many divorce therapists and mediators indicate that well-thought-out co-parenting plans seem advantageous for many and our clinical observations lead us to concur.

In some cases, despite what a judge may decide, the relationship between parents and between parents and child(ren) may take a form, in practice, other than harmonious joint custody. Westman (1983) suggests four possible patterns: 1) parent-centered, with litigation continuing after the divorce; 2) child-centered, in which the children manipulate their parents so that a negative parental relationship persists at an intense level; 3) one parent-one child allied against the other parent; and 4) relative-influenced, in which in-laws "meddle" and grandparents carry on the marital "war."

Glick (1979) estimated that by 1990, only 71% of children in the U.S. under age 18 will be living with two parents, 25% will be living with one parent (16% with mother only and 2% with father only), and the remainder will be living with other relatives, foster parents, or friends. Statistics supplied by the Public Health Service and other agencies look only at children under age 18 as if they are the only ones legally affected by custody decisions. In reality, however, there are other dependent children of divorce, such as those entering or enrolled in college, who, in practice, are also affected by arrangements for their residence and support. Thus Glick's estimates of the number of children affected annually by divorce are underestimates of the actual number of young people whose lives are directly influenced by their parents' severance of marital bonds.

When children are old enough to exercise rational thought, usually about age seven in the eyes of judges, they should be asked their thoughts about their relationships with both parents and the pros and cons they anticipate in residing with each. The older the children, the greater weight their thoughts should have on the custody decision, although, as indicated earlier, we do not believe they should be asked to state a preference since choosing one parent means not choosing the other and asks the young person to violate his/her own sense of loyalty to both parents—a behavior that can produce great guilt and anxiety. It also can set the stage for the young person to manipulate his or her parents to get his/her own way in return for selecting that parent. Yet, not being consulted at all, especially among adolescents, tends to lead to resentment and a sense of helplessness which may contribute to depression. This becomes even more true with respect to visitation schedules (Springer & Wallerstein, 1983). Such resentment affects not only relations with the parents, but attitudes and behaviors in other sectors of the young person's life as well. As the parents discover over time, much as the child(ren) may love the noncustodial parent and cherish visiting with him/her, expanding peer networks and extracurricular interests leading to numerous activities can interfere with the visitation schedule. If such knotty situations are not worked out with due regard for the child's preferences, parent-child relations may suffer. Schedules may need periodic modification to allow for developmental changes in the child and in parents' schedules—which should be dynamic and flexible.

Slowly the literature is beginning to reflect an increasing amount of study of postdivorce parenting which sheds some light on what has previously been merely conjecture. A brief summary of the findings of several of the most significant studies to date follows.

Ahrons (1981) conducted interviews covering a wide range of topics with 54 former pairs in Wisconsin one year postdivorce. It was found that the majority of these no longer married individuals (85%) continued to interact with one another; those who were in contact with the highest frequency were the most supportive and cooperative in their co-parenting roles and reported much satisfaction with the arrangement. As could be predicted, the more fathers remained involved, the less drastic the sense of loss experienced by the children seemed to be. All were mother-custody families. Those parents who rarely or never shared decision making about child-rearing issues were the most conflicted and were significantly less supportive of each others' actions. Generally the men saw themselves as being more involved in sharing child-rearing concerns than did their ex-wives. Ahrons states that such "different perceptions of reality may be responsible for creating conflict in the postdivorce relationship" (p. 423). We would hypothesize that this gets communicated to the children in the form of mothers complaining that dad is insufficiently invested in his children's well-being and fathers bemoaning that they are not appreciated and are disparaged, no matter what they try to do.

In another study, Bowman and Ahrons (1985), as part of Phase 1 of the Binuclear Family Research Project, utilized a sample drawn from public divorce court records in Dane County, Wisconsin. They compared parenting one year postdivorce of 28 joint custodial fathers with 54 non-custodial fathers. The indicators of father involvement which they utilized assess the two dimensions most frequently employed to distinguish joint custody—1) contact and activity with the children, and 2) shared responsibility and decision-making. As might be anticipated, joint custody fathers were found to be much more involved in parenting postdivorce than those in the noncustodial father subsample. They concluded, in accord with earlier findings by Derdeyn and Scott (1984, p. 207), that "there is a marked disparity between the power of the joint custody movement and the sufficiency of evidence that joint custody can accomplish what we expect of it." Nonetheless, the limited empirical evidence to date does suggest that, for those parents who select the option of joint custody, it "appears to be a workable and satisfactory arrangement which permits both parents to continue their parenting roles and relationships after divorce" (Bowman & Ahrons, 1985, p. 184). Our clinical experience indicates further that sound joint custody arrangements enable the children to continue to feel loved by, and important to, both parents and to benefit from the involvement in close relationships to caring adults of both sexes. This in turn helps them in their own identity formation and in gaining confidence about being loveable and valued.

EFFECTS OF DIVORCE ON CHILDREN

The effects of divorce on the children involved, both short- and long-term, have been studied by many researchers (Coddington, 1972; Emery, 1982; Fine, Moreland, & Schwebel, 1983; Goode, 1956; Hetherington et al., 1979; Kalter & Rembar, 1981; Kelly & Berg, 1978; Kinard & Reinherz, 1984; Lamb, 1977; Wallerstein & Kelly, 1980; Wynn & Brumberger, 1982).

In addition to the emotional changes that may occur from the dissolution of the intact family, changes in residence, loss of one live-in parent, etc., children are also likely to become more at risk for poverty, anxiety about support for higher education, and legal problems (Jenkins, 1978). These will vary with who has custody, child and spousal support arrangements, living arrangements, continuing or disrupted relationships with the extended family and myriad other factors including the parents' postdivorce adjustment and whether they are cooperative or conflicted about co-parenting. The gender and age of the children at the time of the divorce are also crucial variables.

Gender Differences

As was indicated earlier, in several studies it has been found that boys tend to react more poorly to divorce, both in intensity and duration of feeling, than girls do (Emery, 1982; Hodges & Bloom, 1984; Kurdek & Berg, 1983). This conclusion has been challenged by Reinhard (1977), Pett (1982), and Kinard and Reinherz (1984), who found no gender differences in their subjects' postdivorce reactions, and by Farber et al. (1983), who found that female adolescents suffered greater stress than male adolescents. Differences in sampling, questions asked, locus of control, and custody arrangements among the respondents in the several studies are some of the factors that may account for these conflicting results.

Hammond (1981) found no significant differences in self-concept, reading achievement, or mathematics achievement between children of intact families and those from divorced families among third to sixth graders. Their teachers, however, rated the boys from divorced families higher on "acting-out" and "distractibility" than boys from intact families, but saw no significant differences among the girls. This may reflect teacher bias rather than reality as far as the boys go. As far as perceptions of behavior, Emery (1982) noted, "girls are likely to be just as troubled by marital turmoil as boys are, but they demonstrate their feelings in a manner that is more appropriate to their sex role, namely, by being anxious, withdrawn, or perhaps very well behaved" (p. 317). A nationwide study of children in first, third, and fifth grades also found poorer adjustment among the boys and older children (Guidubaldi, Cleminshaw, Perry, & McLoughlin, 1983). Hammond found that the girls were more likely to see positive potential in the divorce for themselves, while this was not so for the boys. This may reflect gender differences in maturity more than anything else, as less evidence of gender differences is available for children of divorce at later ages.

AGE DIFFERENCES

Preadolescent Children

Most of the research on the impact of divorce on children has been focused on preschoolers and elementary school-age children. Even with this population, however, the ways in which negative effects are expressed have been shown to differ by age. For example, the preschooler may demonstrate his or her anxiety and distress by regressive behavior and the latency-age child by aggression or withdrawal. Both groups tend to blame themselves for the divorce—the preschoolers because of their basic egocentricity and the older children because they perceive a relation between their overt behaviors and the parental conflicts. Some believe that perhaps if they had not been naughty, their parents would not have fought so often. This is particularly the case when parents have blamed an unwanted and/or unruly child for all their troubles. Other children chastise themselves for failing to be able to somehow find a way to smooth things over and be the "glue" that holds their parents together.

Following the separation, if the resident parent goes out on "dates," the younger children are likely to feel threatened by the parent's new behavior and different kind of absence, whereas the older ones may look askance at the sexuality of their parents that is implied in such activity. Remarriage may similarly affect children differentially depending in part on their age at the time of the event.

In the study by Coddington (1972) alluded to earlier, based on the Holmes and Rahe (1967) study of the effects of life change events on health, more than 3,500 children from preschool through senior high school ranked changes in their family situation for severity of impact. In each of the four subgroups, divorce of parents was second only to the death of a parent in magnitude of change. What is particularly significant in the data collected by Coddington is that the perception of the impact of the divorce increases from preschool to elementary school age, remains high in early adolescence, and then declines in the senior high school years. This is consistent with developmental changes in children. The latency-age child is more aware of and concerned about family identity and traditions than the younger child, while the middle adolescent is beginning to separate more from the family as he/she integrates his or her personal and unique identity, associates more with peers, and is influenced more by friends than by family members (in contrast to younger children).

In a study of children who were pre-Oedipal, Oedipal, and post-Oedipal at the time of parental separation, Kalter and Rembar (1981) found negative correlations between age at the time of divorce and level of emotional disturbance for all of their sample (N = 144 outpatient children). They found that while daughters of divorce who were adolescents when the breakup occurred tended to have drug or alcohol involvement, or to exhibit running away/truancy/sexual acting-out behaviors, latency-age girls did not. Parental separation during the child's latency or Oedipal years was significantly correlated in this study with a higher frequency of academic problems. This supports the earlier assertion of differential demonstration of effects of divorce on children by age.

Kelly and Berg (1978) studied 488 children, aged 9 to 15 years, using a Family Story Test. The test differentiated among children of divorce, those in unhappy but intact families, and those in happy, intact families, and mean scores were derived. The children of divorce expressed several themes in their stories of divorced families: feelings of self-blame leading to feelings of guilt, hopes for reunification of the parents, feelings of being "in the middle" between parents who degraded each other, feelings of increased responsibility as the children took over aspects of the role of the absent parent, and feelings of ridicule from other children. The children of intact but unhappy families expressed the highest fears of abandonment and assigned the greatest amount of blame to parents. Goode (1960) had asserted that "children of divorcé(e)s are aware of their own status ambiguity and usually desire to 'be like other children'" (p. 323). Today, though, the child of divorce is no longer in the minority in school; to the contrary, in many neighborhoods, it is the child in an intact family who is the exception. Under these circumstances, ridicule by other children is less likely to occur. However, the pain experienced is not lessened because they know other children of divorce; the loss and trauma are very personal.

In Hammond's (1981) study of children in Grades 3 to 6, both positive and negative perceptions of divorce were obtained from children in 82 divorced and 83 intact lower-middle-class families. On the positive side, the children said that their parents wouldn't be fighting as much, that they would receive more presents from their parents, that they could celebrate holidays twice, that they would have more attention from their parents, and that they would enjoy visiting the noncustodial parent. On the negative side, the children saw less money for the family and the disadvantage of not seeing one parent as much anymore. On the issue of holidays in particular, however, the "joy" of double celebrations as perceived by younger children is seen as a burden by adolescents (Hagestad, et al., 1984). No matter how evenly attendance at holiday festivities is divided, whether or not the child(ren) may be consulted, each holiday dinner or observance reawakens distress for the older children of divorce, with wishes for the former family "togetherness." Some older adolescents and young adults refuse to go to either parent's home and instead prefer to join their own friends or have dinner alone rather than be confronted anew by their loyalty dilemma. (More on this in the next chapter.)

In a pilot study applying a family system perspective to the analysis of family drawings of children of separation and divorce, Isaacs and Levin (1984) came up with some interesting findings. They administered the Draw-a-Family Test to school-age children (ages 5 to 11 years) during the first year of parental separation and at follow up one year later. They focussed their interpretations on the observed family composition and relative size of each parent in the drawings. They found that children in mother custody families, over time, increasingly omitted their dads from the drawings. Although initially the child saw the father as larger or the same size as the mother, by the second year postseparation, the father was drawn smaller than the mother or omitted. The children seemed to be showing the increasing "peripherality of their fathers" (p. 19). As they omitted their fathers they tended to include people from outside the nuclear family—probably as a compensatory effort to fill the place of the missing father. Another salient finding was that of the 41 children in the study population, nearly one quarter showed a shift by the second year of separation in the direction of a decrease in creativity and an increase in constriction of their family drawings. This raises the question of how well or poorly children of divorce fare over time. The researchers did not see the same drop in the drawings of youngsters who had received preventive family oriented therapy at the time of separation.

The disparities among these and other studies, both in design and in conclusions, led us to the need to do a descriptive study of our own, partially described in Chapter 4 and elaborated upon further now (Kaslow & Schwartz, in press). Beginning with the children of our divorced sample, we sought answers to the questions that arose from conflicting reports in the professional literature. What we found is reported in the following pages. We did not examine the differential impact of varying custody arrangements.

CHILDREN OF DIVORCE: A STUDY

Samples

Approximately two-thirds of our adult sample had children at the time of their divorce. Questionnaires were sent to them either at the parent-respondent's address or at their own residence. Two forms were used: Form IIA, for children 10 years old and younger (the "Babes"), was to be answered by one of the child's parents; Form IIB was answered by the children over 10 themselves (the "Older Kids"). In this chapter, we'll focus on the "Babes" and the comparative data about the two groups. The "Older Kids" portion of the study will be discussed and analyzed in Chapter 9. Separation of the parents, in several cases, occurred when a child was too young to exhibit or express clearly differentiated feelings, or when he/she could not remember years later what the feelings had been. As a result, several questionnaires could not be included in the analysis of postseparation and present feelings.

Children's Feelings

Respondents were asked to indicate how true several "feelings" were at the time of separation and at the time of responding on a scale of 1 = "Very True" to 5 = "Very Untrue." Where there was no response or the item was not applicable for some reason, the item was scored "0" or "6", depending on the item, which altered the mean scores slightly when such cases occurred. A sample of these responses is included in Table 14.

In the case of the younger children ("Babes"), a parent responded and may have unintentionally distorted perceptions or inaccurately recalled the child's reactions. As Young (1983) noted, parents' perceptions of children's adjustment is often "off." It is readily apparent from the figures in Table 14, however, that the younger children seemed to be, in general, less troubled than the older ones at the time of the separation/divorce. This reflects the same pattern that Coddington (1972) found. In several instances, the young child (as recalled by the responding parent) was probably unable to indicate, for example, "feelings of rejection" or "depression." The older children of divorce, in contrast, tended to show a wider range of responses and were more sensitive to their feelings at the time of separation as well as in the present.

Taken as a group, the older children were much angrier initially than the younger ones, but there is somewhat less difference now. They were also markedly more depressed than the younger group at separation, but the gap between the two groups has narrowed over time. Both groups have moved from "some confusion" to relatively low feelings of confusion in the interval between separation and the time of responding.

On the question of feelings of capability, the older subjects have shifted from the negative toward the positive more than is true for the younger children, whose parents tended to see them as "often" feeling capable at both points in time. The older children were much less happy than the younger ones at separation and now, which is not surprising since they were and are more capable of understanding what happened to the family.

The differences shown in Table 14 might be more extreme if those "Older Kids" who were 10 or younger at the time of separation were

Table 14
Comparison of Strength of Feelings of
Older and Younger Children of Divorce

	Children Under 10 (Babes)		Children 10 and Older (Older Kids)	
N	9		24	
X̄ Age at separation	4.22		16.75	
X̄ Age now	6.89		22.38	
	Mean	Range	Mean	Range
Angry				
At separation	3.56	2–5	2.67	1–5
Now	3.67	3–4	3.21	1–5
Feeling capable				
At separation	2.00	1–3	2.54	1–6
Now	2.11	1–6	1.92	1–6
Depressed				
At separation	4.11	2–5	2.83	1–5
Now	4.11	3–5	3.79	1–5
Happy				
At separation	2.56	1–5	3.42	1–5
Now	1.78	1–2	2.50	1–6
Feeling confused				
At separation	2.89	1–4	2.71	1–5
Now	3.78	3–6	3.71	1–5
Feeling rejected				
At separation	3.67	3–5	3.50	1–5
Now	4.11	3–6	3.63	1–5
Total change scores	8.56	−7–30	14.63	−4–30

deleted and moved to the younger group. Combining these "Older Kids" with the "Babes," it can be seen that their recalled feelings are quite similar to those reported by the parents on behalf of the younger children, thus increasing the credibility of the parental reports. The only substantial difference seen here is in the recall of feelings of depression. Since the larger group averaged a year older than the smaller group at separation, their ability to differentiate feelings may be greater, causing the observed difference. Despite the support that Table 15 suggests for the validity of the parental responses for the "Babes," we must be alert to the possibility that the responding parents may have unwittingly answered in terms of how they preferred to believe the child had responded more than in accurate terms that had some base in objective measurement.

The "Total Change Score" summarizes the total shift in feelings in

Table 15
"Babes" and "Under 11s" Compared

	Babes	Under 11s
N	10	20
Angry at separation, $\overline{X}$	3.70	3.35
Happy at separation, $\overline{X}$	2.50	2.80
Depressed at separation, $\overline{X}$	4.10	3.55
Confused at separation, $\overline{X}$	2.80	2.80
Felt rejected at separation, $\overline{X}$	3.80	3.75

item-by-item scores. For example, if a subject indicated a "2" (often true) for feeling confused at the time of separation and a "4" (often untrue) for feeling confused now, the change score for that item equals +2. If a "5" (very untrue) was listed for happiness at the time of separation, and a "2" now, the change score would equal a +3. However, if the subject rated feelings of a capability at "2" for the time of separation and "3" now, the change score equals −1. Since the older children were generally more variable in their self-ratings than the parents were in rating the younger children, it is logical that the "Older Kids" also show a larger mean score for total change over the years than do the "Babes."

DISCUSSION

As previously noted, among the difficulties in research reports on divorce are the use of different time spans (at separation, predivorce, immediately postdivorce, variable periods postdivorce); nonrepresentative, small, biased samples; clinical vs. nonclinical samples; psychometrically unsound measures of adjustment; lack of control groups; the use of "captive audiences"; the number of parental divorces experienced; self-selection of volunteer participants; parents responding for themselves and their children; lack of adequate attention to age and gender differences; and relationships between children of divorce and their parents, siblings, other relatives, and friends (Ellison, 1983; Emery, 1982; Kalter & Rembar, 1981; Kurdek, 1983; Kurdek et al., 1981; Levitin, 1979; White & Mika, 1983).

In the study at hand, there was an attempt to deal with some of these research problems. The sample of divorced adults from which the children's sample was drawn came from 17 states, although they were mostly from Pennsylvania and Florida. They represented a wide range of socioeconomic levels, although the majority had had some college education and were middle or upper-middle class. All subjects were volunteers who responded to a mailed survey, with parents responding for children aged 10 years and younger. All of the adults had been separated or divorced from their first marriage, and none were remarried, reducing the problems attendant upon multiple parentage for the children. Most of the child subjects were in the physical custody of (or in residence with) their mothers. Relatively few had been consulted about custody or choice of residence.

For the younger group, parents reported the dominant feeling at separation to have been capability, followed by happiness and feelings of confusion. According to the parents, there was little depression or anger or feelings of rejection in the young children at the time of separation. There were slight improvements in feelings over time, with total change scores ranging from −14 to +30, but a mean score of only 5.60. These data support the general picture of very young children being minimally troubled by the separation and slightly older ones having more difficulty. Nonetheless, the findings must be interpreted in the light of the fact that they are derived from parental responses rather than direct observation or subject response.

Across the total age range of children of divorce included here, there was a low, positive, nonsignificant relationship between children's change scores and their parents' view of their quality of life now. This does not support the finding generally reported in the literature that children reflect the custodial parent's adjustment to separation and divorce, but may be a function of the wider age span included in this study and/or the self-selection and self-censorship of respondents. Feelings of children of divorce by gender also do not appear as consistent as shown in the literature and may similarly reflect the broad age range, size of sample, or self-selection factors. Of the 36 children of divorce in our sample for whom total change scores could be determined, only five (13.9%) had negative total change scores. All of the others indicated emotional changes over time were positive. Further study of these findings is warranted, as only longitudinal studies, such as the Wallerstein (1984, 1985a) 10-year follow-up, can indicate with some certainty what the long-term effects of divorce are on children.

PARENTAL RESPONSE TO CHILDREN'S BEHAVIORS

Dorfman (1985), a psychotherapist at Hahnemann Medical University in Philadelphia, has prepared an excellent table (see Table 16) which fits exceedingly well with our developmental life cycle model. It relates the child's age to behaviors showing distress that are likely to be exhibited,

Table 16

A Single Parent's Guide to Helping Children
Ages 0–12 Survive Separation and Divorce*

Age	Behaviors	How to prevent these behaviors from becoming serious problems
0–12 months	• fussy, irritable	• Often a reaction to Mother's upset. Eventually the chaos and stress after the Separation will lessen. In the meantime, relax with baby by rocking, stroking and patting. Ask for and accept help and comfort from friends and family.
	• dull, unresponsive	• This is a reaction to Mother's depression that starts as fussiness as infant tries to get Mother to fill the need for stimulation. Because depressed Moms don't want to play, the infant finally gives up. Extended deprivation can affect intellectual and social development. Engage in 2 or 3, 15 or 20 minute daily play sessions. Cooing, peek-a-boo, playful handling and funny faces will go a long way in countering this type of behavior and help to lift Mom's depression too.
1 and 2 yr. olds	• clinging, whining	• Children this age are extremely attached and need Mom nearby to feel secure enough to explore the world. The Separation makes toddler fearful of losing Mother and of anything new. Avoid an assortment of sitters. Allow toddler to have mother substitutes like a worn blanket, stuffed animal or whatever he chooses to drag around.
	• bedtime screaming	• Normal for this age but may be more persistent or severe after the Separation. Do not allow cries to go unattended. Reassure child of your presence by frequent visits to his room. Do not take child to your bed. This would be easier in the short run but harder in the long run.
3, 4, and 5 yr. olds	• wetting, baby talk	• In response to stress a child often regresses to the more secure period of babyhood. Don't panic or punish. Child will regather his energies and be "grown up" again soon.
	• possessiveness, overtidy	• Are attempts to hold on to what is left and to put some order into the disorder. Allow these behaviors while giving reassurance of your continued presence and affection. Always explain beforehand what changes will be occurring.
	• too well behaved	• Preschoolers believe that they are central to all that goes on in the world. They may blame their own "badness" for the Separation, often trying to correct the situation by being too good. Emphasize that the Separation is because of problems between Mom and Dad unrelated to the child.
	• overly aggressive	• Often a sign of child's deeply felt anger over the Separation. Handle as you would any aggressiveness. Restrain from hurting self or others, but do not berate for being "bad."
6, 7, 8 and 9 yr. olds	• drop in grades	• Fantasies about reconciliation, memories, intense sadness, anger and worry keep the child too distracted for learning. Encourage expression of feelings no matter how distressful they are for you. Let the child know that he or she is not alone in these feelings.
	• manipulating	• Parents competing for child's loyalty fall prey to the manipulation of their children for gifts and privileges. Refuse to be a part of what can ultimately damage a child's personality development.
	• overly responsible	• Economics and the emotional needs of Mother often force the child to perform way above expectations for this age. In addition to the babysitting and extra chores, allow for some childish interests. To avoid later resentment, care must be taken so that the burden is not so heavy that the child misses the friends, fun and carefreeness of childhood.

Table 16 (*Continued*)

Age	Behaviors	How to prevent these behaviors from becoming serious problems
10, 11, and 12 yr. olds.	• too grownup	• Girls at this age are prone to sexually provocative behavior especially if Mom has a boyfriend. Jealousy and competition with Mother is likely. Despite mature appearance, child must be treated appropriate to age.
	•mouthiness	• At this age children feel especially betrayed and angry at one or both parents and may be very vocal. They punish and seek revenge often aligning with one parent against the other. Boys especially need the involvement of Father or other male. For girls, remarriage is especially difficult. Extra effort is required to diffuse child's anger and maintain good parent-child relationship.

*Table reproduced with permission of Rachelle Dorfman (1985).

and suggests how parents can prevent such behaviors from becoming serious problems. We are including her table as we have found it quite useful as a conceptual format to utilize with parents in individual and group therapy.

In situations where the mother is awarded primary custody and feels inadequate to the task, her ex-husband, by the nature of his involvement, may help her fail. Isaacs (1982), reported on a "case of a stalemated divorcing process" in which this is indeed what occurred. Kimberly, a nine-year-old girl, was brought by her mom to the Families of Divorce Project in Philadelphia because she was exhibiting screaming tantrums of several hours duration and her mother was unable to control her. In addition, Kimberly did not like to sleep alone so her mom went to bed with her daughter. The problem had begun three years earlier at the time of the parental separation. It was found that the mother had not completed the psychic divorce from her husband. Her incompetent and helpless handling of her child enabled her to turn to and receive support from her ex-husband, thereby maintaining the "phantom family of the past" (p. 234). The child contributed to keeping this fantasy alive by becoming uncontrollable. Her symptomatology enabled her to become closer to and more dependent upon her mother, ensured additional contact between herself and her father, and kept the parental relationship intense and active. The father, who continued to feel guilty about leaving the marriage, was provided by this sequence with an opportunity to assuage his guilt by intervening and helping with the child whenever his ex-wife called upon him. His needs also perpetuated the dysfunctional sequence. The family therapist attempted to break the impasse and enable the mother to make the essential transitions to her new single parent and divorced adult status so that she and Kimberly could both proceed with their individual appropriate developmental tasks. The therapy consisted of preventing the father as rescuer from participating in this way, helping the mother learn how to cope with and manage the specific symptom of the screaming, diminishing the mother/child sleeping together, and returning self-control to the child as mother began to move out and be less dependent upon her for company or to assist her in bringing the ex-husband back into their lives.

We have seen similar cases and utilized some of the above type of interventions in addition to more insight-oriented ones in which all three participants in the drama are helped to become aware of why they precipitate and re-enact this repetitive scenario and how self-defeating it inevitably is.

THERAPEUTIC STRATEGIES

In Table 2 (see pp. 30–31) we have listed when different intervention approaches might be fitting. Here we will describe these in greater detail in terms of the developmental needs of children.

Prior to the actual physical separation of the family unit, which Ahrons (1983b) has aptly dubbed *systemic separation*, the adults may seek marital or divorce therapy or divorce mediation. Once the decision to end the marriage is made, one of the concerns is likely to be how and what to tell the children. This, of course, has to be tailored to the child's age and level of maturity. Some parents can work out a viable plan to do this alone or together. Others may wish to bring their youngster(s) along for one or several therapy sessions so they can tell them in the safe sanctuary of the clinician's office and provide an opportunity for the children, secure in the sense of the therapist's protection, to be free to respond emotionally. Whichever route is chosen, the essence of what is to be conveyed is that the parents realize that they cannot continue to live together because it is no longer a happy union, but that the children were born (or adopted) out of their mutual love and that both will continue to love and be concerned about them, will remain close and involved in decision making, in their activities, and in supporting them in whatever ways are essential.

Following this, and at any time until the child has recuperated well from the family's splitting up and reorganizing itself as a postdivorce family, all treatment should proceed utilizing a family systems framework even though only one member or a subsystem of several members might be seen in any given session or for a certain time period.

Thus, following the realization that the family as it has existed is being dismantled, the child may need to be seen alone or conjointly with his/her siblings. The children may need and want a safe harbor to express their confusion, anger, anxiety about their future, fears of further abandonment, or about feeling torn in half. Often they realize that their parents are so upset that they do not wish to burden them with their grief and worries. If a child has brothers or sisters, building on the sibling bond (Bank & Kahn, 1982) in sibling subsystem therapy can enable them to derive mutual support in their shared experience and in regaining some semblance of control over what is happening to them. For preschool children and through to the latency age years, play and art therapies are probably the most efficacious. For older children, verbal psychotherapy alone or combined with some activities therapy probably constitute the treatments of choice (Kaslow, 1983).

For other children, particularly only children, participation in children of divorce groups, composed of youngsters close in age range, often proves quite helpful. This method is detailed in an article by Kessler and Bostwick (1977). Suffice it to say here that children derive tremendous support, sympathy and empathy from each other as well as from the group leaders or facilitators. Ideally the leaders (from our point of view) should be a heterosexual co-therapy pair who model rationality, warmth, attentive listening, optimism and the ability of a male and female team to respect one another and get along well. If they do, this may offset some of the tendency children have to generalize from their parents' behavior to that of all men and all women; it provides another more positive prototype of interaction. Another compelling attribute of children of divorce groups is the wonderful way the youngsters share their dilemmas and engage in mutual problem solving (Kaslow, 1980).

Periodically parent-child therapy may be in order—to provide a safe forum in which they can confront one another with their profoundly strong and often ambivalent emotions and try to steer a course that leads to closeness but not enmeshment, individuality without rejection or loss of a sense of belonging, improved ability to communicate openly but in a nonhurtful fashion.

Ultimately the family redefines itself (Ahrons, 1983) as the new structure of the postdivorce family becomes stabilized, at least temporarily. If the recovery process is going well and the individuals are reasonably resilient and healthy emotionally, little therapy should be needed at this time.

If and when the unit goes through another transition and transformation with the engagement and remarriage of one or both parents, another disquieting upheaval may occur. If so, any of the modalities elaborated above may again constitute useful therapeutic interventions. It may be necessary to briefly reconstruct the original nuclear family so all can finally finish the remaining work of the separation process. Sometimes both sets of parents need to be assembled conjointly with the children so that the original biological parents can give their children permission to like, accept and get along with the new stepparent(s) and can make it clear that the new stepparent is being asked to share both responsibility and concomitant authority for some aspects of parenting. (Going into the remarriage family in depth is beyond the purview of this book. The interested reader is referred to Sager et al., 1983; Visher & Visher, 1979; and Messinger, 1984, as resource texts on this topic.)

RETROSPECTIVE

Clearly young children are vulnerable to the vicissitudes of the pre-, during and postdivorce experience when their special world is ripped asunder. They generally seem to experience anxiety, confusion, fear of abandonment, and/or worry that their behavior might have contributed to the breakup. Depending on age, some exhibit regression or antisocial behaviors; others manifest their anguish in deteriorating school performance or in psychosomatic symptoms like asthma or gastrointestinal disturbances. Others work hard to defend against the distress they feel and mask their feelings and/or channel their energies into excelling at school, in sports, the arts or other activities. Some attempt to comfort their parents; others defend against tuning into the pain. It is critical that parents not embroil their children in custody disputes and in being carved up or in becoming their constant companion and confidant.

For children to continue to grow in an emotionally and physically healthy manner, it is imperative that the best possible custody and visitation arrangements be worked out. Such plans should insure easy access to both parents and each adult's continuing active and voluntary involvement in nurturing and supporting their child, as evidenced in participating in child-centered activities, helping with homework, chauffering to doctors' visits and after school activities, making an input into key decisions, and providing financial support. Whether the plan is for shared parental responsibility through joint custody or sole custody/visitation, it is essential that the child know that neither parent has nor will be divorced from (loving) him/her.

It appears that children's postdivorce adjustment may be correlated to their parents' adjustment and level of continuing conflict. Thus it becomes incumbent upon parents to cooperate in the best interest of the children they both love and that, if they need assistance with their own emotional turbulence, that they seek it from friends, adult family members, clergy or therapist—but not from their children. It is imperative that children not become parentified, that is, pushed into taking care of their forlorn or overwrought parent(s). They can be expected to have some compassion and be helpful in age-appropriate ways, but the adults must take care of the children—not the other way around!

CHAPTER 9
Older Children
of Divorce

As indicated earlier, most of the studies to date about children of divorce have been focused on preschool and latency-age children affected by marital dissolution, with little attention paid to adolescents and young adults (Tapp, Daniels, Doyle, Olson, & Quiggle, 1985). Therefore this chapter focuses on older children of divorce. Adolescent and young adult children of divorce are often affected at the very point in their lives when separation from their family of origin constitutes a major developmental task for them that becomes more difficult when, instead, one parent separates from them. Given that we have reviewed most of the literature with respect to age differences in Chapter 8, here we will summarize the literature specifically on older children of divorce and then we will present and discuss further the data obtained from questionnaire responses of the "Older Kids" in the Kaslow and Schwartz (in press) study alluded to earlier.

ADOLESCENT AND YOUNG ADULT CHILDREN

Adolescence is generally perceived as a difficult developmental period both by those living through it and by those who live with them. If parents divorce at this stage of a child's development, what impact does the divorce have on these young people? The results of research on this

---

This chapter was originally written for inclusion in *Advances in Family Intervention*, J. Vincent (Ed.), 1987. Permission to reprint in revised form herein was granted by Dr. Vincent.

question are mixed. The Coddington (1972) study suggests that the impact is less than it might be if they were younger. In contrast to the younger children, adolescents and young adults tend to disapprove of the behavior of one or both parents at separation/divorce (Wallerstein, 1983) and to project the blame for the breakup of the family on them. Further, teenagers may feel competition with their dating parents (and vice versa), and want to engage in the same dating behaviors that their parents are modeling.

Schwartzberg (1980) detected three types of reactions among adolescent children of divorce who became patients. There were those who: 1) had prior pathological symptoms become worse, 2) regressed temporarily, and 3) made premature attempts at maturity (sexual acting-out, drug abuse, running away). The adolescents who coped best with the crisis were "those who demonstrated prior good ego strength, good relationships with the custodial parent, and [experienced] minimal parent regression" (p. 399).

McLoughlin and Whitfield (1984), in a study of 64 Australians aged 13–17 years at the time of their parents' separation, found that half of their group saw the divorce as a "relief" because of verbal and/or physical preseparation conflicts between their parents over many months. Although a small percentage of these youths exhibited a deterioration in their school performance as a result of the strain of separation, the other 50% saw an improvement at this time, and most found no deterioration in their relationships with teachers. The majority of these adolescents also experienced no difference in peer relationships. Eighty-four per cent of these Australian subjects planned to marry and expected to have a happy marriage. In their conclusions, McLoughlin and Whitfield stated that "Discretion and sensitivity about entering into new relationships and a parent's conduct in those relationships would also seem to be important to adolescents" (p. 170). Since adolescents are typically very much involved with their own emerging sexuality, they tend to be exquisitely sensitive to their parents' sexuality and are often embarrassed by it, especially if parents flaunt their sexual involvements and are publicly seductive. To what extent the Australian findings are generalizable to adolescents in the United States or elsewhere is uncertain.

Kelly (1981) did a five-year follow-up study of the adolescent subsample in her research with Wallerstein (Wallerstein & Kelly, 1980). She found that the normal de-idealization of parents, growth of autonomy, and the achievement of moral integrity had been speeded up in this group. Yet, 2 of the original 18 subjects had married—disastrously—and 10 were so poorly adjusted that they badly needed therapeutic intervention but had not sought it. The better adjusted members of the sample were dating, but were afraid to commit themselves to long-term relationships. Two-thirds of Kelly's subjects, at the five-year follow-up, were at an age when marriage is often being considered as an option. They still viewed it as an undesirable one.

Wallerstein carried the follow-up of her study with Kelly to the 10-year mark. In a preliminary report, she noted that "In examining the comments of youngsters 19 to 28 years old at the 10-year mark, we had been profoundly moved by the vividness of their memories and their yearning for the intact family of their memory and their fantasy" (1984, p. 447). She also reported that these young adults indicated expectations of betrayal in their interpersonal relationships. Only 9 of the 40 subjects had married, and three-fourths of the remainder expected to marry, though with only cautious optimism (Wallerstein, 1985b). Their feelings may well have been based not only on their preadolescent/adolescent perceptions of the facts of their parents' separation, but also on their sense of having been betrayed by those very adults who were supposed to provide protection and security to them when they were minors. Retrospectively, they still felt saddened by the divorce, and a majority felt that they had lost significant aspects of their childhood and adolescence because of the family dissolution. "Their shared sense was that life had been for them more difficult, more hazardous, and less pleasurable than for their peers whose families remained intact" (Wallerstein, 1985a, p. 550). Although many of these young people were still angry with their parents for the divorce at the 5-year follow-up, only about half still expressed some anger at the 10-year follow-up. Despite the difficulties and wistfulness still expressed, Wallerstein did note two positives at the 10-year follow-up: one was the feeling of being stronger and more independent as a result of the divorce, though the price had been high; the other was the strong support network among siblings (1985a).

According to yet another study, frequency of parental dating tends to be related to an increase in heterosexual social activities among the children, especially if the custodial parent remains single and is dating (Booth, Brinkerhoff, & White, 1984). Clinically, it appears that if the residential parent does not date, feels socially alienated and isolated, and clings to the adolescent for contact and bolstering up, the adolescent's ability to individuate and leave her/him to go to college or take a job away from home is hampered. The young adult perceives, and may be told overtly or covertly, that he/she is needed as a caretaker, and that the rejected parent could not tolerate a second desertion. This is the prime factor that makes separation, at the young adult's initiative, so difficult and sometimes guilt-laden.

For college students, there are even fewer studies from which to draw a picture of the effects of divorce. Hillard (1984) points out that parents of college students may have remained in an unhappy marriage "for the sake of the children" and separate only when the youngest goes off to college or to pursue a career. Although there may be a negative impact on such young adults, whether the youngest or not, the total effect of the parental separation tends not to be as earth-shaking for them as it is for younger children. College students are often geographically removed from the day-to-day situation, involved in their own academic and social activities, and are not subject, as younger children are, to having to choose (or have chosen for them) one parent or the other as legal "custodian."

> College students may react differently to the experience of parental divorce than do younger individuals, both because of their developmental level and because of living in the college environment. Developmentally, the college student is likely to have a relatively mature ego, with the capacity to use relatively higher order defense mechanisms, such as suppression, sublimation, and altruism in dealing with feelings related to divorce. At the same time, however, the developmental tasks of college students, such as consolidation of an independent identity and development of intimacy, may be particularly vulnerable to disruption by stresses of parental divorce. (Hillard, 1984, p. 665)

For some college students, of course, the separation may come as a relief from parental bickering and the intensely conflicted family and home atmosphere of their growing up years. For others, the separation may come as a total shock because their parents had not fought overtly, but had maintained a superficially harmonious facade. In both situations, the young adults may express distress at the pain one or both parents are suffering, but recognize that the parents are better off apart. In contrast to such relatively mature perceptions, university counseling directors found that college students from separated or divorced families, as compared with those from intact families, tended to have greater difficulties in affective adjustment, to evidence more behavior problems, and to have more conflicts in interpersonal relationships (Farber, Primavera, & Felner, 1983). Specific problems cited include depression, anxiety, feelings of abandonment and insecurity, increased drug and alcohol usage, sleeping and eating disturbances, inability to concentrate on studies, peer problems, sexual identity problems, loyalty dilemmas, and financial stress. It should be noted, however, that these directors of college counseling services, as well as Hillard (1984), drew their conclusions from an essentially clinical population, i.e., those students who had sought psychological or psychiatric assistance at this critical time in their lives. There were no control groups of students who were children of divorce and who had not sought therapy.

Recently researchers at the University of Pennsylvania reported finding that the impact of parental divorce on college-aged children is much greater than previously assumed. Hagestad,* Smyer,* Cooney, and Klock's (Bales, 1984, p. 13) preliminary findings reveal that adult children of college age empathize with their parents, even to the degree of making statements about "when we were divorced." Over one half of their 39 student respondents revealed a decline in their own emotional health evidenced in symptoms such as depression, stress, and a sense of insecurity. Many of the respondents expressed grave concern about their parents' future, particularly the mothers', and felt angry at their parents. These researcher/authors indicated that because the subjects are old enough to empathize, "they may be regarded as a valuable source of support for their parents" (p. 13). Nonetheless, and here we agree strongly based on our clinical experience, "In providing empathy for troubled parents, young adults may be placing themselves in a more vulnerable position. The emotions their parents share may become as real for the young adults, making it seem as if they were actually experiencing the divorce themselves" (p. 13).

We have seen students withdraw from college to "go home" to take care of a divorced parent who appears too distraught to manage on his or her own. What is to last for a few months may go on for years as the parent becomes dependent and the adult child feels guilty about wanting to leave because the parent has subtly or overtly communicated that this would be perceived as a second abandonment *and would be intolerable*.

In the Hagestad et al. study, some significant differences were found between male and female adult children of divorce. It was the women who were more likely to report emotional distress at some time during the divorce process. They also expressed more concern about taking sides in the dispute and the authors found this to be in accord with the accepted view of women . . . as family peacemakers and kinkeepers. On the positive side, over half of the respondents stated that they had developed better relations with their mothers postdivorce and about one-third indicated similar positive changes in their relationships with their fathers. Improvements cited were in the areas of communications, understanding, mutual respect, greater relaxation and enjoyment in being together.

Hagestad and her colleagues found that more women than men were angry and their anger tended to be directed at one parent, usually the father. Forty-three percent of the women who reported being angry perceived the father as the lone target of their wrath, while only 14% thought

---

*Hagestad and Smyer, members of the Pennsylvania State University faculty, conducted the research at Penn State, not at the University of Pennsylvania.

it was only directed at their mothers. Male subjects identified the father and mother with equal frequency as objects of their fury.

Unlike younger children, the college-age subjects tended to accept their parents' divorce. Only 15% thought their parents should have stayed together. Nonetheless, their acceptance and understanding of the reasons for the divorce did not seem to be sufficient to insulate them from the disrupting effects of the marital dissolution. The researchers found their interviews with subjects to be very intense and highly emotional; many tears were shed during them. This is borne out in our experiences leading workshops in divorce—the atmosphere whenever some of the participants are divorced or children of divorce, even though they come as professionals for training in divorce therapy, is "heavy" and emotionally charged since few of them have completed the grieving process and been able to "let go" of the anger and disappointment.

In general, the adult children of divorce have found support networks among their siblings, friends, and dating partners. Because of the increased number of children of divorce in recent years, they can find more peers who have experienced family dissolution and who can be genuinely sympathetic.

Although most of the college counseling directors cited above agreed that counseling would be profitable for students confronted with a parental divorce, it is interesting to note that "only 7.2% of the Directors mentioned the availability of any specific support services to students in the midst of this life transition at their education institution (Farber et al., 1983, p. 70). Thus, even if a student sought guidance from a professional knowledgeable about divorce within the institution's counseling service, it is unlikely that one would be found. The student would be obliged to utilize the nonprofessional, peer counseling help that many report having available.

Dating partners and sexual partners are also part of the support network. Students who were children of divorce, as compared with those from intact families and those who had lost a parent by death, have been found to be more likely to engage in premarital sexual intercourse and to be living in a cohabiting relationship (Booth et al., 1984). These researchers hypothesized that such students may be predicating their behavior on that of their parents. At the same time, however, the student subjects reported lack of satisfaction with their (hetero)sexual relationships. This lack of enjoyment may be related to the anticipation of "betrayal of relationships" mentioned earlier by Wallerstein (1984) and Kelly (1981). Nonetheless, these hypotheses must be viewed with caution, as seeking affection to alleviate stress, modeling one's behavior on a parent's behavior (especially if that parent remains single), and having premarital sexual relations are not particularly abnormal phenomena in today's society, nor are they limited to children of divorce.

Some older children of divorce have reported recurrent themes of "increased vulnerability and stress, conflicting loyalties to parents, anger and worries about parents and their future" (Bales, 1984, p. 13). These feelings may be realistic as parents are not always considerate of the impact of their continuing postdivorce conflict on their (grown) children and may attempt to keep them embroiled by using them as confidants. In addition, frequently the family's assets may be divided in ways that negatively affect the children as well as the ex-spouses. Remarriage, for example, causes another restructuring of the binuclear postdivorce family with the addition of new members placing a drain on the family's (limited) monetary resources.

DEPENDENCY AND FAMILY COALITIONS

Tapp et al. (1985) tested eight adult children of divorce—ages 24 to 31, for five hours. The study population was mostly middle-class, well educated and diverse on other demographic variables.

They found that subsequent to the parents' divorce, all adult children (ACs) reported changed relationships with their mothers; 75% described increased positive feelings of closeness, respect, warmth, and compatibility. All cases of positive improvement were related to increased communication, more personal attention, and a mother's improved emotional state. In addition, all reported one parent became more dependent. Most identified the mother; two felt both parents became more dependent. Typically, the dependency took the form of needing additional emotional support. With younger siblings, the dependency became a co-parenting role. The ratio of happy to unhappy feelings about the parental dependency was about equal.

Contrary to the increased independence described in ACs in other studies, Tapp et al. found that AC subjects displayed dependency patterns. Typically, it was on the mother and for financial and problem-solving reasons. The same proportion became more dependent (about half) on the fathers; the reason was strictly financial.

Yet two-thirds of respondents viewed themselves as being as independent of their mothers as they were prior to the divorce. Two-thirds became more father-independent; they cited as reasons coming-of-age and extension of the independence process begun before the divorce. Since Tapp et al.'s sample was quite small, their findings must be viewed with caution.

POSTSECONDARY EDUCATION COSTS

Like custody and visitation, the issues of property and other asset distribution, as well as child support—including college tuition and expenses—are fertile background for continuing skirmishes. This issue is examined now from the point of view of the college-age young adult child of divorce. If who is to cover college costs, how, and in what amounts have not been explicated in a written agreement (usually incorporated in the divorce decree), uncertainty about verbal promises being fulfilled may interfere with the child's ability to plan for higher education and to have confidence in it being supported. The shift in the age of majority from 21 to 18 years of age in the 1970s led to:

> great diversity in the ways in which legislatures and courts have attempted to cope with the continuing need for college support. Some states have steadfastly maintained the age eighteen limitation on the assumed obligation to provide college support. Others have attempted to bring the age of limitation into agreement with the reality that college is attended, [usually] between ages eighteen and twenty-two. The strongest trend, however, has been towards implementing the doctrines of extended dependency or deferred emancipation. (Smith, 1985, p. 618)

The first instance of a court declaring that a noncustodial parent was responsible for a child's college education was *Esteb v. Esteb* in the state of Washington in 1926 (Smith, 1985). By 1983, at least 14 states required that children of divorce be supported for a college education through age 21 and possibly longer. These states include: Colorado, Indiana, Missouri, New York, Iowa, Alaska, Mississippi, California, New Hampshire, Illinois, Washington, New Jersey, and Pennsylania (Smith, 1985). (Note: Alaska's Supreme Court in 1984 overruled an earlier decision and held that a child support order does not have to provide for postmajority support ["Child Support," 1984].)

The rationale underlying this policy is that lack of a college education in today's world handicaps the child in gaining entrance to the career world at an appropriate level. The courts do not uniformly mandate that a noncustodial parent finance a child's postsecondary education; however, the parent's ability to pay and the child's ability to profit from higher education are usually considered. Presumably, if support for college is specified in the agreement, payment is enforceable by the court. Unfortunately, in actuality, sometimes payment is not forthcoming as promised and some courts are hesitant to intervene. And college costs have skyrocketed to such an extent that not all parents can fulfill the guarantees they made a decade or more earlier, despite even the best of intentions.

Adult children of divorce may feel in financial limbo, with their primary residence and loyalty often being with the less affluent parent and their financial dependency resting on the more unpredictable but financially more solvent parent, who resides elsewhere. Therefore, their anxiety may have a rational basis. To derive sufficient funding for college from the nonresident parent, some young adults become persuasive and skilled manipulators or demanding whiners. Similar problems may beset young adults not in college, but who need financial support for their career plans or housing. Conversely, some parents may use the promise of support as a contingent "weapon" to induce their offspring to behave in ways that the parent desires.

OLDER CHILDREN OF DIVORCE: A DESCRIPTIVE STUDY

As indicated earlier, in 1984–85, we (Kaslow and Schwartz, in press) undertook an exploratory study of once-divorced, unremarried adults and of their children of divorce. The questionnaires used were designed specifically for this study (see Appendices). With all subjects, the underlying purpose of the study was to examine the differential impact of the separation/divorce on individuals of varying ages and therefore at different points in their life cycles. There were questions to be answered about gender differences, custodial and noncustodial parent, effects of divorce on school or job performance, feelings at the time of separation and at the time of response, number of siblings and respondent's place in the sequence of children, whether the respondent was consulted about residence and visitation, age and grade level at separation and at time of response, relations with peers/teachers/clients/colleagues at both times, relations with family members at both times, sources of emotional support at separation, and preseparation activities with either or both parents (aid with homework, escort to doctor/dentist/music or art lessons/athletic activities/visits to friends). Possible sources of support were listed (e.g., each parent, maternal grandparents, paternal grandparents, siblings, friends, school counselor) and respondents were to respond with a "yes," "no," or "not applicable." Respondents were also asked whether they planned to marry at some time in the future, whether the parental separation affected their thinking about marriage, and if so, in what ways. Finally, they were asked to add any comments they cared to make about the effects of the separation/divorce on them.

The focus in this portion of the chapter is on those subjects in a single-group, volunteer sample who were aged 11 and older at the time of response. As noted previously, about 1 in 9 divorces occur after 10 years of marriage, with the children in such marriages presumably in or graduating from high school.

Methodology

Questionnaires were sent to 85 adolescents and young adult children of divorce, whom we grouped together as the "Older Kids" subsample. This potential sample was drawn from children of the divorced adult sample in our larger survey, made up from author Kaslow's clinical practice in Florida, from author Schwartz's college campus population in Pennsylvania, from divorced adults both researchers knew personally, and from networking contacts recommended by study participants. Responses were received from 32 young people, or 37.7% of the potential sample. This response rate is consistent with most other questionnaire surveys done by mail. Each questionnaire was sent with an explanation of the study, a consent form, and a prestamped return envelope. One follow-up mailing was sent to nonrespondents approximately one month after the response deadline had passed. (These forms, alluded to earlier, appear in the Appendices.)

Data furnished by the respondents were analyzed using standard descriptive statistics techniques. Most of the questions asked were scored on a 1–5 basis, with 1 = Very True to 5 = Very Untrue, but in some cases, where an item was not applicable (NA) or where no response (NR) was given, the item was scored as a "6," which raised the mean slightly when it occurred. The raw data are available elsewhere (Kaslow & Schwartz, in press).

Sample

All respondents were American born and Caucasian, with half being male and half female. Although the 32 respondents lived in 17 different states, the size and nature of the sample limits the generalizability of the findings. The size of the subsample of those who were age 11 years or older at the time of the family breakup was 21.

Table 17 gives the background of the full group of older respondents in terms of gender, age, and custody variables, while Figure 5 shows the distribution of the subgroup in age at the time of response.

Approximately one-third of our subsample of 21 subjects had been age 13–16 years at the time of the parental separation. Of the remainder, 28.6% were aged 17–18 years when their parents separated, and 8 were no longer minors at this point. Thus the median age of 17.67 years appears to be a more valid "average" age for the "Older Kids" subsample than the mean of 19.33 years. At the time of responding, 13 of the 21

Table 17
Gender, Age at Separation, Age Now,
Custodial Parent, and Consultation on
Custody for Older Children of Divorce (N = 32)

Gender		At Parental Separation	Now
Male	16		
Female	16		
Age		At Parental Separation	Now
Mean		14.09	21.47
Median		16.10	20.50
Range		1–32	11–40
Custodial Parent			
Father	0		
Mother	22		
Joint	3		
NA/No response	7		
Consulted on Custody/Residence			
Yes	9		
No	18		
NA/No response	5		

respondents were of secondary or college age (13–21 years), with the remainder aged 22 years or older (Figure 5). The age range of all "Older Kids" respondents (N = 32) at the time of response was 11–40 years. For the subsample, the lapse in time between the time of separation and the time of response ranged from less than 1 year to 10 years, with the greatest frequency occurring in the 1–3 year range.

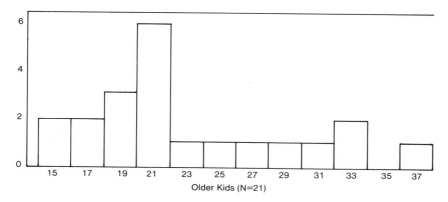

Figure 5. Age of subsample respondents at time of response.

Although 12 of 21 respondents indicated that their mother was the custodial parent, it is obvious from the distribution of ages at the time of separation that some interpreted the question to ask, With whom did they live. Other respondents indicated that "custody" was not applicable to them because of their age. No fathers were cited as the custodial parent. Only 9 of the respondents knew or recalled that they were consulted about which parent should have custody or with whom they would live. Again, in some cases, the question was irrelevant because of age, while in others the young adult simply continued to live in the familial home with the mother. Twelve subjects, however, said that they had been consulted about visitation schedules.

RESULTS AND DISCUSSION

Respondents' Feelings

As can be seen in Table 18, the older children of divorce showed a wide range of answers to questions about their feelings at the time of separation as well as when responding. On the "negative" side, there was still more anger than depression over the divorce, but feelings of hurt had abated about as much as had feelings of depression. Feelings of rejection did not change much over the years following the parental separation, but this may be because the subjects were old enough at the time of separation to recognize that the problem of the divorce was

Table 18
Comparison of Strength of Feelings
at Parental Separation and Now of
Older Children of Divorce (N = 21)

Feeling	At Separation[a]	Now[a]
Angry	2.619	3.328
Competent	2.286	2.190
Depressed	2.667	3.619
Happy	3.571	2.286
Hurt	2.429	3.333
Rejected	3.524	3.905
Total change score		24.476

Note. Scale runs from 1 = Very True to 5 = Very Untrue.
[a] Numbers represent mean scores.

primarily their parents' and had little to do with the parent-child relationship.

On the "positive" side, the older children of divorce reported feeling slightly more competent when responding and somewhat happier than previously, although feelings of happiness were not very strong. The fact that most of the subjects were in their teens or older at the time of separation may also explain why they tended to be "happy" rather than "very happy." They were well aware of why the separation and divorce occurred, yet years later they may still have seen themselves pulled apart emotionally by the divided family situation even though they were functioning well in other realms. (This echoes Wallerstein's [1985a] findings cited earlier.) This feeling of being torn in half may resurface around a college graduation celebration, wedding plans, or birth of a child when both parents should ordinarily be present at the same event.

There is also a carry-over at a statistically significant level of the relationships among feelings at separation and at the time of response. For example, feelings of being happy (or unhappy) at the time of separation are significantly related to feelings of depression in the present $(r = -.527, p < .001)$, feelings of depression at separation are related to feelings of "hurt" now $(r = .469, p < .05)$ and feelings of being rejected now $(r = .585, p < .001)$. In general, it may be said of this sample that the feelings at the time of separation have been relatively persistent over time, though perhaps at a modified and now reduced level. The mean Total Change Score of 24.476, computed from changes in ratings of feelings from one period to the other, suggests that the respondents' feelings have moved in a positive direction over time since the separation.

We were curious to see to what extent the responses of the subsample of "Older Kids" resembled the responses of their age-peers who had been age 10 years or younger at the time of separation, and also the responses of our "Babes" subsample—children who were age 10 or younger at the time of response and for whom a parent completed a questionnaire. The range of scores and means were derived for each of these groups and are shown in Table 19. In terms of total change over time, the subsample of adolescent and young adult children of divorce obviously changed more in a healthy direction than either of the other samples.

When comparing the three groups, it should be remembered that the subsample of "Older Kids," who were 10 years old and younger at the time of separation, were recalling events and feelings from a distance of several years. Similarly, interpretation of the validity of parental responses on behalf of the "Babes" must be cautious as the parents may have unintentionally distorted or inaccurately recalled their perception of their child's feelings.

Table 19

Mean Scores of Children of Divorce on Feelings
at Time of Separation, by Age at Time of Separation

	"Babes" 10 years and under	"Older Kids" 10 years and under	"Older Kids" 11–32 years
	N = 10	N = 11	N = 21
Males	4	7	9
Females	6	4	12
Age at separation	3.900	4.636	19.333
Age at response	6.400	19.273	22.619
Angry at separation	3.700	3.636	2.619
Competent at separation	1.800	4.364	2.286
Depressed at separation	4.100	4.273	2.667
Happy at separation	2.500	4.727	3.571
Rejected at separation	3.800	4.555	3.524
Strong at separation	1.800	4.545	2.857
Hurt at separation	3.300	3.909	2.429
Total change to present	7.700	11.636	24.276

Views of Responsibility

Among both our adolescent and young adult subjects, it appeared that there had been substantial maturation in the years since their parents had parted. Many of them felt that they had assumed more household and family caretaking responsibilities earlier in their lives than they would have assumed had the divorce not occurred. They tended also to have a less romantic, more serious view of marriage than they might have had in the preseparation stage, with many of our subjects indicating that their thoughts about marriage had changed as a response to their parents' divorce.

Although these respondents may still have some regrets at the family's breakup, they have taken a realistic view of the situation. They expressed few, if any, of the hopes and illusions of a parental reconciliation that much younger children of divorce have. Rather than dwelling in the past and regretting the loss of family activities, again as younger children of divorce are wont to do, most of the adolescent and young adult subjects seemed to be facing their own futures and planning ahead.

Comments on Residence, Visitation, and Holidays

Since our subjects were preadolescent or older at the time of the parental separation, one might expect that they would have been consulted about visitation schedules with the nonresidential parent. What we found was that *if* they were consulted about living arrangements, they were also likely to have been consulted about visitation. However, from the subjects' responses, it became apparent that such discussions were not common practice. Consultation about residence was inversely related to age at separation ($r = .710$, $p < .001$), which was not surprising, and to gender ($r = -.432$, $p < .05$), with girls consulted less frequently. Consultation about visitation schedules was also inversely related to age at separation ($r = -.740$, $p < .001$). Since these children of divorce were at an age when peer and extracurricular activities were assuming greater importance in their lives, several respondents indicated that they were still resentful of the fact that they were not given some voice in these matters (and some control over what was happening to them).

Furthermore, for individuals who are chronologically now late adolescents or young adults, and therefore legally no longer "minors," the absence of custody contests does not mean that there are no loyalty dilemmas. Even if the parents reside in the same community, with whom do they spend a holiday? Do they rotate having Thanksgiving dinner at one parent's home and dessert at the other's in alternate years? If the parents live at a distance from each other, how many days of a college vacation are to be spent with each parent, and to which home do they go first? Although we have no quantitative data on this problem, one of our subjects, a young man of 28, commented, for example, "When my parents split a year ago, I thought it would have no effect on me. Was I ever wrong!" A young woman of 20 felt she had no roots after her parents' separation during her second year of college. One parent was in Florida, the other was in New Jersey preparing to remarry, and she wandered between them during her vacations from college feeling as if her only "true" home was at her college dormitory.

Hagestad and her colleagues (Bales, 1984, p. 13) came up with findings very similar to ours regarding college students' attitudes to vacations and holidays. They report that many students indicate that these are a "nightmare" for them and poignantly quoted one student as telling her parents "I'm spending Thanksgiving at McDonald's . . . Then you'll both miss me." Having to shuttle back and forth between two households, and maybe more if grandparents are counted in, means that holidays are rarely relaxing and refreshing; rather they are heavy with travel and tension surrounding how to divide the time available fairly and how not to play into the residual parental conflicts.

The following brief case summary illuminates and illustrates this dilemma:

Rachel came into treatment with me (FK) during the summer of her freshman year in college (1982). Her parents had been divorced in

1980 and her father, who remarried a much younger woman several months after the divorce was final, had continued to live in Florida. They had been, and continued to be, a prominent family in the community—best known for their generosity to various philanthropies. The scandal surrounding the divorce and subsequent, rapid remarriage had been very distressing to Rachel.

Her mother had moved to Manhattan—where she had some friends and where she could detach from the notoriety of her ex-husband's exploits. Her parents lived in suburban Connecticut so she could be close enough to them for some support and far away enough not to become too enmeshed. The paternal grandparents lived about 1 1/2 hours south of the Palm Beach residence of Rachel's father.

This attractive, bright, and sensitive young woman had chosen to go to college in Boston—thus establishing some distance from everyone and shielding herself from the limelight of her well-known family's activities and from some of their ongoing conflicts and turbulence. She was able to commute into New York or Connecticut on occasional weekends to see her Mom and her maternal grandparents. She spent many holidays enjoying the beautiful weather in Florida with her Dad—often much to her Mom's chagrin. She did not wish to offend anyone, yet she wanted to maintain a sense of her own identity and ability to make decisions that were good for her as well as pleasing to everyone else. She often indicated it felt like everyone wanted to carve her up and that she wanted to keep herself in one piece.

One decision which she made in therapy was to apply to spend her junior year abroad, in Israel, a place she had long wanted to visit and be part of. This she was able to expedite and it gave her a much needed breather from the family's ongoing internecine warfare. She returned home in fall of 1984, after a wonderful year abroad, and came in to see me before returning to Boston for her senior year. She had had time in Israel to come into her own and establish her own set of values and a solid core identity minus constant static from her parents and grandparents. She felt much more able to compartmentalize her relationship with each parent and to allocate her own time priorities for holidays and vacations.

Unfortunately, not all children of divorce are as basically healthy, bright and resilient as Rachel.

Yet another example of the concerns of college-age and young adult children reflected in our study is seen in the case of the children of a woman, newly separated, who asked her two questions that exemplified their anxieties: 1) "Are you going to take back your maiden name?" and 2) "Are you going to sell our house?" If she responded "yes" to the first question, this would imply partial rejection of them since they shared the family name with the now absent father. The second question reflected their need, even though no longer residents of the home in which they had spent their childhood, for stability in this period of change.

Support Networks

Support networks for the older children of divorce were strongest with friends and siblings, although if the mother was able to be supportive at the time of separation, there was a strong probability that the father was also ($r = .611$, $p < .001$). Maternal and paternal relatives were generally reported to be supportive at separation if they lived close enough, but in the case of both older and younger children of divorce, grandparents and other relatives often lived at a distance. For the younger children, paternal grandparents were less likely to be of assistance than maternal grandparents, but this appears to be related to the fact that most of the younger children were in the custody of their mothers (even where there was nominal joint custody), and they did not foster visitation. Although the question was not asked directly, some of the subjects volunteered in writing, or in conversation, comments that a neighbor or a friend of one or both parents had also been a source of support to the youth immediately after the separation and since then.

Only six of the older children reported having had support from a school counselor, four from a psychotherapist, and one from group therapy. This is reflected in the negative correlation between therapeutic support and classroom behavior and relationships with relatives and friends, all at statistically significant levels.

General Comments

At the end of the questionnaire, subjects were invited to add any comments they cared to about the effects of the parental divorce on themselves. Some indicated that the separation/divorce came as a welcome relief from parental quarreling and dissension through the years. One of our 19-year-old respondents, whose parents had separated a year earlier, just after her graduation from high school, commented that for her "it was one of the worst and best things that ever happened in my family life. Thank God, it's over. No more 'real' fighting . . . just inner jealousies and such." Another female subject, aged 18 at the time of separation, wrote: "I felt from the start that my parents' separation/divorce was a good thing—a lot of tension left the house with my dad. I wish for my mom's sake that they could have worked it out, but my dad couldn't (and can't) handle closeness. It's been difficult seeing my mom upset (same for my dad), but I've gotten to know both of them better because of their separation."

Some of the subjects gave verbal comments when seen by one of the authors. They often expressed relief that a difficult situation had been resolved, even though the resolution might bring with it new and different problems. For example, one young man said that he was relieved that his father's extramarital relationships were now known to his mother as this secret had been a heavy burden for him to carry in the prior two or three years in which he'd been aware of it.

Still other subjects indicated that they had been and were still involved enough with their own lives that the family dissolution had had little direct impact on them in an emotional sense. These tended to be subjects who were already married or who had been living away from the family home for several years. They did, however, express sympathy for the parents, especially if one had been more hurt by the divorce than the other, which is often the case.

Although no questions were asked about parental remarriages and the subject's relationship with the parent's new spouse or his/her children, some of the subjects did make comments about such relationships. These reflected considerable variation depending on whether the stepparent was perceived as having been instrumental in causing the divorce, how long the parent had been remarried, whether the respondent lived with the remarried parent and new spouse, and age of the respondent at the time of the remarriage. Few of the older respondents, incidentally, viewed the new spouse as his/her "stepparent." Usually the individual was referred to as the parent's husband/wife, suggesting that the respondent was keeping that person at emotional arm's length, that perhaps they did not get together often, and/or they saw them more as a peer than a parent. (None of our adult respondents were remarried, but some of their former spouses, who were part of our study population, were.)

CONCLUSION

In this exploratory and descriptive study, children of divorce ages 11 to 40 years at the time of the family's dissolution were questioned about their feelings at the time of separation and the time of response, about support networks, and about their feelings toward their own potential marriage. No control group of age-peers from intact families was studied as the goal of the survey was to examine a group of young people who have been largely neglected in divorce research and to illuminate areas for further study.

The subsample, aged 14–40 at the time of response ($\bar{X} = 22.6$ years), were all aged 11 years or older at the time of parental separation. They responded to our questionnaire several months to about 10 years after the separation. Their feelings of earlier anger, hurt, and depression had abated to some extent in the intervening period, and they reported feeling somewhat happier and more competent than at the time of separation. As compared with two other subsamples of children who had been younger than 11 at separation, the adolescents and young adults had moved more into a healthier emotional state, even though their original feelings persisted at a modified level. These older children of divorce found siblings and friends to be of greatest emotional support at the time of separation, although parents, grandparents, adult friends of the family, and school counselors and/or psychotherapists also provided aid and comfort in the period of crisis and transition. Most of these older subjects were trying to plan their own futures and, while they had concluded that marriage was part of that future, tended to regard marriage as a state to be approached with caution and serious deliberation.

In postdivorce matters that affected them, the subjects had no illusions that the family would be reunited, and in some cases indicated relief that they would no longer have to live with parental conflicts. They were rarely consulted about custody or visitation schedules, an omission that they still resented. Even where the respondents were legally adults, they found themselves often beset by loyalty dilemmas and financial anxieties, especially with regard to college tuition.

Our subjects' responses indicate a wide variety of reactions to the family crisis, varying with the subjects' age at the time. For those of college age or older, their own involvement with college, work, and/or marriage reduced the direct emotional impact of the separation and divorce. Some of the late adolescents and young adults reported difficulty in the ability to risk making a commitment to a permanent love relationship, ostensibly because they did not want to live through a second divorce—their own. The lack of a clear pattern of response to separation and divorce may reflect the wide age range and differences in personality and coping skills of the respondents, variation in the amount and nature of interaction with both parents, and the ongoing and/or current level of tension between their parents. Further, since this was a voluntary sample, consideration must be given to the possibility that some of those to whom questionnaires were sent and who chose not to respond would have given responses that might have altered our data sharply in one direction or the other. However, the study does suggest that not all older children of divorce were affected negatively by the family dissolution and, indeed, that some were relieved by it. The responses also indicated the more cognitive approach to understanding the reasons for the divorce that this older group had as compared with samples of younger children of divorce.

Clearly, more research is needed about this age group if we are to understand their needs and reactions better so as to improve the empirical base for therapeutic intervention when older children of divorce present for treatment (if it is still an issue for them)—alone, with members of their family of origin, with a potential future spouse, or with their family of procreation. A larger sample, with perhaps less opportunity to refuse responding, might be obtained with the cooperation of family courts in a number of communities. In every instance where a suit for divorce is filed and where the family includes adolescent or young adult children, these young people might be asked to complete a questionnaire exploring their feelings at separation, effects on their school or job performance, support figures, anxieties about the future, and attitudes toward their own possible marriage. Ideally, a follow-up study, three to five years later, could use the same questions to ascertain modifications of these responses over time.

CHAPTER 10

Variable Consequences of Divorce

Although the principal focus of this chapter continues to be on children of divorce and arrangements for their custody, it is appropriate to comment briefly on how the presence or absence of children affects the divorcing parties. Among childless couples, particularly those married for a short while, if the parties never see or hear of each other again, it may be of little importance to them or anyone else. Some may still suffer a sense of shock over the demise of their union and the loss of a partner, but the daily reminders are far fewer when there are no children. Marriages with children, the more frequently seen situation, of course, have consequences of quite a different sort. In this case, lack of contact between the ex-spouses has more serious, more durable, and more wide-ranging effects. These effects permeate not only the lives of the divorcing adults, but, more crucially, the lives of their children as well.

CHILDLESS MARRIAGES

Married couples who have no children are variously pitied, chided, or envied by other people. They may be pitied because they miss the joys of procreation and of helping the next generation grow to maturity, or because they will miss having the comforts allegedly provided by children in later years. Family members, especially would-be grandparents, may berate them for being selfish by not sharing their lives with children or for putting their careers and/or pleasures before parenthood. In yet other instances, the childless couple may be envied, at least some of the time, for their personal freedom which is unhampered by the responsibilities and costs of parenthood.

When divorce occurs in a childless marriage, however, there is often a sigh of relief that at least there are no children to be wounded by the separation. This is especially true if the marriage has been relatively brief. Each of the partners can build a new life without regard to the other, in the same community or in a new locale. They need never have contact, although in some cases the rejected spouse, if the initial move for separation was one-sided, may continue to phone or try to see the ex-mate in hopes of a reconciliation or out of a desire to avenge the "insult" of the divorce.

Of the 22 childless divorced subjects in the Kaslow and Schwartz (in press) study, 9 reported having no contact with the ex-spouse, 10 had limited contact (usually over property matters), and 3 had contact on two or three bases (property matters, expressions of feelings, and/or friendship). Slightly more than half of these subjects had been married five years or less at the time of separation (6 of them were married two years or less). Some found that they could remain friends if not mates; but the majority of comments by these subjects were focused on the pain of divorce, the subsequent loneliness, and fear about future commitments. Comments of those who had been married six or more years, including 1 older respondent who had been married 36 years, were similar. Interestingly, not one of the 22 childless subjects indicated any feelings about their lack of children. They expressed neither regret nor relief that theirs had been a childless marriage.

Our data, shown earlier in Table 11 (see p. 91), do suggest that suicidal thoughts occurred more frequently among the childless than among divorced parents, but the childless also had a slightly better "Total Quality of Life Now" score as compared with same-sexed subjects who had children. Finances appeared to be less of a problem for the childless divorced, which is hardly surprising since no child support payments are involved in such divorces and there is a higher likelihood that the wife has been working and can more easily be self-supporting.

On the whole, as compared with divorces where there were children, there were fewer complications for the childless, but not necessarily less pain. Often relationships with the ex-spouse's family were lost along with the marriage, and there was also loss of their shared history and experiences. On the other hand, since most childless divorced adults are in their 20s or 30s at the time of divorce and unencumbered, they may have a somewhat easier time of rebuilding their lives and perhaps remarrying than do the slightly older group of divorced parents who must consider not only their own preferences, but in what ways new relationships will affect their children.

MARRIAGES WITH CHILDREN

The impact of divorce on individuals, as noted earlier, varies with chronological age, length of marriage, gender, circumstances preceding the separation, and presence or absence of children. Where there are children, the impact will vary further with the number and ages of the children, who has custody, how the children react to the divorce and the custody arrangements, and financial settlement or support agreements.

Preschool and Latency-Age Children

Whether the child is in the sole custody of one parent or travels between the parents in some form of joint custody arrangement, the young child has needs that impose obligations on the parent(s) that differ from those of older children. Clearly, the first consideration is the physical care of the infant or young child if the parent is at work or even out for a few hours of errands, volunteer activities or social life. Although dual-career couples are similarly confronted with child-care needs, in an emergency at least one of them is usually able to be at home with the child. Where there is only one parent available, a child's illness or the closing of a daycare facility may be catastrophic for that parent. Baby-sitters must be hired if the custodial parent wants to go anywhere without the child (and if extended family members or neighbors are not available, which is often the case). Thus, the primary caretaking responsibility brings with it an economic aspect that may represent a real hardship for the parent.

Infants and preschoolers generally function best when there is a consistent, predictable though not necessarily rigid, pattern of life. Stability of environment and familiarity of people around them are important to both the development of the child's interpersonal attachments (bonding and object constancy) and his or her growth in learning. The inexplicable disappearance of one parent, for such young children, raises fears of abandonment by the remaining parent. Routine tends to mitigate that fear. Since these small ones have little comprehension of time, reassurance is also needed that the custodial parent will reappear regularly—at an appointed time, such as after "nap-time," or in time for dinner, for example—if the child is left with a caretaker. Even in a relatively harmonious co-parenting arrangement, the moves from one parent's home to the other's may mean painful repeated partings from a loved and loving adult. The cries accompanying these shifts do not necessarily imply unwillingness to go to the receiving parent, but rather reflect the child's distress at leaving the other parent. If the primary custodial or residential parent employs a specific au pair (nanny/housekeeper), or baby-sitter to whom the child is attached, sometimes arrangements can be made for said person to rotate back and forth with the child to the other parents, thereby providing security, continuity and a positive link between households.

We believe that developmental and personality needs of the child are paramount and that the custody/visitation plan should have a built-in clause for periodic reconsideration of it that coincides with developmental milestones and family life cycle major events. When this is done, the need for change can be anticipated rationally and not happen chaotically when a crisis erupts and one parent frantically calls the other to say "I can't handle Johnny anymore, so you can come and get him and keep him for a few years." Nonetheless, the importance of continuity and predictability must be balanced with responding to changing developmental needs and the parents' differing abilities to be nurturing, responsive and/or limit setting.

Latency-age children can recall how the family "used to be," and are more aware than tots and toddlers of the conflicts that preceded the divorce and those that continue afterwards. They need to be given consistent affection and attention by both parents to maintain their budding self-esteem and to relieve their feelings of grief, (presumed) guilt, and divided loyalty. They also may need periodic interpretation of what is happening around them and expected from them. Although they don't need as much direct physical care as the younger child does, they do still need supervision during nonschool hours, particularly if they are at the lower end of this age range. At the same time, even though the school-age child may assume some new responsibilities in the home, and even take pride in doing these tasks, the child should not be pushed into premature adolescence or into a role reversal where the child becomes "parent" or confidant to the mother or father, nor should he or she be thrust into the growing multitude of "latch key" children. If parents are not home after school, arrangements should be made for either a day care program or a sitter to provide responsible and tender care and supervision.

Among both preschoolers and younger elementary school children, a dominant desire is for the parents to reunite so that the family can be "whole" again. Some children deny the separation and replace it with a fantasy that has the absent parent away on a trip from which he or she will soon return. This fantasy may persist even in the face of dating or remarriage by one or both parents. With the child's talent for magical thinking, the unwanted intruder is simply "wished away" and may be ignored or treated rudely—because the child projects the blame onto this new person for the breakup of the original family—even though he/she may have come into the picture after the legal divorce was final. If the parent's new partner had entered the picture prior to the separation and the child was aware of him or her as an actor in the family drama, the "intruder" label may stick and this person may never be accepted or forgiven, even long after he/she moves into the stepparent role. It is often extremely difficult, if not impossible, for a child to accept a parent's transgression of the ethical/existential and moral ties that bind a family in mutual loyalty. Since it may be untenable to blame one's parent for violation of the family's code of reciprocal integrity, the "intruder" is the recipient of the hostility and blame.

Young adolescents may also feel threatened by the possibility of a new relationship between either parent and another person and create difficulties for the parent reminiscent of the fuss aroused by a 10-month-old suffering from separation anxiety. This may be especially true if the child has become particularly attached to the parent postseparation and perceives another severe wrenching apart and loss.

It is unwise for a dating parent to expose the child(ren) to a succession of "live-in" partners or even to many casual "dates" because of a contrary danger that the child may become attached to the parent's new friends with recurrent grief and anger when those individuals and the parent separate. This simply reawakens the fears of abandonment, rejection, or feelings of being unworthy of an adult's love. If this happens repeatedly, a child may decide not to again become invested in what may prove to be another short-lived relationship. Nonetheless, a parent should also evaluate a date's ability to relate positively to the child if it seems that the friendship is progressing toward a more permanent commitment. In short, the dating parent has to balance his/her psychosocial (and sexual) needs for companionship and affection with the feelings and anxieties of the child(ren) around such relationships and carefully consider how much of their dating should remain personal and private and how much can be shared with children without their becoming vulnerable to sequential losses or too much sexual stimulation in the atmosphere. Far from being free to act on impulse in social or emotional relationships or to have cohabiting relationships, divorced parents experience restrictions and constraints that the childless adult does not have and must seriously consider the impact of their decisions and behavior on their children.

Contact between the parents, unless there is sole legal and physical custody, and one's parental rights are terminated, continues whether or not it is wanted. Progress or problems in school are the business of both parents. Religious instruction and rites are appropriately the concern of both parents. Parental guidelines for the child's activities need to be agreed upon both for the peace of mind of the child and to reduce the possibility of the child playing one parent against the other. If two sets of standards prevail in the two households, the children will need help to shift back and forth without antagonizing either parent, to integrate the validity of the differential expectations and to not feel confused and fragmented by the differences. Other aspects of custody arrangements and their ramifications will be discussed later in this chapter.

Preteens and Adolescents

Although puberty-age children and adolescents may not need as close supervision as younger children, the realities of modern life do dictate a need for some caretaking arrangements for youngsters in this age category. Certainly young teenagers should not be left alone overnight or over a weekend while the parent is away from home. No matter how mature they may seem or how convenient it may be for a parent to do this, it is far better in most situations if they stay at a friend's or relative's home or have someone come and stay with them. The latter may work well for older teenagers who are reliable, self-sufficient, and capable. It is of course important to remember that, legally, parental responsibility for minor children continues until they reach age 18. Again, this means that the parents are likely to have continuing communication with each other as decisions or plans need to be made or when crises arise.

Whether or not the parent is conscientious in his/her efforts to raise law-abiding children, if the minor adolescent gets into trouble over drugs, shoplifting, truancy, arson, or vandalism, evidence of lack of appropriate supervision or outright neglect can be lodged against the parent. This may lead to a modification of the custody arrangements or more severe consequences. As important as a good same-sex role model may be for a latency-age child, it is probably even more essential for the young adolescents who, while seeking to define and integrate their own identity (Erikson, 1963), are subject to increasing peer pressures in their activities. The primary residential parent may carry more weight as the main model for adult behavior than might be the case in an intact marriage and the portrayal he or she gives may be generalized to all men or all women. Obviously, some of the need for a same-sex role model can be fulfilled by other close and important adults *if* they are in the picture—like grandparents, aunts and uncles, teachers, scout leaders or little league coaches, a friend's parents, etc. Sex of child and sex of parent are only one factor to consider; many others, particularly emotional accessibility and stability, and the ability to share the child with the nonresidential parent with minimal animosity, are probably more crucial concerns.

Where younger children may look forward to visits with the "other parent," adolescents may view stipulated visitation schedules as intrusions on their expanding personal or social life. If pressed to adhere to the schedule, by either parent, they may rebel. Since adolescents are also aware that there is no hope of reuniting the family, they may use rebellion in this sphere or in other aspects of daily life to manipulate the parents' behavior toward them and to assert their increasing sense of self, individuation and independence. If family life was filled with conflict prior to the divorce, the adolescent may welcome the new absence of tension in the home. As a few of our adolescent subjects commented, they now feel (postdivorce) that they have a better opportunity to know each parent as an individual and to be respected by each in their own search for identity, meaning and purpose in life.

Adult Children

Even where there are no concerns about baby-sitters, undue negative peer influence, or conflicts about visitation rights and schedules, because the children of a divorced couple are legally adults, the parents still are confronted with the need to be in contact with each other about their children. What should be happy occasions, such as graduations and weddings, or the birth of grandchildren, bring the divorced couple into proximity as they revert to the roles of co-parents. We often read or hear of a child whose wedding plans are being upset because one parent won't attend if the other is to be present, possibly with a lover or new spouse. On less pleasant occasions, such as when a critical illness occurs or in a financial emergency, the parents may need to confer about who will assume some responsibility for helping alleviate the crises. Not all parents are able to work cooperatively, even on behalf of a child. The lack of a united front may not result from malice, but simply from the same incompatible personalities and/or approaches to problem-solving that originally contributed to the demise of their marriage.

The adult child, for his or her part, is confronted with some of the same loyalty dilemmas as younger children, even when he/she no longer lives with either parent. Should he carry family news from one parent to the other? Should she mention having dinner or spending a weekend with one parent to the other, especially if only one parent has remarried? Should an adult son be his mother's escort to social affairs if the alternative is that she won't or cannot attend alone? Should an adult daughter live with her now single father, whether or not she acts as his hostess? How much of a parent's "hurt" or anger should the grown child share? How should the adult child relate to a parent's lover or new spouse?

FREQUENT RESPONSE PATTERNS

Generally, the children have been neither the villains nor the heroes in the marital and divorce conflict; they are its "victims," most often unwillingly. (However, sometimes children do encourage a parent to break away from an untenable situation characterized by spouse and/or child abuse, alcoholism and/or dire poverty. Others are "bad seeds" who do all they can to sabotage their parents' relationship for a variety of reasons they purport are valid.) As one writer stated:

> it is the children who have to adjust to visitation schedules, to moving often to less expensive neighborhoods and schools, to watching a new parental partner take over the place of the child's natural parent. Parents may be much happier on the far side of divorce. But it does not necessarily follow that the children will be, too. (Francke, 1983, p. 57)

The ways in which children perceive and respond to their parents' divorce are numerous, varying not only in accordance with their individual personalities, for children in the same family may react quite differently, but by their ages, gender, availability of emotional support, and also by the amount of pre- and postseparation conflict and the nature of custody-visitation arrangements. Children who were under five years of age at the time of separation tend to have hazy memories of the break, if any at all, when questioned many years later (Wallerstein, 1984). At the time of separation, according to other studies, they tend to blame themselves for the divorce, thinking and saying that if they had behaved better, or been more lovable, the now absent parent might not have left. As they approach school age and the Oedipal/Electra conflict, they may also feel guilty because the wish to be rid of the same-sexed parent has been fulfilled.

Wallerstein (1984), who interviewed her preschool subjects 10 years after the original study when they had reached adolescence, commented that "Considering that these youngsters had spent so few years within the intact family and repressed so much of their early experience, it was interesting to find the persistence of reconciliation fantasies in half the sample" (p. 451). Older elementary school children and adolescents tend to recognize that the divorce is the parents' problem rather than their fault, and that there is little prospect of reuniting the family. In cases where a third party is involved, these children's sense of fairness is violated and the parents' transgression of their marital vows and the family's integrity often leads to anger at the parent who deceived and hurt the other parent and the children. Even this moral position may be modified as time passes, because of such reasons as the desire to see both parents as "good" human beings since part of the child's sense of self-esteem is derived from a belief that they come from "good" parents; the need to resume a relationship with the absent parent because he or she is loved and missed; the desire not to antagonize so as not to be cut off or out financially; and/or the need to identify with the same-sex parent. In one case, for example, and this is fairly common, Mr. J. had the bulk of the economic resources, took the children on trips, and at the same time harshly criticized his former wife (whom he had left for another woman). The teenaged son adopted the father's stance, becoming both verbally and physically abusive to his mother, while his slightly younger sister deplored the situation and supported her mother.

The impact of divorce on school-age children appears to vary by gender as well as age. In a two-year follow-up study of children in Grades 1, 3, and 5, Guidubaldi, Cleminshaw, Perry, Nastasi, and Adams (1984) found that boys tended to adjust less easily than girls both at the time of initial study and two years later, although there had been some reduction related to the sex differences over time. They found significantly greater stability of mental health adjustment over time for girls than for boys, and also better academic adjustment for girls. These findings are corroborated by Hammond (1981), Hodges and Bloom (1984), Emery (1982), and others.

Depending on the circumstances, some children become more mature, more supportive of the resident parent, or better achievers than they might have been had the family remained intact. They recognize the problems that existed prior to separation and the consequences of the divorce in economic as well as emotional terms, and make concerted efforts to contribute to the shrunken family rather than to bemoan the loss of the original family. Differences seen in children according to whether they are only children, are in sole or joint custody situations, and have emotional support networks are among the matters to be explored in the pages to come.

CUSTODY AND RELATED ISSUES

When children are involved in a divorce, there are several matters to be considered. With whom are they to reside? Which of several possible living arrangements is best for the child(ren)? Should the parents share legal and/or physical custody? If one parent has primary physical custody responsibilities, what are reasonable and feasible visitation arrangements for the other parent and for the child(ren)? What amount of child support is equitable for all parties and for how long should it be continued? What privileges do grandparents have in relation to their grandchildren? What provision is to be made for changes in the custody agreement as children's needs change?

Arranging Custody

Parents who decide to dissolve their marriage through adversarial action often prolong the misery of the conflict not only for themselves, but also for their children. The child wonders despondently if there will ever be an end to the fracas; inadvertently he or she may convert the deep anxiety being felt into physical and/or emotional illness. If a psychosomatic illness ensues and the young person realizes, consciously or unconsciously, that when he or she is sick, the parental bickering diminishes and the parents unite in worrying about and caring for him or her, the secondary benefits of the illness may set in and perpetuate the malady. For example:

> Judy was eight when the parental battles became overt. Upset by the screaming and throwing of dishes, she would weep and then start coughing and wheezing. She realized if the wheezing got real bad, her parents would stop yelling and call the doctor. Several times they had to take her to the hospital as she was gasping for breath.
>
> Judy's dad loved her dearly and was worried about leaving his sick daughter so he decided to make another try at salvaging the marriage. Her asthma calmed down as the family grew more peaceful. Two summers later she seemed well enough to go away to overnight camp. Judy believed all was well and that she didn't need to stay home as guardian of her folks' marriage, i.e., she was intuitively willing to be sick if it meant keeping daddy home.
>
> Daddy left while she was away but they did not tell her until she came home. By then dad was beyond the point of no return and although he might come home to help out when Judy had an attack, he was firm in his decision not to reunite and Judy's manipulative behavior no longer served its purpose. (Author FK's case files)

Johnston, Campbell, and Tall (1985) found that, following a prolonged and bitter adversarial divorce, the unhappy situation may continue long after the divorce is granted if the parents cannot come to terms with reality. If child support or alimony payments are in arrears, visitation may be cut off, even in defiance of court orders. While this maneuvering may serve a parent's needs, it is generally destructive to the child's sense of well-being.

As indicated earlier, less time consuming and more peaceful alternatives to adversarial proceedings include arbitration, mediation, and the use of an interdisciplinary committee. There are advantages to these other mechanisms for the parents, in terms of reduction of pain, unpredictability of outcome, costs, and time delays in dissolving the marriage. There are even greater advantages for the children. Mediation, in particular, offers the parents an opportunity to create an agreement regarding child custody, as well as other matters, that reflects a cooperative effort to maintain healthy parent-child relationships rather than to destroy such relationships through fault-finding and attribution of blame. Since the parents will have the responsibility of carrying out the provisions of an agreement, their voluntary compromises in reaching an accord are more likely to ensure its success.

The disservice done to children involved in custody disputes often is the result of differing perceptions of the child custody issue by legal practitioners and mental health specialists. According to Lowery, "for the mental health professional, the evaluation question becomes, 'which parent is a better match for having primary responsibility for raising the child?' . . . the court, on its own, is more likely to ask, 'Which parent is the better adult?'" (1984, p. 379).

The options in child custody are basically sole custody and some form of joint custody. The award of sole custody, that is, both legal and physical custody, to one parent jeopardizes the parent-child relationship with the noncustodial parent. Goldstein, Freud, and Solnit (1973) argued that sole custody, with visitation at the discretion of the custodial parent, minimizes loyalty conflicts and disruptions of routine for the child. They seem to have made light of the following salient facts about the sole custodial parent:

1. He or she may be furious at the former spouse for abandonment and may be retaliating by refusing visitation.
2. He or she may be unable to recognize the other person's worth as a parent and may sabotage visits by being so angry if the child comes home full of junk food, not spic-and-span clean, over-tired, etc., that the child becomes apprehensive about going because of the fear of the scene encountered when he or she comes home happy.
3. He or she may resent the child loving the other parent after what he/she "did to me" and thus make the child feel terribly guilty about and disloyal if they want to be with the noncustodial parent.
4. He or she may fear the child will decide he loves the other parent more and won't want to come home.
5. He or she may not recognize that children need to know both parents will continue to love them and be committed to their well-being.
6. He or she may be too inflexible to work out a new schedule that has continuity and predictability and can include spontaneous phone calls to and planned visits with the other parent.
7. He or she may be domineering and demanding and unable to accord the other parent any rights in their child's life.

Unless one parent is clearly "unfit" because of uncontrollable alcoholism or abusive or incestuous behavior, we have found that sole custody often creates confusion, anxiety and a sense of alienation in the child. Even disturbed parents (may) have a valuable contribution to make to their child's life. If there are concerns about inebriation or abuse, supervised visitation can take place under court or Department of Welfare auspices so that the child does not lose access to the parent; and we incorporate a place in our thinking for the fact that alcoholics do achieve sobriety and some abusers gain control over their behavior through therapy, education, punishment and/or religious experiences.

Nonetheless, if the parent's behavior is objectively evaluated as noxious and detrimental to the child, visitation should be terminated until and unless the behavior changes. It is our opinion that where the desires and the needs of the two parents (to have or withhold visitation) conflict, the needs of the children are paramount and compelling.

Today, joint legal custody and some form of joint physical custody is increasingly the decision in custody cases. Mental health professionals and most lawyers and jurists recognize that divorce may dissolve marital bonds but cannot really sever parents from the children, except under the most dire circumstances. Joint legal custody, regardless of with whom the child actually lives most of the time, means that major decisions on secular and religious education, in health matters except for genuine emergencies, and other matters, must be made by both parents. Day-to-day decisions on routine matters are typically made by the resident parent. Joint legal custody is workable unless the parents are of such diverse opinions or are so hostile to each other that they will not agree on what is best for their child(ren).

Joint physical custody may take three forms: co-parenting, shared but not equal custody, or split custody. Both co-parenting and shared custody demand a cooperative relationship between the parents for optimal effectiveness. In co-parenting, the child usually spends almost equal time with each parent. Possible time arrangements include alternate weeks or months or years with each parent, partial weeks with each parent so arranged that the child moves from one residence to the other approximately every four days, or every two weeks, the child remaining in one place and the parents moving in and out by turns, or some similar schedule. "What is important in co-parenting is that both parents assume a responsibility for meeting a share of all the physical needs, as well as the financial and emotional needs, of their children" (Galper, 1980, p. 16).

The viability of the co-parenting mechanism clearly varies with the age and temperament of the child, apart from any other considerations. For the young child, the constant shifts from one residence to another can be confusing and anxiety-provoking. For school-age children, there may be problems that range from remembering where "home" is on a particular day to leaving needed clothing or assignments at the "wrong" residence. If the child's physical residence is to change frequently, both parents should live in close proximity so that the child can continue to attend one school throughout the year and not have to miss important extracurricular and play activities. This, of course, imposes a strict constraint on the geographical mobility of both parents.

Perhaps one parent has a job opportunity, however, that takes him or her across the country from the other. Equal time may then be figured on an annual basis, with the child(ren) moving from one community to the other each year. This means that the child not only changes domicile annually, but also school attended and friends. A well-adjusted child may be able to do this with relative ease; a child already deeply troubled by the divorce or other aspects of living may well have psychopathological reactions that are functionally disabling. One has only to imagine the disruptive effects of changing school systems every other year, in terms of differential academic expectations and levels of instruction, to fathom what kind of discontinuity in learning this could cause. How can one ever aspire to make a school team, play in the band, hold a class office, etc., if one is only here or there for a year at a time? Good custody plans must consider the consequences of time sharing on the child's maturational and educational processes.

Less geographically confining is shared physical custody, where the child lives primarily with one parent but spends vacations and some evenings and weekends with the other parent. This is a more stable situation for the child, although times spent with the noncustodial parent may be more artificial—in the sense of being a perpetual holiday—than is advisable. In a way, this is unfair to the resident parent who has the primary responsibility and work involved in caring for the child and relatively few of the pleasures. Negative comparisons between the parents that ensue do nothing to rebuild the morale of the custodial parent.

Benefits to the child(ren) of joint custody, legal and/or physical, stem from the maintenance of a continuing, more positive relationship with both parents and the willing acceptance of both adults of their responsibilities. The child then feels neither rejected nor abandoned, as may be the case with sole custody, and has the advantage of close interaction with adults of both sexes.

Although there is psychological literature that suggests that it is better for a child to live with the same-sexed parent (e.g., Santrock & Warshak, 1979), there is little if any support for separating siblings by gender, as is sometimes done in split custody. Not only does this arrangement interfere with the support siblings usually give each other during the pre- and postdivorce periods, but it also raises questions in each child's mind as to why he/she is not living with the other parent. The trauma of losing contact with one or more siblings, added to the impact of losing daily contact with one of the parents, can be devastating to a child and affect his development in very negative ways. Yet, split custody can be advantageous when sibling conflict has been extraordinarily intense and/or if each parent is able to be adequate and competent with one or two children but not with three or more. It does not work well if the rationale is that the children are split like the property—so that each parent has a souvenir or one half of the live marital assets.

Split visitation rights, where the children alternate weekends or vacations in visiting the nonresident parent, can similarly be detrimental to the children. Most children need a stronger sense of togetherness and camaraderie in the sibling subsystem following separation and divorce, not repeated separations from family members. They should be in the same household periodically and be able to maintain frequent, preferably spontaneous, phone contact with one another.

As was mentioned earlier, for several decades, before the "best interests of the child" doctrine became popular in the 1970s, custody awards were typically based on the "tender years" doctrine, with custody awarded to the mother unless she was declared "unfit." Even today, though, except in genuine co-parenting arrangements, in 90% of the cases minor children have their primary physical residence with the mother. What does this do to the father? Unless there is easy access to his children, maternal custody leaves the father feeling lonely, depressed, and distressed at the loss of his children (Hetherington, Cox, & Cox, 1977a). Some fathers, especially those who had previously been close to their children, cannot cope with the repeated separations accompanying their noncustodial, visiting-parent status (Wallerstein & Kelly, 1980). Many fathers develop mental health problems as a result of the loss of their children, even when they have established a new marital relationship. Jacobs concluded that:

> Children deprived of their fathers due to parental divorce may suffer seriously from a wide range of psychopathology. Divorced fathers likewise often suffer from the loss of their children and, like their children, do better following divorce when there is greater continuity of contact. (1984, p. 186)

In those rare cases (figures range from less than 5% of custody agreements to around 10%) where the father is given custody of young children, the fathers report that the arrangement works well for them and the children emotionally. Indeed, in a study of 1,136 volunteer respondents, all single custodial fathers, Greif (1985) found that those who had custody of young children reported having an easier time of it than the fathers who had custody of teenaged children.

Fathers who have sole custody have many of the same problems as mothers with sole custody, and in addition are frequently confronted with role ambiguity and a popular perception of them as being extraordinary people. This means that their needs may not be seen realistically. Understanding their situation involves knowing whether they actively sought custody or merely acquiesced to it because of a variety of circumstances, and whether the mother voluntarily relinquished custody or lost it in court and, if so, why. The six most frequently cited reasons for paternal custody given by Greif's respondents were:

(1) by mutual agreement, (2) because the children picked him, (3) because he offered a more financially and emotionally secure home, (4) because the wife was unable to handle the children, (5) because he won a custody suit, and (6) because his wife deserted the family. (1985, p. 38)

As with single-parent mothers, the single-parent father frequently finds himself overloaded with tasks, from coordinating the household chores to being totally responsible for the child(ren). Fathers may have to make occupational adjustments, such as arranging flexible time schedules and reorienting career goals in order to be at home more. Although mothers have to make these adjustments also, it seems to be more difficult psychologically for men to make the necessary requests of employers. (Greif, 1985). They, like single mothers, have to find satisfactory child-care services for very young children and for the out-of-school hours of older preadolescent children. However, financially this tends to be easier for the fathers as their income is usually significantly greater than that of single mothers.

Depending on their involvement in household responsibilities and child-rearing prior to divorce, as well as when they were married (e.g., early 1960s vs. mid-1970s), the fathers may find some tasks more alien to their experience than others. For example, going to school to confer with a child's teachers may be a new and mutually upsetting experience, with teachers and principals in some locales finding it difficult to deal with fathers rather than mothers. On the other hand, teachers can be very supportive of single fathers, often providing needed information on child development matters (Briggs & Walters, 1985).

Importance of Reevaluation

In the course of normal development, a child's needs and activities change. As the child approaches adolescence, for example, visiting friends and participating in after-school sports become more important. In the child's mind, these activities may take priority over scheduled visits with the noncustodial parent or moves to the joint custodial parent's home. Provision should be made at the time of the final divorce agreement for renegotiation of custodial and visitation arrangements. There may be additional reasons for changes in the existing routine, such as illness of parent or child, religious instruction hours, tutoring or enrichment lessons, that will also necessitate that the parents adjust to the child's changing needs and their own significant changes in circumstances—for instance, debilitating multiple sclerosis, kidney disease, or a paralyzing stroke in a parent.

Reevaluation and renegotiation of custody arrangements are also called for if one or both parents remarry, if one parent has a job opportunity that necessitates a major relocation, or if one parent simply wants to start a new life in another community. In the case of remarriage, an added complexity, varying with the age of the child and other factors, is the degree to which the child is to be integrated into the parent's new family unit. The willingness of the child to be part of the new family, part- or full-time, will also vary with the circumstances of the new relationship (i.e., was it a contributing factor to the divorce or did it evolve after the divorce?).

Although reference is made frequently to "the child," we are well aware that there may have been two, three or more children in the original family. Their relationships as they grow older, their interests, their ability to get along better with one parent than the other, may also dictate changes in the custody arrangements. What must be kept in mind as modifications of the custody agreement are contemplated is how any changes will affect all of the parties, including siblings. Changes should not be made, however, because of a child's machinations of playing off one parent against the other to gain a controlling advantage.

Stacey, now 16, resided with her mother and brother in St. Louis following her parents' divorce when she was 8 years old. Her father described himself to me (FK) in therapy as having been "a good-time Charlie"—not interested in the responsibilities of marriage and fatherhood. Four years later he had moved to Florida, gotten a good job, "grown up a bit"—and married Jeanine, a school counsellor who had never been married before.

The summer Stacey was 13, she and her brother came to visit their dad and stepmother and Stacey thoroughly enjoyed her attractive, vivacious and understanding stepmother and had some good chats and shared activities with her dad. Her mom had also remarried and Stacey disliked her dictatorial, haughty, cold stepfather and having to be her younger brother's primary caretaker (which is a role she had been thrust into). She asked to remain with her dad and Jeanine and they were delighted. Her mom was relieved to finally have one less person to worry about, and consented willingly. Her brother flew back alone—distraught at yet another loss in his inner family circle. Jason is still angry at Stacey, to whom he was extremely attached. Although they spend eight weeks together in the summer (one month at each set of parents) and two weeks at Christmas, he has not forgiven her for her desertion.

Stacey has blossomed with her Dad and Jeanine and is doing well at school and socially. However, a few months ago, she became sexually involved with her boyfriend and to her dismay, her dad and Jeanine reacted vehemently and insisted she break off and commit herself to chastity until age 21. She called her mom, whose reaction was—"I did the same thing at your age and understand—I do hope you're using birth control and enjoying yourself." Stacey began considering returning to Mom's as her more permissive attitude was appealing. Each time Dad or Jeanine "crossed her" by setting limits, she threatened to "go back to my Mom's because she understands and loves me more."

In therapy we've worked toward minimizing Stacey's ability to intimidate through threats. She realizes she prefers remaining with Dad and Jeanine but misses her mom and brother more than she did originally. Since neither set of parents is affluent, Stacey has decided to get a part-time job to earn money toward at least one additional plane trip north each year and Dad and Jeanine are paying for more frequent phone calls.

In this case we are dealing with the *changing needs of six people*, at a minimum. Although the therapeutic goal is the best resolution for all members of this binuclear family system—it may not be possible for Stacey and her brother to each have what's best for them—their needs are not completely consonant. This is one of the sad, inevitable, existential facts that permeate the lives of some postdivorce families. (Here is the kind of situation where use of the Duhl chart [Figure 2, p. 10] can prove illuminating.)

Financial Responsibility

With the rise of "no-fault" divorces, there has been a shift in the way the family's economic resources are divided. In most states, as previously mentioned, the policy is now "equitable distribution" of the couple's assets rather than alimony paid until the payee's remarriage or the payer's death. The primary wage-earner, typically the husband, is responsible for providing "maintenance" and "rehabilitative support" for the ex-spouse for a finite period. (Note: One researcher views "rehabilitative alimony" as an insulting term that "suggests that the homemaker has not been engaged in productive or socially useful work during marriage" [Weitzman, 1985, p. 46].) Assuming that the dependent spouse is the ex-wife, and contingent upon her occupational goals, this support may continue for 3 years or 5 or, at most, 10 years. The payment schedule may even be on a sliding scale, so that payments in the early post-divorce years are higher and then diminish as she is increasingly able to earn an income. Other property is divided by agreement or by court order in line with state statutes.

When there are children involved, however, support payments are usually ordered until the child reaches the age of majority (18 years) or completes a college education. When there is more than one child involved, obviously the payments must be adequate to feed, house, and clothe all of the children. As Mnookin and Kornhauser (1979) wrote:

> Our legal and cultural norms reflect the notion that children should not bear the economic loss, and that, other things being equal, the spouses should bear the loss equally. Because joint consumption implies that the custodial parent and children must essentially share the same standard of living, a dilemma arises: either the children must bear some part of the economic loss, or the noncustodial parent must bear much more of the extra financial burdens imposed by divorce than the custodial spouse. (p. 961)

It is in this dilemma that we see the seeds of poverty that affect so many children of divorce. Until the passage in 1984 of the federal law alluded to earlier that enables employers to withhold delinquent child support funds from an employee's wages, more that 50% of fathers were in arrears on child support payments, some by several years' worth. This has meant, in effect, that the children suffered economically because of their parents' inability to remain married. Although the old alimony laws were, in a sense, punitive for the spouse "at fault," the present laws are punitive for the children inasmuch as even contempt of court citations have proven inadequate to the task of making sure that support payments are made in full and on schedule. Wallerstein (1984) found in her follow-up study that the angriest of the children interviewed "were those who had experienced severe economic deprivation as a result of the father's failure to provide child support that was well within his means" (p. 456). In poorer families, there is not enough to go around and when a support check doesn't come, children may have to go without shoes, food and other essentials. It is hard to love and respect a parent who shirks responsibility or tries to punish the ex-spouse by neglecting the children.

Depending upon what each spouse's resources are, and what plans may have been made in happier days, part of the divorce agreement might include a provision for each parent to contribute to the costs of higher education (equally, or in an equitable share) for their children. Of course, to some extent, the child may be still beset with anxiety about whether one or both parents will withdraw verbally promised support at a later time on some pretext. (Note: This is akin to deciding whether there should be lump sum payments or continuing payments over time [alimony]. If the funds are available for investment, it might be more prudent for the parents to set the money aside in advance in a special account or in zero-coupon bonds so that the funds needed will be available at the appropriate time.)

Despite the award of rehabilitative alimony to an ex-wife, reality may be that the wife must pay so much in child-care costs, which may not be included in child support payments, that she is forced to live in circumstances substantially below her previous standard of living. For any children at home, this means that they, too, suffer as they lose their old home, leave their old neighborhood, and part from their teachers and friends. In instances where the parent does not meet his financial responsibility to his children, it is inadequate and cruel to say to those children, "Tough! Whoever said life was fair?"

It is essential to look at economic factors from the father's viewpoint, too. How much does he *owe* his wife, and for how long, for her contributions to the marriage in terms of services, paid or unpaid, support of his early years in a profession or a job, and affection provided? Obviously the answer to that depends on how long the marriage lasted and the nature of his wife's contributions. Yet another salient factor to be considered is that if her contribution to him ends with the legal divorce, what is the justification for his contribution to her continuing well beyond that cutoff point? What does equity mean here? Does and should the job of homemaker warrant termination pay forever when other jobs provide it for a prespecified time period?

How much does the father owe his children, and for how long? It is the consensus that he owes them support at least until they are 18, longer if unable to support themselves because of physical or mental handicap, and through higher education if possible. This a moral and ethical commitment one makes at the time of conception or adoption of children, at least existentially, and it transcends divorce. But what if he chooses to remarry? Should his second wife (and possible children) be "deprived" because of economic obligations to his first family? The usual legal or judicial response is that this is *his* choice and that the freedom to remarry does not eliminate his prior and primary responsibilities. And the second wife marries him knowing he has these prior commitments!

What if the ex-wife chooses to remarry: To what extent should *her* new husband be responsible for her children's expenses? Or for her further education? These are issues to be explored and resolved as fully as possible prior to remarriage so that there are as few surprises regard-

ing assumptions and expectations as possible and high levels of agreement on financial arrangements and life-style matters (Sager et al., 1983).

Emotional Commitments and Loyalties

Barring those cases where there has been spouse and/or child abuse,
or frequent conflict with one parent clearly more at fault than the other,
children tend to love both of their parents and to expect love from them.
They also need, as we have seen, the affection and nurturance of both
parents for optimal development, again excepting cases of abuse or other
aberration. Although parents fulfill different roles at different stages of
development, they are both needed—as role models, as gender models,
as caring adults. In joint custody arrangements with easy and relatively
frequent access of each parent to the child, most of the desirable effects
of the parent-child relationship are maintained. If both parents mute
their hostilities toward each other and are truly concerned with "the best
interests of their child(ren)," they actively seek to maintain good parent-
child relationships.

In cases where the parents are more concerned with their own needs
and feelings, obviously the relationship fades, or is infected with parental hostility. The young child, not comprehending why the absent parent
remains distant, often blames himself or herself for not being sufficiently
lovable or well-behaved. A slightly older child feels torn between the
parents, what is usually called the 'loyalty dilemma." One parent talks
about all the flaws of the other (absent) parent with the child and tries,
consciously or not, to enlist the youngster on "her side" at the expense
of the father-child relationship. Then, when the child is visiting the
noncustodial or nonresident parent, that adult often does the same. The
child, pulled in both directions, feels guilty if he/she has a happy time
with one parent and hesitates to tell the other parent of these activities.
In some cases, the child does side with one parent and either "spies" on
the other parent or creates situations that add fuel to the fire.

It is less common for the mother to be the absent parent, but in recent
years some women have taken leave of their families to "find themselves." This is a situation made familiar to moviegoers in the film "Kramer vs. Kramer." The children may initially be upset and exhibit regressive or negative behaviors, but in the long run may thrive under the
father's care. Fathers who choose to have custody of their children, it has
been found, tend to be unusually devoted and conscientious in their role
as single parents (Lamb, 1977).

The more frequent event is that the father is the absent parent. Apart
from the absence of a desirable male role model for children of both
sexes, the loss of family income, the social isolation that is more common

for mother-only families, and the removal of a major support figure for the mother, the father's absence typically removes a major socializing and disciplinary agent from the family scene (Lamb, 1977). In some cases, where the mother cannot assume and integrate both parental roles, the child(ren) may exploit the mother's inability to control their behavior, blame her for the father's absence, and transfer an idealized loyalty to the absent father.

When the father has either reduced his visits or withdrawn from the family scene completely in the wake of the separation, the uninformed onlooker may assume that he really doesn't care about his children. This may be a naive as well as an erroneous assumption. In some cases, the ex-wife prevents contact between the father and child(ren). She will not allow telephone conversations, finds excuses to interfere with scheduled visits, and/or poisons the child(ren)'s mind about the father. Legal action can be taken, particularly if visitation is part of the court order, but this may not alter the negative quality of the situation and may only exacerbate the child's confusion in loyalty and commitment.

Some fathers choose to be absent from the child's life because they and the child find the repeated separations at the end of visits too painful. Others believe, incorrectly, that if they're paying only a small amount of child support, they're not entitled to frequent visitation. There are also those who think, again erroneously, that if they don't claim visitation rights, they can avoid paying support. In still other families, especially where there has been remarriage, the new partner is resentful of the child's claims on the father, both emotionally and financially. Two other reasons for father absence suggested by Richards (1982) are attempts to start a new life in some other community without reminders of the past and a disinterest in the children.

Preadolescent, adolescent, and young adult children of divorce are usually cognizant of the factors leading to the divorce and the multiple outcomes stemming from the divorce. They may commit themselves emotionally to one parent or the other on the basis of morality or "fairness." How long this singular loyalty continues tends to be a function of how the parents respond to their children's understanding. Indeed, most studies suggest that children's adjustment to the divorce is directly related to the reasonableness of the parents with respect to each other. If one parent, usually the absent one, has remarried, whole new relationships have to be developed, even between older children and the parent. Sentimental loyalty may remain with the resident parent, yet the child wants to maintain an accord with the other parent. This creates difficulties for the resident parent as well as the child. No matter what her feelings may be toward her ex-spouse, if the mother is sensitive to her child(ren)'s best interests, she does nothing to discourage contact with the father and indeed encourages that parent-child relationship, knowing deep down that ultimately children will evaluate each parent's behavior toward them and in the larger world based on its own merits and not based on tales the other told them years ago. She comes to terms with the need to share holiday observances with the ex-spouse, which may mean that she celebrates some occasions alone or with friends rather than with her children.

SUMMARY

In this chapter, we have discussed the ways in which the impact of divorce differs for the parties involved. The primary differences are seen for the divorcing adults in terms of whether or not they have children. Secondarily, at least on an emotional basis, the length of the marriage affects the response of the adults to divorce, with the separation being a far more wrenching experience for the long-married than for those who had been together for five years or less.

There are economic and social ramifications of divorce as well as emotional ones. This is most clearly seen in divorces where there are children. Custody arrangements affect where the parent(s) will live, in what socioeconomic circumstances, and with how much support in parenting. For the children, divorce can influence not only their relationships with each parent, but also their schooling, friendships, and mental and physical health. Variations are seen by age, gender, and other factors.

Although the elements of physical residence, financial responsibility, and emotional commitments have been discussed more in terms of their negative aspects than the positive ones, this does not mean that all children of divorce are miserable. Given sufficient maturity on the part of both parents and children, all parties to the divorce can build happy and constructive lives for themselves. Regrets about the loss of the original family may continue throughout the children's lives, but do not have to dominate these lives. In many cases, the divorce experience has made the parents more sensitive to their own friends and spouses, and to the impact of their behavior on their children. Over time, the children tend to work out their commitments to each parent, except in families where neglect, abuse, or alcoholism were present before the separation, and reach a rapprochement with each parent with which they can be comfortable.

CHAPTER 11

Extended Family and Friends and Other Community Contacts

Both Bohannon (1973) and Kaslow (1983) discuss the changing aspect of relationships with family, former in-laws, old friends, and new friends as part of the postdivorce period. The first three groups may form part of the divorced adult's support network as early as the predivorce period, continuing through the months or years until the divorce is obtained, and remaining supporters long after the final decree. Other times former in-laws become antagonists to their ex-son or daughter-in-law—particularly where: 1) they opposed the marriage originally, and/or 2) they believe their son or daughter was treated unfairly or cruelly and reject the person accordingly.

The role of the support network changes somewhat in the post-divorce period, in what Bohannon calls the "community divorce" stage. This is partly attributable to the fact that the divorced person's role changes once the divorce is final. No longer is the woman someone's wife, or the man "so-and-so's" husband; the person is now a single adult, whether there are children or not. The divorced woman may be seen as an "economic risk," especially if she has not been employed during the marriage. Despite civil rights and anti-discrimination legislation, if she has not previously had credit in her own name, it may be difficult for her to get a bank loan without a cosigner.

As Maury and Brandwein (1984) have written, the divorced woman's relationships with her children become subject to a public scrutiny that is not true in the two-parent family. Her parents may view her as a dependent child once again and be pleased to welcome their little girl home or be furious that she is again making financial and/or emotional demands on them. Some of her friends may perceive her as a potential threat to their marriages, especially if she is very attractive and appealing. If she is, or is playing, helpless and distraught, and a friend's or neighbor's husband feels sorry for her and becomes helpful and attentive—his wife may indeed have cause for concern, particularly if he likes to feel needed and protective. Or if the newly single woman begins to look and feel very much alive and is stimulating and vibrant, friends' husbands may find her a challenge as she provides an antidote to the repetition and ennui of their long-term marriages. The divorced woman needs to be sensitive to such reactions and not intrude on friends' marriages—seeking her male companions in the singles world—if she doesn't wish to antagonize her old friends and be shut out as an "extra" and too seductive or demanding woman.

Divorced men may be much more welcome by old friends as they usually know women who are eager to meet single men and an extra man seems to be more easily included in social events. However, if he is "broke" by virtue of child support and alimony payments, he too may be considered too encumbered to be of interest to many single women. Married friends may at first pity him but later view him as coming around mostly for a free meal. Some married female friends may attempt to mother him and give too much advice. The need for supportive family and friends must be balanced against the need to grow in independence.

RELATIONSHIPS WITH PARENTS AND SIBLINGS

For many people in the throes of divorce, their parents and siblings are an immediate source of support after separation and continue to be helpful in many ways after the divorce. An older sibling or parent may help the newly single woman, especially, to deal with insurance, taxes, and other business matters attendant upon running a family, if she has not previously handled these details. There may be assistance for individuals of both genders in the matter of making decisions, whether about housing, a job, investments, or other matters of importance. Or the parents and/or siblings may simply be available for listening to the troubled adult's difficulties in the wake of separation and divorce. Where needed and available, they may be able to help care for children while the single parent is absent or help provide financial support temporarily. Sometimes, during the initial transition period, they may provide (temporary) housing. Much of this aid depends, of course, on the proximity of family members to the divorced adult.

There are less common situations, however, where the parents or siblings are so disapproving of a divorce in the family, or so wrapped up in their own concerns, that they furnish little support to the newly divorced person. They neither offer financial aid when it is needed, nor care for the children, nor offer constructive suggestions to the individual. This is most apt to occur when: 1) the family of origin has historically been detached, chaotic, fragmented and/or indifferent; 2) the family's religion prohibits or severely frowns upon divorce and it is totally unacceptable to the family; or 3) it is the first divorce in the family and they are more concerned about "what will people think" and their own humiliation rather than about their son or daughter's pain. In such situations, many individuals have found that friends prove to be more reliable than family, which is a sorry commentary on the original parent-child or sibling relationship.

EX-SPOUSAL CONTACTS

As mentioned earlier, in childless marriages there is little need for the ex-spouses to remain in touch with each other once all the legal and financial matters have been settled. Weiss (1975) pointed out, however, that even without children, it may not be possible to avoid all contact with the ex-spouse without moving physically out of the former geographic locale. If a person decides to relocate a distance away, "it may not be that easy to say farewell to friends, family, and job, to relinquish one's home base and seek to establish onself elsewhere" (p. 112).

Conflicting and alternating feelings of yearning for the ex-spouse and anger or hatred at that person may foster approach-avoidance behavior, drawing the divorced person to the phone or to known haunts of the ex-mate on the one hand and leading to banging down the phone or ducking into a doorway to avoid the ex-mate by turns. Depending on the length of the marriage, there may be some concern if the ex-spouse is ill or in need, with ambivalent feelings about intervening. (The level of ambivalence may vary depending in part on whether the ex-spouse is alone or remarried, living in the same area or not, etc.)

Prolonged feelings of attachment following the divorce impede accomplishing the psychic divorce. Two measures used by Berman (1985) as criteria of continuing attachment were intrusive thoughts about the ex-spouse and preoccupation with the ex-spouse. Although he found several factors significantly related to these criteria, it should be noted that Berman's subjects (60 women, aged 26–53, with at least one minor child at home) had been separated from the ex-husband less than three years at the time of the initial contact and divorced between 1 and 13 months. Since the separation, and more especially the divorce, were still fresh events, it is not surprising that these women were preoccupied with thoughts of and about their former husbands. Nevertheless, Berman's findings are of interest to researchers. He noted that:

> subjects with greater difficulty with the psychological divorce tend to have more minor males [sons], tended not to want a divorce at the time of initial separation, and tend currently to experience more tension and conflict in contacts with the ex-spouse. (p. 387)

Additionally, those subjects who had lower-status jobs and less education tended to have more difficulty completing the psychic divorce than other subjects who had better jobs and more education. It may be that they had more cause to think of their ex-husbands because of their reduced economic position as compared to the married state, and/or had fewer inner resources with which to occupy themselves. Severity of depression at separation, both according to self-report and in terms of symptoms, was also significantly related to intrusive thoughts and preoccupation with the ex-spouse. This is tied to not wanting the divorce when the separation originally occurred, already noted as a principal factor in the continuing attachment to the ex-spouse. It is inevitable that, under the circumstances and in this short interval following the divorce, a woman would think frequently of her ex-husband.

For a divorced couple with children, there is much less opportunity to avoid contact with each other. If they share custodial responsibilities, as 22% of Berman's (1985) subjects did, obviously they must see and/or phone each other about the child(ren)'s needs or welfare. Even when the children are grown, the parents may need to consult each other about a child's problem, or meet at a child's wedding or upon the birth of a grandchild. In another study (Albrecht, 1980, p. 65), only 11% of the subjects reported ex-spousal contact on a continuing basis, and this was generally because of children. "More than 7 out of 10 respondents reported that they had little or no contact with the former spouse, and an additional 18% reported some contact by mail or phone but nothing personal." There is no indication in this study, however, of the extent to which there may have been thoughts of the ex-spouse. By contrast, in our own study, approximately three-fourths of our subjects reported contact with the ex-spouse, but the majority of these respondents had children or were still settling property issues.

In examining the attachments of our subjects, we found that length of marriage was inversely related to contacts with the former spouse and the former in-laws, although the figures were not statistically significant. Those divorced adults who had children were more likely to be in touch with the other parent ($r = .223$), but not necessarily with the ex-in-laws ($r = .046$). If contact was maintained with the ex-spouse (whether childless or not), there was some positive probability that there would also be contact with the ex-spouse's family ($r = .229$).

The support of a lover in the postseparation period was found to be significantly and positively correlated to contact with the ex-spouse ($rho = .352$, $p < .002$). However, since ex-spousal contact was not necessarily affectional or supportive (but was more likely to be related to custody or property matters), and presumably the lover did meet those needs, the correlation could be meaningless. On the other hand, the correlation could indicate that the lover's support, which enhanced the recipient's self-esteem, enabled the individual to deal more effectively with the ex-spouse, when such interactions were necessary.

IN-LAW RELATIONSHIPS

As Weiss (1975) pointed out:

Most important for the further course of a relationship with an in-law is the pre-separation character of the relationship. Should the separating individual and an in-law have maintained only an indirect relationship, seeing one another only because of their shared relationship to the spouse, then the separation is apt to end the relationship. On the other hand, if the separating individual and the in-law like and value one another, they may remain close during the separation. (p. 144)

Since families tend to "stick up" for their own, whether that family member initiated, provoked, or caused the divorce or was the rejected party, it is less likely that the family member's ex-spouse can count on support from his/her in-laws. It does happen, occasionally, where, as Weiss indicated, there is sincere positive feeling between the former in-laws. Even if the being in touch amounts to a phone call once a week, or lunch or dinner together, the former in-law does not feel as if an entire family has been lost along with the marriage.

In many cases, ties with the ex-in-laws are maintained because of the presence of children, who are the nieces, nephews, and grandchildren of both families. Where the mother has custody of minor children, "Social relations of children with paternal kin (grandparents, uncles, aunts) are mediated through their degree of contact with the absent father, which has typically been very limited" (Duffy, 1982, p. 8). Sometimes it is the grandparents rather than the father who maintain the ties and arrange to have the grandchildren at large family gatherings on holidays or special occasions. As we will argue in the next section, it is important to the children's development, particularly their sense of identity, to have such contacts with relatives on both sides.

RIGHTS OF GRANDPARENTS

By mid-1985, all but three states had laws permitting grandparents to petition a court for visitation privileges upon the death, or more relevant, upon the divorce of their adult child, who is the parent of their grandchild. The court then decides whether such visiting privileges are in the best interests of the child. According to Derdeyn (1985), current issues in grandparent visitation actions include:

1. *Animosity among the adult parties (as between parents and in-laws).* Most courts will permit visitation in such cases.
2. *Adoption by a stepparent.* Again, most courts will permit the biological grandparents to visit with the children.
3. *Intrafamilial disputes, i.e., the grandparents against their adult child.* These are such unique situations that the courts tend to decide each such instance on its merits.
4. *Grandparents' visits causing loyalty conflicts.* Derdeyn's conclusion on this issue is that the courts should probably bar the grandparents' visits in order to avoid or prevent further family discord.

In any of the above situations, legal action by the grandparents against the custodial parent(s) may be seen as a "forced entry" action, and is likely to cause additional stress to the grandchildren. On the other hand, grandparents can be a source of support, an emotional cushion, for distressed grandchildren, especially when the custodial parent or both parents are not functioning too well. Foster and Freed (1984), who have urged that the Commissioners on Uniform State Laws draft an act providing for grandparental visitation in the event of separation or divorce as well as death of their adult child, point out that "visitation should not be regarded as the entitlement of the visitation seeker but rather as the need and right of the child to know and associate with the meaningful persons in his or her life" (p. 40).

What is the role of grandparents in the child's life? Grandparents usually provide much affection and very little punishment. They transmit an historical sense of family as they relate incidents of their child's early years, and their own, to the grandchildren. Often they are able to mediate more effectively with the child's parent than the child can, or at least explain to the child what the parent's reasoning is regarding a decision. They certainly can provide tenderness and often understanding when the child is troubled.

Not all grandparents are as warm and caring as those just described. Some exacerbate the conflict between the divorced parents and drag the children further into the loyalty dilemma. Some, not having been too affectionate over the years, are even less welcome in the grandchildren's lives after the divorce. That is why courts often have to determine if grandparent visitation will help or distress the child rather than automatically granting visitation privileges—not visitation rights. In 1982 Florida addressed this issue (Florida Dissolution of Marriage—Children Act, 1982) indicating that "the court may award the grandparents visitation rights of a minor child if it is deemed by the court to be in the child's best interest. Grandparents shall have legal standing to seek judicial enforcement of such an award" (p. 551). This assuaged the fears of many grandparents that they would be excluded from the lives of their grandchildren.

Blau (1984, p. 49) did an evaluative review of the behavioral science literature regarding the role of grandparents in relation to the child and drew the following conclusions from his review:

1. Changes in state laws during the past two decades reflect recognition of the significant positive interaction which can exist between a child and a grandparent.
2. The research strongly suggests that the continuance of an established relationship between a child and a grandparent is likely to provide:
   a. A positive approach to child development milestones.
   b. A sanctuary for the child in times of stress.
   c. A more accepting, esteem-enhancing environment than parents can consistently provide.
   d. A source of positive information and support regarding basic family structure and society's personal and moral values.
   e. A modeling experience which improves the child's capacity to understand and value elders after reaching maturity.
   f. An enhancement of the child's ability to be an effective grandparent two generations hence.
3. Interference with an available, positive grandparent's relationship to a child is likely to have negative psychological effects, both short range and developmentally.
4. Where conflict exists between an available grandparent and the parents of the child, it is in the child's best interests that this conflict be mediated and resolved.

We concur in toto.

OLD FRIENDS

Friends can provide significant support for those going through separation and divorce, but they can also cause the divorcing parties grief if they appear to favor one party over the other. On the positive side, friends stop in if they live nearby, or phone often if they live at a distance. They show that they care if the individual is functioning better today than last week and offer encouragement for tomorrow and the weeks to come. They invite the divorcing person for dinner or a visit, include him or her on a day's outing, and perhaps introduce an eligible "date," if one is available. Principally, they provide reassurance that the individual is still likable and desirable as a friend and help dissipate some of the feelings of sheer loneliness.

Sometimes, however, friends are devoted to both parties to the divorce as individuals and, like the children of divorce, have divided loyalties. Where the decision to divorce was mutual, such allegiances are less troublesome than when one party appears to have treated the other shabbily and the spurned partner feels that continued friendship with him/her is contingent upon renouncing amity with the other. It is sometimes difficult to tell whether the seemingly injured party was a withholder or provocateur, however, so laying blame can be foolhardy. And often, friends only hear a biased elaboration of one side of the story.

There are differences in friendships in terms of age group, duration of marriage, length of the friendship, and bases for the relationship. The loyalty dilemma is more acute when the relationships are long-standing and multifaceted.

Consider, for example, a friendship of 15 or 20 years that is not only social but professional. Husband A is an attorney who has provided services for Couple B in both joint and individual matters. He represents neither party in the divorce, but continues to advise them each separately in other legal affairs. They are each valued as clients. Additionally, Wife A is socially friendly with Wife B, and very angry with Husband B who has rejected and left her friend. When planning a social affair, e.g., wedding, birthday party, do they invite Wife B but not her ex-husband? Do they invite them both at the risk of causing pain to Wife B? How does Wife B respond to her friends' dilemma? (Author LS's case file)

There are no easy answers to the problem, only efforts to maintain friendships sympathetically without becoming embroiled in Couple B's battles as combatants. Much depends, too, on each party's ability to be in the other's company without causing a scene. This is much easier at a large gathering than at a small one. If one of the parties remarries, the complexities and potential emotional difficulties may increase. The ex-wife may be very resentful if her friends come to like and accept the new wife, seeing this as a betrayal of her and a condoning of her ex-husband's actions. In the most rational solution to these problems, the friends will not have to take sides or terminate the friendship with one ex-spouse in order to appease the other, but may need to see them separately whenever possible and not carry stories back and forth.

Even if the loyalty dilemma is avoided by old friends, the divorced individual is confronted by other quandaries. It's very pleasant to be invited for dinner, but at what point does the feeling of being a "fifth wheel" arise? How many times can one expect others to ask a single person to join them at the theatre or for a concert or, worse yet, at a dinner-dance? If the individual expects to be invited frequently, friends may find this burdensome and begin to avoid mentioning their plans. If the individual feels uncomfortable as a "third leg" or "fifth wheel," he/she turns down invitations and is confronted with loneliness and an aching desire to be eligible to be part of the couples' world again.

One solution to the loneliness problem is to make new acquaintances in the singles world, since that is now part of the person's new identity, like it or not. Another solution is to find companionship and refuge in going out with same-sexed friends who are in a similar "singles" position. If mealtime discussions get bogged down, however, in talk of the ex-spouse or of continuing difficulties, this can add to the individual's depression. On the positive side, however, two or more females (or males) can certainly enjoy going places together and engaging in a variety of activities, whether cultural, athletic, educational, or purely social. Despite women's liberation and generally more relaxed social attitudes, the more mature and/or professional woman finds it difficult to spend evenings in bars or cocktail lounges, or to attend a singles' group meeting, even with another woman along for company and support. She tends to regard such settings as "meat markets," and, given all the publicity about AIDS, herpes, and other diseases, is quite leery of becoming involved with casual acquaintances.

The amount of loneliness experienced depends to some extent on the individual. One who has many interests and inner resources, though desirous of company, can manage to keep occupied enough to ward off idle hours being spent dwelling on loneliness. There are also differences by age group, length of marriage, and other commitments, such as to children and parents. Younger women with children may be lonely but may not have time to think about it as they try to deal with more responsibility and less money, homemaking, job, and driving their children to after-school activities or supervising their homework. When they are able to go out socially, they tend to have more opportunities to meet someone with whom to build a new relationship than more mature women have. Middle-aged and older women, who may not have the care of young children to occupy them, tend to be more uncomfortable with strange men and they are confronted by a dearth of men in the 45 + age bracket—and this figure diminishes in terms of the number truly available given that many prefer "younger" women.

Although older women have greater mobility than younger women, they may be reluctant to leave what is familiar and venture off alone. Those who work at least have the opportunity to interact with other people during the day, but may find evenings, weekends, and holidays very lonely and, indeed, even painful. Friends, nestled in their own homes and concerned with their own families, cannot, and should not be expected to, furnish the "complete antidote" to this aspect of loneliness.

CEREMONIES AND RITUALS

A woman in her 50s, divorced for four years and the custodial parent of four daughters aged 12–20, learned about the Holmes-Rahe stress scale at a self-help group. Discussing it with a friend, she said,

Death of a family member was rated at 100 and divorce at 60. That's wrong! They should be reversed. Death is painful but final. Divorce, especially when having children means continuing contact with the ex-spouse, is never final. The wounds just keep being reopened which causes pain all over again. (Author LS's case file)

One key point of this anecdote is the difference between death and divorce in degree of finality. This was discussed earlier in terms of the consequences of widowhood and divorce. Here, however, we need to look at this difference in terms of rituals. Death brings a funeral, along with a wake or sitting shiva (seven day mourning period). There is recognition of the end of a life by relatives, friends, and the community at large. Mourning and expressions of sympathy are an accepted part of the ritual and tears and other open expressions of grief are acceptable, even encouraged. For divorce, there is a court decree, perhaps some sympathetic overtures by those close to the parties, but no public ceremony. And the only person to accompany one to the court hearing is likely to be the attorney. How sad to be virtually alone on such a difficult day! Indeed, for many, even the fact of divorce is quasi-hidden because of shame and/or guilt.

Orthodox and conservative Judaism traditionally have required a religious divorce, granted by a tribunal of three rabbis known as a Beth Din. This divorce must be obtained if one is to remarry within Judaism or subsequent children will be regarded, under religious law, as illegitimate. Only the man can initiate proceedings of the Beth Din. The ritual of granting the "get" or Jewish divorce, however, is a private one. For some individuals, it is demeaning; for others, it provides adequate closure to the marriage.

Kaslow and some other family therapists believe that some kind of formal ceremony of divorce is needed by some clients to help them through the immediate postdivorce period. One approach is to have a public ceremony at one's church or synagogue to which relatives and friends are invited that dissolves the marital tie in a divorce ceremony, thus according religious sanction to the divorce (see Kaslow, 1984a—one such ceremony is included there).

Emanating out of my (FK) growing realization that some people wanted a ceremony to demarcate their married life from the next stage and to bring it to a closure that encompassed the bittersweet quality of their marriage, I have evolved a quasi-therapeutic ceremony over the past three years. It draws from those of Bach (1974) and Close (1977) and is geared to the specific couple who have dissolved their union legally yet want a psychic marker to facilitate the transition to being unwed. We usually hold the ceremony in my office and they are encouraged to bring their children and one close friend each. Some want a sibling(s) or parents present and this is of course acceptable since it is *their* ceremony and the choices are theirs to the extent possible. I also utilize this ceremony in workshops on divorce therapy for mental health professionals—asking individuals who have or are going through divorce to enact husband, wife and friends, and people who are children of divorce to play the part of the children.

Therapeutic/Healing Divorce Ceremony
(Shortened Version)

The adult participants stand facing each other and the children stand facing me. We are in a square or rectangle—depending on number of participants.

FK: Mr. Green—please thank your wife for the good years and happy times you remember.

Mr. G: (Usually puzzled—pauses—chokes and responds—surprised at the positive memories this question evokes. He may say) I really had forgotten—amidst my anger . . . how much I once loved you. You were so lovely, talented, . . .

FK: Mrs. Green—Can you tell your husband about the good things you will always cherish about your marriage?

Mrs. G: (Often teary and barely audible, affirms the sharing, fun and early realizations of her dream and how wonderful she thought he was.)

FK: (To each of the friends separately) Please tell Mr. or Mrs. Green how you are prepared to be available to them during this difficult transition time and what their friendship means to you.

Friends: You can call me at any time to talk, cry, go somewhere with you—I'm here for you in any way that you need me because you're a super person and wonderful friend.

FK: (To children) Can each of you tell your parents what the divorce means to you and what you want from your parents subsequent to the divorce?

Each child: (Something like) I am so sad that this happened but I know you tried your best. I need to know that you will each continue to love me, take care of me, let me love and care about each of you and see you as much as possible. Please do not ask me to take sides or interfere with my relationship to Mom/Dad. (This is usually said with great sadness, wistfulness and through tears.)

FK: (To each parent) Can you tell your children how they were conceived (or adopted) in love, born at a time when you cared very much for each other and were delighted to be having a family? Also, let them know what your thoughts are about your future relationship to them.

Each parent: (Tells in their own words what child has meant to them and affirms that their parental feelings and role will continue.)

FK: (To anyone else at the ceremony) Please tell Mr. and Mrs. Green what is in your hearts as you help them to feel some inner peace and some healing.

When everyone has said what they seem propelled to communicate, depending on the feeling tone being conveyed, I may ask if they all care to hug each other as a goodbye to the family in its present form.

The ceremony is usually quite moving and takes people deep into their feelings, transporting them beyond anger, resentment, or the desire to retaliate to an *affirmation of the value the marriage had* for them for many years and to a realization that *these were not wasted years*; that there is much to still savor and that the children were a significant and lasting joint product of their love. Despite the tears and some bewilderment at the strength of the feelings of happiness and sorrow, many indicate that they feel a profound sense of relief afterwards.

Few people seem ready to address these issues at the time of the legal divorce. I have found the ceremony to be more meaningful when the family comes back together for it anytime subsequent to three months postdivorce. Sometimes it takes several years until they are ready to complete the psychic divorce in this way.

Many professionals are startled by the impact of a simple but eloquent ceremony such as this one. Those participating in the event (and the remainder of the audience at a workshop) are often touched deeply and the children of divorce usually indicate that they had never before said the things that needed to be said which were brought out in this "happening." Some later report contacting their real parents to talk through what had been left unsaid before.

I usually make myself available for consults to people who are quite stirred up and quite a few people have availed themselves of this. Letters from workshop participants afterwards indicate that they find this to be an extremely useful experience personally and professionally.

Ceremonies are not recommended for everyone. There are individuals who would find it too humiliating, too public a display of grief or anger or hurt. Yet even they may wish for some of the kind of support given by family members and the community to mourners of a death in the family. This support can often be found in groups for the widowed and divorced that have arisen in recent years, or with new friends.

THERAPY

At this stage of the postdivorce process, some adults still feel quite troubled. They may be experiencing internal stress—uncertainty and concern about their appeal to others, their integrity and stability, their residual anger and sadness. Simultaneously, they feel the external pressures of bills to be paid, the myriad responsibilities of their new life that must be juggled, the needs and longings of their children and concern that they readjust in healthy fashion, and much more. They may want a genuinely empathic, yet neutral person to enable them to sort out the inner turmoil, and help them confront their contribution to the conflict which led to the dissolution of their marriage. In addition, they may desire someone to serve as a well-informed sounding board with whom to consider how to enrich today and set worthwhile and reachable goals for tomorrow, and/or how to enter a new committed relationship that has a high probability of being healthy and long lasting.

Depending on the time, money and energy a person has available, at this juncture individual therapy or group therapy with others who are divorced probably constitute the treatments of choice. If the person needs all of the attention focused on his or her own issues, individual treatment is advisable. If group support, a feeling of belonging, and learning to function in a heterosexual environment where feedback can be derived from both men and women seem to be essential, then group therapy would appear to be preferable. If parent-child difficulties are causing great consternation, then parent-child treatment should certainly be part of the therapeutic package.

Clearly, a person should seek the best possible therapist he/she can find—someone who practices from a family systems perspective and who understands divorce and its aftermath, with all the nuances and consequences of a process that redirects peoples' lives into often unwanted and uncharted pathways. The therapist should be able to convey optimism, patience, and a sense of the challenges and opportunities the parents can successfully master and how they can help their children handle their new situation with good coping skills.

NEW FRIENDS

The support groups for widowed and divorced adults, such as Parents Without Partners, that have been started in the past dozen years or so resemble support and self-help groups for parents of retarded or handicapped children, relatives of alcoholics, and those actively dealing with a variety of other syndromes. They offer the opportunity for members to share and compare experiences, to learn alternative solutions from each other, and to acquire new information relevant to their problems or status. Speakers are often invited to teach the newly widowed and divorced, for example, how to deal with tax issues or with adolescent children. In addition, there is a period allocated for socializing with other "singles" (rather than with couples) and this provides the opportunity to make new friends and perhaps start dating.

A number of religious institutions and community centers have also undertaken to sponsor special events for singles. These may be religious services at which the emphasis is on rebuilding one's life, or lectures, or dances, or a movie night. Typically, the groups are divided by age, with perhaps one group limited to those up to age 35, another limited to the 35–50 range, and less often a group for those aged 50 and over. The division by age group and the focus on "mingling" lead some singles to regard these as "meat markets" where one seeks a date and/or possible mate for remarriage. Accordingly, those who feel uncomfortable with such settings stay away rather than reawaken the adolescent pain of being "looked over" by members of the opposite sex and possibly being rejected.

"Singles" bars and cocktail lounges are also places to meet new people, but again not everyone finds these appetizing or even comfortable. One woman (a respondent in our study—and her feelings are echoed by many both younger and older) was overwhelmingly depressed by her experience at such a lounge. "There were perhaps 150 people there," she said, "and each of them seemed huddled in his or her own little protective shell, afraid to reach out for fear of being rejected, yet longing for someone else to make an overture. It was horrible!" Then again, others find the opportunity to dance or talk with a member of the opposite sex, even a stranger, to be more welcome than being shut out of heterosexual interaction altogether. Those who have the personal freedom, either being childless or without responsibility for children, of going out casually may seek company actively in the first year or two postdivorce, and then conclude that this is unrewarding. Others enjoy it immensely, learn new skills and become quite socially adept.

For those able to afford it economically, travel with groups offers a change of scenery along with the opportunity to meet new people. Taking courses for advancement or for fun, perhaps a new interest like art or photography or a sport, is another way to be with people and possibly to make new friends. It does take effort on the part of the individual to venture out and explore new worlds, to set shyness aside, to become a new person in a sense. The longer the individual was "so-and-so's" spouse, however, the more difficult it may be to achieve a sole identity.

Another source of friends is the revival of relationships with long-time acquaintances who may not have been part of one's couples' world. Now that single status is shared, other common interests may be recalled that enable the new-old friends to enjoy each other's company under changed circumstances.

Perhaps the critical element in developing new friendships is a willingness to reorganize one's life. If the divorced adult continues to focus on the negative aspects of the ex-spouse and of the divorce, he or she is no more welcome company for others than any other chronically hostile or depressed person. The individual must determine, with therapeutic assistance if necessary, that life has not stopped at the point of divorce and that he/she can face the challenges and opportunities it can afford.

SUMMARY

Both during the months or years before the divorce decree is handed down and during the first few critical years after the divorce is final, the divorcing parties tend to need support from others. One's own parents and siblings tend to be a first line of support, though not always. One's ex-in-laws and other relatives of the ex-spouse are less often willing to play that role. More often, there are complications arising from contacts with the ex-spouse and the ex-spouse's family. Many of these problems derive from the presence of children. What rights do grandparents have in relation to their grandchildren in a divorce situation? Or is it, as we have postulated, that the grandchildren have needs that are best met by interaction with the grandparents and other relatives on both sides of the family? We know from the work of Bowen (1978) that cutoffs in the family tree are dangerous and can leave one quite rootless.

Beyond the family, the divorced adult has to come to terms with the strains the divorce has imposed on old friendships and has to find new ways of relating to old friends that are not dependent on the former couples' bases of interaction. To avoid both the "fifth wheel syndrome" in these old friendships and the loneliness that comes from a lack of social involvement, the divorced person must seek out new friends, perhaps through new activities. For some, "permission" to engage in finding a "new self" comes through a divorce "ceremony" or "ritual," although this is not the avenue of choice for all. For others, through natural inclination or an almost steely determination, isolation and loneliness are reduced through joining singles' support groups or becoming active in adult classes, travel, or professional or religious organizations. What is essential for the newly single is to make a decision that "life must go on," with or without a spouse, but with other people who share their interests. Only then do they become solid "survivors."

CHAPTER 12

Postdivorce—Being in the World Anew

It's over! The divorce decree has been in hand for several years, maybe less; the child custody and visitation agreement is functioning, and the assets (or liabilities) have been divided.

Of necessity, the individual has had to reorder his or her life, adapting to a new residence perhaps, to doing alone or with the assistance of children all of the tasks that had formerly been shared with the spouse, and trying to build a new social network. Divorced people with whom we have spoken frequently indicate that they were never aware, when married, of all the problems (and their variations) of the postdivorce period. Three *practical difficulties, having nothing whatever to do with feelings* toward the ex-spouse or toward the children, that were mentioned time after time were loneliness, time-consuming paper work, and the myriad errands like marketing, going to the cleaners and the hardware store, and the driving of children to their activities without anyone to sometimes pitch in and share the load. If there are elderly parents, again there is no one to share paying attention to their needs. In sum, what divorced people told us was that being divorced may have resolved some problems, but it produced others. Nevertheless, they not only survive, but they adapt, adjust, and sometimes even innovate as they alter their lifestyles.

There are many decisions to be made following the divorce. If awarded the family home as part of the distribution of marital assets, the individual must decide whether to remain there or to move, and if so, where. If possible, this is a decision that should be postponed as long as it can be, for moving is not only expensive, but represents another "separation" from the familiar. Also, if there are children, their needs for continuity in terms of school and friends must be considered and the number of disruptions they undergo should be minimized. A decision to be made by the woman is whether to get a job (this may be a necessity), to change her job, or to remain predominantly mother/homemaker. Several factors enter into this decision, including hours, salary, benefits such as health insurance, alternatives available in an appropriate location, and how all of these mesh with the reality of other commitments, such as to a preschool or handicapped child. Relationships with the ex-spouse's family may or may not be strained, but some decisions have to be made when ex-in-law family celebrations (or funerals) occur about whether or not to attend. Vacation planning is changed, as the divorced individual weighs whether to go with a group or to travel alone or with the children, which places are likely to be comfortable for a "single" and which not, and what age groups patronize different resorts. Ultimately, there may be a BIG question: to remarry or to remain single.

RELATIONSHIPS WITH EX-SPOUSE

In an earlier chapter we discussed conflictual postdivorce relationships between ex-spouses. It is important, however, to look at postdivorce relationships in a larger context also. Among younger divorced couples, those for whom the marriage was short-lived and who had no children, there may be quite amicable contact in the years following the divorce. Many of our younger subjects, for example, indicated that they call each other to talk as friends and to share feelings. Some ex-mates go out to dinner together—as friends—and some even resume a physical relationship. Generally they enjoy and respect each other but are not compatible with/or committed enough to be married to one another. Some do find they still feel a strong mutual attraction and are happier together so they remarry one another later. Others marry a different spouse only to realize they still love their ex-spouse and recognize their yearning to recreate their original nuclear family—to bask in wholeness with their own never before fully appreciated spouse, children (and grandchildren) (Levin, 1984). They go through divorcing the second spouse in order to reunite the family they could not wait to leave several years earlier. Younger children are often delighted to have their fantasy of reunion realized. And the adults may "do it better" the second time around.

If the marriage was relatively short, as many seem to be today, there may not have been time for the deep investment of feelings, energy, and experiences that characterize long-term marriages and make the subsequent divorce more painful. Those who have been married for several decades share a long history of dreaming and building together that is not easily forgotten or replaced.

If both parties remain in the same general locality, they are likely to meet at some point. Tactful family members and friends who are having a small party or gathering may only invite one of the two but, at a larger event such as a wedding, they may feel that they'd like to have both present (if they have remained on friendly terms with both). Both should be asked if they would feel comfortable with the other one in attendance if the hosts are friends who haven't "taken sides." If they have strong feelings about the divorce, then the friends or relatives should ask the one to whom they are closer about inviting the ex-spouse. In families, normally the individual who is part of the family will be invited, but where friendship and kinship overlap, utmost diplomacy must be exercised in inviting the formerly married. (At a sit-down affair, for example, it's possible to seat them at tables as far apart as possible; at a less formal event, each will have to fend for him/herself.)

Continuing contact is of course inevitable where there are children of the marriage. When the children are quite young, noncustodial parent and custodial parent will meet at visitation exchanges. Some couples can handle this reasonably well after the initial disharmony fades. They exchange a few comments on the visit or the arrangements for the next visit, on a child's health or schoolwork, and part until the next time. Other couples unfortunately continue the old battles, too often in front of the children, and exacerbate the old wounds for themselves and the children. They may even go so far as to try to keep the children from seeing members of the ex-spouse's extended family, although today, as indicated in Chapter 11, grandparents can sue for visitation rights in a number of states.

If hostility between the ex-spouses is extremely high, and child support and/or visitation agreements are not being observed, the ultimate escalation of the conflict is kidnapping of the child by the noncustodial parent. This is illegal, and the parents should be so advised by their attorneys. Parental kidnapping is, unfortunately, far more common than most people realize. Many of the missing children whose pictures are being shown on television, milk cartons, and assorted mailings are children who have been kidnapped by a parent. They are not necessarily being mistreated, but they are being kept from their other parent in contempt of a judge's order. No matter what the motivation or intention, kidnapping is frightening and detrimental to the best interest of the child. Little good can come by focusing the controversy on the child and making him/her hide out like a fugitive.

If the children are teenagers, or old enough to drive, visitation confrontations can be avoided. That doesn't mean that all parental contact is eliminated, however, as there are health emergencies, insurance matters, and other quite legitimate reasons for one parent—as parent—to call the other. If all is gone in the relationship, these matters can still be handled with civility if the adults are willing to behave rationally. Some simply can't do this, though, and both they and the children, and often other people close to them as well, suffer for the immaturity and the efforts at undermining or retaliating for past hurts.

Interaction with the ex-spouse can get "stickier" if encounters can't be avoided because of employment in the same firm or similar professions, or of the maintenance of like interests they had shared earlier. Initially, being in the same place at the same time can be very anxiety provoking and even irritating to one or both parties. As time goes on, however, and each begins to lead a more separate life, the inevitability of attending the same church or synagogue, or meeting, or concert becomes less distressing.

In *Friends Through it All*, Stark (1986) cites Ahrons' categorization of divorced couples into four groups—Fiery Foes, Angry Associates, Cooperative Colleagues and Perfect Pals. Ahrons' data, based on a five-year longitudinal study of 98 couples, showed Fiery Foes comprised 24%, Angry Associates—25%, Cooperative Colleagues—38%, and Perfect Pals—12% (many with good joint custody arrangements). Assuming these figures can be generalized beyond the study population, an important conclusion is that at least 50% of divorced couples achieve an amicable postdivorce relationship and we must help revise stereotypical impressions that all remain either permanently embattled or embittered. And this more positive picture may help offset some of the prevalent negativistic view.

ALTERED LIFE-STYLE: TWO SINGLE-PARENT FAMILIES

As Morawetz and Walker (1984) and others have pointed out, the substitution of the term "single-parent family" represents a significant change in public attitudes toward what used to be called a "broken home." However, as we are all aware, the term "single-parent family" can have several meanings.

For example, the birth of a child to an unmarried woman leads to the formation of a family unit which differs from a family in which a parent has died, which in turn differs from a family which lives in hope that the disappearance of the father and husband will be temporary; and all of these differ from a family which has undergone a divorce. (Morawetz & Walker, 1984, p. 8)

We might add that many military families are also de facto "single-parent families" while one parent serves overseas or on the seas or is a POW or an MIA (Kaslow & Ridenour, 1984).

Postdivorce each family subdivides and is restructured into what Sager et al. (1983) call "the double single-parent" family or what Ahrons labels "the binuclear family" (1980b). These terms are more accurate and descriptive than the "single-parent family"—in that both parents are single parents with major responsibility for the children at different times. Our focus here is, of course, on these restructured postdivorce families.

As is true even for families where one parent has died, the physical absence of one parent does not mean that that individual plays no role in the family unit. There are myths, memories, and photographs that keep the absent parent present in one's thoughts and feelings. There are frequent contacts by phone and because of the custody/visitation agreement. There may also be periodic contact because of continuing litigation or the need to modify a custody/visitation plan.

In terms of the children, principally, there are what have been termed "dilemmas and pitfalls of single-parent families." These include:

1. The parent perceiving the child as the embodiment of the absent parent, with particularly deleterious effects if the child serves as a constant reminder of one who has caused great pain and bitterness.
2. Emotional overdependence of the parent on the child.
3. The parent's perception of the child as an overwhelming burden and a hindrance to adjusting to a new life-style.
4. Loss of perspective regarding the child(ren)'s stage of development in the parent's struggle to "survive" following the divorce.
5. Guilt and ambivalence, especially for women who have initiated the divorce, over attempting to meet their own needs.
6. Adolescent-like behavior on the parent's part that may be reflected in similar regression in the child(ren)'s behavior. (Kessler even designates the period postdivorce as "second adolescence" [1975].)
7. Dependence of the parent on his/her family of origin, making him/her, in a sense, a child again. (Morawetz & Walker, 1984, pp. 13–20)

Obviously, not every single parent experiences all of these "pitfalls," but most are confronted by some of them. To aid the single parent in coping with these and other challenges, groups such as "Parents Without Partners" have been formed (see Chapter 11). Like many other self-help peer groups, individuals bring problem situations to meetings and learn how others have handled similar situations. The groups are not necessarily led by professionals, nor are they primarily therapeutic in intent. Their orientation tends, rather, to be a problem-solving one.

One of the major problems of the single parent is his/her relationship with a child's school. There has been relatively little guidance for school personnel in how to deal with divorced families, although generally they seem to be more sensitive today than formerly to the needs of the children of divorce. Apparently there is often an assumption that all post-divorce relationships are adversarial, even when it comes to the children. Individual school principals may decide to open a child's records to either parent, fully in accord with the 1974 Family Educational Rights and Privacy Act (also known as the Buckley Amendment); other principals may choose to open them only to the primary custodial parent. The school's "census"/emergency card may have room for only one parent's name, address, home and work phone numbers. Actually, unless specifically directed otherwise, the school should regard the noncustodial parent as a parent too and provide access to the child's records and welcome him/her to school functions. Where joint custody prevails, this is especially true.

Ricci (1980) has pointed out that schools must become sensitive to alternative family situations. Quoting parental reports, she wrote that:

> parents point to the series of daily reminders that indicate the school/family credibility gap: School textbooks portray the never-divorced family almost exclusively; school forms are designed for one home with two natural parents—not two homes with natural and sometimes stepparents; tickets are issued for one family; presents made in school for Mother's Day and Father's Day are limited to one present per parent per holiday; report cards and notices are sent to only one home. (1980, p. 510)

This is very distressing and unfair where there is co-parenting; where there is one primary parent, these practices tend to shut the other parent out completely unless the custodial parent decides voluntarily to share and relay information. Nor should children have to be responsible for this alone.

We have already indicated the many chores that beset the single parent. These add to the depression and fatigue common in the separation and immediate postdivorce periods, with some individuals never quite getting through this phase. The perceived heavy burden also contributes to increased irritability, self-pity, and less patience with self or children. Therapy for the parent may well be warranted as an aid to becoming less overwhelmed, and therefore better organized and more self-sufficient. This is particularly salient and one might even say almost essential for those who have and have had personality disorders that predate the separation and who have long exhibited dysfunctional behaviors. Therapy may help them gain some insight into their own behavior, thoughts and feelings and inhibit their projecting all blame for their personal problems onto the ex-spouse and the fact of the divorce. As the parent's ability to cope improves, so should the children's.

The difficulties in adjusting to single parenthood for women have been discussed, written about, and studied extensively. The same is not true for divorced men as parents, principally because in the past so few fathers gained custody of their children.

Today, approximately 10% of children of divorce live primarily with their fathers and we understand that in military families this figure may be substantially higher.* The challenges fathers face vary somewhat with the age of the children. It is unclear as yet whether the greatest adjustment for the father comes in the role of parenting preschoolers or adolescents. To date, the scant reports available are mixed. If the father is able to do so, he may hire a person to take care of the child while he is at work, or place the child in a day care center. Some fathers have changed the nature of their work so that they can be at home more during the day, or are fortunate enough to work in a company that has a child care center for children of employees, thus reducing the hours apart from the child and the anguish of wondering if they are receiving good care and supervision. Whatever the age of the child, however, the father now finds that he is either totally responsible for supervision, management, meeting the emotional and other needs of his child(ren), and homemaking, or he must find appropriate people to whom to delegate some of these functions. Rarely has the father had any academic or practical preparation for these roles, such as a course in human development. Nor have many men been socialized emotionally for these functions. It is natural to ask, then, how effective and successful is he at these jobs?

In a study of 27 single-parent fathers of varied ages and socioeconomic backgrounds, Smith and Smith (1981) found that most of the fathers reported having been somewhat involved with their children during their marriage, with two-thirds of them self-described as "authoritarian disciplinarians." Any changes that occurred as a result of becoming a single parent the fathers tended to see as an improvement in their lives and in their relationships with their children, who ranged in age from 18 months to 17 years (average age—10.7 years). Their greatest overall strain was perceived to be time management, although they also indicated that they felt a need to prove themselves to the outside world as being capa-

---

*When author FK was consulting with professional staff members of the Navy Family Service Centers in Norfolk, VA (April 1986) they reported to me that this figure is spiralling rapidly because wives are voluntarily relinquishing custody.

ble of caring for their children. The most successful adjustments to single-parent fatherhood were made, however, by those fathers:

> who were confident in their new roles as single parents; did not feel they had to prove that they could be successful single parents; and had the knowledge and resources to care for their children and themselves emotionally, socially, and materially. (p. 417)

Jacobs (1982, 1984), a psychiatrist, challenges the still prevailing but obsolete stereotypical view that fathers are generally detached and uninterested in child rearing both during marriage and after divorce, while recognizing that this description is true of some men, and some women, too. In terms of postdivorce adjustment, he posits that there is mounting clinical evidence that treatment of the father which emphasizes helping him maintain a good, healthy relationship to his children will have the most salutary effect on the entire family. Thus the therapist must help him identify and resolve the intrapsychic and interpersonal conflicts which impede his achieving this objective.

Echoing the findings of earlier research, Briggs and Walters (1985) assert, in their paper addressed to early childhood educators, that the single-father family is (sometimes) a healthy and constructive family unit. Like Smith and Smith (1981), they point out that life is easier for these families when the father is educationally, occupationally, and economically successful. These authors encourage teachers to share information on child development with fathers. Any presumption that fathers are totally ignorant about this subject would be erroneous and insulting. Briggs and Walters believe that fathers should inform teachers about both the legal stipulations and informal agreements with respect to custody of a child.

The literature available on single-father families does suggest that professionals, if not all of society, are far more optimistic about the success of this arrangement today than was true a generation ago. Fathers as well as mothers have an easier time of single parenting if they have information about this role, a prior good parent-child relationship, and economic resources to support their efforts.

Both single mothers and single fathers who are experiencing difficulty in adjusting to this new role can profit from interaction with their peers and with professionals. One education program, carried out at the University of North Carolina, was designed as a supportive and preventive measure to aid these parents (Warren & Amara, 1985). Groups of four to six parents met with a male-female team of mental health professionals for five sessions in a relaxed setting. As reported, each session had a specific goal rather than being a free-wheeling "group therapy" meeting. The format and content were as follows:

Session 1. Presentation and discussion of information about the reactions of children to their parents' separation and divorce.

Session 2. The focus was on teaching the parents "skills of active listening and direct expression of feelings between parents and children" (p. 85).

Session 3. Discussion of the interaction of divorce issues and discipline, with an emphasis on limit-setting and negotiation skills.

Session 4. Continuing interaction between the ex-spouses and how to handle it. (The authors noted leaders' reports that this was the most emotionally charged session of the series.)

Session 5. Topics included problem-solving techniques, stress reduction, and planning for the future (pp. 83–85).

Warren and Amara report that the subgroup within the 35 participants studied who profited most from the series "included parents who (initially) reported less visitation and less agreement with the noncustodial spouse on child-rearing and parents who reported a major fall in the quality of life since the separation," and who were thus most at risk for having children with problems (1985, pp. 87–89). These authors also found that the information provided and skills taught seemed to be most useful several months after the initial separation, when most of the grief and sense of loss had been worked through and the parents could turn their attention to the children's needs.

RESTABILIZATION—A NEW CONTENTMENT

Both in the professional literature and in the responses to our study, we found that most divorced individuals could and did "move on" from the acute phase of grief, hostility, depression, guilt feelings, and trauma to a new and reorganized life-style. This occurred anywhere from one to four years after the initial separation, with increasing satisfaction with the new life-style as it was refined in later years.

One of our study respondents, Mrs. Q, a woman in her early 50s, had been divorced for more than 20 years. In a discussion with author LLS, she described how she had come to terms with the permanency of her single status, filling her days and evenings with a variety of meaningful work and pleasurable activities. Now relatively satisfied with the pattern, she had recently had it all upset when she met and "fell in love with" a new man. Although she was looking forward to her forthcoming marriage after so many years of being alone (she had raised her two children who are now on their own), there was almost a wistful character to her comments about the satisfaction of having finally achieved contentment in her life and being proud of it.

Restabilizing one's life is not necessarily easy. There are typically numerous economic readjustments, changes in parent-child relationships and with the other parent as parent, and certainly marked alterations in social life. Therapy does help the individual to make the needed modifications emotionally, and may contribute to seeking ways to improve one's social life. Many women, having been part of a couples' world, have to develop new patterns of activity with other women who are also alone. They have not had as much experience as men usually have had with going out for an evening with a friend, or for dinner, or similar activities. And in some conservative communities, women going out without male escorts are at best tolerated but pitied, and at worst thought to be risqué and brazen. Some women view going out with other women as different from having a "social life," which, to them, means having a date with a man.

REMAINING SINGLE

Wanting to date does not necessarily mean that the individual wants to remarry. A number of our female subjects indicated that they were rather proud of having learned to live and function independently, and weren't too sure that they wanted to return to a situation where they had to account for their time and whereabouts to someone else, or had to resume being tied to "Küchen, Kindern, und Kirche." These were primarily the business and professional women to whom relief from some of these chores was welcome, once they recovered from the shock of separation and divorce. Some men also felt that they were ill suited to the commitment and fidelity entailed in a solid marriage and the consideration of the needs and wishes of another that this subsumes. They too preferred remaining single, autonomous, and "free." Both some men and women indicated they enjoy the ability to date a variety of people—finding it less boring than being limited to one partner for life.

For other individuals who consciously choose to remain single after divorce, it may be a matter of having been so pained, of having their trust so abused, that the person vows not to be placed in a similarly vulnerable situation ever again. This is unfortunate for many such people, because it shuts them away from rewarding new relationships that might become warm and lasting friendships, even if not remarriages. If they are afraid to trust anyone again because the one person—their former spouse—whom they thought could be trusted betrayed the marital vows, this can also make them a bitter, even paranoid person. Friends may become less comfortable with them, reinforcing the feelings of distrust as they drift away from the former close relationship.

Others who choose to remain single may do so because they have grown to enjoy their independence. They make their own decisions and don't have to consult a spouse as to his or her preferences. If there are no dependent children for whom the person is custodian or responsible, there is also no need to worry about the hour at which one gets home, whether dinner is ready on time or at all, or similar typical sometimes annoying family concerns. If there are children in the household, the individual may feel that the new smaller family unit is all that can be handled comfortably, and that a new spouse would only complicate matters.

Saul and Scherman (1984) found no significant differences in post-divorce grief or personal adjustment between subjects who were remarried and those who were single in groups 6–18 months after divorce and 19–36 months after divorce. All of their subjects were in the 25–35 year age group. Whether this was a sufficient time period on which conclusions could be drawn is debatable. The fact that the subjects had to have been married only two years to be included in the study also raises some questions, although the authors acknowledge that they were trying to eliminate differences that might be based on age and degree of self-actualization. Certainly the chances for remarriage are greater, as noted earlier, for divorced individuals below 40 years of age than they are for middle-aged people, especially women.

That leads us to those who remain single because of circumstances, rather than because of choice, like the older divorced women who may simply not have the option of remarriage because there are fewer possible suitors available in an appropriate age bracket. Another factor is that many older people experience anxiety about the loss of income, especially Social Security payments, if they remarry. The phenomenon of cohabitation among the elderly may upset their adult children, and few grandchildren expect Grandmom and Grandpa to be living with someone without the legal bonds of matrimony. Yet cohabitation for some is a solution to loneliness, provides affection and sometimes sexual pleasure, ensures a caretaker in case of illness and a companion to have fun with, and does not reduce Social Security benefits. How strange it still sounds to some to hear a grandchild introduce someone as "This is my grandmother's boyfriend" at a family wedding. It certainly throws the picture of the conventional life cycle out of its traditional track.

Whether remaining single is by preference or by circumstance, the individual also has the choice of making a relatively full new life through new friends and new activities, or being a lonely and embittered person. For some, the single life offers an opportunity for freedom and growth that may have been stifled earlier because of the needs of the spouse, or the perception of the spouse that one had certain unchangeable characteristics or personality traits.

It is interesting to observe the metamorphoses that occur in and by some people postdivorce. For example, both some men and women who have been mildly overweight to quite obese lose weight—something they could not seem to do when they were married and their spouse may have been badgering them to do so. The weight decrease may be due to loss of appetite from worries over their deteriorating financial plight or as a by-product of severe depression and/or it might be a manifestation of the assumption of control in one arena of their lives. Others have plastic surgery on their faces or bodies. Some begin and stick to a regular schedule of physical activity such as a toning up program of jogging, doing aerobics, playing tennis or racquet ball, swimming. Yet these same individuals had indicated during their marriages that they had neither the time nor inclination for this. They may have their hair styled and recolored and make other visible changes in appearance. In six months to a year, the divorced individual may look and feel substantially more attractive and physically healthier and more vibrant. If they have been working on unresolved emotional problems concurrently, in therapy or with friends, their mental health may also have improved markedly so that the overall positive change can be quite significant.

In adjusting to the single life, the person may decide to try out different behaviors and roles and find one that is far more comfortable than the former "persona." As the individual makes more decisions alone, self-confidence can grow to an extent that surprises him or her, not to mention the ex-spouse who observes the change. In a sense, this contributes to even more growth as the person feels that he/she has not let the ex-spouse continue to dominate life, even in absentia.

There is another subgroup we have not yet considered—those who decide to divorce because they realize they are homosexual or bisexual and who no longer wish to live an (overtly) heterosexual life-style. When they announce to their spouse and children that they are terminating the marriage and coming "out of the closet," they sometimes wreak havoc above and beyond what departing heterosexual spouses do. During and post divorce they may already have the support of some friends in the gay community, or they may have great difficulty finding a comfortable niche, particularly if word of their sexual preference reverberates in a conservative community and affects their job (despite antidiscrimination policies). Many homosexual individuals decide to remain single and either live alone or with a gay or lesbian roommate. They do not usually remarry—although they may enter a long-term committed living together relationship. Statistically they are counted in census polls as single. When homosexuality is another factor in the decision to divorce, the various effects on children and the former spouse are usually intensified.

REMARRIAGE—STEPFAMILIES AND NEW TIES

Although remarriage is not a major focus of this book, it seems imperative to include some discussion of it here—as for the majority of divorced individuals (about 80%), remarriage marks the culmination of the divorce process. They reach a point of longing for the permanency and security of a marital relationship. It becomes their primary goal and they plan their activities and behavior to see that this will indeed occur.

> It is evident that the precursor to remarriage has been the disruption in all three life cycles: individual, marital and family [nuclear]. The disruption has been an ongoing process, refuelled by each structural change brought about by the marital discord, physical separation, establishment of two single parent homes, and by the divorce. Subsequent dating and courtship of prospective . . . partners adds to the turbulence. (Sager et al., 1983, p. 45)

The motives for remarriage vary, although they are often similar or parallel to the motives for the first marriage. Love and the desire to share one's life on an ongoing basis is probably the most common reason given by the parties. It's a "natural" reason for any marriage, although many people today simply live together without formal sanction of the marriage laws, regarding this arrangement as "less complicated." Another motive for remarriage is to provide a live-in parent for children of the first marriage. The tasks of single parenting can be overwhelming, and the prospect of sharing them with a caring second spouse is very attractive. Some divorced individuals feel so "empty" or "unfulfilled" alone that they actively seek remarriage to rescue them from their very uncomfortable state of disequilibrium. Others remarry to again be supported financially.

Some individuals rush into remarriage, perhaps sealing a relationship that began prior to the divorce; others may not remarry for many years, like the female subject mentioned earlier who had been divorced for more than 20 years. According to Sager et al. (1983), there is an optimum period of time between divorce and remarriage (about three to five years), and the new marriage is likely to be more successful if the spouses have explored the dynamics of their relationships with others in therapy following the divorce (Hyatt, 1977). The remarriage is also more likely to succeed if the new partners deal with their expectations of marriage realistically.

If the remarriage involves children of one or both spouses, a host of factors are relevant to the new situation—the so-called "blended family."

Should an antenuptial agreement be drawn up and signed that provides for the children in the event of a subsequent divorce or the death of the biological parent? (The answer from most attorneys is a clear "yes!") In what ways do members of the blended family relate to each other's extended families and former relatives? What adjustments are needed in child custody agreements with respect to support and visitation? What happens if the couple decides to have children in this marriage, resulting in a "yours," "mine," and "ours" family? What are the strengths of a remarried family? (There are excellent appendices for use with about-to-be-remarried families in the book by Sager et al. [1983] to which the interested reader is referred.)

In a study of 80 remarried families, with children in the home, Knaub, Hanna, and Stinnett (1984) found that there were three significant factors contributing to the strength of these families. One was a supportive environment provided by relatives, friends, and the community in general. A second factor was family income, with a positive correlation between high family income and family strength. The third significant factor was that the family had sought professional help after the remarriage. Knaub et al. suggest that stepfamilies may be more sensitive to potential problem areas "not present within intact units such as the ex-spouse, stepchildren, custody arrangements, visitation schedules, non-custodial parents, stepsibling relationships, and non-custodial children" (p. 53) and therefore they are more likely to seek help rather than to deny the problem.

In addition to these critical issues, the new spouses may find that they have to deal with the shadows of the friends and extended families of the former marriages. In conversation with a middle-aged woman who had been divorced and is now remarried to a widower, these were sources of major adjustment problems in not only a new marriage but also in relocating to a different (his) community. Childless herself, she acquired stepchildren, stepgrandchildren, a host of in-laws and the friends of her new husband. The first two groups were sources of pleasure since she had been childless. The latter two groups were more of a problem since she had little in common with the women.

Much of the adjustment in remarriage depends upon the expectations each individual has of the new relationship. Is romance wanted? Companionship? Financial well-being? How hard are the new partners willing to work to make the remarriage last? Or, having been through one divorce, are they quicker to "throw in the towel"? There are mixed reports as to whether the frequency of divorce is higher in remarriages than in original marriages; generally estimates are at the figure of 50%.

Children and finances constitute two of the potential crisis arenas of the remarriage family. Depending upon their ages at the time of the remarriage, how well relationships were developed before the new marriage, value systems, presence of stepsiblings, attitudes of the other biological parent and grandparents and many other factors, the children may feel very positive toward the new situation—or very negative, or somewhere in between. If there are sufficient funds for both families to live as well as they did before the divorce, finances are not a major stumbling block. However, in the majority of postdivorce families, there is "not enough to go around" and the economic pie gets sliced thin. The first wife may feel very resentful if the second wife lives better than she did in the early years of her marriage, when the husband was struggling up the career ladder. Conversely, the second wife may be horrified when she realizes that the first wife is living totally on the child and spousal support she receives while the new bride must work—and that part of her income goes to defray the living expenses her husband can't afford because he is saddled with huge payments to his former wife. The husband may feel caught between the demands and discontents of both—sensing that no matter what he does, it's a "no win" situation. He may feel quite frustrated when his ex-wife calls claiming the children must have summer camp, orthodontia, or other things he'd like them to have but which just exceed his income and/or interfere with plans made for and with his new family. It's harder sometimes for an absentee father than a residential father to say "I can't afford it" without incurring great wrath.

Conversely, husband number two may find he's asked to pick up the financial slack for his wife's children—even though he didn't expect to—especially if support checks are late or don't arrive at all. All of these possibilities combined with other remnants or ghosts of the prior marriage are not the most promising scenario for a blended family to become a healthy and happy one.

Yet, in Knaub and Hanna's (1984) study of 44 children residing in remarried families, with a mean age of 12.9 years, 70% of the children considered that their families exemplified successful or very successful adjustment. Most of them had known the stepparent (88.6% were living with mother and stepfather) pretty well prior to the remarriage and had come to love him/her. Since the average youngster in this study was only eight years old at the time of remarriage, Knaub and Hanna suggest that this may have contributed to their positive view of the new family. One particularly interesting comment cited deals with discipline, which is often a bone of contention between the new spouses. "When asked about discipline, the predominant theme from the children was for the stepparent to proceed gradually and carefully" (p. 87). Overall, Knaub and Hanna, like Sager et al. (1983), conclude that it is a mistake to regard remarried or "blended" families as inferior or pathological relationships.

In contrast to the rather positive findings of the study just cited, Halperin and Smith (1983) compared the perceptions of 70 children living with stepfathers and 70 children living in intact families. The children were all preadolescents, aged 10–12 years. It was expected that natural fathers would be perceived more positively than stepfathers, but instead, "stepchildren perceived both their stepfathers and their natural fathers less positively and more negatively than the control children perceived their natural fathers" (p. 25). Explanations for this result range from the possibility that the natural father may have abandoned the mother and child(ren), to the feeling of being enmeshed in a triangle consisting of mother, father, and stepfather. Some of the variation may also be attributed to length of the remarriage, age of the child at remarriage, visitation arrangements and frequency of contact with the noncustodial father, and to idealization of the absent father.

A review of 38 studies of the effects of remarriage on children (Ganong & Coleman, 1984) yields few firm conclusions. In the area of cognitive development, "children in stepfamilies were comparable to children in nuclear families in school grades, academic achievement, field independence, and IQ scores" with the exception of one study (p. 401). Despite various weaknesses in the group of studies that are discussed by Ganong and Coleman, the authors concluded "remarriage of parents does not significantly relate to problem behavior or negative attitudes toward self and others in stepchildren" (p. 402). They do point out, however, that the subjects of the studies were so varied in age, residence, which stepparent was involved, and relationships with other family members, that it is difficult to generalize this conclusion to all stepchildren.

Looking at the question of parent-child relationships in remarriages from the opposite point of view, that of fathers, it might be asked how noncustodial fathers react to the new relationships. In a study of 101 men, Tropf (1984) found that where the first wife had remarried, fathers of higher socioeconomic status tended to visit their children more frequently, and those of lower SES visited less frequently. In the realm of support payments, there was a drop in voluntary (noncourt-ordered) support after the wife's remarriage, with some feeling that the stepfather should share some or all of the costs of the children.On the other hand, Tropf also found that if the husband was the remarried party, "80% of second wives accepted their husband's allocation of money to their first children at the time of marriage" (p. 69). This finding is contrary to the popular perception of a high level of resentment on the part of second wives (discussed earlier in this chapter), but may be related to income level.

Visiting patterns may be altered after the remarriage of either party, due in part to changes in geographical proximity, and in part to the second wives' influence. If the father moves a greater distance, the frequency of visits may decrease, but their length typically increases. Tropf concludes, in fact, that "the increases in the duration of visits and the continued use of phone contacts suggest that the parental bond, although affected by the impact of other [new] role commitments, is not readily abandoned by all fathers" (1984, p. 72).

One can conclude from these studies that remarriage offers both the opportunity for new happiness and many obstacles to surmount. Depending on the stage in the remarriage at which observation or study occurs, there might be quite different findings. Early in the remarriage, for example, the new spouses may be very romantically involved while the children are actively hostile toward the new stepparent. A few years later, when the effects of the original divorce have faded and reality has begun to intrude on romance, the children may be more accepting and less hostile and the spouses more ready to admit to less than ideal elements in the marriage. Remarriages have stages of development just as original marriages do. Perhaps what is surprising, given the multiple commitments and complexities of the relational system, is that 50% of remarriage or blended families survive and seem to prosper emotionally as a real testament to resiliency and the human spirit.

SUMMARY

Subsequent to the initial shock of separation and the trauma usually experienced as a result of divorce, individuals find that life does go on. We have been concerned in this chapter with the ways in which life continues and changes in the postdivorce period.

For all ex-spouses, there is a question of how they relate to each other after the divorce. The ways in which they interact will depend on whether they are likely to encounter each other often or seldom, how much hostility was engendered by the separation, whether there is remarriage by either or both parties, and if so, how quickly. If there are children to consider, there is initially a stage of developing two single-parent families and reorienting to binuclearity and its myriad implications. Further adjustments have to be made if one or both of the ex-spouses remarries and depend on what the relationships are within and between remarried or blended families. Another phase commences when the children marry and the divorced spouses become grandparents.

Restabilization of one's life before, after, or in the absence of remarriage involves a wide variety of adjustments and modifications in lifestyle. The individual has many decisions to make, not the least of which is whether to remarry or to remain single. Perhaps the most long lasting and critical decision, however, is whether to regard the postdivorce status as "the end of the world" or as a challenging opportunity to fashion a new life.

CHAPTER 13

The Impact of Children's Divorce on Parents and Some Contributing Factors

Scrutiny of the literature reflects a dearth of shared insights regarding the impact on parents of their children's divorce; their pain and anguish, sense of failure, self-negation, self-examination, dilemmas in coping, humiliation, occasional elation, and the growth possibilities of the experience. A book on divorce would not be complete without a consideration of this phenomenon.

Previously we (Kaslow & Hyatt, 1982) examined the potential positive impact of divorce on those extended family members affected by separation who are able to come to grips with the challenges and opportunities divorce offers for becoming more independent, self-reliant, and self-actualizing. Over time, they utilize divorce as a developmental and not as a destructive experience. There may be a ripple effect so that, for example, a grandmother witnessing her granddaughter going through a divorce and making it a liberating experience may derive sufficient incentive to take part of several days a week out from the 24-hour care of her demanding invalid husband and feel justified in insisting he be cared for by a homemaker or practical nurse. Or the girl's father may no longer be willing to play chauffeur to a wife who has heretofore refused to learn to drive and therefore tied up all of his free time with errands. After 30 years she may finally get her license.

But in that article we did not specifically address the impact on and

This chapter is a rewrite of an article by R. Hyatt and F. Kaslow, which appeared in the *Journal of Divorce*, 1985, 9, (1), 79–92. It is included here with permission of Dr. Hyatt and the *Journal of Divorce*.

responses of the parents of the divorcing parties, an aspect that should not be overlooked if one wants to provide or acquire a kaleidoscopic view of the consequences of divorce.

The senior parents' reactions affect their own life cycle development. And within the context of the cybernetic circular systems model of conceptualization about family relations which we adhere to, it is posited that their reactions impact upon their children's (and grandchildren's) post-divorce readjustment. Thus this chapter is written expressly to consider this phenomenon from a dynamic-developmental and systemic perspective. Given the nature of parent-child relationships, the developmental life cycle history of the family of origin as a unit, and the changing powerful motivations and reactions of other family members to the divorce, such a dynamic, epigenetic approach seems a valid one to take.

SETTING THE STAGE

There is little need to document the dependencies and attachments of the human newborn and infant to the parents; this has been accomplished successfully by others (Bowlby, 1960, 1969; Spitz, 1946; Spitz & Wolf, 1946). The reciprocal transactions between mother and child, taking into consideration the basic temperaments of each, have also been clearly spelled out (Ribble, 1943; Sullivan, 1953). From the moment of first knowledge about the woman's pregnancy, emotionally healthy and eager prospective parents begin to dream, hope, aspire, plan and set expectations for their child. Goals are quickly formulated, often masked in humor ("Johnny will be the first black president of the United States"; "Mary will be the beauty of the neighborhood"; or "Judy will walk away with all the academic honors"). These early fantasies are positive and extend the parents' personal aspirations in life, frequently compensating for deficits in themselves and their living patterns. They hope to have a second chance to fulfill their dreams through their children and long to be wonderful parents offering the best they can emotionally, intellectually, spiritually and materially to their children. (The scenario is quite different in an unwanted pregnancy and this chapter cannot be generalized to apply to undesired, rejected young adults and their parents.)

As the infant progresses, its budding self-control and environmental mastery give rise to a sense of "self." Handling bodily functions is central as the "ego is first and foremost a body ego" (Freud, 1923). Gradually, the identification process takes hold and just as the child incorporates the values, attitudes, and behaviors of the parent, so, too, the parent revels in seeing himself or herself in the offspring, a positive projective identification and a perpetuation of self through time. Egos of all family parties expand as the pride in "that's my child" interlocks with "meet my mom and dad." Each developmental milestone mastered is a shared source of delight to parents and child alike.

Later, conflict is not uncommon when prepuberty and adolescent friends fail to meet the standards of the parent. This may be expressed in phrases like "I don't think Tom is the kind of friend you want to play with"; or "Sandy is not a good influence—in fact, that trio of Sandy, Amy, and Kim are not your kind." During the teen years, of course, the peer group may well be maintained in spite of parental objections, often leading to open family battles. Additional skirmishes and conflicts erupt when the adolescent begins dating, experiencing puppy-loves, and living through early (as well as later) romances. Criteria for "love" and affectional behavior frequently differ vastly between parent and child. "My generation is different" bumps into the concept of "you'll know what we're talking about when you become a parent" and communication cracks wide open. The generation boundaries are and should be very real (Minuchin, 1974). The line between independence-dependence may become dim and fuzzy, inciting rigorous arguments and/or name-calling. In some families, there is virtually no communication for long periods of time if the young adult selects a boyfriend/girlfriend of whom the parents disapprove. Yet this assertion of autonomy is an important aspect of the young person's individuation process (Erikson, 1968).

IN-LAW/OUT-LAW

Ideally, both parent and child strive to shed inappropriate dependency needs throughout their lifetime. Complications may start with the first hint of romantic seriousness, that is, plans for living together or marriage. Even under the best of conditions, in close knit, possessive, perfectionistic, or rigid families, the fiancé(e) may be considered an "intruder." There are new loyalties to be developed as an investment is made in the new relationships being formed. In addition to the fiancé(e), there is the inclusion of an entirely new family structure—the "other" family. "Skeletons" peek out of family closets as facades lift and the "less-than-best-foot-forward" invariably replaces the "best-foot." Eventually, when the context is positive, there is the perceived transition by the family of "losing" a child to "gaining" one. The reflex to safeguard the history of the family (sociobiologists might contend that the "selfish gene" makes for this instinctive protective reaction) slowly gives way, in healthy relationships, to further ego and financial investments in the new family extension. Sharing, as usual, breeds circular intimacy. Relationships bloom meaningfully. Not infrequently the "additional" family member becomes a favored one. More on this later.

THE INTRUDER PHENOMENON

But the perception of the newcomer may indeed remain that of "intruder." If he/she fails to meet the expectations of prospective parents and siblings, powerful defenses are mustered fairly quickly by all. When it becomes clear that in no way is it possible to move into the "inner circle," even a thick-skinned newcomer will give up, prepare counterdefensive maneuvers, and/or go on the offensive. With sensitive, narcissistically oriented, manipulative, competitive personality types, the offensive battle will be fierce. Often, the child of the embattled parents is placed squarely in the middle by the fiancé(e), who may then proclaim: "Make a choice: it's either me or your family." Ambivalences, angers, dependencies are put to the test. Pushed to a forced choice, an intimidated and very much "in love" young adult child frequently selects her/his lover and the lines of demarcation between children and family are solidly drawn. Angers lead to destructive fantasies. Feelings of betrayal abound. Perception becomes blurred, irrational, and very selective. Emotional quicksand swallows all participants. In other families, parents push the forced choice and threaten never to see their child again if they persist with this "crazy" relationship—vowing that they will disown and disinherit their erring offspring who is nonappreciative of all they've done. Fearing their ire and disapproval, and not wanting such a cut off (Bowen, 1978), they cave in and break off—and then carry resentment for many years toward dictatorial parents. A winner-loser model precludes the possibility of any relational growth or rapprochement between the combatants.

As the psychological limits are approached by such confrontation, even a strong-willed, determined child is severely strained. The dramatic push to the forced-choice, that between parents or fiancé(e), may dislodge the romantic cobwebs in the head of many rebellious young adults resulting in the realization that a future partner who would drive a wedge between parent and child will also, in all probability, finally take over the direction of the marital relationship as well. The lack of empathy for ongoing parent-child needs and ties by the newcomer may signal traits of egocentricity, insecurity, inordinate self-sensitivity and insensitivity to others, and need for control. These underlying complexes, often personality disorders, do not easily dissolve or shift.

When the selection of a mate is made between the ages of 16 and 24 years, a time of assertion of one's separate identity and autonomy

(Erikson, 1968), it may well represent the rebellious urges. Thus, a choice that the parents see as "all wrong" may be "so right" because the new mate is indeed unacceptable to the parents and the young adult perceives the choice as his/her declaration of independence.

When there are many differences in background factors and it is an exogamous pairing, the variations that were initially intriguing and exciting to the young people and signalled future trouble to the parents may well become a source of turbulence in the fledgling marriage. The young couple may not share enough in common in terms of attitudes, values, life-style preferences, and goals to be able to live together with a modicum of harmony.

However, when it is the parents who are rigid, controlling and judgmental and think that "no one is good enough for our son/daughter/family," and yet the young adult courageously goes ahead with the marriage, the parents are not likely to relax and switch to a stance that the newcomer will truly be welcome if their offspring is happy with him/her. Unlike the healthy family which is expansive (Kaslow, 1981c), they prefer to extrude the "intruder" because they fear change in the family system and its homeostatic balance and loss of control over a member who is establishing deep ties to an "outsider."

A WELCOME NEWCOMER

Other times, both sets of parents are delighted with their offspring's choice and eagerly embrace their new son- or daughter-in-law—happily expanding and enriching their family circle. The in-law child may be equally pleased with his or her in-laws even to the extent of perceiving them as a second chance family (Lager, 1977). Indeed, he or she may have partially selected them because they were "better" in some ways than his or her biological or adoptive family. Such a situation may jell to the point where the parents may become close or even closer to the in-law child than to their biological offspring—since the residual hurts and annoyances from childhood are absent (except transferentially, perhaps) in this relationship.

HISTORICAL CONSIDERATIONS

Young adults are not alike; each has a unique personality constellation. Variations in temperament are reflected as early as in the hospital nursery (perhaps in utero); these induce specific reciprocal relationships with parents. Birth-order effects are immediate so that too much is often expected of the oldest, for example, or too little from the youngest, last child. Personality variables interplay dynamically with the first signs of compliance, assertiveness, dominance, insecurity and other traits in all family members. Some children are perceived by their parents as "good," others as "bad." Similarly, concepts of the "good" and "bad" mother and father develop in the child (Klein, 1937; Sullivan, 1953). The child's early mastery and achievements play into the ego-needs of the parent and mutual pride is generated. Conversely, lack of obedience and a dearth of skills yield disappointment and shame in both. Attractiveness of the child to others during adolescence adds to the parents' positive feelings—in essence, the popularity of their child as an ego-extension testifies to their own appealing attributes; deficits in this regard hit hard and sensitively at their own negative self-perceptions. In some families, parents who overidentify with or attempt to live vicariously through their children become extremely tense when their children do not socialize and date, fearing they are either unacceptable to the "in group" young people and/or that there is a personality problem that causes them to retreat into aloneness/loneliness. Healthy parents resonate to the hurt their adolescents feel. Today, though career has assumed increasing importance for daughters, the majority of parents still want their children of both sexes to live full lives—which include marriage and children, as well as career. Like Freud (1961), they recognize that a healthy, happy life entails love and work.

If and when their young adult child becomes engaged and gets married to someone of whom they approve, the ego-extension is expanded even further. This may be less true if there is a "living together" pattern which goes counter to the family's value system. Then embarrassment, rage, and disappointment may be prevalent reactions. Once the marriage is consummated, the newcomer can either feed into a positive or negative existing valence. At times there is a neutral tone to the parent-child interactions but typically, at the very least, there is ambivalence. The new in-law child tips the scales to the plus or minus charge. If the newcomer is perceived negatively by the parents, then this tends to validate the status of their own son or daughter as a "bad child." A positively perceived newcomer, on the other hand, may alter parental perceptions and enhance the positive qualities and value ascribed to their child. A reciprocity develops so that opinions about each other and behaviors toward one another, across the two generations, *do* change. Mutual supports evolve and the crooked family tree grows straighter in healthy form (Walsh, 1982).

PARENTAL PRESSURES

An originally "good child" who marries below or in opposition to parental expectations becomes a source of dismay, disappointments, and despair ("How could you have done this to us?"). Unprepared for such a turn of events, and since "good" children tend to be eager to please, are good communicators (at least good listeners), easily manipulated if guilt is played upon, and malleable, there is strong (and unfair) pressure from the parents, and perhaps grandparents, to undo the relationship. Often the family of origin members are successful in this endeavor. At other times, with a child of excellent ego-strength and determination tempered by reasonableness, conflict and anger eventually dissolve after the marriage as parents adopt a posture of acceptance ("I hope she/he knows what she/he is doing"). This occurs when parents understand that their relationship with their child is endangered if they fight against the union or are hypercritical of their child's choice of partner. More positively, sometimes the parents slowly come to the realization that *if they love their child* they should back off, not sabotage, and trust their child to find his/her own way.

Psychological dynamics in this situation are quite complex. Suppose, for example, that the parents' marriage has been rocky and meaningless. The hope that the child will be successful in his/her marriage may become an exaggerated emotion, neurotic in proportion. The mosaic of fantasies about the child which evolved throughout his/her development peak during the child's separation from the household. He/she holds the key to vicarious gratifications. Conversely, an "independent" life for the child, particularly if he/she is an only child or the last of several to depart, connotes for some parents a distasteful being alone together—no longer able to divert their attention to the child or to hold their relationship together for and through the child. This can portend danger for their marriage; thus they shift focus and worry about the child's marriage, sometimes overtly or covertly attempting to undermine it and therefore have the child return to them in order to stabilize their own relationship. Placing such a burden on a child is selfish and unfair—but not uncommon. And such behavior is perpetrated under the guise of love and loyalty.

What is the course of these events? Pent-up angers in the parental relationship explode as the parents' fantasies blow apart. Besides an accretion of frustrations, the parents are likely to experience guilt for their real or fancied ineffectiveness ("Look at what we have done to our child; how could we have produced such an error.") Self-negation and "mea culpa" reactions often lead to an overcompensation for past failures. Parents with neurotic stamina may dive more deeply into the child's marital situation in order to buoy their child. They think they are taking over to save a drowning. Their intrusion is rationalized in an aura of survival. The continuation of the child's "romantic" relationship is equated with doom. Their "generous martyrdom" expressed in emotional concern and/or financial generosity is intended to induce further dependency and gratitude in their child.

Unhappy parents frequently bask in their child's difficulties since it temporarily extricates them from their own ennui and marital doldrums. They find purposefulness, usually unconsciously, in trying to assuage and alleviate their child's floundering, indicating at times—"Our door is always open if you need to come home."

Conversely, parents in a happy marriage, although wary and dissatisfied with their child's choice, will tend to back off and protect the right of the new couple to find their way as they did theirs, hoping that they will not eventually become one of the many of today's marriages that are destined for divorce.

THE DIVORCE

With all of the parental anguish surrounding a perceived ineffective premarital relationship of their child, a divorce rarely occurs without shocking reverberations for all. It represents an end, a finale, and for many—a failure. Just as each member of a divorced dyad and their children rarely escape affective scars, so parents must live with disappointment, agonizing questions, self-doubts, and occasional self-denunciations. Parental satisfactions are meager under most conditions of divorce; "I told you so" brings little joy. When decisions for a breakup are unmistakably sound, coupled with the parents' intellectual understanding, there is little pleasure. Parents who in the past have been hostile and disruptive to the union may feel remorse and guilt when they see their child emotionally distraught and question if the outcome was worth the traumatic turbulence.

There never ceases to be an intergenerational concern for one's children—just as children have loyalties, visible and invisible, to their parents. Progeny's strengths and weaknesses mirror the essence of parents, grandparents, and the entire family line (Boszormenyi-Nagy & Spark, 1973; Bowen, 1978). Achievements as well as inadequate coping of children in the physical, intellectual, emotional and social realms reflect back to their ancestral heritage. Psychological responses to the perceived failures of children are multiple and varied: in addition to the above cited responses, denial, rejection, anger and hostility may be felt and manifested.

There are numerous other complexities when the parental marriage has muddled along its own path of meaninglessness. For example, and not atypically:

In the D. family, after their tearful daughter told them she had separated, at one level there was a form of parental rationalization that "It's tough for *anyone* to make a marriage work these days." On a different level self-deprecation took hold: "If we had been better models, our child would not be so messed up." A vast amount of finger pointing took place with Mr. D. yelling "If you were not such an incompetent, useless bore, *your* kid wouldn't be so screwed up." Mrs. D. countered with "If you had been home more instead of hiding out in your plant, Judy would have known more about men and made a better choice." (Author FK's case file)

Some (selfish and/or dysfunctional) parents may look forward to the child's return in order to add some excitement and meaning to their own lives. Other parents are likely to assert: "We stayed in this marriage for your sake and look at all of us now." Still others resent the renewed financial and emotional burdens ("I thought we were finished with that part of our lives"). Either parent may feel envious and inadequate because their child, in effect, had the courage to terminate an unsatisfactory relationship while they continue to persevere unhappily with their own.

Older parents, still immersed in the anti-divorce value-net of the 1930 to 1960 period, are caught in the strange transitional meanings of divorce; it is one thing to fantasize the possibility, another to live through it. When grandchildren are involved, the pit-in-the-stomach feelings emanating from the fear of loss and disruption gnaw away; in effect, the wound may never heal totally.

In a different vein, when parent-child relationships are healthy, empathy and support are elicited and everyone involved slowly goes through a transformation and reequilibration process (Bohannan, 1970; Kaslow, 1984a; Kessler, 1975). They can and do extricate themselves from the "stuckness" and become present and future oriented.

OTHER FACTORS

With joyous marriages there is a natural expansion of each family to include the in-laws. New friendships are often established between parents-parents as well as siblings-siblings. Divorce obliterates these relationships. Allegiances become sensitive and fragile—always awkward. An in-law child may dearly love the ex-spouse's sibling or parent and want to continue to be close to them. It may prove painful and heart-wrenching although some families work it through and do not sever all bonds. Usually, emotional pieces lay strewn about, rarely to be made whole again.

Many individuals, especially those with passive personalities, cannot express appropriate anger to their former spouse. With cooperative negotiations over child custody, visitation rights, and support payments, there may be a strong masking effect. The absence of acrimony between ex-spouses may be more apparent than real. There is harm in conceal-ment; greater health when emotions are aired. Among other reasons, many children become confused by the "friendship" of parents when they "cannot make it together in marriage." The children should receive a logical explanation as to what makes this possible. Some professionals believe that children of the divorced should be protected from parental explosions and that this is for the adults to deal with. Further, profes-sionals advocate that parents should pledge in their divorce settlement agreements not to disparage each other to their children.

What, then, is the role of the parents of the divorced? Should they incite anger? Is a passive approach meaningful? One step in an effective coping strategy is to be a sympathetic listener, tuning into the pain and ambivalence. Support rather than advice-giving is the recommended avenue. Not being critical or asserting "I told you so" is crucial. So, too, is being careful not to stress one's own embarrassment as to "what people will think."

Understanding the emotional upheaval of the young adult must take precedence over other concerns. But emotional disturbance is not limit-ed to the divorcé(e) alone; parental adjustment is also derailed. Reac-tions of the child to parents are multiple in possibilities—not unlike those of the parents to their child: anger, resentment, guilt, denial, rejection, as well as empathy and support. Reaction formations may cover true feelings. The dynamics between parents and child are very complex, contingent upon the temperaments, personalities, and experiences of each. A reliving of old premarital conflicts is frequently renewed and this reactivation often results in a more pitiful family tragedy—the child taunting: "Now are you satisfied?" or saying plaintively: "If only I had listened to you." The permutations are enormous, and empirical re-search is needed to clarify the nuances of these interactions.

DÉJÀ VU

The cliché "life must go on" is applicable here. And, indeed at times, after a divorce, it seems to grate on and on and on, unhappily and interminably. Sitting home alone, nursing wounds, weighs heavily. For some, dating, at first nerve-wracking, becomes fun. Then eventually, it may be transformed into a "turn-off"—as superficial and empty. For many there is a period of sleeping around, with its accompanying roller-coaster effects and a numbing (Hyatt, 1977). The divorcé(e) and his/her parents may be worried about his/her getting herpes or AIDS, definitely an inhibiting factor.

Parents, although generally sensitive to feelings, ideas, and behaviors of their offspring, can be insensitive to the real emotional highs and lows. On the one hand, they encourage him/her to go out and make new friends; on the other, they are fearful and protective of their child's bruised ego and recognize their vulnerability to being hurt. Should they "push" for activity or leave events to their natural rhythm? The latter is more easily conceived than done. It is difficult to see one's own son or daughter moping around discontented and ill at ease. Should they offer advice when it is not solicited? Not to do so requires enormous self-restraint, wisdom and maturity.

Eventually, many young divorced people reach out and find someone "special." Patterns of behavior, temperament, and personality may be discerned which are similar to those of the first spouse. Scrutiny of the newcomer in depth is almost expected by the parents and their adult child. Discussion, analysis, and forewarning by parents is likely to be interpreted by the child as intrusive; parents view them as hypersensitive; such differences often lead to mini-battles. Little or no communication about the relationship follows and even when the particular person in question is no longer in the picture, the young adult circumvents parental encounters about future dates, as well they should. And parents feel shut out. Defenses and angers once more take center stage. An almost unbelievable circularity of emotional responses between child and parents, similar to those surrounding the first marriage, tend to be repeated. Experiences of "déjà vu" are not uncommon. A high probability exists for the child and/or parents to think: "I should have worked harder at the first one" and "I really haven't seen anyone better out in that strange singles world." Many variations of these themes ripple among multiple cognitive emotional currents.

Wise parents learn to trust their son or daughter's right to their own choices and pull back from overprotective, overpossessive behaviors. They utilize their energies to enrich their own marital relationship. The delightful "happy-ending"—the successful second-time around—is, of course, the idea and ideal of all parties. If remarriage occurs, it may imbue a refreshing spirit in the relationship between parent and child, bringing about a fuller individuation of each from the other plus a new respect for intergenerational and personal boundaries. A positive reanalysis may be made of previous events and historical highlights. All are buoyed with renewed hope and aspirations. A new found environment of contentment may prevail and parents are more likely to have the wisdom to be generally less involved the second time around.

When the divorced child (for want of a better word) is in the over-45 age bracket, particularly if female, chances of remarriage may dwindle. Parents are likely to agonize over their original objections and the chaos to which they contributed. If their offspring is fortunate enough to find a new partner, only very self-centered and/or short-sighted parents would have the audacity to interfere again.

PSYCHOTHERAPEUTIC IMPLICATIONS

Scars invariably mar emotional tranquility and smoothness of function for families of the divorced. Cognitive blind spots interfere with an already elusive sense of human happiness. Anxiety and dysphoric moods weave into an aging parental fabric strained by the formal forces of everyday living. When a child leaves the household to become an independent adult, especially with the love, intimacy, security and protection of a spouse, a warm sense of "having done my job successfully" is generated in the parents. A positive connotation of freedom is experienced: freedom to devote more energy to younger siblings, freedom to plan more fully for their own needs and wants, freedom to relate to the married couples at a more mature level. These freedoms are devastated by divorce, the life cycle is thrown out of kilter, and developmental equilibrium is delayed.

A series of professional psychotherapeutic encounters involving all members of the family can be a restorative experience with significant shortening of negative, nonproductive aspects in the divorce adjustment continuum. Individual, family, and pre-remarriage therapy sessions should be considered depending on the preferred psychotherapeutic modality of the therapist and the needs of the patients. Multigenerational family therapy could be considered in a multiple eclectic approach. Support groups for the parents of the divorced, similar in purpose to groups for children of divorce, could be meaningful as they share experiences and approaches with others in similar circumstances. For parents as well as children, this crisis, like most other crises, can be a tragedy from which they never recuperate or a chance for creative growth and development. When it is utilized as the latter, it affords people a healthy challenge to genuinely examine themselves, their beliefs, values, and relationships.

CHAPTER 14

Toward Integration and Wholeness

In this concluding chapter an endeavor is made to recapitulate and sharpen the major themes, synthesizing them to the extent our current knowledge permits into a meaningful collage. We recognize that our portrayal is necessarily incomplete as it has not been possible to incorporate everything written about divorce; yet we hope we have achieved our aspiration of presenting an accurate and vivid depiction of the process of divorce from a developmental perspective, based on individual and family life cycle formulations. We have attempted to provide an in-depth portrayal of the impact of the period of predivorce conflict and uncertainty, the during-divorce period of trauma, rejection, animosity and turbulence, and the postdivorce period of rebuilding one's life on the divorcing adults, their children, and their extended families.

Rarely is the process simple, gentle or calm. The havoc wrought, intended and unintended, is severe and its effects long lasting. Some of the factors found to be significant in terms of the differential impact of divorce were: age at time of divorce; gender; socioeconomic status; absence or presence of extended family support systems (emotional and financial); for divorcing adults—educational background and occupational skills level; degree of emotional health vs. pathology in the individual and family unit; problem-solving and coping skills; level of realistic optimism; availability of a friendship support network (including playmates, colleagues, self-help groups); and we would add here resiliency, physical health and some "good luck."

In Chapter 1, "A Family Systems Framework and Life Cycle Perspective," we presented a healthy family paradigm as the backdrop against which to view all families. When families go through the divorce process, we believe their overall level of functioning deteriorates—at least temporarily. The system's boundaries to the outer world are, in a sense, violated as one or more members depart from the family unit—often following serious rifts which cause irreparable damage to the family's homeostatic balance.

Such a departure is not directly analogous to the "leaving home" of an adolescent or young adult child (Haley, 1980), yet there may be similarities. For example, when the adolescent leaves home, it may represent a running away from an untenable situation. Some spouses depart because they cannot tolerate living with their mate any longer—the conflicts, dissatisfactions, level of ennui, or unfulfilled "needs" and expectations far outweigh any joy or satisfaction accruing from the marriage. Other adolescents are "thrown out," sometimes being told the parents are "totally fed up with their nonsense" and that "we never want to see your face again." In extreme cases when they've been highly disruptive or behaved totally in opposition to the parents' value system—they may be disowned. In some predivorce separations a spouse who is infuriated over being betrayed or shortchanged may say very much the same things, evicting his/her mate bag and baggage and changing the door locks. Both of these kinds of departures are traumatic, destructive and chilling—and do not occur in optimally functioning families.

In our prototypical healthy family the moving out of a young adult family member to go to college, to relocate to take a job, to live with a friend or to get married is perceived as a predictable life event. It heralds a new phase of independence and self-sufficiency and may be interpreted as a sign that the parents have done their work well in fostering their child's sense of autonomy and confidence. Although there may be some sadness that the launching phase of the family life cycle is ending, it is mixed with pride and joy. It is quite different when a spouse leaves, or rejects the other partner and insists that he/she exit the family home. This is not an anticipated part of the marital and family life cycle, rather it signifies the death of the nuclear family and the inability of the couple to grow and change in tandem in a compatible fashion. This parting is not accompanied by feelings of pride and joy, nor of success. It may be an admixture of anger and relief, shock and confusion.

Another way the family unit's boundary to the external world may have been permeated is the "intrusion" of a lover into the life of one member of the marital dyad before the separation. In a healthy family, any overtures in this direction would be considered inappropriate and would be rejected.

Let us consider only two more of the dimensions of the healthy family, illustratively, to see what happens during the divorce process.

The intergenerational boundary lines often become crossed in ways they should not. If mom disappears and dad is unexpectedly left with the care of two or three young children, he may ask either set of grandparents to temporarily take care of the children—particularly if his job involves a great deal of travel or he feels totally inadequate for the task. When this occurs, grandparents may seem like parents, daddy may seem like a visiting uncle, and mommy like a hazy memory or distant relative. If and when dad remarries and wants to again become a fully in charge residential parent, the grandparents may be reluctant to return the children because they have almost convinced themselves they are the parents.

In a variation on this scenario, currently in my practice (FK), we are seeing both the S grandparents and the T grandparents who are engaged in a custody battle. The S's daughter became pregnant; the T's son was the father. The S's 18-year-old daughter had quit high school and was quite promiscuous. The T's 19-year-old son has been heavily into the drug scene and is considered shiftless and irresponsible. They were referred by the T's attorney wanting an evaluation as to whether the 3-year-old granddaughter had been sexually molested.

Although the mother has legal physical custody, in actuality, the grandparents each have her half of the week. She is a beautiful and captivating youngster, who on clinical and testing evaluation does not show signs of being disturbed. It appears that the sexual charges were a red flag introduced to cast aspersions on the competing family. Each set of grandparents sees in the child another chance to be successful parents and negates the parenthood of their children.

At the moment, treatment is focusing on enabling them to share and not tear apart the child and encouraging them to enable their own young adult children to become more responsible adults. We are urging them to be clear in accurately defining titles and roles of the six adults involved.

Another way generational boundaries are transgressed in divorcing families is when the oldest child becomes parentified—having to comfort a distraught parent, having to take over primary care for younger siblings and/or having to become confidant, companion, provider, etc., for a dependent parent who cannot manage after he or she was "deserted." Such a parentified child of divorce is prematurely thrust into the adult subsystem and sidetracked from attending to what should be his/her major activities—like school work, peer group fun, and sports. Later, if and when the parent finds a new partner, the parentified child may resent being demoted and being expected to again function as part of the child subsystem.

Other characteristics of healthy families that often go awry are good problem-solving, negotiation, and communication skills. The disruptions caused by the separation and divorce are like the tremors of an earthquake. One is uncertain where the lava will fall and what cracks will remain after the major upheaval subsides. If the disenchanted, disaffected party makes a unilateral decision to terminate a marriage, and is convinced it is irrevocable, then the decision is nonnegotiable. Previously useful bargaining and negotiating skills will be rendered useless in the wake of such rigidity. Problem-solving skills may initially shift from earlier pro-active ones to temporarily reactive ones—with the rejectee mustering all of his/her coping abilities to deal initially with one day at a time. And it sometimes is likely to feel futile to attempt to communicate effectively with a former loved one who has become inaccessible. Given all of the above, the frustration mounts and even many couples who might ordinarily function in a very healthy manner look and feel quite chaotic, fragmented and dysfunctional much of the time during the divorce process and in the period of the immediate aftermath. Yet, just as Erikson (1968) posited, at each stage of life one's coping skills and ability to master the essential tasks are predicated on how successfully one was able to cope and make transitions at each prior stage. Predictably then, the individuals who were healthiest and handled transitions well prior to the divorce are most likely to become the successful "survivors" during the resolution and reequilibration phases discussed in Chapter 2 on the "Stages in the Divorce Process." Also in this chapter the individual and family life cycle stages were linked to phases in the divorce process. Here and throughout the book we have indicated which type(s) of therapeutic interventions seem to be most beneficial at various times during the progression of the divorce.

We have shown that causality in relationships is circular rather than linear and that, although on the surface the ostensibly rejecting partner may appear to be "guilty," and the rejected mate may seem an innocent victim—fitting the earlier dominant legal conceptualization that undergirded fault divorce—in actuality the "innocent" partner has often contributed to the demise of the relationship through negative, provocative, or withholding behavior. Thus the contemporary prevailing legal doctrine of "no fault" divorce has much greater concordance with family systems principles of circular causality, morphogenesis and equifinality than assumptions of fault did.

Throughout the book we have reviewed the literature, reporting on the main findings of researchers and clinicians. Bohannon's six stations of divorce (1970, 1973)—emotional, legal, economic, co-parental and child custody, community, and psychic—provided the organizing schema for our own work on stages, feelings accompanying each stage, tasks to be mastered and recommended therapeutic interventions for different family members at the various stages (see Table 2 on pp. 30–31 and Kaslow, 1981b, 1981d, 1983). This was integrated with Duhl's (1981) Chronological Chart, which provides a tool for viewing each family member separately yet simultaneously.

"Causes" of divorce are manifold. They include, but are certainly not limited to adultery; mental cruelty; child and/or spouse abuse; substance abuse (drugs/alcohol); conflict over in-laws and the couple's relationship to them; financial pressures or disagreements over how money should be earned and spent; poor communication; nagging; lack of affection; sexual dysfunction or incompatibility; conflicting value systems and life-style preferences; desire for greater freedom and independence than marriage permits; desire for personal self-actualization which partner is believed to inhibit; growing away from each other; finding the partner increasingly dull, boring or offensive, etc. Here again multiple and circular causality are evident. For example:

> Judi was overly dependent on her possessive parents. This pro-voked her husband's anger, which then interfered with his ability to show affection. Feeling unwanted and not appreciated by Hans, Judi began to drink heavily, which further aggravated and embar-rassed him with his colleagues when they went to business func-tions. After Judi acted seductively and became extremely intoxicat-ed at a dinner party at his boss's home, Hans felt he could tolerate her attention-getting antics no longer. He also saw her as an unfit mother and poor role model for their children. He wanted and needed a different kind of wife now and was not willing, despite Judi's pleas, to reconsider and give her time to go into an alcohol rehabilitation program where she could achieve sobriety and reor-ganize her life.

Clearly, simplistic, linear explanations as to "why" it happened rarely suffice. Although one happening or argument may be the trigger event for the ultimate separation, a series of disagreements based on unaccept-able behaviors and expressed attitudes and feelings have in all probabili-ty been taking place over a prolonged period of time. The final volcanic eruption follows many minor tremors.

Findings from the Kaslow and Schwartz study described earlier, con-ducted in 1984–85 on divorced adults who had not yet remarried and their children, were reported. By dividing the children into two sub-groups—those under 10 years of age (the babes) and those over 11 years of age (older kids), we were able to discern more about the differential impact of divorce according to age of child at the time of the occurrence of the divorce. Main concerns voiced by older children of divorce regarded worries about: their parents' postdivorce adjustment, whether funds would actually be available for college or other postsecondary school education, whether they could make a good choice of a future life partner and a full enough commitment to make a relationship last since they did not wish to have to go through a "second divorce," and feelings that they were still often torn asunder by competitive parental demands and/or expectations.

Our findings are generally consistent with those Wallerstein reported recently from her 10-year follow-up study (1985a). Discussing children of divorce who were now from 19 to 28 years of age, she found they all exhibited or had:

1. Vivid negative memories
2. Depression
3. Resentment toward their parents
4. A sense of deprivation
5. Conservative morality
6. Apprehension about repeating their parents' [unsuccessful] patterns
7. High ideals about marriage

If the kind of data now available to professionals about the negative impact of divorce on children as well as on adults (many of whom experience great sadness, anger, sense of failure, despondency, lack of energy, resentment, inability to trust, etc.) continues to filter out to the general public, one can only speculate whether the realization that divorce is rarely a rainbow with a pot of golden happiness at the other end of the multi-hued arch will serve as a deterrent and cause some portion of the 1.2 million couples who divorce annually to "try harder," to seek good marital therapy, and to become less unrealistic in their expectations. Of course, there are enough stories of a wonderful "life after divorce," of finding oneself and never having been happier, from which many individuals contemplating divorce find encouragement and, for them, optimism outshines the prophecies of gloom and doom. One recent study attesting to the efficacy of the belief that some people do successfully complete the psychic divorce and that a new phoenix can be built from the ashes and solid fragments of what remains and was learned will be presented later. For now that is jumping ahead of our sequence of events.

LEGAL AND ECONOMIC ISSUES AND BATTLEGROUNDS

Much of the bitterness felt may be exacerbated by the legal battles over distribution of assets and child custody/visitation arrangements. All too often litigated divorces deteriorate into ugly fracases—bringing out the worst in the warring contestants. Fifteen percent of all divorces end up as courtroom fights; the remaining 85% are settled out of court. There is to date little data on how satisfactory these resolutions are when the agreements are negotiated primarily by the respective parties' attorneys (Blau, 1986). What we do see and hear is that mediation appears to be a viable alternative dispute resolution strategy and that couples who mediate have a much better chance of fulfilling the provisions of their agreement (Folberg, 1984; Saposnek, 1983; Kaslow, 1984b) because they were instrumental in shaping it and ultimately agreeing to it than do couples who litigate and therefore have an agreement forged by attorneys and/or superimposed by the court. In law it is essential to have standards that are applied rather globally so that all litigants are treated similarly in the various courts of justice. Not very much is left to the individual judge's discretion because he/she may also be influenced by his/her biases, whims and preferences. Some standardization is necessary, yet too much rigidity is ironic in custody matters, given that each child and family is unique and must be treated according to their needs.

We have shown that in this country we have gone through several major changes in the predominant standard for making child custody decisions—shifting from paternal preference to maternal preference, the latter being integrally interwoven with the doctrine of the tender years. This doctrine was predicated on a magical belief in the potency, exclusivity and primacy of the mother-child bond. More recent research on bonding has shown that this closeness is particularly important and special during the first year of the child's life. After that, other significant adults who are extremely nurturing can make very strong two-way attachments with the small child. This finding dovetails with the reports emanating from research on fathers who have sole or shared custody of preschool children. Fathers become quite close, attentive, loving caretakers.

The doctrine of "the best interest of the child" became codified as the standard in the Uniform Marriage and Divorce Act of 1971 as a result of a convergence of several factors, including: evidence of the ability of competent and loving parents of both genders to be primary nurturing caretakers; the desire of some mothers to be liberated from main or sole parental responsibility postdivorce; the increasingly vocal petitions of fathers to share in single parenting more fully; and the realization by mental health professionals and those shaping social policy that children need access to both parents and the continuing love and active involvement of both. Although maternal preference still colors the decisions of particularly some of the older and more conservative judges, the "best interests" standard is currently one of the major precepts adhered to in 48 of the 50 states.

Unfortunately, much of the expressed adherence to this presumption is verbiage. In many instances, each parent and their respective attorneys construes the child's best interest to be whatever they say it is—to suit their narcissistic needs, to penalize their spouse, to punish the child, or as a bargaining chip to get the other partner to succumb to the terms of a "guerrilla campaign" (Blau, 1986). Dad, for instance, might say it's in the best interest of his sons to be awarded to him—knowing that he is away a great deal and he'd have to hire a live-in housekeeper. Further, he knows his wife is a fine, devoted and available mom and very much wants primary physical custody. Because this is her main area of sensitivity and vulnerability, he is using the threat of a custody fight to intimidate her into making major financial concessions by "voluntarily" abdicating part of her claim to what she would be legally entitled under equitable distribution or community property laws. Such tactics nullify the essence of "the best interest of the child" doctrine and ultimately interfere with sound planning and wise and reasonably harmonious parental co-parenting relations. These tactics violate consideration of the rights and needs of children; model unethical and reprehensible behavior by parents to their children—causing them to fear and even hate, rather than to love and respect, the offending parent; and make them pawns in a vicious chess game entitled "custody" that is a mask for "money."

No knowledgeable and astute mediator will permit such bargaining ploys. Generally custody issues are dealt with separately from financial considerations and the avowed emphasis is on what does *this* child need at *this* time, what can each parent provide and how do these interface, and how can each share the co-parenting in the most efficacious manner. This is a very different starting point and perspective and apparently leads to more peaceful, workable outcomes in the best interest of all involved parties.

Currently, the "best interest" standard is intertwined in many states with preference for joint custody. The terms joint custody, co-custody, joint parental responsibility, and shared parenting can be interpreted in a variety of ways. Therefore, in each agreement, we recommend that the intended meaning be clearly defined and that it rationally incorporate a feasible shared parental responsibility arrangement—flexible enough to allow for the changing developmental needs of the child(ren) and major modifications in parental circumstances *and* structured and definitive enough to enable predictability and continuity in the child's life.

Few lawyers and judges are trained in the vast areas of child development and family dynamics. They are not likely to be astute in understanding the subtleties of manipulation and chicanery that masquerade under the umbrella phrase "best interest of the child." Therefore, we urge that before the court awards custody in disputed cases, the children be fully evaluated by a child psychologist or family therapist, such assessment to include personality and intelligence tests. Further, the evaluation should include observation of each child interacting with each parent, a home visit to each parent's residence to see the living environment they will be providing for the child and the child's degree of comfort with the milieu, and a clinical interview with each parent separately to assess their parenting skills and attitudes.

The report to the court (or the mediator if requested by same) should present findings and *not* make a recommendation. The ultimate decision-making authority is delegated by our society to the court and not to the clinician. The report tendered should comprise primary data upon which the decision can be predicated (Blau [personal communication, March 1984], 1986). The report should also recommend periodic reassessments of the child at approximately three-year intervals to see how the child is progressing at times of significant developmental milestones.

If this is done, and the couple is following a mediated agreement, this recommendation may coincide with a similar one made by the mediator for occasional reevaluations of how well the custody/visitation plan is operating. If what becomes apparent is that some modifications need to be made truly "in the best interest of the child," these can be done in the sane atmosphere of the safe sanctuary of the mediator's office and then taken to the attorney to file at court. No legal struggle need ensue, thus avoiding another debilitating scene and tying up the courtroom dockets.

Despite the 6% decline in the divorce rate in the early 1980s from 5.3 per 1,000 population in 1981 to 5.0 per 1,000 population in 1982 (the most recent national statistics we could obtain [National Center for Health Statistics, 1985]), the phenomenon is so widespread and raising such national concern that on June 3, 1986, NBC-TV produced a special white paper entitled "Divorce Is Changing America," which was narrated by Jane Pauley. The alarm bells which resounded on that program highlighted some of the issues and trends we have analyzed in the foregoing chapters. Given that Wallerstein and Weitzman were two of the participants, and we have liberally cited their work, this concurrence would be expected. The program addressed one of the most measurable aspects—the economic aftermath of divorce.

The most current data presented (with interpretations interspersed by the current authors) indicated that contemporary America is now experiencing the unanticipated and latent consequences of no-fault legislation and the women's liberation movement with its thrust for equality. Weitzman posited that 85% of divorced women receive no alimony and that 50% of the men who are supposed to pay child support (two million of them), under the provisions of their divorce decrees, fail to do so. Some divorced men disappear, so that despite laws which provide for the attachment of wages, there are no known wages to attach. The people charged with tracking down errant fathers are overloaded and in some states this task is not given high priority. Some men are sent to jail; others who refuse to meet their obligations (incurred by virtue of bringing a child into this world *and* by court mandate) were depicted as "stealing from their kids."

It is no wonder then that divorced women who have primary physical custody and receive no child support rapidly experience a decline in their socioeconomic status and their ability to provide for the children's basic survival needs. And, according to the White Paper, the problem is of mammoth proportions and growing.

Certainly financial stress, often to the extreme of dire poverty, does not bode well for the postdivorce adjustment of these mothers and their children. It's hard to minister to the psychological and social needs of one's children and oneself when survival concerns about having adequate shelter and sufficient nourishing food are paramount. Earning a living and/or "getting on welfare" are overriding preoccupations. Bitterness, resentment and anger do not fade when an ex-spouse absconds, totally abandoning his family and leaving them to cope without any financial or emotional assistance from him. In such instances, children may learn to distrust, even "abhor" the parent who disappears. It is hard to be loyal when one is betrayed. The consequences of such behavior by a parent are long lasting and we have seen instances where they are irreversible.

A balanced overview must also present the alarm being sounded from the other corner of the ring, that of concern for men's rights (Siller, 1986). Siller, a practicing matrimonial lawyer with over three decades of experience, posits that "the ultimate goal, greater power, always remains the same. So it is in the war between the sexes" (p. 26). He cites the most recent *O'Brien vs. O'Brien* decision, handed down by the New York Appellate Court on December 26, 1985, decreeing a medical license to be "marital property" as a "landmark divorce decision with devastating implications." The court accepted the valuation of Dr. O'Brien's license at $475,000, based on the testimony of an expert witness who had considered such factors as his income, age, and life expectancy. His wife's distributive share was set at 40%, or $188,800 of his future earnings—in addition to the other items she was to receive in the settlement. Siller interpreted this precedent-setting decision as "the most damaging economic incursion by any state in the country." Previously, 20 state courts had refused to consider a medical license as a marital asset.

The O'Briens had no children during the 14 years of their marriage. Dr. O'Brien claimed that his wife made no direct financial contribution toward his medical training in Mexico; he held that all told his wife and her parents contributed $16,000 to their support during his education and training years. There were innuendos that Dr. O'Brien was guilty of marital misconduct (adultery) and that he had "abandoned" his wife two weeks after he obtained his medical license. Even though under New York law marital misconduct is not supposed to be a factor considered in the equitable distribution of assets, Siller implied that there was an attempt to appropriately compensate her for his alleged transgressions.

Siller holds that the valuation was made predicated on an assumption that the doctor would practice surgery and that he would not become incapacitated. He holds that "the court's opinion is manifestly inequitable, since once made, equitable distribution decisions are incapable of being modified!" (1986, p. 26). (What can be modified are child support allotments and child custody arrangements.) He implies that other states may follow suit and that persons holding a variety of professional and business licenses may find themselves in situations similar to Dr. O'Brien's. Interestingly, he does not address the fact that today husbands are also helping to send their wives through medical school, law school, etc., and that the equitable distribution of a professional practice as part of a marital settlement could also apply to the women's practice and future earnings being divisible.

We have all seen cases in which the husband was or felt "fleeced"; where the wife trumped up charges that she was unable to work and the lawyer helped her secure a physician's testimony that she had something like "chronic back pain." We have seen men so overburdened with child support and alimony payments that they cannot maintain a decent standard of living and are unable to remarry or, if they do, they really struggle to make ends meet. These cases may fall into the 15% not discussed by Weitzman and they merit attention also.

Although an ex-wife's contribution to the husband ends with the divorce, his economic entwinement with her never ends if she is awarded permanent alimony. He not only continues to be a father, which he should be, as this role does not end with divorce, but economically he remains her partial source of financial support. This usually means he cannot complete the psychic divorce either, as his resentment is likely to remain quite conscious. Society should address the justice (or injustice) of this. Certainly, if the wife is legitimately unable to work due to physical and/or emotional impairment, or if she has been married for many decades, has not worked during that time, and is too old to be trained for the workaday world, then the ex-husband who wants a divorce should assume some responsibility for her solvency. But, whether this is "fair, just and humane" in the case of younger and healthy wives is open to question.

Power is a theme which has emerged several times but which has not been addressed as a composite with many linked and competing facets—some minuscule, some mid-sized, and others huge and overwhelming. Ideally one conceptualizes that the decision to divorce belongs to the couple. After all, usually, at least in the United States and most western cultures, it is they who selected each other and decided to marry. Their marriage represented a contract undertaken voluntarily. Even if the woman were pregnant prior to the decision to marry—unless she was raped—the sexual liaison was entered into by choice. They decided to have the baby rather than to seek a termination of the pregnancy through abortion and sometimes of the relationship through "breaking up."

Couples who marry may prefer to do so with or without parental blessing; parental sanction is required only when young people are declared to be legally under age to enter into a marital contract. They do not need the permission of the legal system to wed although they must fulfill legal requirements such as passing a blood test and getting a license in a civil ceremony. Many, but certainly not all, couples prefer to be married by a clergy person in a religious ceremony and to also receive a religious document that the union is consecrated—such as the ketubah in Judaism. But under law, in the United States and many other countries where church and state are separate, one only need obtain a civil license for the marriage to be recognized as bona fide and accorded all the rights, privileges and responsibilities granted to married couples.

Divorce appears to be handled differently. There may be a great disparity in the bargaining leverage each member of the couple brings to divorce negotiations. If they enter mediation, the mediator will attempt to redress the power imbalance by strengthening the ability of the weaker partner to negotiate and convincing the stronger mate to do so in good faith and in accord with principles of equity.

Otherwise, one or both parties may seek the most powerful attorneys they can find and afford—delegating to them power over distribution of their assets and over critical decisions about their children's future lives. Further, society has endowed judges with seemingly extreme power in making ultimate decisions, in the form of the provisos of the divorce decree. Stir into this boiling cauldron the fact that one's children may well try, over and over, to stop the movement toward divorce through tears, suicidal efforts, psychosomatic symptomatizing, truanting, etc., and one realizes children also attempt to exercise power and influence over the divorcing couple. So do some senior generation parents who respond with fury, threats of heart attacks or ulcer flare-ups, talk of disinheriting, or total denial of the events transpiring. Like the children, they are endeavoring to persuade the couple "not to go though with it, for our sake—we couldn't tolerate the pain and humiliation."

In some countries like Israel, Finland, Argentina, and Italy, where there is not a definite demarcation of church and state, organized religion wields a great deal of power over those desirous of divorcing. (One need only consider that in June 1986 Ireland upheld its mandate of "no divorce" to realize how strong an influence some churches exert on their congregants' lives.) Where traditionally divorce has been labelled a sin, as in some Catholic countries, those wishing to terminate their marriages have been unable to secure divorces and have had to instead settle for annulment. This procedure declares their marriage to be null and void, based on it having been entered into under false pretenses, such as hiding a history of mental illness, on the part of one party. It seems incomprehensible to us that a religious establishment and member of it can act as if what existed, sometimes for many years, can be erased and eradicated. It happened, and existentially the memories linger. If there were children, their legal and religious status as legitimate progeny of two adults, wed to each other, may be jeopardized. What a horrible fate to innocent victims, and propagated under the guise of being God's will.

Equally baffling, when practiced ostensibly for humanitarian reasons, are the obstacle courses one must hurdle before a religious divorce is granted by the Rabbinate in Israel and in other countries where observant Jewish people cannot remarry unless they obtain a religious as well as a civil divorce. It can take years of waiting if the divorce is contested. And the male Rabbinic court is chauvinistic in favoring the husband's wishes for or against the marital dissolution. Sometimes civil and religious dictates conflict, further complicating the situation.

It is hoped that this kaleidoscopic overview will make it apparent that the couple as a unit may well feel, and accurately so, that a decision which should be *their choice* is governed instead by myriad other people and forces including their parents' wishes, pressure from their children, and interventions by lawyers, judges, clergy, and religious institutions. Their personal power may well be diminished under the weight of external pressures from family, religious, and civil law not to divorce. Yet, to remain married when there is abuse, alcoholism, extreme incompatibility, a high level of unresolvable conflict and even hatred, is a travesty and a tragedy.

BEYOND LEGALITIES

The theme of loss emerges as a substantial and perhaps overpowering one. In the termination of one's union, the entire dream, which has beckoned since one's days of being read fairy tales, of getting married and living happily ever after, vanishes into nothingness. To the extent that this dream represents a pivotal part of one's personal life plan for oneself and one's children, and that one's family of origin also has a stake in it, its demise leaves one adrift in a now uncharted sea and without a mooring.

As Rice and Rice (1986) indicate, one loses his/her main *love object* and, in so doing, the reality as well as the fantasy of sharing fully and intimately one's life with another—the joys and sorrows, the inadequacies and competencies, the frustrations and accomplishments. In addition, Rice and Rice point out that the loss of a central *role*, that of husband or wife, undermines one's sense of self, as an important aspect of one's being has been lived out in and defined by that role. Although one remains a parent, at least part-time (with loss associated with missed parts of one's child's life), one's identity as a spouse becomes nonexistent. One is no longer part of the couples' world and so a further loss may occur if and when one perceives he/she no longer has entrée to the usually comfortable and familiar couples' world that most of his/her friends inhabit. In some social circles, when one ceases to be Mrs. Somebody, she can no longer go to her husband's clubs or business activities; she may be less welcome on philanthropic and civic committees because she has lost access to her husband's wealth and stature. In some socioeconomic, ethnic, and religious groups, a divorced woman loses status as the prevailing belief system holds that there is fundamentally something wrong with her if she couldn't hold the marriage together.

In terms of Wynne's (1984) relational systems epigenetic model for understanding family development alluded to in Chapter 1, in divorcing couples something has gone amiss in several if not all of the areas in which contentment and fulfillment should evolve if a marriage is to be viable and enduring. These areas are: attachment, caregiving, communication skills, joint problem solving that is conducive to mutuality, and ultimately, the kind of intimacy which blossoms from sharing and trust in the realms of sexual passion, feelings, fantasies, and meaningful experiences. The end of the marriage signifies the demise of involvement in any of the above areas in which it did eventuate, another dimension of the losses sustained.

It is only in a relatively small segment of society that it is perhaps stylish to become and be divorced and where sophisticated observers, like social historians and some therapists, have begun to include divorce as a stage in adult life cycle development.

Logically, for people to restabilize or reequilibrate and complete their progress toward the psychic divorce, they must rebuild their shattered ego, regain a sense of self-esteem by defining and acquiring new and meaningful roles and relationships, and ultimately draw a different life map in which they take the stewardship for its fulfillment. Because this is a mammoth and complex task, it is little wonder that it takes several years until the losses become less acute and one acquires a sense of internal consistency and peace and a sense of belonging in the external world again. For some over 55 years of age, this may never occur.

We have pointed out that members of one's extended family, friends, colleagues, peers, playmates, and neighbors can be quite helpful during and after the divorce process. Emotionally, they can offer sympathy, empathy, availability to listen and do things together, support, and encouragement. At the adult level, they may pitch in with child care or temporary financial assistance. Realizing one is not abandoned by everyone and doesn't have to go through the bumpy transition alone is comforting.

Support groups for newly single adults and separate ones for children of divorce can prove extremely beneficial. Many children need a place, either in group therapy, individual therapy, or children of divorce groups to talk out how depressed and bewildered they feel. Dr. Neil Kalter (Pauley, 1986), on the NBC White Paper, indicated that without such opportunities, 20% to 30% of the children of divorce will have severe problems, including premature sexual acting out, unwed pregnancies, abortions, school failures, and/or running away from home. These statements seem inconsistent with those of Wallerstein that the young adult children of divorce become morally conservative and our findings that many become overly enmeshed with their parents and unable to leave home.

We interpret this discrepancy to mean we cannot overgeneralize the findings from any one study to all groups of young people. To be highly generalizable, a study would need to have a huge number of subjects and be representative of the whole spectrum of racial, religious and ethnic groups that comprise our pluralistic society, and also span the entire socioeconomic and educational continuum of families. In addition, it would have to be longitudinal, like Wallerstein's study.

We have suggested that for some people, a divorce ceremony helps them to bring closure to the prior marital-divorce phase of their lives. Others just need time and new relationships to readjust and heal. Along with Kessler (1975), Hyatt (1977), Sager et al. (1983) and others, we believe many people survive well and do go on to a satisfying "life after divorce." Where the former partners handle themselves well, treat each other civilly, and continue to love their children and be part of their lives—we believe the experience can be constructive and not destructive. We further agree, from our clinical and research findings, with the studies cited earlier that indicate children of divorces which are handled humanely and fairly fare better than children who grow up in physically intact but highly conflicted and pathological families.

One recently reported study (Tuzlak & Hillock, 1986) adds support to this outlook. They interviewed 57 women in the metropolitan Toronto area who had been separated or divorced for at least one year and who had primary custody of their child(ren). Their findings indicated that "the 96 children of the subjects were functioning well in their school, had good relationships with their peers and their mothers." Fewer than "half of the mothers reported a decline in their children's relationships with the father" and they found "no significant differences between the female and male children" (p. 86), a finding they realize contradicts earlier study results.

Tuzlak and Hillock responsibly state that there are difficulties in generalizing their findings since their subjects did not experience a sharp decline in their standard of living after the dissolution of the marriage and that their results were based totally upon mothers' perceptions and memories. They point out, however, that Pett (1982) found that parents and children significantly agree with one another on reactions to divorce. They are dismayed that society perpetuates the myth, cited by Bernard and Nesbitt (1981, p. 40), that "divorce has inordinate power to hurt people regardless of the mental health and maturity of the adults and children involved." Instead, they conclude that their study of well-functioning female-headed families indicates that some new postdivorce family systems can and do become "as strong or stronger than their intact predecessors," joining others like Kurdek and Siesky (1980), the aforementioned Bernard and Nesbitt (1981) and Pett (1982) in stating that separation and divorce need not be devastatingly traumatic experiences. They suggest, and we concur, that we must conquer "divorceaphobia" and give due attention and respect to those "who make it"—those whom we have previously called "the survivors." They are the healthy individuals who are capable of handling transitions, mastering tasks, and entering the next phase of their life cycles with a sense of competency, humor, and creativity.

Given that 75% of divorced women and 83% of divorced men remarry, obviously they decide to risk trusting and caring deeply again. We would like to close on an optimistic note, relating some of the principles we have found that are conducive to good marriages—first or second time around—and that seem characteristic of the preponderance of healthy, happy marriages.

1. The partners in a healthy marriage are strong individuals but feel stronger being a couple. Sometimes they enjoy being alone—but often they take pleasure in each other's company and feel strengthened by their closeness.
2. They have fun with each other. They laugh together at life's little absurdities. And they take time for play—making sure they go on vacations and have nights out together.

3. They don't take each other for granted. Intuitively these couples know that to remain important in each other's lives, they must spend time together.
4. They respect each other's privacy. They're interested in each other's activities—but if one spouse wants to do something alone, the other won't intrude.
5. Each may feel comfortable playing tennis or golf without facing accusations like "You don't love me" or "You're being inconsiderate."
6. Healthy couples don't try to become exactly like each other. Each partner knows he or she is distinct.
7. They don't expect their marriage to be smooth sailing. They know life has its ups and downs—and anticipate problems such as illness or job-related troubles.
8. They have a high level of trust in each other. This trust helps them sidestep quarrels over things like money problems or jealousy. And even if one partner violates the trust, his or her mate can feel secure that it won't happen over and over.
9. They don't assume conflicts will resolve themselves. They continually work toward improving communication.
10. They keep sex in perspective. To them, sex is an expression of affection, passion and love—not a weapon used to get their own way or gloss over conflicts.
11. They are attuned to each other's needs. Each encourages the other to grow and change.
12. They do not expect their partner to know automatically their thoughts, so they speak out when they have something on their mind.
13. Finally, happy couples have positive outlooks and attitudes. They feel they're giving *to* the relationship and to each other—not giving up something *for* the relationship or giving *in* to the partner.

Appendix A: Letter Sent to Second Batch of Potential Subjects (Rewrite of First Letter)

THE PENNSYLVANIA STATE UNIVERSITY
COMMONWEALTH EDUCATIONAL SYSTEM

The Ogontz Campus

1600 Woodland Road
Abington, Pennsylvania 19001

March 20, 1985

Your name has been suggested to one of the investigators listed below as a possible participant in a study we are doing on the effects of separation and divorce. We are seeking information from formerly married adults and from (or about) children of separated and divorced parents.

As you will read in the enclosed explanation of the study, all responses will be kept confidential. All signed consent forms will be separated from the questionnaires and sent under seal to the office of the University's Vice-President for Research and Graduate Studies at University Park.

Relatively little is known about the effects of separation and divorce on people of different ages or genders, or those who have been apart from their first marriage for varying lengths of time. Your cooperation in responding to the enclosed questionnaire will be a valuable contribution to research in this field.

If you are willing to participate, we would appreciate having your response as soon as possible—before April 20th. A stamped self-addressed envelope is enclosed for your convenience in returning the questionnaire and consent form. Many thanks for your cooperation and participation in this research project.

Sincerely yours,

Lita Linzer Schwartz, Ph.D.
Professor of Educational Psychology
Principal Investigator

Co-Investigator: Florence W. Kaslow, Ph.D.
Director, Florida Couples and Family Institute

Appendix B: Questionnaire I—Divorced Adults

This questionnaire is part of a study on the effects of separation and divorce on the parting spouses in relation to their gender, age, and length of marriage. As indicated on the attached "informed consent" form, all of your responses will be kept confidential.

The first set of questions focus on background information. The second set deal with the separation/divorce itself. Please answer all questions. Mark the appropriate answers with an "X" unless a more specific answer is being requested.

Demographic Background

Are you the wife _____ husband _____ in the former marriage?   Today's
   date _____
Birthdate _____ Current Age _____ Age at marriage _____ Age at
   physical separation _____ Age at divorce _____
Level of education:
   Self: HS grad. _____ HS+ _____ College grad. _____ Grad./Prof.
   degree _____
   (Ex)spouse: HS grad. _____ HS+ _____ College grad. _____ Grad./Prof.
   degree _____
In your former marriage, did the wife work:
   Before Marriage? No _____ P/t _____ F/t _____   Was it a career _____ or
   Job? _____
   During marriage: No _____ P/t _____ F/t _____   Was it a career _____ or
   Job? _____
   Since sep./div.: No _____ P/t _____ F/t _____   Is it a career _____ or
   Job? _____
Husband's occupation at time of separation? _____
Wife's occupation at time of separation? _____

Income:
  Your current earned annual gross salary _____
  Annual income from interest, dividends, real estate, other investments _____
  Annual income received in child support payments _____
  Annual income received in alimony payments _____
Expenses:
  Annual amount paid in child support _____
  Annual amount paid in alimony _____
Assets:
  Please estimate total assets:
  Less than $10,000 _____ $10–15,000 _____ $15–20,000 _____
          $20–25,000 _____ $25–30,000 _____ $30–50,000 _____ $50–75,000 ____
          $75–100,000 _____ Over $100,000 _____
Husband's religion _____ Wife's religion _____
Husband's ethnic background _____ Wife's ethnic
  background _____
Where there children of this marriage? Yes _____ No _____
If yes, what were their ages at the time of the separation?
  Oldest _____ #2 _____ #3 _____ #4 _____ #5 _____ #6 _____
Who is the primary custodian of the child(ren)? H _____ W _____ Joint _____
Are any of the children exceptional (mentally/physically/emotionally handi-
  capped? Gifted? Talented?)? If so, give number of child (see question above) and
  nature of exceptionality.
  # _____ # _____ # _____
Do you live in a: City _____ Suburb _____ Rural area _____ ?
Do you live in: Marital home _____ Apartment _____
                Different house than marital home _____
                Different community than former spouse _____

Separation and Divorce

1. Who sought (requested) the separation? H _____ W _____ Joint
   decision _____
2. Was the other party (mark all that apply):
   Agreeable _____ Surprised _____ Distressed _____ Frantic _____
3. Length of marriage to physical separation?
   1–2 years _____ 3–5 years _____ 6–10 years _____
   11–15 years _____ 16–20 years _____ 21–25 years _____ 26–30 years _____
   31–35 years _____ 36–40 years _____ 41–45 years _____ 46–50 years _____
4. Was there a period of disillusionment and/or conflict before the decision to
   separate? Yes _____ No _____ If so, how long did it last? _____
5. Did your spouse exhibit any of the following behaviors before the decision
   to separate? (Mark all that apply)
   Severe depression _____ Hypercritical _____ Aggressive _____
   Bizarre _____ Irrationally accusatory _____ Self-focused _____
   Withdrawn _____ Staying away from home more _____
   Argumentative _____
6. Length of period from separation to divorce?
   Not yet divorced _____ Less than 1 year _____ 1–2 years _____ 2+
   years _____

7. How were issues resolved (property, custody, etc.)?
   Mediation _____ Litigation _____ Still unsettled _____ Made own agreement _____
8. Following the decision to separate and divorce, did you ever contemplate suicide? Yes _____ No _____
9. How long has it been since you were divorced?
   a. Divorce not yet granted _____ 1–2 years _____ 3–5 years _____ 6+ years _____
   b. Divorce suit filed or granted in: (State) _____ (Year) _____
10. In the period following the separation, did you receive emotional support from:

Your family of origin (parents/siblings)?	Yes _____ No _____
Your children?	Yes _____ No _____
Extended family (aunts/uncles/cousins)?	Yes _____ No _____
Neighbors?	Yes _____ No _____
Friends?	Yes _____ No _____
Lovers?	Yes _____ No _____
Colleagues at work?	Yes _____ No _____
Psychotherapist?	Yes _____ No _____
Others (specify) _____	Yes _____ No _____

11. In the period following the separation, what were your relations with your (ex-)spouse's parents and/or siblings?
    Frequent positive contact _____ Frequent negative contact _____
    Some contact _____ No contact _____
12. Do you still have contact with your former spouse? Yes _____ No _____
    (Mark all that apply on both questions)
    If yes, is it by: Phone _____ Mail _____ In-person _____
    If yes, are these contacts with regard to:
    Child(ren) _____ Property _____ Feelings _____ As friends _____
13. Do you have any thoughts about remarriage?
    Would like to remarry _____ Unsure _____ No such desire _____
    Have already remarried _____
14. Has your (ex-)spouse remarried? Yes _____ No _____ Not applicable _____
15. With regard to the quality of your life since the separation, would you say that it is *now* the same or changed?

	Much Worse	Worse	Same	Better	Much Better
Emotional					
Financial					
Occupational/Vocational					
Physical health					
Social					

16. Indicate which feelings were characteristic of you in each period, using a scale of 1 (=very true), 2 (=often true), 3 (=somewhat true), 4 (=rarely true), 5 (=never true). Place the appropriate number in each column for each characteristic:

	At separation	6 mos. later	1 yr. later	Now
Angry				
Anxious				
Bitter				
Capable				
Competent				
Confused				
Depressed				
Desire to retaliate				
Empty				
Fearful				
Happy				
Healthy				
Hurt				
Jealous				
Joyful				
Pleased				
Powerful				
Relieved				
Resentful				
Sorry				
Strong				

17. Please list the major problems you have experienced since your separation:

    a.

    b.

    c.

    d.

18. If you have any thoughts you would like to add, please do so in the space below:

Thank you for your cooperation.

Appendix C: Questionnaire IIA—On Children Under 10 Years of Age

This questionnaire is part of a study of the effects of separation and divorce on children, especially in the area of academic performance. The results of the study, after analysis of the data, should be helpful to school counselors, therapists, and mediators interacting with divorcing couples. As noted on the attached "informed consent" form, all of your responses will be kept confidential.

The first set of questions focus on background information. The second set deal specifically with the effects of the separation and/or divorce on your child(ren). For each child under 10, please respond as factually as you can in terms of the period immediately following separation and again for right now. For those of school-age, please include, if possible, specific course grades or cumulative average for each period.

Demographic Information

Are you the mother? _____ or father? _____   Today's date _____
How long were you married at the time of the separation? _____
How long has it been between the date of physical separation and today? _____
Who is the primary custodial parent of your child(ren)?
   Mother _____ Father _____ Joint _____
Was your child consulted about:
   Custody arrangements? Yes _____ No _____
   Visitation with noncustodial parent? Yes _____ No _____

For the following items, please use this scale:

	Much Worse (1)	Worse (2)	Same (3)	Better (4)	Much Better (5)

	At Separation	Today
1. School Performance (as compared with preseparation) Grades		
Classroom behavior		
Relations with classmates		
Relations with teachers		
2. Relations with others With you		
With siblings		
With other parent		

For the next group of items, please indicate Yes, No, or NA (Not applicable):

3. Did this child have emotional support from:	Yes	No	NA
You			
Other parent			
Siblings			
Maternal grandparents			
Paternal grandparents			
Other maternal relatives			
Other paternal relatives			
Friends			
School counselor			
Psychotherapist			
Small therapy group			

For the next group of items, please indicate Father, Mother, Both, or NA:

	Father	Mother	Both	NA
4. Who helped this child with homework prior to separation?				
5. Who took this child (prior to separation): To doctors				
To dentists				
To music/art lessons				
To athletic activities				
To visit playmates/parties				

6. If you care to add any comments about the effects of separation/divorce on this child, please do so in the space below:

Thank you for your cooperation.

* * * * * * *

Child # _____ Born: _____ / _____ / _____   Boy _____ Girl _____

Separation and Divorce

	At Separation	Today
Age		
Grade level		

Feelings and behaviors: (Scale: 1 = very true, 2 = often true, 3 = sometimes true, 4 = rarely true, 5 = not true)

Angry		
Bitter		
Capable		
Competent		
Confused		
Depressed		

Anxious		
Fearful		
Happy		
Healthy		
Hurt		
Hostile		
Joyful		
Pleased		
Powerful		
Rejected		
Relieved		
Resentful		
Sorry		
Strong		
Supportive (of you)		

Appendix D: Questionnaire IIB—For Children 11 Years Old and Older

This questionnaire is part of a study of the effects of separation and divorce on children. The results of the study, after analysis of the data, should be helpful to school counselors, therapists, and mediators interacting with divorcing couples. As noted on the attached "informed consent" form, all of your responses will be kept confidential.

The first set of questions focus on background information. The second set deal specifically with the effects of your parents' separation/divorce on you. Please respond as factually as you can in terms of the period immediately following your parents' separation and again for right now. If you were in school (or are now), please include specific course grades or cumulative average for each period.

Demographic Information

Are you male _____ female _____ ?   Today's date _____
Of the children in the family, are you:
   Oldest _____ #2 _____ #3 _____ #4 _____ #5 _____ #6 _____
How many brothers and sisters do you have? _____
Your date of birth: _____   Your age today? _____
How long were your parents married at the time of their physical separation?
_____
How long has it been between the date of separation and today? _____
Who has been (or was) the primary custodial parent for you?
   Mother _____ Father _____ Shared _____ Not applicable _____
Were you consulted about:
   With whom you would live? Yes _____ No _____
   Visitation with your other parent? Yes _____ No _____

For the following items, please use this scale:

	Much Worse (1)	Worse (2)	Same (3)	Better (4)	Much Better (5)

	At Separation	Today
1. School or College Performance (as compared with preseparation) Grades		
Classroom behavior		
Relations with classmates		
Relations with teachers		
If you were working at either time: Job effectiveness		
Relations with customers/clients		
Relations with colleagues on the job		
2. Relations with others Mother		
Father		
Siblings		
Friends		

For the next group of items, please indicate, Yes, No, or Not Applicable (NA):

	Yes	No	NA
3. Following the separation, did you have emotional support from: Mother			
Father			
Siblings			
Maternal grandparent(s)			
Paternal grandparent(s)			
Other maternal relatives			
Other paternal relatives			

	Yes	No	NA
Friends			
School counselor			
Psychotherapist			
Colleagues on the job			
Small therapy group			

If you were or are in school/college, for the next group of items, please indicate Father, Mother, or Both:

	Father	Mother	Both
4. Who helped you with your homework at the time prior to separation?			
5. Who took you (prior to separation) to: Doctors			
Dentists			
Music/art lessons			
Athletic activities			
To visit playmates/parties			

6. Do you expect to marry at some time in the future?
   Yes _____ Maybe _____ No _____
   Has your parents' separation affected your thinking about marriage?
   Yes _____ No _____
   If yes, how? _____
7. If you care to add any comments about the effects of separation/divorce on you, please do so in the space below:

Thank you for your cooperation.

* * * * * * *

Separation and Divorce

	At Separation	Today
Age		
Grade level		

Feelings and behaviors: (Scale 1 = very true, 2 = often true, 3 = sometimes true, 4 = rarely true, 5 = not true)

	At Separation	Today
Angry		
Anxious		
Bitter		
Capable		
Competent		
Confused		
Depressed		
Fearful		
Happy		
Healthy		
Hostile		
Hurt		
Joyful		
Pleased		
Powerful		
Rejected		
Relieved		
Resentful		
Sorry		
Strong		
Supportive of one parent		

Appendix E:
Informed Consent Form

Title of Investigation: An Investigation of the Effects of Separation and Divorce
                        on Parting Spouses and the Children of Divorce
Principal Investigator: Lita L. Schwartz, Ph.D.
Co-Investigator: Florence W. Kaslow, Ph.D.

Date: 30 June 1984

    This is to certify that I, _____ .
                                                 (Print Name)
hereby agree to participate as a volunteer (or to permit my minor child to participate) in a scientific study as an authorized part of the educational and research
program of The Pennsylvania State University under the supervision of Drs. Lita
L. Schwartz and Florence W. Kaslow.

    The investigation and my (child's) part in it have been defined and fully
explained to me by the researchers and I understand their explanation. The
procedures of this study and their risks have been described to me in writing.

    I have been given an opportunity to ask whatever questions I may have had
and all such questions and inquiries have been answered to my satisfaction.

    I understand that all answers to questions will remain confidential with re-
gard to my identity. I further understand that I am free to deny any answer to
specific items or questions in interviews or questionnaires.

    I certify that, to the best of my knowledge and belief, I have no physical or
mental illness or weakness that would increase the risk to me of participation in
this investigation.

    I further understand that I am free to withdraw my consent and terminate my
participation at any time.

_____   _____
  (Signature of Subject or Parent/Guardian)   (Date)

We, the undersigned, have defined and fully explained the investigation in writing to the above subject.

_____   _____

(Investigator's Signature)   (Date)

_____   _____

(Co-Investigator's Signature)   (Date)

Appendix F:
Explanation of Study
(Adults' Form)

Purpose of the Study

Through this study, we hope to identify and document differences in the effects of separation and divorce on the separating/divorced parties according to age, gender, and length of marriage, and the effects on the children of divorce, according to their gender, age at the time of the parents' separation, and custody arrangements.

Procedures to Be Followed

Questionnaires are being distributed, by mail, to separating/divorced persons, both with and without children, in several geographical areas of the country. Parents of children under 10 are asked to respond for those children, but children over 10 and young adults are being asked to respond for themselves. The questions asked are about you and your family's experiences from the time of physical separation from the marriage to the present.

Upon receipt by the researchers, all questionnaires will immediately be coded by subject number only so that your name will not be associated with your questionnaire and your answers will be kept confidential.

An informed consent form, enclosed with each questionnaire, is to be signed by you. When these are returned to the principal investigator, they will be sent to the Office of the Vice-President for Research and Graduate Studies of The Pennsylvania State University in envelopes with special seals that are used for sensitive studies.

No risks or discomforts to you are foreseen as a result of responding to the(se) questionnaire(s).

Potential Benefits

It is expected that the results of this study will contribute to public and professional understanding of the effects of divorce on people of different ages and life stages. Furthermore, it is expected that the results obtained can be used by therapists, school counselors, and other professionals to assist adults and children to deal with the separation/divorce crisis in as constructive and healthy ways as possible.

Period of Time Required: approximately 30 minutes.

After reading the above explanation, you are requested to read and sign the enclosed consent form, and to fill out the enclosed questionnaire. If you have any questions, please contact Dr. Schwartz or Dr. Kaslow. Thank you for your cooperation and participation.

Lita Linzer Schwartz, Ph.D.
Professor, Pennsylvania State University
Principal Investigator

Florence W. Kaslow, Ph.D.
Director, Florida Couples & Family Institute
Co-Investigator

Appendix G: Explanation of Study (Children's Form)

Purpose of the Study

As part of a larger project, we are studying the effects on children of separation and divorce by their parents. We are seeking information about possible differences of effects on boys and girls according to their age when the parents separated and according to custody arrangements.

Procedures to Be Followed

Questionnaires are being sent to separated and divorced adults and to children of divorced parents in different parts of the country. Older children and young adults are asked to answer questions about themselves and their family's experiences from the time their parents last separated until now. You will be asked questions about your feelings about your parents' separation, your school/work performance then and now, and people who have been helpful to you in this situation.

When the questionnaires are returned to the investigator, they will be numbered so that no names are attached to them. The attached consent form will be sent separately in a sealed envelope to the Office of the Vice-President for Research and Graduate Studies of The Pennsylvania State University for safekeeping and to protect your privacy.

No risks or discomforts to you are anticipated as a result of taking part in this project.

Potential Benefits

After the answers to the questionnaires have been analyzed, it is expected that the information learned from them will be used by school counselors, therapists, and other professionals to help other children to deal with their parents' separation and divorce in as healthy ways as possible.

Period of Time Required: about 30 minutes.

After reading the above explanation, please read and sign the informed consent form and fill out the questionnaire. If you have any questions, please contact Dr. Schwartz or Dr. Kaslow.

Thank you for your cooperation and for taking part in this study.

Lita L. Schwartz, Ph.D.
Principal Investigator

Florence W. Kaslow, Ph.D.
Co-Investigator

Appendix H:
Note to Parents of
Older Children

Whether or not you are participating in this study, we hope you will encourage, without undue pressure, your child(ren) to answer the enclosed questionnaire. Please go over the explanation of the study and the consent form with your child(ren), and assure your child(ren) of the right not to answer specific questions. If a child doesn't understand something (word or rating scale, for example), please explain it or allow the child to call one of us.

Thank you.

Principal Investigator: Lita L. Schwartz, Ph.D.
Co-Investigator: Florence W. Kaslow, Ph.D.

Appendix I:
Sample Mediation Contract

Kaslow Associates, P.A.
2617 North Flagler Drive
Suite 204
West Palm Beach, FL 33407

We are consulting you together to discuss and mediate the possible dissolution of our marriage.

We realize that the issues we will be discussing are complex. They may include alimony or spousal support; custody, visitation and child support; division of assets; and tax impacts. Our interests may conflict on some of these issues. We believe that we are capable of dealing with those issues cooperatively in mediation and of drawing up a tentative memorandum of understanding with your guidance that reflects our wishes and thoughts.

We realize that:

1. You do not represent either of us during the mediation.
2. You will not represent either of us in any legal proceeding related to the dissolution of our marriage or child custody arrangements.
3. Each of us may discontinue the mediation at any time and proceed individually through our own attorneys. Similarly, you may discontinue the mediation if you believe we have reached an impasse or if you believe the mediation process is being abused by either of us.
4. Each of us pledges to fully disclose, when pertinent, all of our income and assets, and to produce whatever records and tax returns are requested.
5. During mediation, if prior to the divorce, neither of us will transfer or dispose of any assets except in the usual course of business without advance notice to the other.

6. Conferences generally will be held with both of us present. If it becomes advisable, periodically, for you to meet individually with one of us, you may do so, providing the other partner consents.
7. You will work with us while we try, in good faith, to negotiate a settlement and, if we are successful, you will use your best efforts to prepare a written document that reflects our agreement.
8. Each of us is (encouraged) to retain separate and independent legal counsel to advise us of our rights, if necessary, and to review any agreement before we sign and formally adopt it.
9. Under certain circumstances, such as the presence of child abuse or threatened harm to any family member, it may be necessary for you to notify the appropriate authorities and not adhere to confidentiality restrictions.

You have agreed to work with us only with the stipulation that neither of us will call you or permit you to be called as a witness in any matrimonial matter in which we are involved. You are to be *immune from testimony or deposition*.

Each of us is aware that, if our negotiations break down and we become courtroom adversaries, the information disclosed during mediation will be available to the other without the legal procedures that are commonly used to compel disclosure of information.

We know that your fees will be calculated at $ an hour for conferences, research, writing memoranda, consulting with advisory counsel, or any other time spent on our behalf. In addition to fees, we agree to pay the costs incurred for all expenses undertaken on our behalf. Mediation often requires hiring impartial experts to evaluate assets and financial holdings (such as real estate, pensions, personal property, businesses, tax returns and financial reports). We agree to pay the costs of hiring those experts and for secretarial services in preparing memoranda.

Our initial payment is enclosed. We know that fees are to be paid each session. If we do not pay your fee promptly as billed, you may terminate your services.

When signed by us, this letter becomes a binding agreement.

Very truly yours,

_____

Date _____   _____

References

Abroms, G. (1978). The place of values in psychotherapy. *Journal of Marriage and Family Counseling, 4*(4), 3–18.

Ahrons, C. R. (1979). The coparental divorce: Preliminary research findings and policy implications. In A. Milne (Ed.), *Joint custody:A handbook for judges, lawyers and counselors*, (pp. C1–C9). Portland, OR: Association of Family Conciliation Courts.

Ahrons, C. R. (1980a). Divorce: A crisis of family transition and change. *Family Relations, 29*, 533–540.

Ahrons, C. R. (1980b). Redefining the divorced family: A conceptual framework. *Social Work, 25*(6), 437–441.

Ahrons, C. R. (1981). The continuing coparental relationship between divorced spouses. *American Journal of Orthopsychiatry, 51*, 415–428.

Ahrons, C. R. (1983a). Predictors of paternal involvement postdivorce: Mother's and father's perceptions. *Journal of Divorce, 6*(3), 55–69.

Ahrons, C. R. (1983b). *The binuclear family: Parenting roles and relationships*. Unpublished paper.

Albrecht, S. L. (1980). Reactions and adjustments to divorce: Differences in the experiences of males and females. *Family Relations, 29*, 59–68.

Albrecht, S. L., Bahr, H. M., & Goodman, K. L. (1983). *Divorce and remarriage: Problems, adaptations, and adjustments*. Westport, CT: Greenwood Press.

American Bar Association (1973). Proposed revised Uniform Marriage and Divorce Act. *Family Law Quarterly, 7*, 135–165.

American Bar Association (1981). *Model code of professional responsibility*. Chicago: National Center for Professional Responsibility.

American Bar Association (1985). Pension plans and divorce. *Family Advocate, 8*(2), 2–45.

American Psychiatric Association (1980). *Diagnostic and statistical manual of mental disorders* (3rd ed.). Washington, DC: Author.

Bach, G. R. (1974). Creative exits: Fight therapy for divorcées. In V. Frank & V. Burtle (Eds.), *Women in therapy: New psychotherapies for a changing society* (pp. 307–325). New York: Brunner/Mazel.

Bahr, S. J. (1983). Marital dissolution laws: Impact of recent changes for women. *Journal of Family Issues, 4*, 455–466.

Bahr, S. J., & Galligan, R. J. (1984). Teenage marriage and marital stability. *Youth and Society, 15*, 387–400.

Bales, J. (1984). Parents' divorce has major impact on college students. *APA Monitor, 15*(8), 13.

Bank, S. R., & Kahn, M.D. (1982). *The sibling bond*. New York: Basic Books.

Baruch, G., Barnett, R., & Rivers, C. (1983). *Love prints: New patterns of love and work for today's women*. New York: New American Library.

Bateson, G. (1979). *Mind and nature: A necessary unity*. New York: Dutton.

Berkowitz, D. A. (1984). An overview of the psychodynamics of couples: Bridging concepts. In C. C. Nadelson & D. C. Polonsky (Eds.), *Marriage and divorce* (pp. 117–126). New York: Guilford.

Berman, W. H. (1985). Continued attachment after legal divorce. *Journal of Family Issues, 6*, (3), 375–392.

Bernard, J. M., & Nesbitt, S. (1981). Divorce: An unreliable predictor of children's emotional predispositions. *Journal of Divorce, 4*,(4), 31–42.

Bertanlaffy, L. (1968). *General systems theory: Foundations, development, application*. New York: Braziller.

Blau, T. H. (1984). The role of the grandparent in the best interests of the child. *American Journal of Family Therapy, 12*(4), 46–50.

Blau, T. H. (1986, June 7). Writing child custody and visitation plans. Plenary address presented at the Florida Association of Professional Family Mediators Annual Conference, Panama City, FL.

Bloom, B. L., & Hodges, W. F. (1981). The predicament of the newly separated. *Community Mental Health Journal, 17*, 277–293.

Bloom, B. L., White, S. W., & Asher, S. J. (1979). Marital disruption as a stressful life event. In G. Levinger & O. C. Moles (Eds.), *Divorce and separation: Context, causes, and consequences* (pp. 184–200). New York: Basic Books.

Bodin, A. M. (1982). Explaining divorce to children. In P. A. Keller & L. G. Ritt (Eds.), *Innovations in clinical practice: A source book*, Vol.1 (pp. 382–385). Sarasota, FL: Professional Resource Exchange.

Bohannon, P. (1970). The six stations of divorce. In P. Bohannon (Ed.), *Divorce and after: An analysis of the emotional and social problems of divorce* (pp. 29–55). New York: Doubleday.

Bohannon, P. (1973). The six stations of divorce. In M. E. Lasswell & T. E. Lasswell (Eds.), *Love, marriage and family: A developmental approach* (pp. 475–489). Glenview, IL: Scott, Foresman.

Booth, A., Brinkerhoff, D. B., & White, L. K. (1984). The impact of parental divorce on courtship. *Journal of Marriage and the Family, 46*(1), 85–94.

Boszormenyi-Nagy, I., & Spark, G. (1973). *Invisible loyalties*. New York: Harper and Row. (Reprinted 1984, New York: Brunner/Mazel.)

Bouton, K. (1984, October 9). Women and divorce: How the new law works against them. *New York*, pp. 34–41.

Bowen, M. (1978). *Family therapy in clinical practice*. New York: Jason Aronson.

Bowlby, J. (1960). Separation anxiety. *International Journal of Psychoanalysis, 41*, 89–113.

Bowlby, J. (1969). *Attachment and loss: Vol.1—Attachment*. New York: Basic Books.

Bowman, M. E., & Ahrons, C. R. (1985). Impact of legal custody status on fathers' parenting postdivorce. *Journal of Marriage and the Family, 47*, 481–488.

Briggs, B. A., & Walters, C. M. (1985). Single-father families: Implications for early childhood educators. *Young Children, 40*(3), 23–27.

Buckley, W. (1967). *Sociology and modern systems theory*. Englewood Cliffs, NJ: Prentice-Hall.

Cain, B. S. (1982, December 19). Plight of the gray divorcée. *The New York Times Magazine*, pp. 89–95.

California Assembly Bill #1480 (1979, April 29), and Chapter 915 (Custody), (1979, September 21).

Carter, E., & McGoldrick, M. (Eds.). (1980). *The family life cycle*. New York: Gardner Press.

Child support. (1984, July). *Fairshare, 4*(7), 13–14.

Chiriboga, D. A., & Cutler, L. (1977). Stress responses among divorcing men and women. *Journal of Divorce, 1*(2), 95–106.

Close, H. (1977, Spring). Service of divorce. *Pilgrimage, 5*(1), 60–66.

Coddington, R. D. (1972). The significance of life events as etiologic factors in the diseases of children—II: A study of a normal population. *Journal of Psychosomatic Research, 16,* 205–213.

Cohen, H. N., & Hillman, A. S. (1985). New York courts have not recognized women as equal marriage partners. *Equitable Distribution Reporter, 5*(9), 93–104.

Colarusso, C. A., & Nemiroff, R. A. (1981). *Adult development: A new dimension in psychodynamic theory and practice.* New York: Plenum.

Coogler, O. J. (1978). *Structured mediation in divorce settlement.* Lexington, MA: D. C. Heath.

Daniels-Mohring, D., & Berger, M. (1984). Social network changes and the adjustment to divorce. *Journal of Divorce, 8*(1), 17–32.

Dell, P. F. (1982). Family theory and the epistemology of Humberto Maturana. In F. W. Kaslow (Ed.), *The International Book of Family Therapy* (pp. 56–66). New York: Brunner/Mazel.

Derdeyn, A. P. (1985). Grandparent visitation rights: Rendering family dissension more pronounced? *American Journal of Orthopsychiatry, 55,* 277–287.

Derdeyn, A. P., & Scott, E. (1984). Joint custody: A critical analysis and appraisal. *American Journal of Orthopsychiatry, 54,* 199–209.

Dicks, H. (1963). Object relations theory and marital studies. *British Journal of Medical Psychology, 36,* 125–129.

Dorfman, R. (1985). A single parent's guide to helping children, ages 0–12, survive separation and divorce. Philadelphia: Unpublished manuscript.

Duffy, M. (1982). Divorce and the dynamics of the family kinship system. *Journal of Divorce, 5*(1/2), 3–18.

Duhl, F. (1981). The use of the chronological chart in general systems family therapy. *Journal of Marriage and Family Therapy, 7*(3), 345–352.

Ellison, E. S. (1983). Issues concerning parental harmony and children's psychosocial adjustment. *American Journal of Orthopsychiatry, 53,* 73–80.

Emery, R. E. (1982). Interparental conflict and the children of discord and divorce. *Psychological Bulletin, 92,* 310–330.

Erikson, E. H. (1963). *Childhood and society* (2nd ed.). New York: Norton.

Erikson, E. H. (1968). *Identity: Youth and crisis.* New York: Norton.

Farber, S. S., Primavera, J., & Felner, R. D. (1983). Older adolescents and parental divorce: Adjustment problems and mediators of coping. *Journal of Divorce, 7*(2), 59–75.

Financial planning update. (1986, April), pp. 3–4.

Fine, M. A., Moreland, J. R., & Schwebel, A. I. (1983). Longterm effects of divorce on parent-child relationships. *Developmental Psychology, 19,* 703–713.

Fisher, B. (1981). *Rebuilding when your relationship ends.* San Luis Obispo, CA: Impact.

Florida Dissolution of Marriage—Children Act, 82–96 (1982), pp. 549–553 of Senate Bill No. 439.

Folberg, J. (1983). A mediation overview: History and dimensions of practice. *Mediation Quarterly, 1,* 13–14.

Folberg, J. (1984). *Joint custody and shared parenting.* Washington, DC: Association of Family Conciliation Courts.

Foster, H. H., & Freed, D. J. (1984). The child's right to visit grandparents. *Trial, 20*(3), 38–45.

Francke, L. B. (1983). *Growing up divorced.* New York: Linden Press/Simon & Schuster.

Freud, S. (1923). The ego and the id. In J. Strachey (Ed. and Trans.), *The standard edition of the complete psychological works of Sigmund Freud* (Vol.19, pp. 13–66). London: Hogarth Press.

Freud, S. (1961). *Civilization and its discontents* (J. Strachey, Ed. and Trans.). New York: Norton.

Freud, S. (1963). *The sexual enlightenment of children.* New York: Collier Books.

Friedman, J. T. (1984). *The divorce handbook: Your basic guide to divorce* (updated ed.). New York: Random House.

Froiland, D. J., & Hozman, T. L. (1977). Counseling for constructive divorce. *Personnel and Guidance Journal, 55,* 525–529.

Galper, M. (1980). *Joint custody and co-parenting: Sharing your child equally.* Philadelphia: Running Press.

Ganong, L. H., & Coleman, M. (1984). The effects of remarriage on children: A review of the empirical literature. *Family Relations, 33,* 389–406.

Garber, B. (1984). Parenting responses in divorce and bereavement of a spouse. In R. S. Cohen, B. J. Cohler, & S. H. Weissman (Eds.), *Parenthood: A psychodynamic perspective* (pp. 183–203). New York: Guilford Press.

Gardner, R. (1976). *Psychotherapy with children of divorce.* New York: Jason Aronson.

Glasser, W. (1983, May). Reality therapy and divorce. Workshop presented at Allentown, PA.

Glendon, M. A. (1984). Family law reform in the 1980's. *Louisiana Law Review, 44,* 1553–1574.

Glick, P. C. (1979) Children of divorced parents in demographic perspective. *Journal of Social Issues, 35*(4), 170–182.

Goldstein, J., Freud, A., & Solnit, A. J. (1973). *Beyond the best interests of the child.* New York: Free Press.

Goode, W. J. (1956). *After divorce.* Glencoe, IL: Free Press.

Goode, W. J. (1960). Pressures to remarry: Institutionalized patterns affecting the divorced. In N. W. Bell & E. F. Vogel (Eds.), *A modern introduction to the family* (pp. 316–326). Glencoe, IL: Free Press.

Greif, G. (1985). *Single Fathers.* Lexington, MA: Lexington Books.

Guidubaldi, J., Cleminshaw, H. K., Perry, J. D., & McLoughlin, C. S. (1983). The impact of parental divorce on children: Report of the nationwide NASP study. *School Psychology Review, 12,* 300–323.

Guidubaldi, J., Cleminshaw, H. K., Perry, J. D., Nastasi, B. K., & Adams, B. (1984, August). Effects of divorce on children: NASP-KSU two-year longitudinal study. Symposium presented at the 92nd annual convention of the American Psychological Association, Toronto.

Hagestad, G. O., Smyer, M. A., & Stierman, K. (1984). The impact of divorce in middle age. In R. S. Cohen, B. J. Cohler, & S. H. Weissman (Eds.), *Parenthood: A psychodynamic perspective* (pp. 247–262). New York: Guilford.

Haley, J. (1973). *Uncommon therapy: The psychiatric techniques of Milton Erikson.* New York: Norton.

Haley, J. (1980). *Leaving home: The therapy of disturbed young people.* New York: McGraw Hill.

Halperin, S. M., & Smith, T. A. (1983). Differences in stepchildren's perceptions of their stepfathers and natural fathers: Implications for family therapy. *Journal of Divorce, 7*(1), 19–30.

Hammond, J. M. (1981). The effects of divorce on children's self-concept, academic achievement, school behaviors, and attitudes. *Scientia paedogogica experimentalis, 18*(1), 70–82.

Hansson, R. O., Knopf, M. F., Downs, E. A., Monroe, P. R., Stegnan, S. E., & Wedley, D. S. (1984). Femininity, masculinity, and adjustment to divorce among women. *Psychology of Women Quarterly, 8,* 248–260.

Haynes, J. (1981). *Divorce mediation.* New York: Springer.

Haynes, J. (1982). A conceptual model of the process of family mediation: Implications for training. *American Journal of Family Therapy, 10*(4), 5–16.

Hetherington, E. M., Cox, M., & Cox, R. (1977a). Divorced fathers. *Psychology Today, 10*(11), 42–46.

Hetherington. E. M., Cox, M., & Cox, R. (1977b). The aftermath of divorce. In J. H. Stevens, Jr. & M. Mathews (Eds.), *Mother-child, father-child relations* (pp. 149–176). Washington, DC: NAEYC.

Hetherington, E. M., Cox, M., & Cox, R. (1979). Stress and coping in divorce: A focus on women. In J. E. Gullahorn (Ed.), *Psychology and women: In transition* (pp. 95–128). New York: John Wiley.

Hillard, J. R. (1984). Reactions of college students to parental divorce. *Psychiatric Annals, 14*(9), 663–670.

Hodges, W. F., & Bloom, B. L. (1984). Parent's report of children's adjustment to marital separation: A longitudinal study. *Journal of Divorce, 8*(1), 33–50.

Hoffman, L. (1980). The family life cycle and discontinuous changes. In E. Carter & M. McGoldrick (Eds.), *The family life cycle: A framework for family therapy* (pp. 53–68). New York: Gardner Press.

Hollingshead, A. B. (1957). *Two-factor index of social position.* New Haven: Author.

Holmes, T. H., & Rahe, R. H. (1967). The Social Readjustment Rating Scale. *Journal of Psychosomatic Research, 11,* 213–218.

Holy Bible. (1952). (New Catholic ed.). New York: Catholic Publishing.

Howell, R. J., & Toepke, K. E. (1984). Summary of the child custody laws for the fifty states. *American Journal of Family Therapy, 12*(2), 56–60.

Hughes, S. F., Berger, M., & Wright, L. (1978). The family life cycle and clinical intervention. *Journal of Marriage and Family Counseling, 4*(4), 33–40.

Hunt, M. (1966). *The world of the formerly married.* New York: McGraw-Hill.

Hurowitz, N. (1981). *Divorce: Your fault, my fault, no fault.* Bridgeport, PA: Law-Trac Press.

Hyatt, R. (1977). *Before you marry . . . again.* New York: Random House.

Hyatt, R., & Kaslow, F. (1985). The impact of children's divorce on parents: And some contributing factors. *Journal of Divorce, 9*(1), 79–92.

Hyde, L. M., Jr. (1984). Child custody in divorce. *Juvenile and Family Court Journal, 35*(1), 1–3, 17–38, 57–72.

Isaacs, M. B. (1981). Treatment for families of divorce: A systems model perspective. In I. R. Stuart & L. E. Abt (Eds.), *Children of separation and divorce.* New York: Van Nostrand Reinhold.

Isaacs, M. B. (1982). Helping mom fail: A case of a stalemated divorcing process. *Family Process, 21*(2), 225–234.

Isaacs, M. B., & Levin, I. R. (1984). Who's in my family? A longitudinal study of drawings of children of divorce. *Journal of Divorce, 7*(4), 1–21.

Jacobs, J. W. (1982). The effect of divorce on fathers. *American Journal of Psychiatry, 139,* 1235–1241. (Reprinted in *International Journal of Family Therapy,* 1984, *6*(3), 177–191.)

Jenkins, S. (1978, March–April). Children of divorce. *Children Today,* pp. 16–20. (Reprinted in S. Chess & A. Thomas (Eds.), *Annual progress in child psychiatry and child development,* 1979, (pp. 283–292). New York: Brunner/Mazel.)

Johnston, J. R., Campbell, L. E. G., & Tall, M. C. (1985). Impasses to the resolution of custody and visitation disputes. *American Journal of Orthopsychiatry, 55,* 112–129.

Kaffman, M., & Talmon, M. (1982). The crisis of divorce: An opportunity for constructive change. *International Journal of Family Therapy, 4,* 220–233.

Kalter, N., & Rembar, J. (1981). The significance of a child's age at the time of parental divorce. *American Journal of Orthopsychiatry, 51,* 85–100.

Kaslow, F. W. (1979/80). Stages of divorce: A psychological perspective. *Villanova Law Review 25,* 718–751.

Kaslow, F. W. (1980). History of family therapy in the United States: A kaleidoscopic overview. *Marriage and Family Review, 3*(1/2), 77–111.

Kaslow, F. W. (1981a). A diaclectic approach to family therapy and practice: Selectivity and synthesis. *Journal of Marital and Family Therapy, 7*(3), 345–351.

Kaslow, F. W. (1981b). Divorce and divorce therapy. In A. S. Gurman & D. P. Kniskern (Eds.), *Handbook of family therapy* (pp. 662–696). New York: Brunner/Mazel.

Kaslow, F. W. (1981c). Profile of the healthy family. *Interaction, 4*(1/2), 1–15. (Reprinted in *The Relationship,* 1982, *8*(1), 9–24.)

Kaslow, F. W. (1981d). Group therapy with couples in conflict: Is more better? *Psychotherapy: Theory, Research and Practice, 18,* 516–524.

Kaslow, F. W. (1982a). Portrait of a healthy couple. *Psychiatric Clinics of North America, 5*(3), 519–527.

Kaslow, F. W. (1982b). Group therapy with couples in conflict. *Australian Journal of Family Therapy, 3*(4), 199–204.

Kaslow, F. W. (1983). Stages and techniques of divorce therapy. In P. A. Keller & L. G. Ritt (Eds.), *Innovations in clinical practice: A sourcebook* (Vol.2, pp. 5–16). Sarasota, FL: Professional Resource Exchange.

Kaslow, F. W. (1984a). Divorce: An evolutionary process of change in the family system. *Journal of Divorce, 7*(3), 21–39.

Kaslow, F. W. (1984b). Divorce mediation and its emotional impact on the couple and their children. *American Journal of Family Therapy, 12*(3), 58–66.

Kaslow, F. W. (1987, in press). The emotional process of divorce and its interface with the mediation process. In J. Folberg & A. Milne (Eds.), *Divorce mediation: Theory and practice.* New York: Guilford Press.

Kaslow, F. W., & Hyatt, R. (1982). Divorce: A potential growth experience for the extended family. *Journal of Divorce, 5*(1/2), 115–126.

Kaslow, F. W., & Lieberman, E. J. (1981). Couples group therapy: Rationale, dynamics and process. In P. Sholevar (Ed.), *Handbook of marriage and marital therapy* (pp. 347–362). New York: SP Medical and Scientific Books.

Kaslow, F. W., & Ridenour, R. I. (Eds.). (1984). *The military family: Dynamics, structure and treatment.* New York: Guilford Press.

Kaslow, F. W., & Schwartz, L. L. (in press). Older children of divorce: A neglected family segment. In J. Vincent (Ed.), *Advances in family intervention.* Greenwich, CT: Jai Press.

Kaslow, F. W., & Steinberg, J. L. (1982). Ethical divorce therapy and divorce proceedings: A psychological perspective. In J. Hansen & L. L'Abate (Eds.), *Values, ethics, legalities and the family therapist* (pp. 61–74). Rockville, MD: Aspen Systems.

Kelly, J. B. (1981). Observations on adolescent relationships five years after divorce. *Adolescent Psychiatry, 9,* 133–141.

Kelly, J. B. (1982) Divorce: The adult perspective. In B. B. Wolman (Ed.), *Hand-*

book of developmental psychology (pp. 734–750). Englewood Cliffs, NJ: Prentice-Hall.

Kelly, R., & Berg, B. (1978). Measuring children's reactions to divorce. *Journal of Clinical Psychology, 34,* 215–221.

Kessler, S. (1975). *The American way of divorce: Prescription for change.* Chicago: Nelson Hall.

Kessler, S., & Bostwick, S. (1977). Beyond divorce: Coping skills for children. *Journal of Clinical Psychology, 6,* 38–41.

Kinard, E. M., & Reinherz, H. (1984). Marital disruption: Effects on behavioral and emotional functioning in children. *Journal of Family Issues, 5*(1), 90–115.

Kitson, G. C., & Langlie, J. K. (1984). Couples who file for divorce but change their minds. *American Journal of Orthopsychiatry, 54,* 469–489.

Kitson, G. C., & Sussman, M. B. (1982). Marital complaints, demographic characteristics, and symptoms of mental distress in divorce. *Journal of Marriage and the Family, 44,* 87–101.

Klein, M. (1937). *The psychoanalysis of children* (2nd ed.). London: Hogarth Press.

Knaub, P. K., & Hanna, S. L. (1984). Children of remarriage: Perceptions of family strengths. *Journal of Divorce, 7*(4), 73–90.

Knaub, P. K., Hanna, S. L., & Stinnett, N. (1984). Strengths of remarried families. *Journal of Divorce, 7*(3), 41–55.

Kohlberg, L. (1969). Stage and sequence: The cognitive development approach to socialization. In D. A. Goslin (Ed.), *Handbook of socialization theory and research.* New York: Rand-McNally.

Krantzler, M. (1974). *Creative divorce.* New York: M. Evans.

Kulka, R. A., & Weingarten, H. (1979). The long-term effects of parental divorce in childhood on adult adjustment. *Journal of Social Issues, 35*(4), 50–78.

Kurdek, L. A. (1983). Concluding comments. In L. A. Kurdek (Ed.), *Children and divorce* (pp. 83–87). San Francisco: Jossey-Bass.

Kurdek, L. A., & Berg B. (1983). Correlates of children's adjustment to their parents' divorces. In L. A. Kurdek (Ed.), *Children and divorce* (pp. 47–60). San Francisco: Jossey-Bass.

Kurdek L. A., Blisk, D., & Siesky, A. E., Jr. (1981). Correlates of children's long-term adjustment to their parent's divorce. *Developmental Psychology, 17,* 565–579.

Kurdek, L. A., & Siesky, A. E. (1980). Effects of divorce on children: The relationship between parent and child perspectives. *Journal of Divorce, 4*(2), 85–99.

Lager, E. (1977). Parents in law: Failure and divorce in a second chance family. *Journal of Marriage and Family Counseling, 3*(4), 19–24.

Laiken, D. S. (1981). *Daughters of divorce: The effects of parental divorce on women's lives.* New York: William Morrow.

Lamb, M. E. (1977). The effects of divorce on children's personality development. *Journal of Divorce, 1,* 163–174.

Lazarus, A. (1981). *The practice of multi-modal therapy.* New York: McGraw-Hill.

Levin, M. J. (1984, October 14). Divorced couples who are reunited. *Philadelphia Inquirer,* pp. 1-f, 12-f.

Levinger, G. (1966). Sources of marital dissatisfaction among applicants for divorce. *American Journal of Orthopsychiatry, 36,* 803–807.

Levinson, D. J., Darrow, C. N., Klein, E. B., Levinson, M. H., & McKee, B. (1978). *The seasons of a man's life.* New York: Knopf.

Levitin, T. E. (1979). Children of divorce: An introduction. *Journal of Social Issues, 35*(4), 1–25.

Lewis, J., Beavers, W. R., Gossett, J. T., & Phillips, U. A. (1976). *No single thread: Psychological health and the family system.* New York: Brunner/Mazel.

L'Hommedieu, T. (1984). *The divorce experience of working and middle class women.* Ann Arbor: UMI Research Press.

Liddle, H. A. (Ed.). (1983). Clinical implications of the family life cycle. *Family Therapy Collections.* Rockville, MD: Aspen Systems.

Little, M. (1982). *Family breakup.* San Francisco: Jossey-Bass.

Lowery, C. R. (1984). The wisdom of Solomon: Criteria for child custody from the legal and clinical points of view. *Law and Human Behavior, 8,* 371–380.

Luepnitz, D. A. (1982). *Child custody: A study of families after divorce.* Lexington, MA: Lexington Books.

McLoughlin, D., & Whitfield, R. (1984). Adolescents and their experience of parental divorce. *Journal of Adolescence, 7*(2), 155–170.

Maslow, A. (1968). *Toward a psychology of being.* New York: Van Nostrand.

Maury, E. H., & Brandwein, R. A. (1984). The divorced woman: Processes of change. In C. C. Nadelson & D. C. Polonsky (Eds.), *Marriage and divorce: A contemporary perspective* (pp. 193–206). New York: Guilford Press.

Messinger, L. (1984). *Remarriage: A family affair.* New York: Plenum.

Minuchin, S. (1974). *Families and family therapy.* Cambridge: Harvard University Press.

Mnookin, R. H., & Kornhauser, L. (1979). Bargaining in the shadow of the law: The case of divorce. *Yale Law Journal, 88,* 950–997.

Morawetz, A., & Walker, G. (1984). *Brief therapy with single-parent families.* New York: Brunner/Mazel.

Nadelson, C. C., & Polonsky, D. C. (1984). *Marriage and divorce: A contemporary perspective.* New York: Guilford.

National Center for Health Statistics (1984). Advance report of final divorce statistics, 1981. *Monthly Vital Statistics Report, 32*(9), Suppl. (2). DHHS, Publication No. (PHS) 84-1120. Hyattsville, MD: Public Health Service.

National Center for Health Statistics (1985, December 26). Advance report of final divorce statistics,1983. *Monthly Vital Statistics Report, 34*(9), Suppl. (9). DHHS Publication No. (PHS) 86-1120. Hyattsville, MD: Public Health Service.

Neville, W. G. (1984). Divorce mediation for therapists and their spouses. In F. W. Kaslow (Ed.), *Psychotherapy with psychotherapists,* (pp. 103–119). New York: Haworth.

Oakland, T. P. (1984). *Divorced fathers: Reconstructing a viable life.* New York: Human Sciences Press.

O'Brien v. O'Brien (1982). 114 Misc., 2nd 233, 452 NYS 2nd 801.

O'Brien v. O'Brien (1985, December 30). 12 *Family Law Reporter,* (BNA) 2001, N.Y.L.J., December 30, 1985, at 4.

O'Brien v. O'Brien, New York Superior Court, December 1985.

Olson, D. H., Sprenkle, D. H., & Russell, C. (1979). Circumplex model of marital and family systems: I. Cohesion and adaptability dimensions, family type, and clinical applications. *Family Process, 18,* 3–28.

O'Neill, G., & O'Neill, N. (1972). *Open marriage: A new lifestyle for couples.* New York: M. Evans.

Pauley, J. (1986, June 3). NBC News White Paper: Divorce is changing America. National Broadcasting Company TV Network.

Perlman, J. L. (1982). Divorce—a psychological and legal process. *Journal of Divorce, 6*(1/2), 99–114.

Pett, M. G. (1982). Correlates of children's social adjustment following divorce. *Journal of Divorce, 5*(4), 25–40.

Pettit, E. J., & Bloom, B. L. (1984). Whose decision was it? The effects of initiator status on adjustment to marital disruption. *Journal of Marriage and the Family, 46*, 587–596.

Pietropinto, A. (1985). Effect of unhappy marriages on children. *Medical Aspects of Human Sexuality, 19*(2), 173–181.

Pollack, S., Kaslow, N.J., & Harvey, D. (1982). Symmetry, complementarity and depression: The evolution of an hypothesis. In F. W. Kaslow (Ed.), *The international book of family therapy,* (pp. 170–183). New York: Brunner/Mazel.

Rahe, R. H., Ryman, D. H., & Ward, H. W. (1980). Simplified scaling for life-change events. *Journal of Human Stress, 6*(4), 22–27.

Raschke, H. J. (1977). The role of social participation in postseparation and postdivorce adjustment. *Journal of Divorce, 1*, 129–140.

Reinhard, D. W. (1977). The reaction of adolescent boys and girls to the divorce of their parents. *Journal of Clinical Child Psychology, 5*, 21–23.

Retirement Equity Act of 1984, (REA) (1984, August 23). Washington, DC: P.L. 98-397.

Reusch, J., & Bateson, G. (1951). *Communication: The social matrix of psychiatry.* New York: Norton.

Rhodes, S. L. (1977). A developmental approach to the life cycle of the family. *Social Casework, 58*, 301–311.

Ribble, M. (1943). *The rights of infants.* New York: Columbia University Press.

Ricci, I. (1980). *Mom's house, Dad's house.* New York: MacMillan.

Rice, J. K., & Rice, D. G. (1986). *Living through divorce: A developmental approach to divorce therapy.* New York: Guilford.

Richards, M. P. M. (1982). Post-divorce arrangements for children: A psychological perspective. *Journal of Social Welfare Law*, 133–151.

Richardson, L. (1985). *The new other woman.* New York: Free Press.

Rubenstein, D., & Timmins, J. F. (1978). Depressive diadic and triadic relationships. *Journal of Marriage and Family Counseling, 4*, 13–14.

Sager, C. J. (1976). *Marriage contracts and couple therapy: Hidden forces in intimate relationships.* New York: Brunner/Mazel.

Sager, C. J., Brown, H. S., Crohn, H., Engel, T., Rodstein, E., & Walker, L. (1983). *Treating the remarried family.* New York: Brunner/Mazel.

Santrock, J. A., & Warshak, R. A. (1979). Father custody and social development in boys and girls. *Journal of Social Issues, 35*(4), 112–125.

Saposnek, D. T. (1983). *Mediating child custody disputes.* San Francisco: Jossey-Bass.

Satir, V. (1964). *Conjoint family therapy.* Palo Alto: Science and Behavior Books.

Saul, S. C., & Scherman, A. (1984). Divorce grief and personal adjustment in divorced persons who remarry or remain single. *Journal of Divorce, 7*(3), 75–85.

Schwartz, L. L., & Kaslow, F. W. (1985). Widows and divorcées: The same or different? *American Journal of Family Therapy, 13*(4), 72–76.

Schwartz, S. F. G. (1984). Toward a presumption of joint custody. *Family Law Quarterly, 18*, 225–246.

Schwartzberg, A. Z. (1980). Adolescent reactions to divorce. *Adolescent Psychiatry, 8*, 379–392.

Shakespeare, W. (1968). *As you like it* (overseas ed.). London: Oxford University Press.

Siller, S. (1986, June). Men's rights. *Penthouse,* p. 26.

Smith, R. M., & Smith, C. W. (1981). Child-rearing and single-parent fathers. *Family Relations, 30,* 411–417.

Smith, W. (1985). New rules, new burdens. *Family Advocate, 8*(2), 4–8.

Spanier, G. B., & Casto, R. F. (1979). Adjustment to separation and divorce: An analysis of 50 case studies. *Journal of Divorce, 2,* 241–253.

Spanier, G. B., & Hanson, S. (1981). The role of extended kin in the adjustment to marital separation. *Journal of Divorce, 5*(1/2), 33–48.

Spanier, G. B., & Thompson, L. (1984). *Parting: The aftermath of separation and divorce.* Beverly Hills, CA: Sage.

Spitz, R. A. (1946). Anaclitic depression. *The psychoanalytic study of the child.* New York: International Universities Press.

Spitz, R. A., & Wolf, K. M. (1946). The smiling response: A contribution to the ontogenesis of social relations. *Genetic Psychological Monographs, 34* (Whole No. 57–125).

Springer, C., & Wallerstein, J. S. (1983). Young adolescents' responses to their parents' divorces. In L. A. Kurdek (Ed.), *Children and divorce* (pp. 15–27). San Francisco: Jossey-Bass.

Stark, E. (1986, May). Friends through it all. *Psychology Today, 20*(5), 54–60.

Stuart, I. R., & Abt, L. E. (1981). *Children of separation and divorce: Management and treatment.* New York: Van Nostrand Reinhold.

Sullivan, H. S. (1953). *The interpersonal theory of psychiatry.* New York: Norton.

Tapp, J. L., Daniels, T., Doyle, P. M., Olson, D. G., & Quiggle, N. (1985). *Effects of divorce on adult children.* Unpublished paper, University of Minnesota.

Tcheng-Laroche, F., & Prince, R. (1983). Separated and divorced women compared with married controls: Selected life satisfaction, stress and health indices from a community survey. *Social Science and Medicine, 17*(2), 95–105.

Thompson, L., & Spanier, G. B. (1983). The end of marriage and the acceptance of marital termination. *Journal of Marriage and the Family, 45*(1), 103–114.

Trafford, A. (1984). *Crazy time: Surviving divorce.* New York: Bantam Books.

Tropf, W. D. (1984). An exploratory examination of the effects of remarriage on child support and personal contacts. *Journal of Divorce, 7*(3), 57–73.

Turner, N. W. (1980). Divorce in mid-life: Clinical implications and applications. In W. H. Norman & T. J. Scaramella (Eds.), *Mid-life: Developmental and clinical issues* (pp. 149–177). New York: Brunner/Mazel.

Tuzlak, A., & Hillock, D. W. (1986). Single mothers and their children after divorce: A study of those "who make it." *Conciliation Courts Review, 24*(1), 79–89.

U.S. Department of Health and Human Services (1985). *Wage withholding for child support: An employer's guide,* OCSE Publication No. 103. Rockville, MD: Office of Child Support Enforcement.

Visher, E. B., & Visher, J. S. (1979). *Stepfamilies: A guide to working with stepparents and stepchildren.* New York: Brunner/Mazel.

Wallerstein, J. S. (1983). Children of divorce: The psychological tasks of the child. *American Journal of Orthopsychiatry, 53,* 230–243.

Wallerstein, J. S. (1984). Children of divorce: Preliminary report of a ten-year follow-up of young children. *American Journal of Orthopsychiatry, 54,* 444–458.

Wallerstein, J. S. (1985a). Children of divorce: Preliminary report of a ten-year follow-up of older children and adolescents. *Journal of the American Academy of Child Psychiatry, 24,* 545–553.

Wallerstein, J. S. (1985b). The overburdened child: Some long-term consequences of divorce. *Social Work, 30*(2), 116–123.

Wallerstein, J. S. (1986). Women after divorce: Preliminary report from a ten-year follow-up. *American Journal of Orthopsychiatry, 56*, 65–77.

Wallerstein, J. S., & Kelly, J. B. (1979). Divorce and children. In I. N. Berlin, L. A. Stone, & J. D. Noshpitz (Eds.), *Handbook of child psychiatry IV: Prevention and current issues* (pp. 339–347). New York: Basic Books.

Wallerstein, J. S., & Kelly, J. B. (1980). *Surviving the breakup: How children and parents cope with divorce.* New York: Basic Books.

Walsh, F. (Ed.). (1982). *Normal family processes.* New York: Guilford.

Warren, N. J., & Amara, I. A. (1985). Educational groups for single-parent fathers: The parenting after divorce programs. *Journal of Divorce, 8*(2), 79–96.

Weiss, R. S. (1975). *Marital separation.* New York: Basic Books.

Weiss, R. S. (1982). Attachment in adult life. In C. M. Parkes & J. Stevenson-Hinde (Eds.), *The place of attachment in human behavior.* New York: Basic Books.

Weitzman, L. J. (1985). *The divorce revolution: The unexpected social and economic consequences for women and children in America.* New York: Free Press.

Wertlieb, D., Budman, S., Demby, A., & Randall, M. (1984). Marital separation and health: Stress and intervention. *Journal of Human Stress, 10*(1), 18–26.

Westman, J. C. (1983). The impact of divorce on teenagers. *Clinical Pediatrics, 22*, 692–697.

Westoff, C. F., & Goldman, N. (1984). Figuring the odds in the marriage market. *Money, 13*(12), 33–42.

Whitaker, C. A., & Miller, M. H. (1969). A reevaluation of psychiatric help when divorce impends. *American Journal of Psychiatry, 12*(6), 57–64.

White, S. W., & Bloom, B. L. (1981). Factors related to the adjustment of divorcing men. *Family Relations, 30*, 349–360.

White, S. W., & Mika, K. (1983). Family divorce and separation: Theory and research. *Marriage and Family Review, 6*(1/2), 175–192.

Wise, M. J. (1980). The aftermath of divorce. *American Journal of Psychoanalysis, 40*, 149–158.

Woody, J. D., Colley, P. E., Schlegelmilch, J., Maginn, P., & Balsanek, J. (1984). Child adjustment to parental stress following divorce. *Social Casework, 65*, 405–412.

Wynn, R. L., & Brumberger, L. S. (1982). A cognitive developmental analysis of children's understanding of family membership and divorce. Paper presented at the Twelfth Symposium of the Jean Piaget Society, Philadelphia.

Wynne, L. C. (1984). The epigenesis of relational systems: A model for understanding family development. *Family Process, 23*, 297–318.

Young, D. M. (1983). Two studies of children of divorce. In L. A. Kurdek (Ed.), *Children and divorce* (pp. 61–69). San Francisco: Jossey-Bass.

Index

alimony granted to, 148
discrimination against, in divorce court, 66
in divorce and in widowhood, 61–64
divorced, employment of, 149–153
as divorced mothers, 106–108
divorce initiated by, 47
in divorces in 1940s, 39
early marriages of, 103
economic consequences of divorce on, 154–155
gender-related issues in, 94–95
living alone, 59, 60
permanent alimony granted to, 275
postdivorce decisions of, 236

postdivorce restabilization by, 244
socioeconomic class and life expectations of, 136–137
see also Divorced women; Mothers
Women's liberation movement, 42, 273
Work, *see* Employment
Wright, L., 15
Wynne, L. C., 17–22, 36, 278

Young, D. M., 168
Young adults, 177–183
courtship by, 255–258
leaving home by, 266
love relationships feared by, 158–159
Young children, *see* Children